Making our Way through the World

How do we reflect upon ourselves and our concerns in relation to society, and vice versa? Human reflexivity works through 'internal conversations' using language, but also emotions, sensations and images. Most people acknowledge this 'inner dialogue' and can report upon it. However, little research has been conducted on 'internal conversations' and how they mediate between our ultimate concerns and the social contexts we confront. Margaret Archer argues that reflexivity is progessively replacing routine action in late modernity, shaping how ordinary people make their way through the world. Using interviewees' life and work histories, she shows how 'internal conversations' guide the occupations that people seek, keep or quit; their stances towards structural constraints and enablements; and their resulting patterns of social mobility.

MARGARET S. ARCHER is Professor of Sociology at the University of Warwick. She has written over twenty books including *Structure, Agency and the Internal Conversation* (Cambridge, 2003) and *Being Human: The Problem of Agency* (Cambridge, 2000).

D1237139

Making our Way through the World

Human Reflexivity and Social Mobility

Margaret S. Archer

University of Warwick

CAMBRIDGE UNIVERSITY PRESS

Cambridge, New York, Melbourne, Madrid, Cape Town, Singapore, São Paulo

Cambridge University Press
The Edinburgh Building, Cambridge CB2 8RU, UK

Published in the United States of America by Cambridge University Press,
New York

www.cambridge.org
Information on this title: www.cambridge.org/9780521696937

First published 2007

Printed in the United Kingdom at the University Press, Cambridge

A catalogue record for this publication is available from the British Library

ISBN 978-0-521-87423-6 hardback
ISBN 978-0-521-69693-7 paperback

To the memory of
Luminiţa Caibăr

Who made her way lovingly through the world

Contents

Acknowledgements

This book was an adventure. After commuting to the University of Warwick for thirty years, I finally got to know the city of Coventry. To do so means unpacking 'the decline of British manufacturing' into the painful lived reality of many people: the young without work, the families with first-hand knowledge of redundancy, and the older ones who will try anything rather than say 'I'll never work again.' My first and deep thanks go to those who generously gave hours of their time to being interviewed and shared the good, the bad and the mundane so openly. I sincerely hope that I have given their life stories the respect and understanding they deserve – and not only because these are the book.

Secondly, my thanks go to the ESRC for funding this project and its successor. Without the award there would have been no research team and, without the team . . . Its international mix is what excites me about globalisation – an excitement that remains despite and after reciting its catalogue of errors. In order of appearance, thank you Hazel Rice (UK), research secretary; Andrew Timming (USA), pilot statistician; Man Wing Yeung (Hong Kong), project statistician; Nana Zhang (China), pilot interviewer; Sergey Petrov (Russia), IT assistant; Inga Aleksandravici (Lithuania) and Adina Bozga (Romania), preliminary interviewers; and especial gratitude to Nicoleta Cinpoeş (Romania) for checking every chapter, for teaching me some rules of English grammar we don't learn over here, as well as for correcting the Conclusion at 35,000 feet.

Some good old friends helped, as usual, through discussions, suggestions and much-needed encouragement; thank you again Pierpaolo Donati, Doug Porpora, Andrew Sayer and Wes Shumar. Through various conferences, the book made some new friends. I'm especially grateful for helpful comments from Vincent Colapietro, Dave Elder-Vass and Norbert Wiley, which I hope have been put to good use.

Finally, my apologies are owed to an anonymous female attendant at the New York Metropolitan Museum of Art, whom I seriously affronted in November 2004 by using my camera to snap the unauthorised version of the cover painting.

viii

Introduction: reflexivity as the unacknowledged condition of social life

Reflexivity remains a cipher in social theory. Neither what it is nor what it does has received the attention necessary for producing clear concepts of reflexivity or a clear understanding of reflexivity as a social process. These two absences are closely related and mutually reinforcing. On the one hand, the fact that there is no concept of reflexivity in common currency means that just as Molière's Monsieur Jourdain spoke prose all his life without knowing it, everyone from the founding fathers, through all normal lay people, to today's social theorists have constantly been referring to reflexivity or tacitly assuming it or logically implying it under a variety of different terms.

On the other hand, because the terminology that subsumes reflexivity is so varied – from the portmanteaux concepts of academics, such as 'consciousness' or 'subjectivity', through Everyman's quotidian notion of 'mulling things over', to the quaint, but not inaccurate, folkloric expression 'I says to myself says I' – the *process* denoted by reflexivity has been underexplored, undertheorised and, above all, undervalued. Reflexivity is such an inescapable, though vague, pre-supposition and so tacitly, thus non-discursively, taken for granted, that it has rarely been held up for the scrutiny necessary to rectify its undervaluation as a social process. Because reflexivity has been so seriously neglected,[1] redressing this state of affairs means making some bold moves. The intent behind the present book is finally to allow this Cinderella to go to the ball, to stay there and to be acknowledged as a partner without whom there would be no social dance.

Our human reflexivity is closely akin to our human embodiment, something so self-evident as not to have merited serious attention from social theorists until 'the body' was 'reclaimed' during the past two or three decades. However, whilst all passengers on the Clapham omnibus would

---

[1] The main exceptions being American pragmatism and social psychology; the former contribution was discussed in my *Structure, Agency and the Internal Conversation*, Cambridge: Cambridge University Press, 2003, ch. 2 and the latter will be examined in the companion volume to this book, *The Reflexive Imperative*.

concur that, indeed, they have bodies, most would be stumped by 'reflexivity' if asked whether or not they practise it. In fact, as will be shown in chapter 2, nearly all subjects agree that they do if the question is rephrased to avoid using the word. Because the term is ill-defined and not in everyday use, let us begin from the ordinary activities to which it refers amongst ordinary people: ones that they do recognise and can discuss if ordinary language is used.

At its most basic, reflexivity rests on the fact that all normal people talk to themselves within their own heads,[2] usually silently and usually from an early age. In the present book this mental activity is called 'internal conversation' but, in the relatively sparse literature available, it is also known *inter alia* as 'self-talk', 'intra-communication', 'musement', 'inner dialogue' and 'rumination'. Indeed, it seems probable that some people engage in more internal dialogue than external conversation at certain times in life and under particular circumstances: those living alone and especially the elderly, those employed in solitary occupations or performing isolated work tasks, and only children without close friends. What are they doing when they engage in self-talk? The activities involved range over a broad terrain which, in plain language, can extend from daydreaming, fantasising and internal vituperation; through rehearsing for some forthcoming encounter, reliving past events, planning for future eventualities, clarifying where one stands or what one understands, producing a running commentary on what is taking place, talking oneself through (or into) a practical activity; to more pointed actions such as issuing internal warnings and making promises to oneself, reaching concrete decisions or coming to a conclusion about a particular problem.

Two things are clear about this (non-exhaustive) list. Firstly, not all of these activities are fully reflexive, because they lack the crucial feature of the 'object' under consideration being bent back in any serious, deliberative sense, upon the 'subject' doing the considering. For example, a worker tackling a new procedure or someone erecting a wardrobe from a flat-pack asks herself 'What comes next?' and often answers this by consulting an external source such as the manual or instruction leaflet. Of course, this could be viewed as weakly reflexive because their question also stands for 'What do I do next?' But it is weak because the response is to consult the rule-book rather than thrashing it out through internal

---

[2] 'Human beings have a wholly unique gift in the use of language, and that is that they can talk to themselves. Everybody does it, all the time' (note that the last phrase will receive some refinement in this text). Samuel C. Riccillo, 'Phylogenesis: Understanding the Biological Origins of Intrapersonal Communication', in Donna R. Vocate (ed.), *Intrapersonal Communication: Different Voices, Different Minds*, Hillsdale, N.J., Lawrence Erlbaum, 1994, p. 36.

deliberation about subject in relation to object and vice versa. Hence, the dividing line between reflexive and non-reflexive thought is far from clear cut because anyone's thoughts can move back and forth between the two.

Secondly, not all of the mental activities listed above concern social matters because the object over which a subject deliberates need not concern people or society. For example, solo climbers talk themselves through handholds and footholds, and riders ask themselves how many strides their horses should fit in before jumping an obstacle. However, it can always be maintained that sporting activities like these are weakly social; they are usually reliant upon manufactured equipment, often entail human artefacts, such as route maps and fences, and frequently presume some social context, such as the existence of mountain rescue or the right to jump some farmer's hedges. Although it is usually possible to invoke some social element of the above type, neither analytically nor practically are such elements primary to the activity. The dividing line can be fuzzy in practice, although the analytical distinction is clear enough.

The present book deals only with strongly reflexive processes and its concern is with reflexive deliberations about matters that are primarily and necessarily social.[3] Reflexivity itself is held to depend upon conscious deliberations that take place through 'internal conversation'. The ability to hold such inner dialogues is an emergent personal power of individuals that has been generally disregarded and is not entailed by routine or habitual action. Myers summarises the unwarranted neglect of this personal property as follows:

[The importance of] self-dialogue and its role in the acquisition of self-knowledge, I believe, can hardly be exaggerated. That it plays such a role is a consequence of a human characteristic that deserves to be judged remarkable. This is the susceptibility of our mind/body complexes to respond to the questions that we put to ourselves, to create special states of consciousness through merely raising a question. It is only slightly less remarkable that these states provoked into existence by our questions about ourselves quite often supply the materials for accurate answers to those same questions.[4]

Precisely because our reflexive deliberations about social matters take this 'question and answer' format, it is appropriate to consider reflexivity as being exercised through internal conversation.

---

[3] The Weberian distinction between 'action' and 'social action' is maintained here. Not all of our personal powers or the actions that we conceive and carry out by virtue of them can legitimately or usefully be considered as social: for example, the lone practice of meditation or of mountaineering. See Colin Campbell, *The Myth of Social Action*, Cambridge: Cambridge University Press, 1996 and also Archer, *Structure, Agency and the Internal Conversation*, ch. 1, 'The Private Life of the Social Subject'.

[4] Gerald E. Myers, 'Introspection and Self-Knowledge', *American Philosophical Quarterly*, 23, 2, April 1986, p. 206.

The following definition is used throughout the present work: *'reflexivity' is the regular exercise of the mental ability, shared by all normal people, to consider themselves in relation to their (social) contexts and vice versa.* Such deliberations are important since they form the basis upon which people determine their future courses of action – always fallibly and always under their own descriptions. Because this book focuses upon people's occupational concerns and patterns of social mobility – in order to have a concrete point of reference for the discussion of reflexivity – the contexts involved are social contexts. However, let us return to the basic question, namely what are people doing when they engage in self-talk?

Some of the subjects interviewed,[5] and also certain social psychologists, respond in a derogatory manner to the idea of 'talking to oneself'. Indeed, this is probably the worst vernacular formulation through which to ascertain anything about their internal conversations from the population at large. At best, it elicits a wary assent, sometimes immediately followed by the qualification: 'But I'm not daft.' Interestingly, in languages as different as English and Romanian, the association persists between talking to oneself and 'being simple' or 'off one's head', and it is not eliminated by emphasising that internal dialogue is conducted silently. Resident English speakers are much readier to assent that they engage in inner dialogue and to amplify upon their self-talk if the activity is described to them as 'silently mulling things over' or 'thinking things through in your own head'. The origins of this negative reaction are obvious, but its duration may have been prolonged by psychologists as different as Piaget and Vygotsky, who held that 'speaking out loud' either disappeared or was internalised with age and, thus, its absence in adults represented a sign of mental maturity. Equally, social psychologists often display considerable negativity towards 'rumination', which is seen as interfering with routinised schemes that are regarded as providing quicker and more reliable guides to action.[6]

Folk wisdom can be recruited in praise of routine action, as in the following verse:

> The centipede was happy, quite, until the toad in fun
> Said, 'Pray which leg goes after which?'
> This worked his mind to such a pitch,
> He lay distracted in a ditch, considering how to run.

---

[5] Details about the empirical framework on which this study is based are found in chapter 2 and in the Methodological appendix.

[6] See the *Journal of Personality and Social Psychology* from 1970 to date. For example, see Timothy D. Wilson and Jonathan Schooler, 'Thinking Too Much: Introspection Can Reduce the Quality of Preferences and Decisions', *Journal of Personality and Social Psychology*, 60, 2, 1991.

The book which approvingly reproduced this nursery rhyme expatiates upon reflexivity as 'the curse of the self': '[T]he capacity to self-reflect distorts our perceptions about the world, leads us to draw inaccurate conclusions about ourselves and other people, and thus prompts us to make bad decisions based on faulty information. The self conjures up a great deal of human suffering in the form of negative emotions . . . by allowing us to ruminate about the past or imagine what might befall us in the future.'[7] Instead, we would do better to stick with tried and trusted routines. However, traditional routines work only in recurrent and predictable circumstances. Certainly, some newly acquired skills may later become embodied and operate as 'second nature', as with driving on 'auto-pilot' – until an emergency occurs. But others remain intransigently discursive, defying routinisation (as in writing a book). Where novel situations are concerned, the more appropriate piece of folk wisdom is 'Look before you leap.'

Contrary to this negativity towards internal conversation, the thesis defended in the present book is that reflexivity is the means by which we make our way through the world. This applies to the social world in particular, which can no longer be approached through embodied knowledge, tacit routines, or traditional custom and practice alone – were that ever to have been the case for most, let alone all, people. Although reflexive deliberation is considered to be indispensable to the existence of any society, its scope has also been growing from the advent of modernity onwards. In the third millennium, the fast-changing social world makes it incumbent on everyone to exercise more and more reflexivity in increasingly greater tracts of their lives. Justifying the decline and fall of routinisation is the theme of the next chapter. The need to incorporate reflexivity more prominently in social theorising is its corollary.

Incorporating reflexivity

The reasons for promoting reflexivity to a central position within social theory are summarised in the following proposition. *The subjective powers of reflexivity mediate the role that objective structural or cultural powers play in influencing social action and are thus indispensable to explaining social outcomes.* This proposition raises three key questions about the nature of human action, which are listed below and will be examined in turn. The argument running through them and serving to justify the proposition is that none of these questions about the nature of human action in society is answerable without serious reference being made to people's reflexivity:

[7] Mark R. Leary, *The Curse of the Self*, Oxford, Oxford University Press, 2004, p. 19.

1 Why do people act at all? What motivates them and what are they (fallibly) trying to achieve by endorsing given courses of action? This entails
   an examination of their personal *concerns* and inner reflexive deliberations about how to go about realising them.
2 How do social properties influence the courses of action that people
   adopt? This involves a specification of how objective structural or cultural powers are reflexively *mediated*.
3 What exactly do people do? This requires an examination of the *variability* in the actions of those similarly socially situated and the
   differences in their processes of reflexivity.

1 The reflexive adoption of projects

'Social hydraulics' is the generic process assumed by those who hold that
no recourse need be made to any aspect of human subjectivity in order to
explain social action. All necessary components making up the *explanans*
refer directly or indirectly to social powers, thus rendering any reference
to personal powers irrelevant or redundant. Although few social theorists
will go quite as far as that, if only because of the need to acknowledge our
biological endowments, the growth of sociological imperialism comes
extremely close to doing so. Indeed, the model of agency promoted by
social constructionists, which I have characterised elsewhere as 'society's
being',[8] subtracts all but our biological properties and powers from us as
people and accredits them to the social side of the balance sheet. In consequence, each and every sociological explanation can be arrived at from
the third-person perspective because any references to first-person subjectivity have already been reduced to social derivatives and, at most, permutations upon them. In consequence, anything that might count as
genuine human reflexivity effectively evaporates. It lacks causal powers
and represents only phenomenological froth. 'Hydraulic' theorising,
which construes what we do in terms of the pushes and pulls to which we
are subjected, is resisted throughout this book, in all its reductionist versions – social, philosophical or neuro-biological.

In contradistinction, internal conversation is presented as the manner
in which we reflexively make our way through the world. It is what makes
(most of us) 'active agents', people who can exercise some governance in
their own lives, as opposed to 'passive agents' to whom things simply
happen.[9] Being an 'active agent' hinges on the fact that individuals

---

[8] Margaret S. Archer, *Being Human: the Problem of Agency*, Cambridge, Cambridge
University Press, 2000, ch. 3.
[9] For this distinction, see Martin Hollis, *Models of Man: Philosophical Thoughts on Social
Action*, Cambridge, Cambridge University Press, 1977.

develop and define their ultimate concerns: those internal goods that they care about most,[10] the precise constellation of which makes for their concrete singularity as persons.[11] No one can have an ultimate concern and fail to do something about it. Instead, each person seeks to develop a concrete course of action to realise that concern by elaborating a 'project', in the (fallible) belief that to accomplish this project is to realise one's concern. Action itself thus depends upon the existence of what are termed 'projects', where a project stands for any course of action intentionally engaged upon by a human being. Thus, the answer to why we act at all is in order to promote our concerns; we form 'projects' to advance or to protect what we care about most.

If projects were optional, in the strong sense that people could live without them, the social would be like the natural world, governed only by the laws of nature. Human beings are distinctive not as the bearer of projects, which is a characteristic people share with every animal, but because of their reflexive ability to design (and redesign) many of the projects they pursue. If we are to survive and thrive, we have to be practitioners, and the definition of a successful practice is the realisation of a particular project in the relevant part of the environment. The ubiquity of human projects has three implications for the relationship between subjects and their natural environment, which includes the social order.

Firstly, the pursuit of any human project entails the attempt to exercise our causal powers as human beings. Since this takes place in the world, that is, in the natural, practical and social orders, then the pursuit of a project necessarily activates the causal powers of entities which belong to one of these three orders. Which powers are activated (beneficially or detrimentally) is contingent upon the nature of the project entertained and, of course, it is always contingent whether or not a particular project is adopted at all. *The key point is that any human attempt to pursue a project entails two sets of causal powers: our own and those pertaining to part of natural reality.* Generically, the outcome is dependent upon the relationship between these two sets.

Secondly, these two kinds of causal powers work in entirely different ways once they are activated. On the one hand, the properties of objects in the natural order, artefacts in the practical order, and structural and cultural properties in the social order are very different from one another, but nevertheless the exercise of their causal powers is *automatic*. If and when these emergent properties are activated, then, *ceteris paribus*,

---

[10] See Harry G. Frankfurt, *The Importance of What We Care About*, Cambridge, Cambridge University Press, 1988, ch. 7. and A. McIntyre, *After Virtue*, London, Duckworth, 1981, pp. 187ff.   [11] Archer, *Being Human*, ch. 9.

they simply work in a specific way in relation to other things. Thus, water has the power to buoy up certain entities and it does so by virtue of its constitution in relation to the specific density of objects – logs float and stones sink. On the other hand, most, though not all, human powers work reflexively rather than automatically.[12] We have the power to lift various objects in our vicinity but also the ability to determine whether we do so or not.

Thirdly, when our causal powers as human beings are interacting with those of different parts of the world, the outcome is rarely just a matter of their primary congruence or incongruence. Certainly, once the causal powers of objects, artefacts, or structural and cultural properties are activated, they will tendentially obstruct or facilitate our projects to very varying degrees. Conversely, the reflexive nature of human powers means that actual outcomes are matters of secondary determination, governed by our inner deliberations about such obstructions and facilitations, under our own descriptions. We often have the capacity to suspend both: suspending that which would advance our aims by engaging in inappropriate action and suspending that which would impede our aims by circumventory activities. Generically, we possess the powers of both resistance and subversion or of co-operation and adaptation. Clearly, our degrees of freedom vary in relation to what we confront, but whether or not and how we use them remains contingent upon our reflexivity.

Thus, our physical well-being depends upon establishing successful practices in the natural world; our performative competence relies upon acquiring skilful practices in relation to material artefacts; and our self-worth hinges upon developing rewarding practices in society. It follows that the attempted realisation of any project immediately enmeshes us in the properties and powers of the respective order of natural reality in relation to our own.

Hence, in nature, the project of swimming, whether conceived of by design or through accident, ineluctably entails the interaction of two sets of causal powers. Of course, if *per impossible*, no one had ever sought to swim, then the natural power, which enables us to float in water, would have been unrealised for humanity. Yet this power is nonetheless real even if it had never been exercised. However, the project of swimming quite literally plunges us into the causal powers of rivers, pools and the sea. We do not instantiate them; rather we have to interact with them and to discover whether accommodation between their powers and our own can lead to a successful practice, in this case, swimming. Some people never do swim,

---

[12] Obviously, there are many of our bodily liabilities, such as their responses to cancer or falling from heights, which are automatic rather than reflexive.

because reflexively they doubt the water's real powers and also lack sufficient reason for overcoming their frightened incredulity.

Similarly, in the practical world, we entertain such projects as throwing a spear, getting through a door or using a computer. But these cannot become skilful practices unless and until we learn how to interact with the causal powers of the objects in question, powers which are usually termed affordances and resistances. A door latch affords a means of opening a door, if used properly, but reflexivity can leave the power of the latch unexercised if our experience has persuaded us that this door, or doors in general, open by being pushed. Improper usage, such as pushing against a latch,[13] will simply meet with resistance. Successful practice depends upon accommodating ourselves to such affordances and resistances, as we do all the time when driving a car.

Matters are no different in the social order where many of the projects that we pursue necessarily involve us with constraints and enablements. As with the other two orders of natural reality, life in society is impossible without projects; each one of its members has myriads of them every day. Of course we do not usually think of such things as catching buses, going to the pub or taking the dog for a walk in these terms. Nevertheless, a change of circumstances can make us realise that this is precisely what they are, namely successful social practices which have become taken for granted as embodied knowledge. Yet, any rail strike makes getting from here to there a serious reflexive project. Prohibition had the same effect for acquiring a drink, as did foot-and-mouth regulations for finding somewhere to exercise the dog. As in the other two orders, meeting with serious social constraints incites not only reflexive circumvention by some but also resignation to the abandonment of such projects by many.

To summarise, the pursuit of human projects in the social domain frequently encounters structural properties and activates them as powers. In such cases there are two sets of causal powers involved in any attempt to develop a successful social practice: those of subjects themselves and those of relevant structural or cultural properties. The causal powers of structures are exercised *inter alia* as constraints and enablements which work automatically, even though they are activity dependent in both their origin and exercise, whereas human powers work reflexively. Certainly, it is the case that the perception (or anticipation) of constraints or enablements can serve as a deterrent or an encouragement, but this is the same in both the natural and the practical orders and, in any case, this effect is a result of our (fallible) reflexive judgements. Finally, under all but the most

---

[13] For a variety of practical examples, see Donald Norman, *The Psychology of Everyday Things*, New York, HarperCollins, 1988.

stringent constraints, agents have the capacity to suspend the exercise of constraints (and enablements) through their circumventory (or renunciatory) actions. In turn, these actions depend upon our knowledgeability and commitment. The establishment of a successful social practice is dependent upon the adaptive ingenuity of reflexive subjects. They must necessarily take account of the causal powers of social properties, under their own descriptions, but are not determined by them in the conception, the pursuit or the realisation of their projects.

2 The reflexive mediation of structural and cultural properties

Whilst resisting 'social hydraulics', it is necessary to allow for a milder form of objective 'social conditioning'. Central to an acceptable account of such conditioning is Roy Bhaskar's statement that 'the causal power of social forms is mediated through social agency'.[14] This is surely correct, because unless the properties of structure and culture are held to derive from people and their doings and to exert their causal effects through people and their actions, theorising would be guilty of reification. Nevertheless, the linking process is not complete *because what is meant by that crucial word 'though' has not been unpacked.*

Vague references to the process of 'social conditioning' are insufficient. This is because to condition entails the existence of something that is conditioned and, since conditioning is not determinism, this process necessarily involves the interplay between two different kinds of causal powers: those pertaining to structures and those belonging to subjects. Therefore, an adequate conceptualisation of 'conditioning' must deal explicitly with the interplay between these two powers. Firstly, this involves a specification of *how* structural and cultural powers impinge upon agents, and secondly of *how* agents use their own personal powers to act 'so rather than otherwise' in such situations. Thus, there are two elements involved, the 'impingement upon' (which is objective) and the 'response to it' (which is subjective).

On the whole, social theory appears to have conceptualised the objective side satisfactorily in terms of cultural and structural properties impinging upon people by shaping the social situations they confront. Often this confrontation is involuntary, as with people's natal social context and its associated life chances. Often it is voluntary, like getting married. In either case, these objective conditioning influences are transmitted to agency by shaping the situations that subjects live with, have to confront, or would confront if they chose to do x, y or z.

[14] Roy Bhaskar, *The Possibility of Naturalism*, Hemel Hempstead Harvester, 1989, p. 26.

Sometimes they impinge as constraints and enablements upon various courses of action and sometimes by distributing different types of vested interests or objective interests to different (groups of) people, which can enhance or reduce their motivation to undertake a given course of action.

However, what this non-deterministic account of 'conditioning' usually omits is why people do not respond in uniform fashion under the same structured circumstances. Subjects who are similarly situated can debate, both internally and externally, about appropriate courses of action, and come to different conclusions. This is one of the major reasons why Humean constant conjunctions are not found between structural and cultural influences and action outcomes. At best, what are detected are empirical tendencies in action patterns, which are consonant with objective influences having affected them. These must remain nothing more than trends, partly because external contingencies intervene, given that the social system is open, but partly because a second causal power is *necessarily at play*, namely the personal power to reflect subjectively upon one's circumstances and to decide what to do in them or to do about them. Such inalienable powers of human reflexivity would generate variations in action responses even if it were possible to achieve conditions of laboratory closure. In short, the conceptualisation of this process of mediation between structure and agency is usually not fully adequate because it does not fully incorporate the role played by human subjectivity in general. In particular, it omits the part reflexivity plays in enabling subjects to design and determine their responses to the structured circumstances in which they find themselves, in the light of what they personally care about most.

Let me now attempt to improve upon this generic account of social conditioning by presenting it as mediated by human reflexivity. The process of 'conditioning' has been seen to entail the exercise of two sets of causal powers: those of the property that 'conditions' and those of the property that is 'conditioned'. This is clearest where constraints and enablements are concerned, the obvious point being that a constraint requires something to constrain and an enablement needs something to enable. These are not intransitive terms because if, *per impossible*, no subject ever conceived of any project, he or she could be neither constrained nor enabled.

For example, the mere existence of a centralised educational system does not constrain curricular variations, unless and until somebody advances the policy of, say, introducing geographical or linguistic variants. Only when that project is mooted does centralisation become a constraint, *ceteris paribus*. Equally, in the cultural realm, if there is a contradiction between two beliefs or two theories it remains a purely logical matter, existing out there in the 'Universal Library',[15] but is inert until and unless someone wants to uphold one of those ideas, assert one of those ideas or do something with one of those ideas. In other words, *for an objective structural or cultural property to exercise its causal powers, such powers have to be activated by agents.*

The proper incorporation of personal powers into the conceptualisation of conditioning entails the following three points. Firstly, that social properties or, more exactly, the exercise of their powers, are dependent upon the existence of what have been termed 'projects', where a project stands for any course of action intentionally engaged upon by a human being. These projects, *as subjectively conceived of by people*, are necessary for the activation of social properties, that is their transformation into powers. Secondly, only if there is a relationship of congruence or incongruence between the social property and the project of the person(s) will the latter activate the former. Congruity or incongruity need not be the case. For example, if someone's project was to engage in regular private prayer, no structural power on earth could prevent it though, of course, socio-cultural influences might be at work discouraging the activity of praying. When congruence prevails, it represents a structural enablement and where incongruence exists, it constitutes a structural constraint. Thirdly, and most importantly, subjects have to respond to these influences by using their own personal powers to deliberate reflexively, always under their own descriptions, about how to act in such situations. What is unique about the reflexivity of human beings is that it can involve anticipation. A constraint or an enablement need not have impinged or impacted, it could just be (fallibly) foreseen. Hence, the efficacy of any social property is at the mercy of the subjects' reflexive activity.

In the case of any such property, outcomes vary enormously with agents' creativity in dreaming up brand new responses, even to situations that may have occurred many times before. Ultimately, the precise outcome varies with subjects' personal concerns, degrees of commitment and with the costs different agents will pay to see their projects through in the face of structural hindrances. Equally, they vary with subjects' readiness to avail themselves of enablements. The one result that is rarely, if ever, found is a complete uniformity of response on behalf of every person who encounters the same constraint or the same enable-

---

[15] See Margaret S. Archer, *Culture and Agency: the Place of Culture in Social Theory* Cambridge, Cambridge University Press, 1998, ch. 5. Metaphorically, the Universal Library is where all World Three items of knowledge are lodged.

ment. The deliberative process involved has nothing in common with cost–benefit analysis. It is emotionally charged, rather than being a simple exercise in instrumental rationality, because it is maintained that our emotions (as distinct from moods) are commentaries on our concerns,[16] which supply the 'shoving power' leading to action (or the resistance resulting in inaction).

To deal adequately with this variation in subjects' responses, when agents are in the same social situation, does indeed mean addressing their subjectivity. It entails acknowledging their *personal powers*, in particular their power of reflexivity to think about themselves in relation to society and to come to different conclusions that lead to variable action outcomes. In short, without knowledge about their internal deliberations, we cannot account for exactly what they do. This can be quickly illustrated by considering another potential structural power, namely the differential placement of agents in relation to the distributions of resources and the impossibility of deducing determinate courses of action from such positionings alone. Suppose a collectivity of agents is well placed in terms of remuneration, repute and representation – or 'class', 'status' and 'power'. These positionings cannot in themselves be assumed to engender reproductive projects, despite this group having much to lose objectively if they do not adopt them. To begin with the most obvious reason, not all people are guided by their objective interests; they can choose to marry downwards, to take vows of poverty, to renounce titles or to say a plague on the rat-race. Thus, at best, this leaves a probability statement about the doings of 'most people most of the time', but to what actual courses of action do these probabilities attach?

Since there is no answer to that question, we are thrown back upon empirical generalisations such as 'the greater the cost of a project, the less likely are people to entertain it'. Not only is that no explanation whatsoever (merely another quest for Humean constant conjunctions) but also, far from having eliminated human reflexivity, it relies upon a banal and most dubious form of it. Instead, sociologists covertly recognise that subjectivity cannot be ignored. Yet, more often than not, this 'recognition' consists in it being smuggled in by social theorists *imputing subjective motives* to agents, rather than examining the subject's own reflexively defined reasons, aims and concerns. Analytically, the result is the 'Two-Stage Model' presented in Figure 1. Effectively, this model transforms the first-person subjective ontology[17] of the agent's internal

---

[16] Margaret S. Archer, 'Emotions as Commentaries on Human Concerns', in Jonathan Turner (ed.), *Theory and Research on Human Emotions*, Amsterdam, Elsevier, 2004, pp. 327–56. Thus, I do not follow Max Weber in representing 'affectual action' as a separate form of action.

The Two-Stage Model

1 Structural and/or cultural properties *objectively* shape the situations that agents confront involuntarily and *exercise powers of constraint and enablement* in relation to –

2 Subjective properties imputed to agents and assumed to govern their actions:

- promotion of vested interests   (critical realism)
- instrumental rationality   (rational choice theory)
- habitus/induced repertoires   (Bourdieu/discourse theory)

Figure 1 The Two-Stage Model

conversation into a third-person 'objectivist' account proffered by the investigator.

Social realists have often been guilty of putting imputed responses to vested interests or objective interests into accounts of action as a kind of dummy for real and efficacious human subjectivity. There are many worse exemplars, and probably the worst is rational choice theory, which imputes instrumental rationality alone[18] to all subjects as they supposedly seek to maximise their preference schedules in order to become 'better off' in terms of some indeterminate future 'utiles'. Subjectively, every agent is reduced to a bargain hunter and the human pursuit of the *Wertrationalität* is discountenanced.[19] Bourdieu, too, frequently endorsed an empty formalism about subjectivity, such that people's positions ('semi-consciously' and 'quasi-automatically'[20]) engendered dispositions to reproduce their positions. Such theoretical formulations seem to lose a lot of the rich and variable subjectivity that features prominently in his *La Misère du Monde*. In the cultural counterpart of the above, discourse 'theory' simply holds these ill-defined ideational clusters to have gained unproblematic hegemony over the subjectivity of a given population.

The inadequacies of any version of the 'Two-Stage Model' can be summarised as follows: (1) the failure to investigate anybody's subjectivity; (2) the imputation of homogeneous concerns and projects to some given

---

[17] Internal conversations have what John Searle calls a 'first-person ontology' because of their subjective mode of existence: 'each of my conscious states exists only as the state it is because it is experienced by me, the subject'. John Searle, *Mind, Language and Society*, London, Weidenfeld and Nicolson, 1999, p. 43.

[18] See Margaret S. Archer and Jonathan Q. Tritter (eds.), *Rational Choice Theory: Resisting Colonisation*, London, Routledge/Taylor and Francis, 2001.

[19] Martin Hollis, 'Honour among Thieves', *Proceedings of the British Academy*, 75, 1989, 163–80.

[20] Pierre Bourdieu, *Outline of a Theory of Practice*, Cambridge, Cambridge University Press, 1977 and *The Logic of Practice*, Oxford, Polity Press, 1990.

group or collectivity; (3) the endorsement of 'passive agents'; and (4) the foundational denial that the personal power of reflexivity needs to be understood. Sociology can neither dispense with reflexivity nor make do with such impoverished acknowledgements of it. If this personal property and power is to be given its due, to do so entails replacing the third-person imputation of subjectivity by its first-person investigation.

It is proposed that 'reflexivity' be incorporated as a personal property of human subjects, which is prior to, relatively autonomous from and possesses causal efficacy in relation to structural or cultural properties. Clearly, this means that only limited tracts of people's subjective lives are pertinent to social theory. For example, I presume no one would suggest that a dislike of spinach has causal powers beyond a capacity to disrupt family tea time. However, I want to defend the much more concrete response, namely that the aspect of 'subjectivity' which should be given its due is our reflexivity. In other words, 'reflexivity' is put forward as the answer to *how* 'the causal power of social forms is mediated *through* human agency'. Our internal conversations perform this mediatory role by virtue of the fact that they are the way in which we deliberate about ourselves in relation to the social situations that we confront, certainly fallibly, always incompletely and necessarily under our own descriptions, because that is the only way we can know or decide anything.

3 Reflexivity and the endorsement of different courses of action

Reflexivity, exercised through internal conversation, is advanced as the process which not only mediates the impact of social forms upon us but also determines our responses to them. Firstly, reflexive mediation is essential for giving an account of precisely what we do rather than a statement about probable courses of action. And, in relation to constraints and enablements, agential responses can vary greatly: from evasion, through compliance, to strategic manipulation or subversion. Secondly, if it is held that agential subjectivity has itself been moulded by social influences, such as ideology, 'habitus' or, for argument's sake, 'discourse', it is impossible to ascertain for whom this is and is not the case without examining their inner dialogue. It cannot be the case for all, because 'the sociologist' has seen through these *attempts* at ideational misrepresentation in order to be able to describe them, but cannot claim a monopoly on this ability.

Certainly, because we are not infallible, it can be maintained that social factors affect agents' outlooks without people's awareness. That would be the case for ideological influences or for members of a social class overestimating an objective obstacle, like those working-class parents who used to turn down grammar school places on the grounds that 'they are not for the likes of us'. Again, however, we cannot know that this is the case without examining agents' subjectivity, their reflexive internal conversations. Without that we cannot discover what 'ideology' or 'social class' has encouraged one person to believe but failed to persuade another to accept. What cannot be assumed is that every ideological effort will or can be successful in instilling all people with the beliefs in question. Ideologies, however hegemonic, are not in themselves influences, but rather attempts to influence. They too, as a cultural counterpart of structural factors, involve both impingement upon the subject and reception by the subject. Reception is obviously heterogeneous, or no one would ever have accepted a grammar school place for their working-class child and no counter-ideology would ever have been formulated.

In brief, it will be argued that our personal powers are exercised through reflexive inner dialogue and that internal conversation is responsible for the delineation of our concerns, the definition of our projects and, ultimately, the determination of our practices in society. It is agential reflexivity which actively mediates between our structurally shaped circumstances and what we deliberately make of them. There is an important caution here: people cannot make what they please of their circumstances. To maintain otherwise would be to endorse idealism and to commit the epistemic fallacy.[21] Indeed, if people get their objective circumstances badly wrong, these subjects pay the objective price whether or not they do so comprehendingly. To believe incorrectly that one can service a heavy mortgage results in foreclosure, with further objective consequences for obtaining alternative accommodation. What reflexivity does do is to mediate by activating structural and cultural powers, and in so doing there is no single and predictable outcome. This is because subjects can exercise their reflexive powers in different ways, according to their very different concerns and considerations.

Thus, an alternative 'Three-Stage Model' is advanced, one that gives both objectivity and subjectivity their due and also explicitly incorporates their interplay through the process of reflexive mediation.

Stage 1 deals with the kind of specification already developed about how 'social forms' impinge and impact on people by moulding their situations. This I summarised as follows in an earlier work:

Given their pre-existence, structural and cultural emergents shape the social environment to be inhabited. These results of past actions are deposited in the form of current situations. They account for what there is (structurally and culturally) to

---

[21] The 'epistemic fallacy' is the substitution of how matters are taken to be for how they in fact are, even if we cannot or do not know the latter. See Andrew Collier, *Critical Realism*, London, Verso, 1994, pp. 76–85.

be distributed and also for the shape of such distributions; for the nature of the extant role array, the proportion of positions available at any time and the advantages/disadvantages associated with them; for the institutional configuration present and for those second order emergent properties of compatibility and incompatibility, that is whether the respective operations of institutions are matters of obstruction or assistance to one another. In these ways, situations are objectively defined for their subsequent occupants or incumbents.[22]

The Three-Stage Model

1 Structural and cultural properties *objectively* shape the situations that agents confront involuntarily, and *inter alia* possess generative powers of constraint and enablement in relation to
2 Subjects' own constellations of concerns, as *subjectively* defined in relation to the three orders of natural reality: nature, practice and the social.
3 Courses of action are produced through the *reflexive deliberations* of subjects who *subjectively* determine their practical projects in relation to their *objective* circumstances.

Figure 2 The Three-Stage Model

However, these social features only become generative powers, rather than unactivated properties, in relationship to subjects' projects.

Doubtless, it will be asked, 'Don't these social factors affect people's motivation and thus the very projects they pursue?' There are indeed structural properties, such as vested interests, and cultural properties, such as ideology, which can motivate by encouraging and discouraging people from particular courses of action without their personal awareness. These are the unacknowledged conditions of action, yet, whilst it may seem paradoxical, it is maintained here that they have first to be found good by a person before they can influence the projects she entertains. How is this seeming paradox resolved? The answer lies in being precise about what a subject needs to be aware of in order to be influenced. Let us first take a structural example. For a person to find a vested interest good does not entail that she has full discursive penetration of that property, as if she were endowed with all the qualities of the best sociologist. Subjects do not and cannot know everything that is going on, or there would be no such things as 'unacknowledged conditions'. There are indeed, but all those conditions need to do in order to shape a subject's motivation is to shape the situation in which she finds herself.

[22] Margaret S. Archer, *Realist Social Theory*, Cambridge, Cambridge University Press, 1995, p. 201.

Take a young academic, whose mother tongue is English. What she recognises and takes for granted about her situation are aspects of its ease: books are quickly translated into English, which is also one of the official languages at conferences, is used in the best-known journals and so forth. What she does not need to possess is discursive penetration about *why* her situation is so comparatively easy and rewarding. She does not need to acknowledge that she is a beneficiary of neo-colonialism, which has given English the academic status it has today. In order for her motivation towards her academic career to be enhanced and for her to follow courses of action to this end, all she has to recognise consciously and to find good is, for example, the ease and fluency with which she makes interventions at her first international conferences.

Unacknowledged cultural conditions work in exactly the same way, by shaping situations. This same young academic might rapidly be appointed to the editorial board of a journal and regard this as a further indication of her success. However, at successive board meetings she finds her interventions being interrupted, her suggestions ignored and her reservations overridden. What she feels in this situation is unease, and her motivation to participate or even to attend declines accordingly. Her discomfort is all she needs to know in order for her to back out of this potential opening. It is not necessary for her to understand that she had been an instance of female 'tokenism' in order to explain her increasing silence and gradual withdrawal.

Structural factors also operate as deterrents – capable of depressing agential motivation and discouraging certain courses of action. They do so by attaching different opportunity costs to the same course of action (such as house purchase) to different parts of the population. This is how 'life chances' exert causal powers, but it must be noted that their outcomes are only empirical tendencies. And what no tendency can explain is why x becomes a home owner and y does not, when both are similarly socially situated. That is a question of the subjects' own concerns and their internal deliberations, which govern whether or not particular people find the cost worth paying. The simple fact that somebody is faced with a deterrent, in the form of an opportunity cost, does not mean that they are necessarily deterred, any more than does the fact that people inherit vested interests mean they are bound to defend them – Tony Benn renounced a title in order to sit in the House of Commons.

In short, there are a number of ways in which both structural and cultural factors can affect people's motivation and, hence, the projects that they will formulate. However, for such social factors to be influential, they *do not first have to become internalised as part of a subject's dispositions*. Indeed, some of the ways in which they work – such as giving (situational) encouragement or discouragement – are incompatible with the notion of prior internalisation. Someone's projects cannot be discouraged, and thus reduced in the light of their circumstances if their expectations had already been adjusted downwards. In that case, discouragement would never occur.

Certainly, an accumulation of discouraging (or encouraging) experiences *may* become internalised as expectations. Once again, it is impossible to know for whom this is or is not the case without examining the form that their reflexive deliberations have taken during the course of their biographies. And subjects are not uniform in this respect. Thus, we will later meet Billy, an unskilled worker who had been made redundant four times as a victim of the progressive decline in manufacturing industry. On each occasion, his response was to pick himself up and resume the struggle to 'work himself up'. Equally, those who 'accept' discouragement do not simply give up and become 'passive' victims of their circumstances. Instead, they actively use their reflexivity to devise 'second' or 'third' best projects for themselves, as will be seen with Joan in chapter 3. These are not 'passive agents', dispositionally reconciled to their experiential lot. They are reflexively aware of unfairness, regretful about foreclosed opportunities, but continue to do what they can about what they care about most in circumstances not of their making or choosing.

Stage 2 examines the interface between the above and agential projects themselves for, to repeat, it is not personal properties that interact directly with structural or cultural properties, but subjects' powers as expressed through the pursuit of their projects that activate the powers of social forms. The generic questions posed by a subject over her lifetime and the answers she gives herself during her life course can be distilled into two: 'What do I want?' and 'How do I go about getting it?' The answer to the first question is undoubtedly influenced by what a subject knows or finds out, because such information is not evenly distributed throughout society. Nevertheless, an active subject is still required to actualise such influences, which are not hydraulic determinants. The readiest way of activating these social powers is when a subject can answer the question 'What do I want?' from within her natal context and does so without looking any further. She thus confirms her context by confining her subjective deliberations to it. However, the majority of interviewees could not and did not do so. Some temporised (usually by staying on at school), whilst others actively courted experience and sought information from beyond their social backgrounds.

In other words, the fact that there are indeed socially inegalitarian distributions of information does not generate a uniformity of response from those similarly situated in relation to them. How individual people answer the above two questions involves a dialectical interplay between their 'concerns' – as they reflexively define them – and their 'contexts' – as they reflexively respond to them. The answers that they give to themselves are arrived at through internal conversation. To explain their actions entails understanding their intentions – as arrived at through external 'inspection' and inner dialogue.

In relation to the question, 'What do I want?', I have earlier conceptualised the internal process of answering it as the 'DDD scheme',[23] representing three significant moments that can be distinguished as phases of the life-long internal conversation: discernment, deliberation and dedication. (1) Discernment is fundamentally about the subject putting together reflective, retrospective and prospective considerations about the desiderata to which she is drawn through an inner dialogue that compares and contrasts them. It is an inconclusive moment of review; at most, this self-talk begins to clarify our relationship to our reigning concerns because, as 'strong evaluators',[24] we cannot be lacking in concerns. It does so by clarifying our predominant satisfactions and dissatisfactions with our current way of life. Thus, the moment of discernment serves to highlight our positive concerns without discriminating between them. It is a process of book-marking in which actual and potential items of worth are registered for further consideration. Sifting of a negative kind is involved because, out of the plenitude of possible concerns available to anyone, only those that have been logged in constitute topics for further deliberation.

(2) Deliberation is concerned with exploring the implications of endorsing a particular cluster of concerns from those pre-selected as desirable to the subject during the first moment. This is performed by disengaging the demands, the merits and the likely consequences of that constellation of concerns were the subject to embrace them. This phase of the inner dialogue ranges from the one extreme of discarding projects, through comparing the worth of contesting concerns, to the opposite pole of preliminary determination. Deliberation produces a very provisional ranking of the concerns with which a subject feels that she should and can live. Often, this phase of the process entails a visual projection of scenarios seeking to capture, as best the subject is able, the *modus vivendi* that would be involved, whilst listening to the emotional commentary that is provoked and evoked when imagining that particular way of life. Such musings are still inconclusive, but as Peirce insisted: 'every man who does accomplish great things is given to building elaborate castles in the air'.[25]

---

[23] For a fuller discussion, see Archer, *Being Human*, ch. 7.

[24] Charles Taylor, 'Self-Interpreting Animals', in his *Human Agency and Language*, Cambridge, Cambridge University Press, 1985, esp. pp. 65–8.

[25] Charles Sanders Peirce, cited in William H. Davies, *Peirce's Epistemology*, The Hague, Martinus Nijhoff, 1972, p. 63.

We should be cautious about restricting acts of the imagination to 'great things' or 'golden deeds', because there is nothing necessarily heroic or idealistic about deliberation. What subjects warm to during this dialogical phase might be 'concerns' that are ignoble, associated 'projects' that are illegal and ensuing 'practices' that are illegitimate.

(3) Dedication represents the culminating moment of experimentation between thought and feeling that has occupied the preceding phases. In it, the subject has to decide not only whether a *particular modus vivendi* is, in her view, worth living, but also whether or not she is capable of living such a life. Thus, the moment of dedication is also one of prioritisation because the very accentuation of someone's prime concern is simultaneously the relegation or elimination of their others. Within internal conversation, dedication is a phase of inner dialogical struggle because the completion (*pro tem*) of the dialogue has to achieve both prioritisation of and alignment between the concerns endorsed, but also resignation to those relinquished.

It is Stage 3 that has generally been neglected in social theorising, but which appears essential in order to conceptualise the process of mediation properly and completely. In Stage 3, by virtue of their powers of reflexivity, people deliberate about their objective circumstances in relation to their subjective concerns. They consult their projects to see whether they can realise them, including adapting them, adjusting them, abandoning them or enlarging them in the deliberative process. They alter their practices such that, if a course of action is going well, subjects may become more ambitious, and, if it is going badly, they may become more circumspect. It is this crucial Stage 3 that enables us all to try to do, to be or to become what we care about most in society – by virtue of our reflexivity.

This final stage of mediation is indispensable because, without it, we have no explanatory purchase on what exactly agents do. The absence of this purchase means settling for empirical generalisations about what 'most of the people do most of the time'. Sociologists often settle for even less: 'Under circumstance x, a statistically significant number of agents do y.' This spells a return to a quest for Humean constant conjunctions and, in consequence, a resignation to being *unable* to adduce a causal mechanism. Equally wanting is the procedure in which subjectivity is not properly investigated, but is improperly imputed, precisely because it cannot be eliminated.

In contradistinction to both of these unsatisfactory conclusions is an approach which gives the personal power of reflexivity its due. It is to this end that the present book is devoted. To accord reflexivity its due entails fully acknowledging three points about how we make our way through the world.

1 That our unique personal identities, which derive from our singular constellations of concerns, mean that we are radically heterogeneous as subjects. Even though we may share objective social positions, we may also seek very different ends from within them.

2 That our subjectivity is dynamic, it is not psychologically static nor is it psychologically reducible, because we modify our own goals in terms of their contextural feasibility, as we see it. As always, we are fallible, can get it wrong and have to pay the objective price for doing so.

3 That, for the most part, we are active rather than passive subjects because we adjust our projects to those practices that we believe we can realise. Subjects regularly evaluate their social situations in the light of their personal concerns and assess their projects in the light of their situations.

Unless these points are taken on board, our way through the world is not a path that we ourselves help to chart and the various trajectories that we describe remain without explanation.

Part I

1   Reflexivity's biographies

This chapter is devoted to two macroscopic considerations about reflexivity – taken to be the regular exercise of the mental ability, shared by all normal people, to consider themselves in relation to their (social) contexts and vice versa.[1] The first issue concerns the proposition: 'no reflexivity; no society'. In other words, reflexivity is held to be a transcendentally necessary condition of the possibility of any society, though one that is rarely acknowledged. The second consideration takes up the bulk of this chapter and defends the proposition that some forms of social organisation foster greater reflexivity amongst their members than others. It is maintained that reflexivity has increased in scope and in range from the earliest societies to the one global society now coming into being. This latter proposition is contentious. It is denied from opposed viewpoints: by Ulrich Beck, announcing subjective freedom as a *rerum novarum* of 'reflexive modernization' (now we have it; then we didn't) and by Pierre Bourdieu, maintaining that reflexivity has always played a minor role in the guidance of social action, in the past as in the present.

No reflexivity; no society

Through those inherited dichotomies between the primitive and the modern, mechanical and organic integration, *gemeinschaft* superseded by *gesellschaft* and, most general of all, tradition versus modernity, early forms of social organisation became stereotyped as ones in which reflexivity was neither known nor required. Instead, culture, generically defined as a 'community of shared meanings', fully orchestrated the doings of primitive 'cultural dopes'. This view was epitomised in Evans-Pritchard's characterisation of the Azande, the life of whose minds derived from their coherent tribal culture:

[1] This definition is not intended to cover every aspect of reflexivity (such as checking one's arithmetic), but concerns only those reflexive processes which are explicitly social. As a distinction, it parallels that between 'action' and 'social action'.

In this web of belief every strand depends upon every other strand, and a Zande cannot get out of its meshes because it is the only world he knows. The web is not an external structure in which he is enclosed. It is the texture of his thought and he cannot think that his thought is wrong.[2]

It became conventional to accept that the members of 'old and cold' societies blindly followed traditional norms, beliefs and practices, making all action routine action and thus giving no quarter to reflexive deliberation.

Elsewhere,[3] I have called this the 'myth of cultural integration' and traced its origins from the early anthropologists until it became canonical for generations of sociologists. Specifically, this myth has led to generalised beliefs about the nature both of 'individuals' and of 'culture' in early societies, the effect of which is to exclude reflexivity or any need for it. Conversely, 'no reflexivity; no society' is reinforced by a minority of anthropologists, such as Ernest Gellner, who doubted that the minds of tribespeople were thoroughly orchestrated by tribal culture and who allowed them a much more generous quantum of self-reflexive thoughts. Gellner's Berbers could indeed reflect upon themselves in relation to their circumstances: they 'long ago sized each other up: each knows what the other wants, the tricks he may get up to, the defences and countermeasures which, in a given situation, are available, and so on'.[4] Far from being unable to think that his socialised 'thought is wrong', an individual Berber, with an ounce more gumption than his fellows and an eye to the main chance, may well have concluded that he could do far better for himself by thinking otherwise.

Equally, Gellner was no believer in a seamless web of consistent belief that characterised primitive society. Sometimes, an individual Berber had to exercise his ingenuity if he was to square the contradictions inherent in his role, such as the holy man (*agurram*) who must be generously hospitable but also appear unconcerned about the wherewithal for his openhandedness.[5] Such activities are supremely reflexive ones, entailing consideration of the self in relation to the social context and vice versa, but are also indispensable to the very working of that society.

---

[2] E. E. Evans-Pritchard, *Witchcraft, Oracles and Magic among the Azande*, Oxford, Oxford University Press, 1937, p. 195.

[3] Margaret S. Archer, *Culture and Agency: the Place of Culture in Social Theory*, Cambridge, Cambridge University Press, 1988, ch. 1; also in *British Journal of Sociology*, 36, 3, 1985.

[4] Ernest Gellner, *Thought and Change*, London, Weidenfeld and Nicolson, 1964, p. 154.

[5] '. . . an *agurram* who was extremely generous in a consider-the-lilies spirit would soon be impoverished and, as such, fail by another crucial test, that of prosperity'. Ernest Gellner, 'Concepts and Society', in Bryan R. Wilson (ed.), *Rationality*, Oxford, Blackwell, 1979, p. 44.

The reasons justifying 'no reflexivity; no society' are summarised as follows:

1 *Reflexive first-personhood is indispensable to traditional society.* A continuous 'sense of self' (as distinct from any social 'concept of the self') is a condition of social life in general. Without it, no rule, expectation, contract, obligation, responsibility or entitlement could be incumbent upon anyone in particular, unless each subject knew himself to be one and the same person *to whom* it had been ascribed. For example, it would be futile for a Zande to utter, in the third person, 'This is when a young Azande warrior takes a wife,' *without reflexive first-person awareness* that the expectation applies to him himself.[6]

This signals that the idea of a society, all members of which live life in the third person, is a contradiction in terms. It indicates the *impossibility* of a society whose members are all 'self-blind', like Sydney Shoemaker's[7] George, who can comprehend mental states in a third-person manner, but lacks the reflexive self-awareness that any such state – of belief, feeling, intention or memory – pertains to him himself. Possibly, a few 'Georges' might get by socially, doing things by imitating others and behaving as normative conventionalists. But they could do so only by following others who knew their own minds sufficiently well to give a lead when norms failed to cover every eventuality. In other words, what can be true for each 'George' cannot be true for all members of society. Whether tribal or otherwise, a society of the reflexively 'self-blind' is not possible because all societies are open systems and hence no normative canon covers all contingencies. Each 'George' would be waiting on the rest to give a lead, which no one would be capable of doing. It is only the long, cold *durée* which gives the *appearance* that the members of traditional societies are non-reflexive automata, whose actions are puppeteered by the third-person normative system of the tribe.

2 *Traditional practices require reflexivity.* Considerable emphasis is always placed upon the importance of practical action in early societies – upon tacit knowledge and embodied skills – which is non-discursive in nature and often held to work as 'second nature'. Elsewhere,[8] I have argued that our relations with the practical order and the skills deriving from interaction with artefacts – as in hunting, driving or computing – are vital in every social configuration. However, it is a mistake to leap from

---

[6] See Lynne Rudder Baker, 'The First-Person Perspective: a Test for Naturalism', *American Philosophical Quarterly*, 35, 4, 1998.

[7] Sydney Shoemaker, 'On Knowing One's Own Mind', in his *The First-Person Perspective and Other Essays*, Cambridge, Cambridge University Press, 1996.

[8] Margaret S. Archer, *Being Human: the Problem of Agency*, Cambridge, Cambridge University Press, 2000, chs. 4 and 5.

the fact that these skills are tacit and embodied to the assertion that they represent routine actions the exercise of which does not require reflexivity. In all of the above examples, things go wrong, we make human errors, the unexpected occurs and choices have to be made. Indeed, it is the very speed and readiness with which practitioners react in these circumstances that generates the illusion that these responses too are 'second nature'. They cannot be, otherwise one is committed to the notion that there is a complete codification of 'emergency procedures', which is a contradiction in terms. So, too, is the notion that such procedures as do exist work as non-reflexive habitual action. From experience, any motorist knows how much self-control it takes to follow procedural advice and 'steer into a skid', rather than intuitively slamming on the brakes.

Perhaps the disinclination to admit that reflexivity plays an indispensable part in the smooth exercise of practical skills comes from the erroneous assumption that since they are non-discursive in nature, then self-monitoring cannot be reflexive because self-consciousness entails internal *linguistic* deliberations. This is to model our intra-personal communications far too closely upon inter-personal ones. Instead, the knowledge that something is wrong, which takes us off auto-pilot, may simply be a sense of unease – that the car *feels* wrong or the *feeling* that something has upset the herd – about which we then, but only then, attempt to diagnose discursively.

3 The workability of tradition depends upon reflexivity. It has already been indicated that no culture is so coherent in its composition and no structure is so comprehensive in its organisation that it is free from internal contradictions or gaps, such that all the contingencies people confront are covered by clear expectations about appropriate courses of action. Yet, given life in the open system that is society, such situations must arise. When they do, it is up to those affected to bridge the gaps by improvisation or to deal with the contradictions by choosing what action to take. Both are reflexive activities and traditional forms of social life owe their apparently smooth functioning to this reflexive papering over of their gaps and personal coping with their disjunctions.

Moreover, the workability of tradition depends upon more than 'positional' prescriptions and expectations, on the one hand, and a 'dispositional' readiness to act, on the other. There are interactive processes to be accomplished that are unscripted and situations in which interaction itself places the script in the actors' hands.[9] Even the quiet accomplishment of everyday, routine interactions has been shown by Garfinkel[10] to

---

[9] Nicos Mouzelis, *Sociological Theory: What Went Wrong?*, London, Routledge, 1995, pp. 101f.   [10] H. Garfinkel, *Studies in Ethnomethodology*, Oxford, Polity Press, 1984.

involve constant 'reflexive accounting', as a constitutive feature of all forms of social life. This is what produces smoothly patterned relations between those involved and it is what maintains this patterning.

However, for tradition to remain workable, there has to be some means of coping with the frictions arising from interaction, be these personal antagonisms, factional grievances or bids for power. This is the case for every social formation; all that differs in traditional societies is that these events should appear to be resolved traditionally. Such resolution entails reflexivity twice over: about what to do, on the part of those with the power to act decisively, and about how to justify their actions, which often involves the elaboration of tradition itself. For example, in the Kenyan Masai Mara, villagers frequently go into town, which is permitted, but also get up to some traditionally prohibited activities on their visits. Recently, a Masai leader, speaking in front of his people, stated that there had never been a case of AIDS in the surrounding six villages – any incidence of which would have implied interactions unacceptable to tradition. However, he added, their community suffered disproportionately from tuberculosis, which carried no such implication, but merely embroidered upon TB long having been endemic in Kenya. Tradition is malleable, syncretic and adaptive, but it needs the exercise of reflexivity to make it so.

This brief excursion into anthropology was intended to indicate that reflexive self-consciousness was a transcendental condition of the possibility of any society and one for which empirical evidence can be adduced: for primitive, modern and the most recent social formations. In that respect there is no difference between them; in all of these societies some degree of reflexivity is practised by their component members.

'Reflexive modernisation': a catchy phrase to capture a phase

It will not have escaped any reader's attention that the adjective 'reflexive' is in vogue for describing current high, late or second-wave modernity. It is worth a brief examination of how 'reflexivity' is employed by Bauman, Beck, Giddens, Lash et al. to ascertain whether or not this property is regarded as being exclusive to late modernity or, rather, to have intensified with it. If the former, it traduces 'no reflexivity; no society'; if the latter, it raises the question about what currently induces more reflexivity and why. The notion that some social formations and ways of life generate *more reflexivity than others* appears reasonable and not impossible to substantiate empirically.

The term 'reflexive modernisation' was used independently by Beck, Giddens and Lash[11] before they collaborated in 1994 and published their book of the same name.[12] The concept appears to herald a new process governing the social in late modernity. The co-authors seem agreed that they are advancing a 'theory of reflexive modernisation',[13] whose governing process is that of reflexivity itself,[14] which exerts causal powers with consequences such as 'individualisation'.[15]

Nevertheless, there are considerable problems about pinning down the central concept and, ten years later, one reviewer is still asking the key question: 'what does Beck count as reflexive *processes?*'[16] This puzzlement is understandable because there is a paradox at the heart of the concept 'reflexive modernisation'. On the one hand, 'reflexivity' always entails self-monitoring and some ensuing form of self-control. On the other hand, 'modernisation', of the 'late' variety, is characterised by Giddens as the 'runaway society', the 'juggernaut' out of control, and similarly by Beck as a cluster of globally dangerous and uncontrolled 'side effects'. How can these two contradictory components, making up the term 'reflexive modernisation', fit together? It will be maintained here that they cannot. No real meaning can be attached to the notion of *systemic* reflexivity (that is, a property possessed by the social system as an ensemble of institutional 'parts'), which the concept of 'reflexive modernisation' suggests adjectively. Instead, what I believe is being proposed is that 'late' modernity fosters increased personal reflexivity at the *social level* (that is, a property pertaining to the members of society).

In what sense is *systemic reflexivity* held to exist and how does it work as a process? Is this process the cause or the consequence of increased *social* reflexivity? Indeed, how does Beck answer the question put to him about

---

[11]   See Ulrich Beck, *Risk Society: Towards a New Modernity*, London, Sage, 1992 (first published in German in 1986); Anthony Giddens, *The Consequences of Modernity*, Cambridge, Polity Press, 1990 and *Modernity and Self-Identity*, Cambridge, Polity Press, 1991; and Scott Lash, 'Reflexive Modernization: the Aesthetic Dimension', *Theory, Culture and Society*, 10, 1, 1993.

[12]   Ulrich Beck, Anthony Giddens and Scott Lash, *Reflexive Modernization: Politics, Tradition and Aesthetics in the Modern Social Order*, Cambridge, Polity Press, 1994.

[13]   Beck refers to the 'theory of reflexive modernisation', *Risk Society*, p. 87, and to an 'empirically oriented, projective theory', *Risk Society*, p. 9, and Lash to 'reflexive modernisation theory', in Beck et al., *Reflexive Modernization*, p. 112.

[14]   Giddens refers to modernisation's 'intrinsic reflexivity', *Modernity and Self-Identity*, p. 19. Beck states that 'Western (capitalist, democratic) industrial society . . . is becoming global or, simply, reflexive', 'Reply' in Beck et al., *Reflexive Modernization*, p. 175.

[15]   Again in terms of causal efficacy, Giddens refers to 'the thoroughgoing *reflexivity* which is the third major influence on the dynamism of modern institutions'. Beck et al., *Reflexive Modernization*, p. 20.

[16]   Mick Smith reviewing *Conversations with Ulrich Beck*, Cambridge, Polity Press, 2004, in *Sociology*, 39, 3, 2005, p. 547 (my italics).

what *processes* count as reflexivity, especially at the *systemic* level? Although the term 'reflexive modernisation'[17] is used repeatedly, it is not defined in *Risk Society*. It is endowed with causal efficacy: social classes, the nuclear family, science, democracy 'and their foundations begin to crumble and disintegrate *in the reflexivity of modernization*'.[18] But what is the *reflexivity* of the modernised system that is held to be causally responsible? In his contribution to the volume on *Reflexive Modernization*, Beck allows that the application of the term 'reflexivity' to the social system is misleading:

[T]he concept of 'reflexive modernization' . . . does not imply (as the adjective 'reflexive' might suggest) *reflection*, but (first) *self-confrontation* . . . This type of confrontation of the bases of modernization should be clearly distinguished from the increase of knowledge and scientization in the sense of self-reflection on modernization. Let us call the autonomous, undesired and unseen, transition from industrial to risk society *reflexivity* (to differentiate it from and contrast it with *reflection*). Then 'reflexive modernization' means self-confrontation with the effects of risk society that cannot be dealt with and assimilated in the system of industrial society.[19]

Hence, Beck is not discussing 'reflexivity' at all, and 'self-confrontation' comes from a different stable because it is not initiated reflexively by those *responsible* for undesirable side effects but by the *recipients* of those unintended consequences, who force their progenitors to confront these matters.[20]

Yet, why should a well-established term like 'reflexivity', with its stable denotations of self-monitoring and self-control, be used to refer to its precise opposite?[21] That it does just that, Beck makes clear in his 'Reply', without justifying this perverse usage:

In pointed terms, the 'reflexivity' of modernity and modernization in my sense does not mean reflection on modernity, self-relatedness, the self-referentiality of modernity, nor does it mean the self-justification or self-criticism of modernity . . . modernization *undercuts* modernization, unintended and unseen, and therefore also reflection-free.[22]

At the end of the day, 'reflexive modernisation' is simply a catchy phrase to capture a phase,[23] whose salient features (side effects) escape both the

---

17 Beck, *Risk Society*, p. 12.   18 Ibid., p. 14 (my italics).
19 Beck et al., *Reflexive Modernization*, p. 6.
20 'Modernization risks, then, can only be "forced on" the sciences, "dictated to them", from the *outside*, by way of public recognition . . . the *publicly transmitted criticism of the previous development becomes the motor of expansion*' Beck et al., *Reflexive Modernization*, pp. 160–1 (my italics).
21 Ibid. Underscoring the fact that science and technology possess no reflexively guided processes of control is Beck's statement that they have no 'brakes or a steering wheel'. Ibid., p. 180.   22 Ibid., p. 177.
23 When writing their joint 'Preface', Beck et al.'s best collective recommendation for the concept is that since 'the protracted debate about modernity and postmodernity has

classic 'progressive' portrait of modernity and the playful figure of post-modernity.

However, there is an important claim being advanced about *social* reflexivity, as distinct from the rodomontade about *systemic* reflexivity. It asserts that there is an increase in *social* reflexivity, a pressure upon individuals to become more reflexive, as global society progressively distances itself from traditionalism, and it is one that is worth taking seriously. Fundamentally, Beck goes on to maintain that globalisation fosters a greater amount of *individual or agential* reflexivity than ever before, with a far-reaching impact upon life-styles and personal biography. If this statement is warranted, it should be highly consequential for the way in which we 'make our way through the world' in the third millennium.

Individual reflexivity: its increasing tasks and burdens

The thesis about the increase in *social* reflexivity starts from the statement that 'in reflexive modernity, individuals have become ever more free of structure; in fact they have to redefine structure (or as Giddens puts it, tradition)'.[24] The main line of argument concentrates upon what Beck had already heralded in *Risk Society*, that is, 'the beginning of a *new mode of societalization*, a kind of "metamorphosis" or "categorical shift" in the relation between the individual and society'.[25] *Risk Society* had emphasised the contemporary *disintegration* of entrenched structures from which people were 'liberated' and, consequently, propelled towards 'individualisation'. In turn, this implies much higher demands being placed upon each individual's reflexivity to choreograph his or her own life course.

Globalisation increasingly freed people from the traditional restraints of 'common values' and replaced the burden of conformity with the imperative to elaborate a 'self-culture' and express it in 'a life of one's own'. In parallel, the traditional social groupings structured by industrial society (class, status and gender) *dissolved*, thus shattering the frail unity of shared life experiences which had lasted until the 1950s. Simultaneously, individuals became 'disembedded' from the old ties of kinship, neighbourhood, regional culture and geographical location through their progressive entry into the labour market which, given sufficient affluence and welfare provisions, intensified the '*dissolution* of lifeworlds associated with class

Footnote 23 (*cont.*)
   become wearisome', then the 'idea of reflexive modernization, regardless of whether or not one uses that term as such, breaks the stranglehold which these debates have tended to place on conceptual innovation'. *Reflexive Modernization*, p. vi.   [24] Ibid., p. 177.
[25] Beck, *Risk Society*, p. 127.

and status group subcultures'.[26] Gone were the old industrial 'zombie categories', such as social classes or housewives, which encouraged their members to coalesce around interests common to them. Shifting occupational requirements and the mobility associated with employment opportunities enforced a permanently nomadic existence because, in Bauman's words, '[t]here is no "re-embedment" prospect at the end of the road taken by (now chronically) disembedded individuals'.[27]

The decline of *routine action* is the direct consequence of these changes: 'In the place of binding traditions, institutional guidelines appear on the scene to organize your own life . . . *The crucial difference is that modern guidelines actually compel the self-organization and self-thematization of people's biographies.*'[28] Not only are individuals *compelled* to develop elective 'do-it-yourself biographies', but they are also newly burdened with sustaining this tightrope act, with daily renewing the inter-personal relationships (love, marriage, parenthood), enabling them to keep their balance, and also charged with regularly updating their own choreography. If this scenario carries conviction, is de-routinisation accompanied by an intensification of reflexivity, which takes over from routine in providing the guidelines for action? At first glance, this appears to be Beck's assumption, given the part played by self-definition, self-realisation and, above all, self-determination in making a 'life of one's own'. However, it should be underlined that increased reflexivity is not an automatic consequence or corollary of decreased routinisation. One alternative could be a growth in 'spontaneity', perhaps rooted in the impulses of Mead's rather mysterious 'I';[29] another could be Baudrillard's capricious 'playing with the pieces', in postmodernist fashion.[30] On the whole, Beck's exemplifications of living a 'life of one's own' show closer kinship with such forms of spontaneous action than with reflexive deliberation.

Despite his persistent (if often perverse) references to 'reflexivity', Beck takes no interest in it as a process. Although he makes frequent use of the self- prefixes, indicative of reflexivity, the concept itself remains pallid and unexamined. Paradoxically, reflexivity is not accorded the centrality one would necessarily expect if, as Beck and Beck-Gernsheim argue, '[t]he choosing, deciding, shaping human being who aspires to be the author of his or her own life, the creator of an individual identity, is the central character of our time'.[31] If not, why not?

---

[26] Ulrich Beck and Elizabeth Beck-Gernsheim, *Individualization*, London, Sage, 2002, p. 31.
[27] Zygmunt Bauman, 'Foreword', in Beck and Beck-Gernsheim, *Individualization*, p. xvi.
[28] Beck and Beck-Gernsheim, *Individualization*, pp. 23–4 (my italics).
[29] G. H. Mead, *Mind, Self and Society* [1934], Chicago, University of Chicago Press, 1974, pp. 113f.   [30] J. Baudrillard, 'On Nihilism', *On the Beach*, 6, 1, 1984, p. 24.
[31] Beck and Beck-Gernsheim, *Individualization*, pp. 22–3.

Central conflation and its incompatibility with reflexivity

The explanation of this lack of engagement with reflexive processes is argued here to derive from Beck's 'central conflationism', that is, his elision of structure with agency, which means that the interplay between them cannot be examined. Unlike Giddens, who has made a principled and theoretical attempt to transcend the distinction between the two through his notion of 'duality',[32] Beck's conflation of structure and agency is empirically based. It stems from his description of what 'structures' and 'agents' have become during late modernity. Whether central conflation is endorsed theoretically or empirically, it remains incompatible with what is required by any workable notion of reflexivity. By definition, reflexive deliberation depends upon a clear subject–object relationship. It can neither work nor be examined if there is any tendency to conflate the two, that is, to elide the properties and powers pertaining respectively to 'structure' and to 'agents'. As Mouzelis argues,

> it is only when the objective–subjective distinction is maintained that it is possible to deal in a theoretically congruent manner with cases where situated actors distance themselves from social structures relatively external to them in order to assess, more or less rationally, the degree of constraint and enablement these structures offer, the pros and cons, the chances of success or failure of different strategies, etc.[33]

Reflexivity depends upon a subject who has sufficient personal identity to know what he or she cares about and to design the 'projects' that they hope (fallibly) will realise their concerns within society. Equally, it depends upon the objectivity of their social circumstances which, under their own (fallible) descriptions, will encourage them to follow one course of action rather than another. Deliberation consists in people evaluating their situations in the light of their concerns and evaluating their projects in the light of their circumstances. Any form of conflation fundamentally precludes examination of this interplay. It is submitted that Beck and Beck-Gernsheim's concept of 'institutionalised individualism',[34] as the new structure of late modernity, could not be more conflationary in its clamping together of structure and agency.

They do not argue that 'de-traditionalisation' should be equated with 'destructuring', because 'in modern societies new demands, controls and constraints are being imposed on individuals'[35] through a network of

---

[32] Anthony Giddens, *Central Problems in Social Theory*, London, Macmillan, 1979, pp. 69f.
[33] Nicos Mouzelis, 'Habitus and Reflexivity', unpublished manuscript.
[34] Authors' 'Preface', in Beck and Beck-Gernsheim, *Individualization*, p. xxi.
[35] Beck and Beck-Gernsheim, *Individualization*, p. 2.

regulations, conditions, provisos, such that individualisation does not represent unfettered subjectivity. Nevertheless, 'liberation' from traditional structural constraints and the proportional surge of individualisation means that, 'under the tidal wave of new life designs, of do-it-yourself and tightrope biographies', the 'structures of the "social" are having to be renegotiated, reinvented and reconstructed'.[36] In other words, any notion of a 'systemic' level, with sufficient durability for its properties and powers to be disengaged, activated and exerted, has been rendered obsolete. Additionally, the newly institutionalised 'network of regulations' is open to so many personal trial-and-error permutations that it is not seen as a generative mechanism exercising causal powers. Therefore, it is unsurprising that Beck and Beck-Gernsheim conclude that their analysis has nullified the premise of 'social-structural analyses' because, '[w]ith the emergence of a self-culture, it is rather a *lack* of social structures which establishes itself as the basic feature of the social structure'.[37] Or, to put their central conflation in a nutshell, 'individualization is becoming *the social structure of second modern society itself*'.[38]

As structural powers recede, social determinism diminishes and the scope for individual decision-making increases:

Individualization in this sense means that each person's biography is removed from given determinations and placed in his or her own hands, open and dependent on decisions. The proportion of life opportunities which are fundamentally closed to decision-making is decreasing and the proportion of the biography which is open and must be constructed personally is increasing.[39]

If it is the case that macro-influences do recede, we should anticipate greater variability at the micro-level of individual agents, as the exercise of their personal powers is freed from external controls. However, the paradox of Beck and Beck-Gernsheim's *agential* portrait is that increased individualisation is *not* accompanied by increased individuation. There is no growth in real personal differentiation, and thus in the heterogeneity of the population. This explains their lack of interest in the *process* of reflexivity itself, in the types of subjective deliberations linking different personal concerns to correspondingly different biographical outcomes.

In this version of central conflation, both structures and agents are characterised by such indeterminacy that they can have no determinate consequences for one another. As far as structure is concerned, it is not seriously allowed that different groupings of agents face truly different objective 'circumstances', which they take into account, under their own descriptions, in the process of their subjective decision-making. Instead,

---

[36] Ibid., p. 14.   [37] Ibid., p. 51.   [38] 'Authors' Preface', ibid., p. xxii.
[39] Beck, *Risk Society*, p. 135.

their circumstances (not of their making or choosing) are levelled out.[40] For example, extremes of poverty and wealth are deprived of significance by the observation that, for the majority, their positions on society's wealth distribution are not durable but are readily transposed a few years later. Thus, social inequality becomes 'ambivalent' rather than influencing different courses of action. A general, homogeneous feeling of anxiety is held to replace the *heterogeneous* strategies by which differently placed individuals once sought to advance themselves or to protect themselves in relation to social stratification.

Even if it were granted, for argument's sake, that the ambivalence and indeterminacy of agents' 'circumstances' meant that these made little difference to the process of decision-making, the same does not follow for the decision-makers. If agents have gained increased scope for action, then individual differences, exercised as personal properties and powers, should make more of a difference to their actions – arrived at reflexively. This is what will be ventured here, on the basis that our personal identities are defined by our 'constellation of ultimate concerns' and that our quests for social identities are deliberative attempts to secure positions (occupational, familial, institutional, voluntary) in social contexts which allow these concerns to be realised.[41] But 'the importance of what we care about', as Harry Frankfurt[42] puts it, is disallowed by Beck and Beck-Gernsheim as being constitutive of personal identity. To them, such commitments form the (revisable) core of no one. Either these concerns are merely the 'preordained, unquestioned, often enforced ties of earlier times' (and thus not personally distinctive) or our commitments today are strictly 'until further notice' (and thus too unstable to define identity).[43]

To Beck and Beck-Gernsheim, personal biography is discontinuous in nature. It is subject to breakdown, reconstitution and reinvention. Its only continuity is not one of underlying and enduring concerns but of the narrative form imposed upon it by the fickle and non-binding 'decisions' of its narrator. In other words, their social being is ultimately an ideational self-construct rather than a seat of action. The active agent is dispersed into and conflated with his or her risky environment; at most, he becomes *provisional man* and she is *pro tem* woman. As such, their capacity for inner deliberation may have increased, but it is capricious and kaleidoscopic in its nature and effects. Although every life is lived electively, because (revisable) choices are made in the opacity and uncertainty of modern society, 'the self-focused individual is hardly in a position to take the

---

[40] Beck and Beck-Gernsheim, *Individualization*, pp. 49–51.
[41] Archer, *Being Human*, chs. 7, 8 and 9.
[42] Harry Frankfurt, *The Importance of What We Care About*, Cambridge, Cambridge University Press, 1988, ch. 7.   [43] Beck and Beck-Gernsheim, *Individualization*, p. 3.

unavoidable decisions *in a rational and responsible manner*, that is, with reference to the possible consequences'.[44] The decisions taken, and what reflexively went into their making, become uninteresting because they are *given* all the interest of people playing the lottery.[45]

Therefore, contrary to the present study, reflexivity is not tracked as the mediatory process which charts different trajectories through the world, according to differences in the mode of reflexivity practised by various groups of agents. Nevertheless, the growth of business now open to the internal conversation does invite that enterprise. Reflexivity need not be consigned to the free-form construction, deconstruction and reconstruction of life narratives; it can be examined as the causally powerful relationship between deliberation and action in people's social lives.

The demise of routinisation

In one major respect it does seem that the protagonists of 'reflexive modernity' are indeed correct: specifically, *about the decline of routine action*. As Bauman puts it, 'in a nutshell, "individualization" consists in transforming human "identity" from a "given" into a "task" . . . No more are human beings "born into" their identities.'[46] Although this statement seems to over-accentuate the *lack* of personal autonomy in traditional and earlier modern societies in order to highlight the contrast with late modernity, the conclusion drawn appears substantially correct. Lash makes the same point as Bauman when he argues that 'after the transition to reflexive modernity, *the new individualism does not become routinized*'.[47]

Beck and Beck-Gernsheim draw the conclusion that must follow from this accord about de-routinisation: 'the individual is becoming the *basic unit of social reproduction* for the first time in history'.[48] Individualization is the antithesis of collective class experience, or any other collective experience, because collectivities no longer share common lives; they are now more like aggregates in their constitution – and shifting ones at that. Once, it could be presumed that '[c]lass, social layer, gender presuppose a collective moulding of individual behaviour – the old idea that, by knowing that someone was a Siemens apprentice, you also knew the things he said, the way he dressed and enjoyed himself, what he read and how he voted. This chain syllogism has now become questionable.'[49]

[44] Ibid., p. 48 (my italics).
[45] One indicator of the fact that 'reflexivity' is accorded little sustained interest is that it merits only five references in the index to *Individualization*.
[46] Bauman, 'Foreword', p. xv.
[47] Lash, 'Foreword', Beck and Beck-Gernsheim, *Individualization*, p. viii (my italics).
[48] 'Authors' Preface', Beck and Beck-Gernsheim, *Individualization*, p. xxii (my italics).
[49] Ibid., p. xxiv.

'Habitualisation' and the challenge of change

One of the things that its questionability challenges is the continued applicability and relevance of Bourdieu's central concept of 'habitus'; indeed the example given about the Siemens apprentice seems to have this concept in mind. The new array of shifting, temporary and precarious positions is too fluid to be consolidated into correlated dispositions, which are inherited and shared by those similarly positioned. On the contrary, to Beck and Beck-Gernsheim, '[i]t is precisely this level of preconscious "collective habitualizations", of matters taken for granted, that is breaking down into a cloud of possibilities to be *thought about and negotiated*. The deep layer of foreclosed decisions is being forced up to the level of decision making.'[50] The implication is that the relevance of Bourdieu's 'semi-unconscious' and 'quasi-automatic' 'habitus' peters out towards the end of the twentieth century.

The conditions (arguably) propitious for generating social reproduction through habitualised dispositions have undergone fundamental transformation by the third millennium. Henceforth, any underwriting of a relatively stable system of social stratification by the entrenchment of reproductive dispositions is decreasingly possible. 'What is historically new is that something that was earlier expected of a few – to lead a life of their own – is now being demanded of more and more people and, in the limiting case, of all.'[51] From this, Lash draws the conclusion that 'reflexive modernization means that *increasingly modernization will be accompanied by increasing reflexivity, that is, by the increasing ability of agents to reflect on structure*'.[52]

When social contexts are characterised by rapid change, this poses an obvious problem for any theory emphasising routine or habitual action as the (main) means by which we make our way through the world. American pragmatists confronted this issue by making a distinction between those relatively unchanging circumstances, in which routine furnished a ready and effective guide to action, and those circumstances the novelty of which demanded the thoughtful formulation of an appropriate response. For Peirce, Mead and Dewey,[53] when routine action was blocked, for whatever reason, this triggered internal conversation in order

---

[50] Beck and Beck-Gersheim, *Individualization*, p. 6 (my italics).   [51] Ibid., p. 8.

[52] Scott Lash, 'Pierre Bourdieu: Cultural Economy and Social Change', in Craig Calhoun, Edward LiPuma and Moishe Postone (eds.), *Bourdieu: Critical Perspectives*, Oxford, Polity Press, 1993, p. 204 (my italics).

[53] See Norbert Wiley, *The Semiotic Self*, Chicago, University of Chicago Press, 1994 and his 'Pragmatism and the Dialogical Self', paper given at the annual meeting of the Society for the Study of Symbolic Interaction, August 2005.

to overcome the problem by reflexively generating an innovative solution. Thus, pragmatists agreed that the portion of daily life (and of life in general) that could be handled by routine practices was *variable*, and thus not total. Accompanying this was a corresponding acknowledgement that the scope for reflexivity *expanded* when subjects confronted unfamiliar and problematic situations. Is the same the case for Bourdieu's theory of 'habitus', a term deriving from the Latin 'habitual or typical condition' and defined as 'an acquired system of generative schemes objectively adjusted to the particular conditions in which it is constituted'?[54]

Bourdieu's foundational premise is that 'there exists a correspondence between social structures and mental structures', that is, between objective social position and subjective disposition. Wacquant summarises this correspondence as follows:

> Bourdieu proposes that social divisions and mental schemata are structurally homologous because they are *genetically linked*: the latter are nothing other than the embodiment of the former. Cumulative exposure to certain social conditions instills in individuals an ensemble of durable and transposable dispositions that internalize the necessities of the extant social environment, inscribing inside the organism the patterned inertia and constraints of external reality.[55]

In other words, dispositional durability derives from structural stability and then serves to reproduce the social circumstances from which the habitus itself originated. Thus, a habitus ensures the continued appropriateness of its own embodied practices *by prolonging contextual continuity*.

What about historical social change even if, in Bourdieu's view, its sources are predominantly exogenous? Will this not cut short the 'durability' of a given habitus because of the mismatch induced between the practical mastery acquired in a prior context and the practices now required in the new and discontinuous context? It should be noted that Bourdieu consistently downplayed historical variability, just as he always minimised the importance of comparative structural variations.[56] Hence, he maintained that the same homology between mental dispositions and traditional social structures persisted in the high modernity of the twentieth century. Even were his (questionable) minimisation of earlier historical change to be offset by the relative slowness with which social configurations succeeded one another – thus allowing time for dispositional adjustment – the

---

[54] Pierre Bourdieu, *Outline of a Theory of Practice*, Cambridge, Cambridge University Press, 1977, p. 95.

[55] Pierre Bourdieu and Loïc Wacquant, *An Invitation to Reflexive Sociology*, Oxford, Polity Press, 1992, p. 13.

[56] Margaret S. Archer, 'Bourdieu's Theory of Cultural Reproduction: French or Universal?', *French Cultural Studies*, 4, 1993, 225–40 and 'Process without System: Bernstein and Bourdieu', *Archives Européennes de Sociologie*, 26, 1983, 196–221.

same cannot be said today. The speed and novelty of global change must raise the question of any homology with mental states being sustained or sustainable.

However, Bourdieu insisted that any habitus was constituted by *transposable* dispositions, that is, tacit and practical skills transferable between non-identical contexts, because 'habitus' is not mere 'habit', but possesses the generative capacity to supply adaptive (if not creative) practices.[57] Thus, he maintained that habitus is 'the strategy generating principle enabling agents to cope with unforeseen and ever-changing situations'.[58] Two questions seem pertinent here. Firstly, how much contextual discontinuity is compatible with the adaptability of a given habitus? The answer cannot be 'substantial' because, if so, the lower-class habitus would not have served to confirm and reproduce members' natal positions but would have adjusted to the educational and occupational opportunities becoming available and promoting upwards mobility.

Secondly, since the habitus is always held to be the *embodiment* of a strong practical sense, giving a feel for the game, one can seriously question whether today's novel global games *can be played* by virtue of embodied practical mastery. In other words, new games with such names as 'external investment', 'labour mobility', 'foreign exchange dealing', 'multi-lingualism' or 'permanent software upgrading' need to be mastered by an intensively *discursive and deliberative approach*, one exceeding the possibilities of *embodied* skills – how can stock exchange trading or computer programming be embodied? Here, the traditional pragmatist would invoke the distinction between areas where habitual action sufficed and those calling for internal conversation, resulting in reflexively defined innovation. Significantly, when Bourdieu acknowledged a certain affinity with Dewey, he did so by elasticating the creativity of 'habit', as he also does with 'habitus', so that both can meet the new problems posed by changed circumstances.

Thus, Bourdieu argued 'that the theory of practical sense presents many similarities with theories, such as Dewey's, that grant a central role to the notion of habit, understood as an active and creative relation to the world'.[59] However, it should be noted that Dewey himself did not engage in such concept-stretching for the term 'habit'. Rather, he claimed it was 'mind' that functioned as the 'active and eager background which lies in wait and engages in whatever comes its way' – including passing judgement upon the appropriateness of habit. 'Mind', to Dewey, did indeed

---

[57] Pierre Bourdieu, interviewed in Bourdieu and Wacquant, *An Invitation to Reflexive Sociology*, p. 122.   [58] Bourdieu, *Outline of a Theory of Practice*, p. 72.

[59] Bourdieu interviewed in Bourdieu and Wacquant, *An Invitation to Reflexive Sociology*, p. 122.

engage in conscious and deliberative reflexivity, in the form of internal conversation, precisely when habitual action was blocked by unfamiliar circumstances. For Dewey,

deliberation is a dramatic rehearsal (in imagination) of various competing possible lines of action. It starts from the blocking of efficient overt action . . . Then each habit, each impulse, involved in the temporary suspension of overt action takes its turn at being tried out. Deliberation is an experiment in finding out what the various lines of possible action are really like. But the trial is in imagination, not in overt fact.[60]

Instead, the concept of habitus is stretched beyond a repertoire of responses appropriate to 'sedimented situations' alone. Yet, any given habitus must surely cease to be pertinent when situations themselves are in fast flux. If every habitus derives from 'socialised subjectivity', change is now too rapid and appropriate practices now too evanescent for inter-generational socialisation to take place. Children have to know what their parents could not and occupy positions that did not exist for the parental generation.

Central conflation and its squeeze on reflexivity

Habitus is Bourdieu's central mediating concept between subject and object, structure and agency, and objectivism and subjectivism, *inter alia*, by means of which he aims to transcend these dualisms. In other words, his project of theoretical transcendence has much in common with that of Giddens, the difference being that, whilst a crucial element of Giddens' strategy is to accentuate the knowledgeability of lay actors about their social circumstances, an equally vital part of Bourdieu's project depends upon the habitus working 'semi-unconsciously' and hence necessarily behind actors' backs.[61] Nevertheless, both theorists are what I have termed 'central conflationists'.[62] That is, they do not attempt to transcend these dualisms by upward or downward reduction of either referent, but rather regard each pair as being mutually constitutive. In other words, they constitute an amalgam whose properties and powers are completely inter-dependent and ineluctably intertwined. As Wacquant describes this,

the relation between the social agent and the world is not that between a subject (or a consciousness) and an object, but a relation of 'ontological complicity' – or mutual 'possession' as Bourdieu recently put it – between habitus, as the socially

---

[60] John Dewey, *Human Nature and Conduct* (1922), New York, Modern Library, 1930, p. 190.   [61] Richard Jenkins, *Pierre Bourdieu*, London, Routledge, 1992, p. 95.

[62] Archer, *Culture and Agency*, ch. 4 and *Realist Social Theory: the Morphogenetic Approach*, Cambridge, Cambridge University Press, 1995, ch. 4.

constituted principle of perception and appreciation, and the world which deter-mines it.[63]

This creates difficulties for Bourdieu, as it did for Beck and as it does for all central conflationists, about *how* reflexivity proper can take place at all. The nub of these difficulties is that Bourdieu's agents do not confront circumstances, but are an integral part of them. The definition of the reflexive process employed in this book points to subjects reflecting upon themselves in relation to their circumstances and vice versa. And that is predicated upon maintaining the subject and object distinction. But if there is mutual 'possession' or 'ontological complicity' between the two, there can be, at most, only distorted internal communication – though Bourdieu never discusses intra-personal dialogue – not the reflexive inter-nal conversation, which *requires* separation between subject and object. Yet, if we view our habitat through the lens of a habitus, their 'mutual pos-session' deprives human subjectivity of the necessary degree of indepen-dence from its habitat to reflect upon it (evaluate it, find it wanting, determine to change it and so forth). Moreover, since it is impossible to slough off this habitus, we are condemned to misrecognise the habitat to which it corresponds.[64] It follows that the loss of (lay) reflexivity is the cost paid for transcending the dualisms of subject and object and subjec-tivity and objectivity. That leaves us with the paradox of the later Bourdieu as the champion of reflexive sociology, to which we will return.

The expulsion of lay reflexivity is the price paid for promoting the habitus to represent our subjectivity, but it is not the sole payment. Subtracting this mental ability from the subject's repertoire of powers entails a domino effect to which further powers sequentially fall – specifi-cally, consciousness, accountability and intentionality. Separately, these 'losses' have been noted by various commentators, but it is their common cause in the banishment of reflexivity that is worth accentuating here. This is because the difference between actively making our way through the world or our passively bearing the weight of the world pivots upon the presence or absence of reflexivity.

Firstly, through the habitus, Bourdieu wanted to show how action and its outcomes were not the products of unsocialised individual wills. Therefore, each agent, 'willy nilly, is a producer and reproducer of objec-tive meaning. Because his actions and works are the product of a *modus operandi* of which he is not the producer and has no conscious mastery,

---

[63] Bourdieu and Wacquant, *An Invitation to Reflexive Sociology*, p. 20.
[64] Pierre Bourdieu and Jean-Claude Passeron, *La Reproduction*, Paris, Editions de Minuit, 1970. See the discussion of teachers and their necessary misrecognition of their own 'pedagogic action'.

they contain an "objective intention", as the Scholastics put it, which always outruns his conscious intentions.'[65] Secondly, given this lack of consciousness, it is pointless to solicit agential accounts of their doings because the tacit nature of their practical competence precludes them from accounting for their accomplishments. This means that the in-depth interviewing upon which the present book is based is bound to fail. It invites subjects to reflect verbally upon matters that are inaccessible, because unconscious, and ineffable, because embodied rather than dis-cursive. Consequently, exalting the habitus also valorises the investigator over the subject because it 'privileges analytical understanding as ineluctably superior to the native understanding of the world'.[66] It thus entails the substitution of third-person accounts for first-person ones.

Thirdly, the way has been paved for the derogation of human intention-ality, which becomes illusory:

Individualistic finalism, which conceives action as determined by conscious aiming at explicitly posed goals, is indeed a well-founded illusion: the sense of the game which implies an anticipated adjustment of habitus to the necessities and probabilities inscribed in the field does present itself under the appearance of a successful 'aiming at' a future.[67]

But to take these appearances for reality and then to construe action as being rational and calculative is to succumb to the illusion which misleads rational choice theorists. However, to hold human intentionality to be illusory disallows far more understandings of action than Elster's alone. As Jenkins puts it, we

know, on the basis of our own experience if nothing else, that actors do, some of the time, make decisions which they attempt to act upon and that they do, some-times, formulate and adopt plans which they attempt to carry out. Any model or theory of social practice which does not recognise this experiential truth will be at least as flawed as the proposition that conscious decision-making is *all* we need to understand.[68]

This depletion of personal powers for reflexive deliberation again derives directly from the 'central conflationist' conception of the human subject as inextricably entangled with his or her social position: 'persons, at their most personal, are essentially the *personification* of exigencies actu-ally or potentially inscribed in the structure of the field or, more precisely,

---

[65] Bourdieu, *Outline of a Theory of Practice*, p. 79.

[66] Jenkins, *Pierre Bourdieu*, p. 56. As Jenkins also comments: 'Further questions are also raised about the degree to which the testimony of research subjects is, by definition, unreliable and about the limits within which they can reflect adequately upon their own practice.'

[67] Bourdieu interviewed in Bourdieu and Wacquant, *An Invitation to Reflexive Sociology*, p. 125.   [68] Jenkins, *Pierre Bourdieu*, p. 74.

in the position occupied within this field'.[69] The main victim of this tilt towards objectivism[70] is reflexivity itself. What people think, plan, determine or say is never allowed to originate 'within their own heads', because internal deliberations always have to be referred backwards and outwards to the external conditions of their formation, which their habitus reflects; Bourdieu presents us with 'a world where behaviour has its causes, but actors are not allowed their reasons'.[71]

The sociologist, the subject and the possibility of reflexivity

Two defining features of the habitus and its workings are fundamental to Bourdieu's discountenancing of reflexive deliberation as common to all lay subjects: the 'semi-unconscious' operation of the habitus, held to work as 'second nature', dispenses with the need for deliberation and its embodiment prevents subjects from explaining their doings, even to themselves. Thus, 'principles em-bodied in this way are placed beyond the grasp of consciousness, and hence cannot be touched by voluntary, deliberate transformation, cannot even be made explicit'.[72] It will be argued that neither feature is (or could be) consistently upheld within his theorisation of the acting subject and that Bourdieu himself breaks with both features when dealing with one specific category of acting subject – the sociologist.

Firstly, the close adjustment between subjects and their contexts in which (subjective) individual dispositions mirror (objective) social positions relies upon the development of habitus through socialisation and experience. Such complicity between habitus and habitat implies, as Sayer notes, 'a model of a perfectly malleable human, a model which makes it impossible to understand how anyone could react against and resist at least some parts of their habitat'.[73] The model assumes a correspondence between the two, when this is, in fact, an empirical question. Yet, if we ask *how* the habitus works to produce actual practices which reproduce the habitat, it is clear that this model of 'perfect malleability' (the completely 'passive agent') simply does not do for the theory itself. Certain human properties of consciousness and self-awareness have to be called upon for action to ensue. For example, the habitus is held to generate the practices which result in reproduction through people's 'subjective expectation of

---

[69] Pierre Bourdieu, *La Noblesse d'Etat. Grands corps et Grandes écoles*, Paris, Editions de Minuit, 1989, p. 449.

[70] J. B. Thompson, 'Editor's Introduction' to Pierre Bourdieu, *Language and Symbolic Power*, Cambridge, Polity Press, 1991, p. 11.　　[71] Jenkins, *Pierre Bourdieu*, p. 97.

[72] Bourdieu, *Outline of a Theory of Practice*, p. 75.

[73] Andrew Sayer, *The Moral Significance of Class*, Cambridge, Cambridge University Press, 2005, p. 31.

objective probabilities', such as the possibilities of entering a *lycée*, to which parental actions are accordingly adjusted. This raises some awkward questions: 'How do people know what the objective probabilities are? How, if not at the conscious level, do people act upon these perceptions of probability? . . . How can an expectation be anything other than conscious?'[74]

However, the argument against conscious deliberation is held to be reinforced because the 'practical sense', used in 'embodied practice', employs 'the fuzzy logic of practice' and depends upon a 'feel for the game', neither of which is susceptible of conscious explication. Although I have argued elsewhere[75] that practical knowledge is indeed procedural rather than declarative in kind, this does not entail the *opposition* Bourdieu posits between 'totalising' scientific knowledge and 'the logic of practice which understands only in order to act'. What justifies his imposing an epistemological barrier, which hermetically seals off different forms of knowledge from one another and makes them inaccessible to other than their practitioners – who are assumed to be different people? After all, our embodied knowledge lends itself to the public codification of practice in the discursive domain, through maps, knitting patterns, cookery books and sheet music, which is consciously appropriated by others. Equally, this works both ways. Any given practitioner receives a constant flow of technical artefacts (applied science) whose usefulness to his practice requires conscious deliberation because their very novelty precludes their usage being 'second nature'.[76]

During the 1990s, Bourdieu made significant concessions about becoming conscious of and resistant to one's habitus through his advocacy of sociological reflexivity. Obviously, this raises the question of whether or not what can be true for the sociologist can be common to all. His primary concern was how to lay bare 'the *social and intellectual unconscious* embedded in analytical tools'[77] of sociology and the 'unthought categories of thought which delimit the thinkable and predetermine the thought'.[78] This could be accomplished through *collective debate* and *mutual critique* amongst all members of a scientific field. Such discursive critique allows academics to detect and correct *unconscious* forms of heteronomy because it

enables us to monitor, up to a certain point, some of the determinisms that operate through the relation of immediate complicity between position and dispositions. At bottom, determinisms operate to their full only by the help of the unconscious, with the complicity of the unconscious. For determinism to exert itself unchecked,

[74] Jenkins, *Pierre Bourdieu*, p. 82.   [75] Archer, *Being Human*, ch. 5.
[76] See Archer, *Being Human*, pp. 177–90.
[77] Bourdieu and Wacquant, *An Invitation to Reflexive Sociology*, p. 36.
[78] Pierre Bourdieu, *Leçon sur la leçon*, Paris, Editions de Minuit, 1982, p. 10.

dispositions must be abandoned to their free play. This means that agents become something like 'subjects' only to the extent that they consciously master the relation they entertain with their dispositions. They can deliberately let them 'act' or they can on the contrary inhibit them by virtue of consciousness.[79]

Thus, Bourdieu conceded the *possibility of reflexivity*, as an *option* open to certain agents, but this (major) concession still left his theorising far short of recognising the *necessity of reflexivity* for social life and life in society.

Moreover, because the *realisation* of reflexivity in academia is presented as necessarily being a *collective* enterprise, which can develop amongst those whose job it is to critique one another's ideas, it follows that this necessary condition for consciously correcting one's dispositions will be lacking for the vast majority of people – academia being 'a world apart'.[80] Yet, the development of conscious reflexivity is never allowed to be a lone, autodidactic exercise. Hence, Bourdieu's latter-day insistence that 'social agents are determined only to the extent that they determine themselves', *through their very non-reflexivity*, does not mean endorsing the view that most people are potentially reflexive subjects whose deliberations can help them to make their own way through the world.

Exaggerating historical continuity?

Bourdieu's concept of habitus and its applications are generally lacking in historical specificity but, rather, gesture towards universality. Despite occasional admissions that the effects of these socialised dispositions may be more pervasive in traditional societies,[81] the fact that Bourdieu moves backwards and forwards between his earlier anthropological fieldwork in North Africa and his later analyses of contemporary France serves to reinforce the timelessness of his theorising. Consequently, social embeddedness and the absence of choice about one's social positioning, or the presence of what I term 'contextual continuity', are taken to be the rule for all time.

Indeed, the continuing pertinence of the dispositional habitus *depends* upon the endurance of the positions with which it is intimately linked, 'in a manner that inhibits the possibility of any strong theory of *social change*'.[82] In other words, as Calhoun comments, the non-reflexive workings of habitus assume 'a high level of homology among fields, an absence of

---

[79] Bourdieu, interviewed in Bourdieu and Wacquant, *An Invitation to Reflexive Sociology*, pp. 136–7.

[80] Pierre Bourdieu, 'The Intellectual Field: a World Apart', ch. 9 in his *In Other Words: Essays Towards a Reflexive Sociology*, Oxford, Polity Press, 1990.

[81] Bourdieu, *In Other Words*, p. 65: 'in societies where *codification* is not very advanced, the habitus is the principle of most modes of practice'.

[82] Lash, 'Pierre Bourdieu: Cultural Economy and Social Change', p. 203.

systemic contradictions, and therefore a tendency towards social integration and stable reproduction of the encompassing field of power'.[83] Only given this high and lasting degree of 'contextual continuity' can the subjective dispositions constituting the habitus ensure a pre-adaptation of individuals to the objective probabilities inscribed in their social positions. Only then can Bourdieu argue that the 'most improbable practices are therefore excluded, as unthinkable, by a kind of immediate submission to order that inclines agents to make a virtue of necessity, to refuse what is anyway denied and to will the inevitable'.[84] Thus, the notion and working of the habitus is admitted to be antithetical to 'unpredictable novelty'.[85]

Hence, the 'timeless' workability of Bourdieu's concept of habitus is dependent upon a history of structural and cultural morphostasis. He described his project as one of 'uncovering some of the universal laws that tendentially regulate the functioning of all fields' and went on to speak of 'transhistorical invariants, or sets of relations between structures that persist within a clearly circumscribed but relatively long historical period'.[86] These statements raise two serious questions. Firstly, how well can his approach, based as it is upon structural and cultural continuity and the close correspondence between them, deal with past social disjunctures which 'circumscribe' historical periods when morphogenesis introduces discontinuities in structure, culture and life experience? Secondly, how satisfactorily can his analytical framework be projected forward to deal with the transformations represented by nascent globalisation, which were coming into view towards the end of his life? The answers to the two questions are closely linked.

They are contained in his brief discussion of 'crisis' which appears to concede that, during major social disruptions, 'routinised action' cannot be appropriate and that people then do cope with change through conscious decision-making. However, in the following quotation, what he gives with one hand, he then takes away with the other:

Times of crisis, in which the routine adjustment of subjective and objective structures is brutally disrupted, constitute a class of circumstances when indeed 'rational choice' often appears to take over. But, this is a crucial proviso, it is habitus itself that commands this option. We can always say that individuals make choices, as long as we do not forget that they do not choose the principals [sic] of these choices.[87]

---

[83] C. Calhoun, 'Habitus, Field and Capital: the Question of Historical Specificity', in C. Calhoun et al. (eds.), *Bourdieu: Critical Perspectives*, Cambridge, Polity Press, 1993, p. 82.
[84] Pierre Bourdieu, *The Logic of Practice*, Cambridge, Polity Press, 1990, p. 54.
[85] Ibid., p. 55.
[86] In L. Wacquant, 'Toward a Reflexive Sociology: a Workshop with Pierre Bourdieu', *Sociological Theory*, 7, 1, 1989, p. 36.   [87] Ibid., p. 45.

But this 'crucial proviso' means that our (apparently) conscious coping strategies remain orchestrated by the non-reflexive habitus, which furnishes the principles that less-than-consciously guide our actions.[88] Logically, it is hard to see how this can be – how routine principles of action, adjusted to a very different earlier setting, can supply appropriate guidelines for acting once 'contextual continuity' has been 'brutally' displaced. Instead, this seems to be a formula for generating practices inappropriate to what is needed in the new context or, for that matter, in any new field to develop – such as the global fields emerging in the late twentieth century.

What the enduring focus upon habitus cannot encompass is how global morphogenesis[89] produces circumstances that 'reward' new categories of people, who pursue the situational logic of 'opportunity'; how it generates 'new characters' who, even if they come from the old *héritiers*, are highly aware that they must reflexively select, suppress and supplement features from their inherited repertoire of routines; and how the practices they develop entail creative, reflexive thought about what courses of action do *constitute* mastery in and of the new context. Nascent globalisation rewards an innovative spirit that is the precise antithesis of any form of routinisation.

Traditionalism to modernity

As far as their treatment of reflexivity is concerned – which is my only concern with the theories of 'reflexive modernisation' and of 'habitus' – these theories appear to have equal but opposite defects. While theorists of 'reflexive modernity' assign an excessive freedom of subjective identity formation to social subjects today, the usage of the concept of 'habitus', under such changed circumstances, assumes an exaggerated continuity in the socialisation of personal identities. Both the dichotomous view in which traditionalism is held to give way to reflexive modernisation (thus making reflexivity a 'newcomer') and the relatively timeless morphostatic panorama (meaning that nowhere has reflexivity 'arrived') fall equally wide of the mark. In their different ways, both theories contain unacceptable assumptions about the *history of routinisation and reflexivity*.

There is not space here to provide even a cursory summary of the combinations of morphostatic and morphogenetic scenarios that have

---

[88] Jenkins, *Pierre Bourdieu*, p. 77.
[89] A term first coined by Walter Buckley, *Sociology and Modern Systems Theory*, Englewood Cliffs, N.J., Prentice Hall, 1967. Morphogenesis refers 'to those processes which tend to elaborate or change a system's given form, structure or state' (p. 58). It is contrasted to morphostasis which refers to those processes in a complex system that tend to preserve the above unchanged.

successively dominated in different historical formations,[90] save briefly to indicate their implications for reflexivity and its overall growth in scope (the proportion of those practising it intensively) and reach (the range of issues addressed reflexively). At the macroscopic level, it is the *relationship* between the structural system (materially grounded) and the cultural system (ideationally grounded) that conditions whether the social is characterised by morphostasis or by morphogenesis. The most stable social scenario, that of traditional societies, is generated from the co-existence of structural and cultural systems, which are both morphostatic and the elites of which are superimposed. This corresponds to ancient India and China, as Weber analysed them, and is the closest exemplar both of the 'traditionalism' portrayed in the theory of 'reflexive modernisation' and of the 'almost perfect homology between structure and culture', presented by Bourdieu.

At the start of this chapter, it was maintained that no culture was so coherent in its composition and no structure was so consistent in its organisation as to constitute an enduring form of life without constant resort to the reflexively governed actions of its members. This is the case despite cultural and structural morphostasis being mutually reinforcing in traditional societies. In other words, some reflexivity was required from all, but its practice was not life-transforming for most people, or transformatory of the social context – which is why we can still justifiably talk about traditionalism. The justification consists in the fact that the *co-existence of cultural and structural morphostasis together generated a high and lasting degree of everyday 'contextual continuity' for the population in question*: repetitive situations, stable expectations and durable relations.

Such continuity is underpinned by a low level of structural differentiation and an equally low degree of ideational diversification – the two, again, being mutually reinforcing. Thus, the structural elite was trapped in the only form of cultural discourse in parlance, in the absence of an alternative fund of ideas; similarly, the cultural elite was enmeshed in existing leadership roles, given the lack of any other form of social organisation. Cultural morphostasis, through the stable reproduction of ideas amongst a unified population, generates an ideational environment that is highly conducive to structural maintenance. Equally, structural morphostasis, through perpetuating social subordination and controlling marginality, makes a substantial contribution to cultural maintenance. When the context remains continuous over many generations, then very large tracts of everyday life come under the tutelage of routine action and remain there. Induction, initiation and imitation suffice for the transmission of this

---

[90] See Archer, *Culture and Agency*, pp. 209–73 and *Realist Social Theory*, pp. 308–24.

repertoire and for the conduct of most repetitive activities. Reflexivity is vital for the correct appropriation of rights and duties by those to whom they are ascribed, for the self-monitoring of their performance and, above all, for bridging the gap between formal expectations and actual eventualities. However, what reflexivity does not and cannot do in traditional societies is to enable its members to re-envisage either the self or the social, because they lack the ideational and organisational resources for doing so.

With the transition to modernity, the most fundament change is that both traditionalism's ideational unification and its unitary power hierarchy give way, although either cultural or structural morphogenesis can lead the way. Consequently, modernity is ultimately constituted by the growth of both diversification in the realm of ideas and differentiation amongst social groups. Since it is impossible to do justice to the complexity of the transition to developed modernity but equally illegitimate to ignore this long period during which morphogenesis slowly engaged, three points alone will be highlighted because of their bearing upon reflexivity and its increase in both scope and range.

Firstly, the kinds of processes responsible for the advent of modernity were not ones that involved the *active participation of more than a minority of the population*. Prototypically, the process involved a struggle between a traditionalist elite and its modernist assailant: Church and State, Court and Parliament, Privileged Estates and Third Estate, Monarchy and lower Samurai or Nobility and Intelligentsia. As the two locked in contest for the advancement versus the defence of vested interests, their protagonists had to engage in innovative thought and action: in elaborative argument and counter-argument to legitimate their claims and in strategic manoeuvres to gain or to retain positional advantage. For those involved, such activities were highly reflexive. There are no routine guidelines for action once 'contextual discontinuity' prevails precisely *because* it is being persistently pursued by some. Temporarily, the majority of the population can continue with their traditional practices undisturbed; most are illiterate and remain unacquainted with the new ideas in circulation and most are distant from the capitals in which key confrontations took place. Thus, it is impossible to present the decline of traditionalism as a simple trajectory with homogeneous effects for all at any given time.

Secondly, the very slowness of the modernisation process, together with its differential impacts (on the urban and the rural, the political players and the populace, advanced countries and less advanced), meant that 'contextual discontinuity' and 'contextual continuity' co-existed cheek by jowl for different sections of any given population at any particular time. Nevertheless, the fact that ideational pluralism proliferated and recruited increased (sectional) support also precluded the re-establishment of old-style cultural morphostasis. The resumed reproduction of a traditional, uniform conspectus of ideas is impossible in the face of sectionalised socio-cultural groupings. Similarly, the interaction of a growing variety of interest groups, each of which became articulate in its own defence and capable of detecting self-interest in the claims of others, was sufficient to prevent any drift back to unquestioned structural morphostasis. These dynamics sounded the knell for *traditionalism*, but did routine action decline in direct proportion? Despite the *systemic* discontinuities then marking the Western world, was it not possible for new forms of 'contextual continuity' to be established at the *social level* during the same period – in the form of class culture, urban communities, denominational groups, occupational solidarity and so forth? Given the relative lack of social mobility, this seems to have been the case. But if it is, then does this not mean that re-routinisation had time to develop? It seems quite plausible that *new* forms of 'contextual continuity' favouring *newly routinised, collective guidelines to action* could become entrenched during the transition to urbanisation and industrialisation.

Thirdly, if the restructuring of modernity does not obviously promote intensified reflexivity except amongst its elites and other organised and articulate contenders for advancement, are the concurrent effects of cultural morphogenesis more positive? With the transition to modernity underway, the organised contenders for power and position adopt countervailing ideas to legitimate their aims. To oversimplify greatly,[91] those defending their positions pursued a situational logic of *correction*, in which they conceded a little ideationally in order to buttress the consistency of their defence, with the aim of (re-)establishing ideational *unification* at the socio-cultural level. Correspondingly, those who challenged them promoted antithetical ideas, whose contradiction with the dominant conspectus reflected the situational logic of *elimination* of both the dominant and their legitimating ideas. During the great age of ideological debate, the populace did not remain immune in a cocoon of cultural traditionalism. Sooner or later they became the targets of efforts to mobilise and manipulate them in order to determine the outcomes of issues that were not of their making. As they were dragged into the ideological fray, popular awareness of alternative ideas grew – and to be aware of an alternative to tradition spells the end of traditionalism.

Cultural cleavages proliferated, as more and more groups gained 'voices' with the approach of high modernity. This entailed considerable

[91] Archer, *Culture and Agency*, developed the theme that the *logical* relations between the ideas in social circulation (the Cultural System at any given T1) had a *causal* influence upon the type of cultural integration (Socio-Cultural relations at T2) because of the different *situational logics* in which upholders of any corpus of beliefs/theories/ideologies were embroiled.

public reflexivity (external conversation) as new collectivities promoted further 'contextual discontinuities' in order to advance their own agendas. The baton passed from class-based parties to ethnic and feminist groups and on to those asserting the legitimacy of difference – the gays, the countrysiders, single parents and so forth. It seems probable that their mobilisation intensified private reflexivity (internal conversation) as people deliberated, for example, about gendered roles in the family or coming out of the closet.

Nevertheless, three features still bound such movements to the lineaments of modernity: they were essentially struggles for *incorporation* into the organised social structure, they were by definition *collective* and participation remained *optional*, even amongst covert supporters. In short, the scope and range of reflexivity had expanded as modernity developed, but it remained limited and when not limited, then still voluntary. Even in the most developed parts of 'high modernity' there was no general situational logic of *opportunity* inducing the majority of any population to embrace 'contextual discontinuity' – by consciously matching their skills in a novel manner to new but complementary outlets – and thus establishing a *modus vivendi* by individual deliberation.

Nascent globalisation and the situational logic of 'opportunity'

Again with considerable oversimplification, the emergence of globalisation is first the consequence and later the condition of unmitigated morphogenesis within and between the cultural and structural domains. Vertiginously, the generative mechanism of morphogenesis – for variety to stimulate yet greater variety – had begun to engage fully and to manifest its tendential effects.

In a prescient book, Teune and Mlinar[92] maintained that as sources of innovative ideas became concentrated within the (cultural) system rather than being distributed across and controlled by different social institutions (as with the industrial inventions and technological innovations of modernity), this induced a novel pattern for their assimilation. Instead of a process of collective social *interaction* (for example, between management and the unions) being necessary for the appropriation and application of 'variety', its concentration within a single cultural system, free from local gatekeepers, prompted a new form of *transaction* between the systemic source and those individuals who saw advantages to be derived

---

[92] Henry Teune and Z. Mlinar, *The Developmental Logic of Social Systems*, London and Beverly Hills, Sage, 1978.

from it. This abstract analysis becomes more vivid when concretised in the new quotidian transactions taking place between the Internet and its users.

Without implying, as do some sociological commentators, that all which had seemed solid had melted into the ether, the suggestion is nevertheless advanced that those features of modernity, most preservative of 'contextual continuity' in local and daily living, were now weakening. Specifically, the lack of *penetration* of radical change amongst the general population, the *slowness* of social change that permitted the re-establishment of 'contextual continuity' plus associated forms of routinised action and, above all, the situational logics of cultural 'protection', 'correction' and 'elimination', which had restrained the logic of *opportunity*, all gave way simultaneously.

Indeed, a distinctive feature of the globalisation process is its penetration and penetrative potential – to the extent of affecting everyone on the planet. Progressive penetration means that we all become denizens of one world; the problem is that we have not become citizens of it.[93] Not only is globalisation unaccompanied by new forms of government and governance, but it systematically disempowers those previous and hard-won agencies for social guidance and participation – representative democracy, the institutions of civil society, trade unionism and citizenship – once associated with development in modernity. The decline of collective forms of participation, as opposed to demonstration, widens the gap between the relatively unaccountable corporate giants and the vast majority of people, now subject to systematic deregulation. Increasingly, the responsibility for their life trajectories is passed down to the individual level, in transaction with the global system. For the first time ever, there are pressures upon everyone to become *increasingly* reflexive, to deliberate about themselves in relation to their circumstances; not freely, because unequal resource distributions, life chances and access to information have intensified dramatically on a world scale, but nevertheless self-consciously, given the demise of collective agencies shouldering the burden for them.

Next, the speed of change is fundamentally destructive of 'contextual continuity' in the more 'advanced' parts of the world: both destroying the ways of life continuous from the past and defying the re-establishment of new continuities on the basis of residence, community, occupation, religion or kinship, as in modernity's past. What is novel is that in so far as some succeed in constructing or strenuously maintaining a small shelter

---

[93] Margaret S. Archer, 'Social Integration, System Integration and Global Governance', in Ino Rossi (ed.), *Frameworks for Globalization Research*, New York, Springer, forthcoming.

of 'contextual continuity' for themselves and some significant others, this now comes at a price. The costs are in terms of a refusal to become geographically mobile, of declining occupational promotion and of rejecting educational advancement. This is no longer the romanticised endurance of, for example, the working-class community; it is a choice, it has to be made, it carries a price-tag, it is based upon personal commitment and is hostage to it. Thus, in no sense is 'contextual continuity' a default option or a fall-back position. It is just as much a deliberate choice about *modus vivendi* as are the more obviously self-conscious modes of embracing 'contextual discontinuity' and determining to make a particular form of it one's own.

Finally, for the first time in human history, the situational logic of *opportunity* is becoming predominant. The prizes go to those who can manipulate concomitant cultural compatibilities, that is, items of information or elements lodged in 'World Three', between which there is no necessary connection but the complementarities of which can be exploited to advantage. Its forerunners were those disciplinary combinations, such as bio-chemistry, radio-physics and computerised design, but as variety spawns further variety, they take generic names – systems analysis, informatics or logistics – the common denominator of which is synergy. For the individual, the name of the game is 'transferable skills' and 'human resource development' is a life-long enterprise. In this new context of changing posts and change of postings, of serial partnering and repartnering, of inter-continental changes of address, the scope for routine action, common to all, reduces to things like regularly brushing our teeth.

Nevertheless, under nascent globalisation, the inducements towards increasing the scope and range of personal reflexivity and a corresponding decrease in routinised guidelines to action are not synonymous with Beck's notion of 'making a life of one's own'. We never do make history, including our life histories, under the times and circumstances of our choosing. We never live in an unstructured environment, even if the structural contours of global society are still in formation. Individuals still start from differentially advantageous places, with different life chances, encounter constraints and enablements and causes to truncate or elasticate their aspirations and designs. Hence the necessity for more and more people to respond with increased reflexivity; the only alternative is to become a passive agent and, as nascent globalisation intensifies, that means becoming more and more of a loser. The new global distribution of resources enforces 'passivity' on large tracts of the population in the southern hemisphere but also places a higher premium on 'activity' in the north.

The 'reflexive habitus' – an oxymoron?

In sum, the foregoing argument has sided with the view of protagonists of 'reflexive modernisation' that routinisation has declined with globalisation, but with the important caveat that social structure – the constraints and enablements or the distribution of interests which help to shape 'projects' for action – has not shrunk to the proportions of 'institutionalised individualism'. Conversely, whilst it has disagreed with Bourdieu about the enduring pertinence of routine action – even allowing for the generative adaptability of habitus – it has sided with his fundamental premise that social stratification persists, albeit in a very different form from the class structure he continued to endorse.

Confronted with much the same inability to come down with conviction on either side, certain authors have worked for a compromise between them, which seeks to have the best of both worlds. In advancing the concept of a 'reflexive habitus', they aim to project Bourdieu's *dispositional* analysis forward, despite contemporary *positional* transformations, associated with nascent globalisation.

This is the compromise, as summarised in Sweetman's words:

What is being suggested here is that, in conditions of late-, high-, or reflexive-modernity, endemic crises . . . lead to a more or less permanent disruption of social position, of a more or less constant disjunction between habitus and field. In this context reflexivity ceases to reflect a temporary lack of fit between habitus and field *but itself becomes habitual, and is thus incorporated into the habitus in the form of the flexible or reflexive habitus.*[94]

The compromise concept of a 'reflexive habitus' itself seems to be compromised: it is either vacuous or an oxymoron. Moreover, it unhelpfully elides two concepts which Bourdieu consistently distinguished: the dispositions constituting habitus and reflexivity as self-awareness of them.[95]

On the one hand, it points to the necessary intensification of reflexivity under the conditions prevailing in the third millennium, as has been maintained in this chapter. Therefore, what does calling this a 'habitus'

[94] Paul Sweetman, 'Twenty-first Century Dis-ease? Habitual Reflexivity or the Reflexive Habitus', *The Sociological Review*, 51, 4, 2003, p. 538 (my italics). This quotation continues: 'To the extent that Bourdieu's "non-reflexive" habitus depends upon relatively stable conditions and on "lasting experience of social position", his analysis may thus be said to apply more to simple- or organised- modernity, where the comparative stability of people's social identities allowed for a sustained, coherent, and relatively secure relationship between habitus and field.'

[95] For a useful discussion of this point, see Dave Elder-Vass, 'Reconciling Archer and Bourdieu in an Emergentist Theory of Action', paper by courtesy of the author.

add? Presumably, that people now have a *disposition* to be reflexive about their circumstances. But does this not simply re-describe what they do and, to some extent, have always done? In that case, is it any different from those pseudo-explanations by means of which psychologists sometimes presume to account for actions by subsuming them under a personality trait? For example, observed regularities in behaviour, such as being out-going, are 'explained' nominalistically by designating those who display them as 'extroverts'. Perhaps it could be argued that what serves to distinguish such a 'disposition' from nominalism is that it implies 'preparedness'. But, if so, to be prepared must be used transitively; one must be in a state of preparation for something determinate. Otherwise, to possess the disposition boils down to the statement that most people now *expect* to have to think about the choices they make or maintain. Well, yes, they do, but it is still hard to see how calling this a 'habitus' explains anything either about their deliberative processes or about what they do. In fact, given how 'habitus' stressed the pre-adaptation of people to circumstances and the 'semi-conscious', 'quasi-automatic' nature of its operations – all of which Sweetman accepts – it is hard to think of any concept less helpful for dealing with conscious deliberations and the determination of choices.

On the other hand, Sweetman maintains that 'certain forms of habitus may be *inherently* reflexive, and that the flexible or *reflexive* habitus may be both increasingly common and increasingly significant due to various social and cultural shifts'.[96] What does 'inherently' mean here, given that Bourdieu consistently held the formation of any habitus to be the result of socialisation? What type of socialisation can provide a preparation for the unpredictable and novel? This seems to be a contradiction in terms, unless it slides into vacuity, into something like the Boy Scouts' intransitive motto: 'Be Prepared!' At least, tying knots and lighting fires without matches 'prepared' for certain, relatively improbable, survival situations, but that is not possible here, given the unpredictable contexts confronted under nascent globalisation. There are only two ways out of this impasse.

One path is taken by Mouzelis who, consistent with Bourdieu, attempts to provide an answer in terms of a socialisation that could result in the development of a 'reflexive habitus'. He refers to

a reflexive disposition acquired not via crisis situations, but via a socialization focussing on the importance of 'the inner life' or the necessity to 'create one's own goals'. For instance, growing up in a religious community which stresses meditation and inner contemplation can result in members of a community acquiring a

---

[96] Sweetman, ' Twenty-first Century Dis-ease?', p. 530.

type of *reflexive habitus* that is unrelated to contradictions between dispositions and positions.[97]

Although it seems probable that such an experience might indeed enhance what I later term 'meta-reflexivity' (reflecting upon one's reflections), this does not seem a convincing response. To begin with, whatever is in fact the case about the continued decline or relative revival of religious communities, retreat centres and so forth, it cannot be suggested that these provide the general form of socialisation current in nascent modernity, where what is at issue is the intensified reflexivity of the majority of people. Furthermore, in the Western world, such communities can only be entered by adults and thus select from amongst the pre-socialised rather than supplying their socialisation.

The other path entails abandoning any claim that it is acquired through socialisation, but accepts that it is accrued from the individual's own life experiences. The various transformations, which represent 'reflexive modernisation', 'contribute towards a continual and pervasive reflexivity that itself becomes habitual, however paradoxical this notion may at first appear'.[98] Again, what does calling reflexivity 'habitual' add to noting that it is 'continual and pervasive', given that it cannot be the motor of habitual action, as the author agrees? Finally, when the concept is voided of all connection with courses of action, paradox gives way to contradiction. For example, Ostrow writes that there 'is no clear path from dispositions to conduct. What does exist is a protensional field, or perspective, that contextualises all situations, setting the pre-objective framework for practice, without any express rules or codes that automatically and mechanically "tell" us what to do.'[99] What perspective could possibly 'contextualise all situations', especially unpredictable and unintended ones? Fatalism alone fits the bill.

If all that is meant by those introducing this concept is that people now grow up disposed to expect change, its force is unobjectionable. But it only confuses matters to use the term habitus to cover such expectations. From Bourdieu's own perspective, it seems valid to ask in what sense a disposition can justifiably be called a habitus, when it derives from personal experience rather than from parental socialisation? When it is not the source of habitual action or a generative mechanism for appropriately playing the game? When it provides no directional

---

[97] Mouzelis, 'Habitus and Reflexivity', p. 5 (my italics).
[98] Sweetman, 'Twenty-first Century Dis-ease?', p. 538.
[99] James Ostrow, 'Culture as a Fundamental Dimension of Experience: a Discussion of Pierre Bourdieu's Theory of Human Habitus', in Derek Robbins (ed.), *Pierre Bourdieu*, Vol. I, London, Sage, 2000.

guidance for the subject's actions? Moreover, in ceding Bourdieu's belief in the durability of social class to Beck's reduction of social structure to 'institutionalised individualism', the implication is that people's subjectivity is unconstrained by structural properties – and unenabled by them too. In that case, all they have to be reflexive about is their own eclectic life-styles.

Because of the conviction that there is no such entity as an unstructured society, including nascent globalisation, my aim is to hang on to the original definition of reflexivity – an individual reflecting about herself in relation to her circumstances and vice versa. This involves an acceptance of increasing disembeddedness, of a decline in traditional routinised action and of intensified reflexivity. But it also entails people with real personal concerns exercising their reflexivity in relation to real structural constraints and enablements, under their own fallible descriptions. To launch the analysis that takes up this volume, let us begin by meeting some of the new young people who have grown up under nascent globalisation. All are aged around thirty, all are living in situations of 'contextual discontinuity', all have distinctive personal concerns and, to make headway with their projects, all have had reflexively to confront the restructuring of the world.

Meet the new cosmopolitans

Raphael is the urbane son of a Thai judge, a multi-lingual, cybersmart, frequent flyer, who gained a first degree in law from Bangkok, followed by another from the UK. His long vacations are spent in Kobe acquiring Japanese in order to extend the family firm's clientele and he is currently surfing the net for American law schools. He can tell a real from a fake Rolex at a glance and knows that Highland malt is better than the most expensive blended whisky. Raphael is a cosmopolitan; he has much less in common with the people of Thailand than his father, let alone his mother. He shares precious little with his parents beyond their communal interest in the firm, the resources of which have been an enablement to his becoming an international lawyer. Raphael thus follows the situational logic of opportunity; he does not spurn the assets sunk in the family firm or invested in his own education, but he migrates – courting 'contextual discontinuity' – in order to acquire the complementary qualifications to transform the firm into a global enterprise. Although highly privileged, he still has to harness these advantages so as to chart his own trajectory and to do so through personal reflexivity because his own knowledgeability exceeds that of his background.

Dana comes from a large Romanian family, living far from the capital, whose parents were engaged in routine factory production. Her education was continually constrained by shortages of money, she completed her degree through a combination of scholarships and coaching private pupils, and finally obtained a permanent academic post in her home town. Since her overriding concern was to gain academic recognition as a specialist in English literature, she engaged in a high-risk strategy to circumvent the constraints she confronted. This entailed resigning her lectureship, embracing 'contextual discontinuity' by starting all over again on an MA in England, and then gritting her teeth for another four years of financing herself through a PhD. Dana has been a book-stacker, cinema usherette and envelope-filler, she has been homesick and hospitalised, she has eaten on a budget of five pounds a week or less, and still has no guarantee that her strategy will pay off by (re)gaining her a lectureship in England. There are no routine guidelines for the course of action she has adopted; each step has entailed a reflexive monitoring of herself and her project in relation to new and unpredictable situations. She, too, follows the situational logic of opportunity, seeking a foreign complement to her acquired skills, and will continue to do so in the knowledge that it is too late for the return of the native.

Leo had all the objective advantages of a British middle-class background: professional parents, private schooling and graduating debt-free. He rejected the prospect of becoming a 'suit' and conceived his own project for adventure tourism, in line with his passion for mountaineering, whilst still an undergraduate. Yet, he was constrained by both lack of capital and his inappropriate academic training, despite plenty of informal experience of climbing and mountain rescue. Again, a high-risk strategy was adopted in following the situational logic of opportunity. For three years Leo and his fiancée held an average of four jobs between them at any one time, they spent nothing, owned nothing and saved more than forty thousand pounds, which founded their hands-on enterprise abroad. In the course of his earlier work in bars, security and a nightclub, and in view of the diversity of their current clients (from London lawyers to Preston plumbers), Leo reflexively shed evidences of his background: his accent became intentional Essex, his dress, outdoors-for-indoors, and his vehicles came from Ministry of Defence disposal sales. Over five years, he and Annie have worked up an impressive portfolio of skills, have diversified the courses they offer, and design expeditions to the long-haul places in which they want to climb themselves. Reflexive pursuit of his concerns is now paying off, but only by embracing and actively accentuating his 'contextual discontinuity'.

Mick comes from precisely the opposite background: traditional, manual working-class parents, inner-city comprehensive schooling, marrying early and having a child. However, he acquired a skilled trade and, given the pay that this can now command, his project turned the national shortage of such skills into a considerable enablement for him. Soon after becoming qualified, Mick and a loose group of fellow ex-apprentices pooled their variety of skills and combined to form a small outlet offering comprehensive house maintenance. Until demand built up, Mick had no reservations about taking a couple of weeks' construction work from the Job Centre. Putting the two types of experience together, he saw a new opportunity. The team itself could buy and renovate derelict properties, using the profits from the sale of the first to purchase the next. Several years and a divorce later, Mick now has three bought-to-let houses of his own in the Midlands and one in Spain, where he spends increasing amounts of his time, given that his ex-wife has child-custody. When I phoned him recently to replace a cistern, he was 'unavailable' – busy winterising his yacht in Santander.

There are five points to make about these new, young cosmopolitans, who were chosen purely for purposes of illustration rather than for their typicality.

Firstly, their socialisation appears to have played a negligible role in the courses of action they have adopted to date. Indeed, all can be interpreted as intentionally turning their backs upon 'traditionalism', if this is taken to mean pursuing the life trajectories to which their social origins would typically have led.

Secondly, they have 'picked and mixed', selecting something from their backgrounds or early experiences as their ultimate concern, but then seeking to supplement it with complementary items taken from extraneous contexts which, they hope, will enable them to realise their concerns. Precisely because they have followed the situational logic of opportunity, they have also become 'contextually discontinuous' from their natal and national origins and all are now, at least partly, living abroad. In other words, 'disembeddedness' is not something that 'just happens' to people passively, there is often an active and voluntary component involved.

Thirdly, all had conceived of 'projects', in line with their concerns, which gave distinctive shapes to their lives and the manner in which they were making their way through the world – even if these are later rescinded or revised. 'Projects' themselves were matters of commitment rather than rational choice (some might say Dana and Leo had made the worst out of a good hand), and each one took considerable reflexive discernment and constant self-monitoring to sustain and advance it.

Fourthly, in the process, all had to confront constraints and enablements, both structural and cultural. Their reflexivity was required to diagnose these in relation to what they cared about, to deliberate strategically about how constraints could be circumvented and enablements harnessed to their concerns, and, finally, to determine upon courses of action that they believed were sustainable and that they could sustain as a *modus vivendi* – at least in the short to mid-term. The early days of a young cosmopolitan are not the easiest of times.

Fifthly, the career trajectories they had sketched to date bore no more relationship to positional reproduction than they themselves did to dispositional replication, even for Raphael who comes closest to playing the international exchange market in cultural, educational and financial capital. These are not Bourdieu's people, but aliens to his theory in their quest to make positions for themselves and to remake themselves for positions in the new globalised world. But they are not Beck's people either, because the personal biographies and social identities they are forging are not subject to capricious narrative revision or reducible to the superficiality of self-presentational life-styles – for all, they have been far too strenuous and costly for that.

Conclusion

In this chapter it has been argued that 'contextual discontinuity' intensifies throughout modernity, and especially during the transition to nascent globalisation, with the consequence that routine or habitual action becomes decreasingly appropriate for all. However, this growing 'disembeddedness' coincides with a shifting opportunity structure: global society is undergoing restructuring, rather than becoming destructured. In conjunction, these changes mean that personal reflexivity acquires an unprecedented importance in determining how we make our way through the world.

Reflexivity does so by *mediating deliberatively* between the objective structural opportunities confronted by different groups and the nature of people's subjectively defined concerns. Each life will describe a trajectory, shaped by structural properties and powers, as reflexively interpreted and activated by individuals. If our reflexive deliberations indeed play this mediatory role, then the outcomes will correspond neither to the endurance of stable social reproduction, generated by a lasting habitus, nor to extreme social volatility, produced by unbridled narrative inventiveness. Thus, these three divergent biographies of reflexivity – all of which are speculative – lead to diverging expectations about the process and pattern of social stratification under conditions of nascent globalisation. This book goes to the heart of the dispute and investigates the place of reflexivity in the current patterning of social mobility.

2   Reflexivity in action

Reflexivity is the 'unknown soldier' of social science: hats are doffed to it but nothing is done to establish its identity. However, 'unknown soldiers' represent the unknowable, their anonymity is their identity and, if their names could be inscribed on cenotaphs, other 'unknowns' would replace them to memorialise nameless sacrifices. This makes sense, whilst failing to get to know about reflexivity does not. Hence the oddity of the last chapter, where disagreements about 'reflexivity's biography' went deep without the nature of reflexivity becoming clear.

This book is a contemporary investigation of reflexivity in action. The present chapter examines preliminary questions. Firstly, what is internal conversation? Is it simply external conversation, minus the sound? Secondly, does it play a part in determining the courses of action undertaken by normal members of society? If so, does it help them define what they care about most and what they could do to realise it? Thirdly, what goes on during reflexive inner dialogue? Is it much the same in form and content for everybody and can this be established one way or the other? Fourthly, does the nature of self-talk differ with social origins and make a difference to social outcomes? Fifthly, because a nail is needed on which to hang the discussion, do our reflexive deliberations influence our occupational positions? If that is the case, does internal conversation also affect the pattern of social mobility characterising our life courses? Finally, if satisfactory answers are given to these questions, can we improve upon speculation when discussing the role of reflexivity in the immediate past and future?

As long as all histories of reflexivity remain speculative, there is little prospect of arbitrating between them. For example, Gagnon[1] argues that

---

[1] John H. Gagnon, 'The Self, its Voices, and their Disaccord', in Carolyn Ellis and Michael Flahery (eds.), *Investigating Subjectivity*, Newbury Park, Calif. and London, Sage, 1992, pp. 232–8. 'The domain of the private has ineluctably grown as cultures have become more complex and the intrapsychic, that is the domain of the self has become the crucial mediator in a world in which the collective connections between meaning and action, meaning and meaning, and action and action have grown less compelled and hence less compelling' (p. 239).

there has been a massive increase in the extent, complexity and variety of inner speech throughout the past two centuries, whereas George Steiner[2] maintains that, from the seventeenth century onwards, inner speech has become progressively impoverished as more and more of our 'speech selves' have been expended in external conversation. Although I have taken the former view, the argument for the increase of reflexivity with the growth of modernity could be erroneous. Were that to be the case, it would not affect the significance attached to reflexivity today. The rest of the book is contemporary in focus; it is left open whether or not Vygotsky's[3] request for a 'historical theory of inner speech' can ever be met satisfactorily.

Internal conversation: what it is and why it matters

Reflexivity is exercised through people holding internal conversations. This capacity to conduct inner dialogue is a personal emergent property (PEP) which is dependent upon, though irreducible to, a neurological base. As an emergent, self-talk is a relational property deriving from self-consciousness in conjunction with the acquisition of symbols, the most important being natural language, through which we can interrogate the world we inhabit. The key feature of *reflexive* inner dialogue is silently to pose questions to ourselves and to answer them, to speculate about ourselves, any aspect of our environment and, above all, about the relationship between them. However, such reflexivity, including meta-reflexivity in which we reflect upon our own reflections, is not exhaustive of internal conversation. This also includes non-reflexive self-talk – which is not of concern in this volume – for example, abstract inner dialogue (such as solving mathematical problems), imaginative inventiveness (creating Middle Earth or the spinning jenny) and the extrapolation of ideas (as in science fiction).

This starting point accords with Vygotsky's conviction that 'inner speech is for oneself. External speech is for others.'[4] He, too, recognised that he was dealing with an emergent stratum of human reality: 'Inner speech is not the interior aspect of external speech – it is a function in itself,' one he called 'a distinct plane'.[5] In *Structure, Agency and the Internal Conversation*, I made the case that the core features of the life of our minds, as expressed in internal conversation, were threefold. Firstly, inner dialogue constitutes a genuinely *interior* phenomenon, one under-writing a private life for the social subject. Secondly, its *subjectivity* means

---

[2] George Steiner, 'The Distribution of Discourse', in his *On Difficulty and Other Essays*, Oxford, Oxford University Press, 1978, p. 94.

[3] L. S. Vygotsky, *Thought and Language* (1934), Cambridge, Mass., MIT Press, 1964, p. 153.   [4] Ibid., p. 131.   [5] Ibid., p. 148.

that it has a first-person ontology, thus precluding any attempt to render it as a third-person phenomenon. Thirdly, internal conversation possesses *causal efficacy*,[6] one of its causal powers being the subject of the present book. However, I do not want to repeat the philosophical defence of reflexive inner dialogue, but to focus upon its exercise as a power by ordinary people in living out their social lives.

In everyday terms, what would we lack if we did not possess this property and exercise it as a power? Tomlinson's response is that without 'an effective inner voice, it is very difficult to initiate ideas, develop thought, be creative, and respond intelligently to discourse, plan, control our feelings, solve problems, or develop self-esteem'.[7] This list includes some activities that are internal to people (controlling their feelings) and some which involve external interaction (responding to other speakers). Both are vital. Internally, it is through self-talk that we define our ultimate concerns and thus our personal identities, since our singularity as persons is constituted by our particular constellation of concerns.[8] Externally, we first seek to realise these concerns in society through further inner dialogue which identifies those roles through which they can be expressed. Afterwards, we seek to acquire the roles in question. Finally, our social identities arise from the manner in which we personify such roles in line with our concerns.[9] In other words, internal conversation is not 'idle'; one of its most important causal powers is reflexively to conceive and to conduct those courses of action by which we navigate our way through the social world.

However, identities are not formed under circumstances of people's choosing. Not only is everyone involuntarily born into a particular natal context, with its associated life chances, but every voluntary decision they subsequently take also brings with it a quota of involuntary features. This then raises questions about the relationship between two sets of emergent properties: the personal property of reflexivity (a PEP) and the structural and cultural emergent properties of the social (SEPs and CEPs), which people ineluctably confront. As has already been outlined in the Introduction, the causal powers of SEPs, such as constraints and enablements and vested or objective interests, and of CEPs, such as the situational logics shaped by different combinations of cultural contradictions or complementarities, do not work hydraulically. Both require *activation* by the PEP, by the 'projects' which subjects define and seek to accomplish.

[6] Margaret S. Archer, *Structure, Agency and the Internal Conversation*, Cambridge, Cambridge University Press, 2003, ch. 1.
[7] Brian Tomlinson, 'Talking to Youself: the Role of the Inner Voice in Language Learning', *Applied Language Learning*, 11, 1, 2000, p. 123.
[8] See Margaret S. Archer, *Being Human: the Problem of Agency*, Cambridge, Cambridge University Press, 2000, ch. 7.   [9] Ibid., ch. 9.

In other words, reflexive internal conversation (PEP) is responsible for *mediating* the impact of SEPs and CEPs because it is the subjects' objectives and internal deliberations about their external feasibility that determine *how* they confront the structural and cultural circumstances whose presence they cannot avoid.

In short, our internal conversations are seen as crucial to how we make our way through the world today. They are so because they account for our being 'active agents',[10] people who make things happen, not 'passive agents' to whom things happen. However, precisely because so little is known sociologically about the workings of internal conversation, theoretical debate soon becomes sterile unless anchored in empirical investigation. Yet, one cannot investigate social action as a whole. Therefore, to tell the story of how we actively make our way through the social world, rather than (semi-)passively bearing its weight, the focus will be upon social mobility, upon our internal dialogical part in designing and monitoring the trajectories – ones of stability, mobility or volatility – that we are found to have taken, are taking or plan to take. That is why internal conversation matters, but before it is justifiable to begin discussing its consequences and how reflexivity operates, the concept itself requires clarification.

What is internal conversation?

Because this book is a contribution to sociology, reflexivity – as a crucial part of internal conversation – was defined earlier as 'the regular exercise of the mental ability, shared by all normal people, to consider themselves in relation to their social contexts and vice versa'. However, others from a large array of disciplines have been interested in the phenomenon of internal conversation for entirely different but perfectly legitimate reasons and have proffered definitions appropriate to their purposes. For example, Siegrist, a cognitive psychologist concerned with the role of inner speech in mediating self-consciousness, defines 'inner conversations as talk to oneself about oneself',[11] thus making no explicit reference to the subject's social circumstances. This tendency to produce definitions tailor-made for different substantive research problems has the consequence that it is not by consulting this array that a general understanding of internal conversation can be reached.

So, let us begin the other way round, with the earliest and most comprehensive definition available, that of Plato: thinking is 'the conversation

---

[10] See Martin Hollis, *Models of Man*, Cambridge, Cambridge University Press, 1977.
[11] Michael Siegrist, 'Inner Speech as a Cognitive Process Mediating Self-consciousness and Inhibiting Self-deception', *Psychological Reports*, 76, 1995, p. 260.

which the soul holds with itself in considering anything'.[12] This intro-duces two issues about internal conversation that have remained contro-versial ever since. (1) By using the term 'conversation', is it being asserted that inner dialogue is a silent version of external conversation – one that uses the public medium of natural language in the same way?[13] (2) Is all thought a matter of inner dialogue? Only those issues directly relevant to reflexivity will be considered here.

1   The relationship between internal conversation and natural language

Three positions are taken in relation to this question, although none is homogeneous. Firstly, there is the assertion that inner 'dialogue' has con-siderable *independence* from the medium of natural language. Usually, the arguments in its favour are phenomenological and derive from reports of 'wordless' but meaningful intra-personal communication as attested by various parties: prominent scientists, mathematicians and religious con-templatives. For example, the mathematician Van der Waerden held that only graphical and motor representations were necessary for the under-standing of geometrical concepts such as a 'circle' or 'Pascal's helix';[14] Einstein maintained that he worked primarily in terms of images, mainly 'visual and, some, of muscular type', and generalised this by asking, 'Has not every one of us struggled for words although the connection between "things" was already clear?';[15] St John of the Cross and St Teresa of Avila alike avow near defeat in attempting to use language to capture contem-plative experiences: experiences that 'relate to things so interior and spiri-tual that words commonly fail to describe them', for 'something is passing within the soul beyond that which can be expressed by the tongue'.[16]

Do such illustrations lead to Buyssens' conclusion that expressing experiences to ourselves is 'outside language',[17] this representing the

---

[12] Plato, *Theaetetus*, ed. Bernard Williams, Cambridge and Indianapolis, Hackett, 1992, 189e.

[13] A second important issue is raised simultaneously, namely that of who is speaking to whom in the internal conversation in a manner paralleling the external dialogical part-ners, but I have already dealt with this at some length. See Archer, *Structure, Agency and the Internal Conversation*, pp. 95–107.

[14] B. L. Van der Waerden, 'Denken ohne Sprache', *Acta Psychologica*, 10, 1–2, 1954.

[15] A. Einstein, *Ideas and Opinions*, New York, Crown, 1954, p. 336. See also J. Hadamard, *An Essay on the Psychology of Invention in the Mathematical Field*, Princeton, Princeton University Press, 1945.

[16] St John of the Cross, 'Prologue', *Living Flame of Love*, ed. E. Allison Peers, Tunbridge Wells, Burns and Oates, 1987, pp. 20, 13. See also Margaret S. Archer, 'Western Mysticism and the Limits of Language', in Margaret S. Archer, Andrew Collier and Douglas V. Porpora, *Transcendence*, London, Routledge, 2004.

[17] E. Buyssens, 'Speaking and Thinking from the Linguistic Standpoint', *Acta Psychologica*, 10, 1–2, 1954, pp. 164f.

strongest version of the *independence* thesis? That seems over-hasty because it confines 'language' to natural language, including *parole*. More moderate is John-Steiner's conclusion, after interviewing a group of fifty 'experienced thinkers': 'I would suggest that the internalization of experience and of the modality-specific ways in which experience is shaped are not mirror-images of the external communicative process'.[18] This she presses in order to fend off the notion that internal communication represents sub-vocal speech. Nevertheless, to maintain that intra-personal communication is not a mirror image of external communication, as I believe is correct, does not justify regarding the former as language-independent. There is an alternative, which entails modifying this position still further, namely to extend the referents of language well beyond 'natural' language. Artificial languages, such as mathematical symbols or musical notation, may indeed be the terms in which their adepts communicate internally on these matters. Equally, the tradition of religious symbolism and imagery could constitute the equivalent for the Western contemplatives, who relied heavily upon metaphorical extrusion when they reached the limits of (natural) language. But they still managed to talk to and write for an external audience,[19] because of the familiarity of writers and readers alike with the same corpus of tropes. Such considerations seriously modify the language-independent argument, yet only for those highly proficient in a given area. However, where this argument has a valid point for everyone is in its insistence that our inner dialogues are not *exclusively* dependent on language, natural or otherwise. They are supplemented by visual and auditory images, mental pictures, diagrams and symbols, together with emotional and visceral sensations – none of which can (usually) be deployed in the course of external conversation.

Secondly, there is the more popular position in which internal conversation is presented as being completely dependent upon and indeed derivative from (natural) language. At its simplest, for example, is Arendt's conception of inner dialogue being like speaking to a friend.[20] The notion of internalisation of the public linguistic medium, constituted by shared collective meanings, is central to Mead's notion of the inner dialogue. Above all, it is what makes it possible for Mead's 'generalised other' to operate as an internal interlocutor. Sokolov puts forward the bluntest formulation of this thesis: 'inner speech, far from being an

---

[18] Vera John-Steiner, *Notebooks of the Mind*, Albuquerque, N. Mex., University of New Mexico Press, 1985, p. 213.
[19] Often, irreducible religious metaphors were used, those which are elucidated only by reference to further tropes. See Janet Martin Soskice, *Metaphor and Religious Language*, Oxford, Clarendon Press, 1985, pp. 105f.
[20] Hannah Arendt, *The Life of the Mind*, Orlando, Fla., Harcourt Brace, 1978, p. 189.

independent entity, is a secondary phenomenon derived from external speech – auditory perception of the speech of other persons and active mastery of all the forms of the spoken and written word'.[21] Just as trenchantly, he seeks to take away the point accredited to the first position concerning the role of (non-linguistic) visual imagery and symbolism in internal conversation: 'Early mastery of the verbal system of concepts ensures that virtually all other forms of thinking (objective-pictorial and objective-practical) will occur within the conceptual framework of language, i.e., on the basis of previously acquired concepts which are retained in memory and are subsequently actualized in the form of concealed or inner speech.'[22] Yet on closer inspection, the argument for the *dependency* of internal conversation upon natural language turns out to be one that does *not* deprive inner dialogue of emergent properties – properties that are both distinctive and irreducible.

Initially, in his discussion of the personal and internal use of graphic imagery instead of words, Sokolov makes a telling clarification: 'such substitutions are more likely in inner speech, whose vocabulary frequently assumes a very individual, subjective significance'.[23] In this he differs from Mead, to whom both the external *and* internal use of any 'significant symbol' entails 'a language gesture', which constitutes 'a stimulus that reverberates and calls out the same attitude in the individual who makes it as it does in others who respond to it'.[24] Sokolov draws no such conclusion about the social standardisation of the meaning of words. On the contrary, use of the public language medium does not preclude its elements acquiring a 'very individual, subjective significance'. Meanings can be personal and idiosyncratic rather than collective and shared. He and Vygotsky are also quite clear that *which* matters we dwell upon mentally and *what* notions we come up with are in no sense determined by the linguistic medium employed, even though they depend upon it for their encoding or expression. In short, the *contents* of our internal conversations are independent of the fact that they depend upon the use of natural language as a tool.

Equally independent is the *form* of internal conversation. The argument for dependency does not imply that internal and external dialogue are 'the same' or even similar to one another. To Vygotsky, inner dialogue is substantially contracted compared with external speech, being an 'expression of thought in condensed form' using 'a greatly reduced number of words'.[25] Sokolov endorses this 'laconism' or brevity of inner speech,[26]

[21] A. N. Sokolov, *Inner Speech and Thought*, New York, Plenum Press, 1972, p. 1.

[22] Ibid., p. 3.   [23] Ibid.

[24] G. H. Mead, '1927 Class Lectures in Social Psychology', in D. L. Miller (ed.), *The Individual and the Social Self*, Chicago, University of Chicago Press, 1982, p. 136.

[25] Vygotsky, *Thought and Language*, p. 141.   [26] Sokolov, *Inner Speech*, pp. 120–1.

which requires unfolding if it is to be conveyed verbally to others. Thus, neither the form nor the content of internal conversation is determined by its dependency upon natural language. This is because inner speech is indeed regarded as an emergent property. We have already seen that Vygotsky referred to it as a 'distinct plane' and Sokolov, too, endorses emergence when he states that our 'concepts are relatively free relative to the concrete forms for their expression, but still they cannot exist separate from their forms'.[27] Thus, the argument for dependence ends by disavowing any form of linguistic determinism of inner dialogue and by making dependency less than total. What it does not impugn, because inner speech is regarded as an emergent property, is its interiority and subjectivity, much less its causal efficacy, since the whole thrust of both above thinkers was to maintain that 'external speech is functionally dependent upon inner speech'[28] – especially for creativity and originality.

The third position, that of co-dependence, strikes a balance between the previous two. It is advanced most clearly by Peirce and forms part of his overall attempt to combine our concrete singularity with our undoubted sociality, without allowing the balance to slip one way or the other. Specifically, internal conversation – which is how he himself conceptualises the life of the mind – is held to depend upon a *plurality* of intersubjective signs. Since such signs are not confined to natural language alone, it is more accurate to say that the individual's internal conversation is reliant upon a variety of elements drawn from the public cultural system,[29] which is why I have termed it the argument for co-dependence.

What Peirce offers is a developmental account of how a subjective perspective is elaborated from the objective affordances of culture to furnish a private 'inner world' into which we can withdraw – the domain of internal conversation. The crucial point about this 'inner world' is that it relies upon the private use of public media. The dependence of our inner dialogue on the external cultural realm is upheld, without this in any way being allowed to determine what we do with it. In the following description, Peirce is at pains to stress the *plurality* of public media that are drawn upon – and the more the better for maximising the causal powers of internal conversation. As Colapietro summarises Peirce's overview:

When I enter into the inner world, I take with me the booty from my exploits in the outer world, such things as my native language, any other languages I might know, a boundless number of visual forms, numerical systems and so on. The more booty I take to that secret hiding place, the more spacious that hiding place

[27] Ibid., p. 3.   [28] Ibid., p. 65.
[29] See Margaret S. Archer, *Culture and Agency: the Place of Culture in Social Theory*, Cambridge, Cambridge University Press, 1988, ch. 5.

becomes . . . the domain of inwardness is not fixed in its limits; the power and wealth of signs that I borrow from others and create for myself determine the dimensions of my inwardness.[30]

There are four points to note in this summary statement. Firstly, natural language is one among many sets of inter-personal signs that make up the 'inner world'. Peirce is one of the few to acknowledge that multi-lingualism, presumably including mastery of dead languages, extends the range of things we can say to ourselves. Secondly, he explicitly includes 'visual forms' and 'numerical systems', which, since they are called 'boundless', may be taken to include artificial languages, notational systems and established forms of artistic symbolism, such as those introduced in connection with the 'independence argument'. Thirdly, he includes signs that the subject 'creates for himself', which would also cover the cascading metaphors created and deployed by those such as St John of the Cross when he had tensed language to its limits.

Finally, what do the above points contribute to the purpose (and indeed to the causal powers) of internal conversation according to Peirce? For Colapietro, the answers derive from the 'capacity to retreat into inwardness [which] creates the possibility of performing imaginary experiments (i.e. experiments in the imagination)'.[31] There is no doubt about the huge importance that Peirce attached to this mental source of innovation – in creative thought and action in the world. To him, our internal conversation, like all emergent properties, was also held to have internal powers (to modify ourselves through self-talk by self-criticism and self-control) and external powers (to modify society by generating exemplary ways of life). Therefore, even if inner dialogue does take place (partly or mainly) in words, language is not deterministic: 'language is not something *to* which I conform myself; it is something *by* which I transform myself'.[32]

In short, the private and innovative *use* made of the public linguistic medium is just as significant as the fact that natural language is an indispensable tool for the emergence of the private inner world in the first place. As the home of internal conversation, the inner world is a domain of privacy fabricated from public materials; as a 'plastic theatre' of inner drama, it is dependent upon my imaginative construction and use and is thus a first-person world; as the bearer of causal powers, its exercise can modify both us ourselves and our social environment. Thus, Peirce's 'argument for co-dependency' neatly balances the 'independence' and the 'dependency' that the other two positions had respectively exaggerated at

---

[30] Vincent M. Colapietro, *Peirce's Approaches to the Self: a Semiotic Perspective on Human Subjectivity*, Albany, N.Y., State University of New York Press, 1989, pp. 115–16.
[31] Ibid., p. 102.   [32] Ibid., p. 110.

times. Simultaneously, it accords internal conversation the genuine interiority, subjective ontology and causal powers which are defended here.

2 Thought: internal conversation and external language

If we now scrutinise Plato's aphorism that 'thinking is the conversation which the soul holds with itself in considering anything', the previous discussion shows that it consists of two distinct questions. The first, which amounts to asking 'Is thinking the same process as engaging in external conversation?', is now distinct from the second, which asks 'Is thought synonymous with internal conversation?' The conclusion to the previous section was that internal and external conversations were significantly different, in particular because external dialogue[33] consists of natural language, whereas inner dialogue is far from being confined to it.

It seems that there are few advocates of thought being similar to external conversation and thus to natural language. Although textbooks regularly pit Piaget and Vygotsky against each other over the independence of thought from speech or the dependence of thought upon speech, in fact both firmly rejected the notions that thought is the same process as external speech or that it entails the use of natural language, at least in its externally recognised form. It is this rejection which underlies Piaget's rather dismissive treatment of children's lone external (or 'egocentric') speech and his belief that it disappears during early childhood, without detriment to the development of higher mental activities. However, Vygotsky, who talked about its 'internalisation' rather than its 'disappearance', never maintained that thought entailed the sub-vocalisation of natural language (that is, external speech without the sound). Even the later generations of Russian linguistic psychologists, who did defend the sub-vocalisation thesis in relation to thought, were quite explicit that *what* was sub-vocalised was completely different in form from natural language.[34]

Thus, it is quite difficult to find a modern proponent of the first proposition. The closest is probably Blachowicz,[35] who maintained that inchoate and 'fuzzy' ideas require internal verbal articulation in natural language as

[33] Note that this is strictly a statement about *dialogue* because this assertion is not true of non-dialogical communication, such as television adverts, which can manipulate visual imagery and 'atmospherics' through use of music, sound-effects and symbolism. Equally, once the topic has been introduced in natural language, proficient mathematicians can communicate *seriatim* in math symbols. Were it claimed that they can hold a dialogue in math symbols, I would not resist this because all it shows is that human beings can learn artificial languages just as they can learn foreign languages in which they then converse.

[34] See the conclusions of Sokolov, *Inner Speech*, pp. 259–63.

[35] James Blachowicz, 'The Dialogue of the Soul with Itself', in Shaun Gallagher and Jonathan Shear (eds.), *Models of the Self*, Exeter, Imprint Academic, 1999.

a logical condition for the self-understanding of our own thoughts. Of course, even here, the prior existence of the 'fuzzy' component means that the entirety of the thought process is not held to be identical with external speech. In the next section I will argue that Blachowicz's 'internal articulation' is a requirement for one specific function of internal conversation alone and, hence, is not the predicate of self-understanding in general. Thus, where thought is concerned, there appears to be substantial agreement with Peirce's general position that, in so far as thinking is held to depend upon internal conversation, such inner speech is considered to be quite different from external speech.

The more contentious question is whether or not thought is synonymous with internal conversation. This proposition has been asserted by Mead, Vygotsky and Sokolov. Here, I want to argue for a qualified assent based upon a proviso. The proviso is that the Peircian characterisation of inner speech be accepted: our internal conversation is constituted as much by symbols, images, emotions and remembered sensations as it is by components of natural languages. The qualification limits the proposition to stating that *reflexive thought* does indeed take place through internal conversation. Potentially, that could leave substantial tracts of thinking outside its bounds, but it is not relevant to the present study to take a position on this broader issue. In parenthesis, nothing seems inherently implausible about the notion of 'wordless meditation', as in the contemplative 'prayer of quiet', or about mathematical hunches or metaphorical leaps. What should be noted is that these kinds of thoughts, like the most practically orientated ones, may 'drift' in and out of reflexivity, because it is always open to the subject to ask herself why she is doing something, whether or not she is doing it well and so forth. Thus, to reiterate, the boundaries of reflexive thinking are not clearly demarcated and are certainly not fixed.

Why is reflexive thought held to be synonymous with internal conversation – perhaps being distinctive in this respect from non-reflexive thinking? Quintessentially, reflexivity involves a subject considering an object in relation to itself, bending that object back upon itself in a process which includes the self being able to consider itself as its own object. If we review the tasks undertaken by reflexivity or the functions of reflexive processes, we come up with that long list of mental activities bearing the 'self-' prefix: self-observation, self-monitoring, self-criticism, self-evaluation, self-commitment and so forth. All of these have a common denominator. In each and every such activity, we are asking ourselves questions. In everyday language, their respective exemplars are 'How do I look?', 'Am I getting this right?', 'Can't you be more exact?', 'Why did you slip up there?' or 'Could I really do that?' And to each of these kinds of questions we give ourselves answers, fallible as they are. In other words, by questioning and answering we are holding an internal conversation with ourselves and *inter alia* about ourselves. This is the nature of reflexive thought. Obviously, we can play at questioning and answering in many areas, such as wondering what the weather will be like tomorrow and concluding that it looks set to be fine. However, in no sense is that a reflexive thought because the answer may simply draw upon observing a 'red sky at night'.

Reflexive thought is synonymous with internal conversation because reflexivity is *not* a vague self-awareness but a *questioning* exploration of subject in relation to object, including the subject as object, one which need not have any practical outcome or intent. What seems more profitable than pursuing the general lines of the 'thought and language' debate is to explore the distinctive nature of internal conversation and how it works in relation to the particular features of reflexive thinking.

The distinctive features of internal conversation

Considering how little sustained interest has been taken in internal conversation, once the high tide of American pragmatism was over, those who have studied it show a remarkable degree of consensus about its characteristics. Specifically, it is always *contrasted* with external conversation and consequently, it is held erroneous to model it upon social dialogue. Although the 'inner voice is crucially different from the public voice . . . it does use a variety of the same language in order to achieve its functions. In this sense it is different from the mentalese posited by some philosophers and cognitive psychologists as a universal mental code.'[36] However, accord about the features of internal conversation is not paralleled by an equivalent agreement about its functions. With the exception of Wiley's work,[37] inner dialogue has not been systematically examined in relation to the exercise of reflexivity. Therefore, in the discussion that follows, the characteristics held to be distinctive of self-talk are also briefly examined in terms of their implications for the ten tasks of reflexivity as explored in the empirical part of this study.[38]

Silence and privacy

Because internal conversation takes place in silence, what 'I says to myself says I' is also a matter of privacy. This means that anything goes, which is

---

[36] Tomlinson, 'Talking to Yourself', p. 125. For 'mentalese', see S. Pinker, *The Language Instinct*, London, Penguin, 1994.

[37] Norbert Wiley, *The Semiotic Self*, Oxford, Polity Press, 1994.

[38] These are 'mulling over', 'planning', 'imagining', 'deciding', 'rehearsing', 'reliving', 'prioritising', 'imaginary conversations', 'budgeting' and 'clarifying'.

not the case in external dialogue. There is no question of observing good manners or conversational conventions. We cannot offend ourselves (though we may later deem our thoughts to have been offensive), we can interrupt ourselves as often as we please, start dialogues where we wish and abandon them when we will, we never apologise for dwelling interminably on some preoccupation or breaking off in mid-sentence, and we can curse our heads off or bawl our hearts out – all because questions of self-presentation, public accountability or consideration for others do not arise. Abrogation of convention also embraces contravention of social norms. In the absence of external censorship, the most immoral, illegal and inhumane excesses can be contemplated and mentally indulged, just as the most imprudent acts of generosity or self-sacrifice may be contemplated. In brief, as Wiley neatly puts it, 'we are little gods in the world of inner speech'.[39]

Secondly, because speaker and listener are one and the same person, we talk silently to ourselves without misunderstanding. In self-talk, each of us knows what we mean and is never in the position of a third party who is necessarily an interpreter. As Davidson maintains, 'there can be no general guarantee that a hearer is correctly interpreting a speaker; however easily, automatically, unreflectively and successfully a hearer understands a speaker, he is liable to general and serious error. The speaker cannot, in the same way interpret his own words . . . cannot wonder whether he generally means what he says.'[40] Within internal conversation, the question of interpretation does not arise; in speaking to oneself, a person's deliberations are made up of internal sayings whose meaning she knows and her comprehension rate approaches one hundred per cent.[41] Of course, anyone may be wrong *in* her beliefs, but not *about* the fact that she holds them. What she does with self-warrant[42] is to question and answer herself about her mental states and the relations between them, knowing what she means as she deliberates with herself about them. In so doing, she does what no one else can. In basing her private and (some of her) public conduct upon her reflexive deliberations, she draws *directly* on meanings known to her, which can only be known *indirectly* and *fallibly* by others.

[39] Norbert Wiley, 'The Sociology of Inner Speech: Saussure Meets the Dialogical Self', paper presented at the meeting of the American Sociological Association, August 2004.
[40] Donald Davidson, 'First-Person Authority', *Dialectica*, 38, 2–3, 1984, p. 110.
[41] John R. Johnson, 'Intrapersonal Spoken Language: an Attribute of Extrapersonal Competency', in Donna R. Vocate (ed.), *Intrapersonal Communication: Different Voices, Different Minds*, Hillsdale, N.J., Lawrence Erlbaum, 1994, p. 176. What she will not comprehend are all the implications of what she knows.
[42] For a discussion of self-warrantedness, see William Alston, 'Varieties of Privileged Access', *American Philosophical Quarterly*, 8, 3, 1971.

Putting these points together, their implication for 'mulling over' – the most general of reflexive mental activities – is to underscore the fact that reflexivity is first-person in kind. Its consequences are that no communality of social background, no similarity in social circumstances, and no uniformity of stimulus, opportunity or constraint will be reflected upon in the same way: involving the same considerations, entailing the same evaluations or proceeding according to the same deliberative schema. The causal power of exercising this PEP is to throw the cat amongst the pigeons, meaning that no external generative mechanism will ever lead to an empirical uniformity of outcomes. Neither *Homo economicus* nor any of his relatives will ever behave with predicted conformity.

Ellipsis and the accordion effect

Perhaps the most commonly cited feature of internal conversation is its contracted form. It is generally agreed to be characterised by syntactical and semantic ellipses, rendering it 'lean and fast' in comparison with external speech. Because we know what we mean, abbreviations and short cuts are employed in inner dialogue. Vygotsky considered this to be the central distinguishing factor of inner speech: 'inner speech is almost without words';[43] Mead concurred that we need very few vocal gestures in conversation with ourselves 'compared with those we need when talking to others. A single symbol is enough';[44] and Sokolov echoes this: 'inner speech departs ever farther from vocal, audible speech', with its abbreviated character resulting 'in an ever increasing condensation of sense into a single word or, even, hint at a word', until these 'elements, carriers of generalized sense, become, metaphorically speaking, quanta – condensed particles of thought'.[45] Wiley gives a nice commonplace illustration: of the thousand and one things other people do which can annoy me, all I need in order to voice a particular grievance internally 'is the word "bastard" along with a specifier. The specifier can be a visual image of the look on their face, an auditory image of what they said, the emotion of wrongness that we attribute to their action – or even some fringe words (e.g. "lying bastard").'[46]

In brief, external speech entails a great redundancy of communicated information, whether in spoken or written form, which linguists estimate at 60–70 per cent.[47] In contrast, Korba[48] has estimated that inner dialogue

[43] Vygotsky, *Thought and Language*, p. 145.
[44] G. H. Mead, *Movements of Thought in the Nineteenth Century*, Chicago, University of Chicago Press, 1936, p. 381.   [45] Sokolov, *Inner Speech*, pp. 121–2.
[46] Wiley, 'The Sociology of Inner Speech', p. 8.
[47] Sokolov, *Inner Speech and Thought*, p. 260.
[48] R. J. Korba, 'The Rate of Inner Speech', *Perceptual and Motor Skills*, 71, 1990, 1043–52.

is approximately ten times faster (in terms of words per minute) which, in conjunction with its leanness, pares redundancy to the bone. From this, what is usually accentuated is the economy of internal speech as a cognitive resource, particularly in relation to the demands of external conversation. Its contracted nature provides us with a running commentary on the utterances of our interlocutors whilst they are speaking and gives us time not only to react internally but also to prepare our verbal response.

In turn, consensus about the elliptical nature of inner dialogue has led various commentators[49] to associate the internal conversation with Basil Bernstein's early work on linguistic codes and educational performance.[50] Tomlinson draws a direct parallel: 'This linguistic code [our inner voice] is similar to the restricted code claimed to be typical of the speech of the lower working classes by Bernstein in that it is fundamentally elliptical, vague, implicit, concrete, descriptive, and narrative; in that it uses a narrow range of vocabulary and structures; and in that it relies to a great extent on such nonverbal features as intonation and stress.'[51] This parallelism seems misguided for three reasons.

Firstly, it is drawn from the stance of linguistics alone, because the comparison of *language codes* obliterates the role of imagery and symbolism from inner dialogue, which have been argued to be vital in differentiating internal conversation from natural language usage. To focus exclusively upon semantic and syntactical ellipses ignores Peirce's insight that the more multi-media 'booty' is incorporated from the outer world, the richer the life of the mind becomes.

Secondly, as Wiley maintains, 'the resemblance of inner speech to the restricted code is misleading. Inner speech seems restricted because it is efficient to speak to oneself in this way. But this is merely the way the crushed or condensed feature of inner speech looks – not the way it has to be.'[52] Indeed, in its abbreviated syntax and lack of crucial parts of speech (for example, the subject) it might also seem to resemble pidgin language, yet, if 'it actually were pidgin it could not handle complex ideas. But the syntax of inner speech is just as involved, if not more so, as ordinary speech. Still, all the parts of speech are there, and they could be produced in all their complexity merely by unfolding the internal utterance.'[53]

The above points seem well made, but in making them there is a danger in allowing the linguists to stake out the territory for their own purposes. This consists in accepting their focus on the single function of internal dialogue vis-à-vis external dialogue. In other words, it is dangerous to

---

[49] Alistair Mutch, 'Review', *Journal of Critical Realism*, 3, 2, 2004, 384–9.
[50] Basil Bernstein, *Class, Codes and Control*, Vol. I, London, Routledge and Kegan Paul, 1971.
[51] Tomlinson, 'Talking to Yourself', p. 125.
[52] Wiley, 'The Sociology of Inner Speech', p. 7.   [53] Ibid., p. 6.

move unwarily between the concepts of 'inner speech' and 'internal conversation'. This underlies the third objection to Tomlinson's parallel between Bernstein's restricted code and the *form* taken by inner dialogue. I would question Tomlinson's characterisation of self-talk as being *generically* 'elliptical, vague, implicit, concrete, descriptive and narrative'. Instead, which of these adjectives is appropriate will vary from one internal conversation to another. What their applicability varies with is the *reflexive task* that any given internal conversation performs.

On the one hand, in the case of 'budgeting' – be it in terms of money, time or effort – my inner dialogue may indeed be elliptical and implicit. For example, on spotting some attractive shoes in a shop window, the tentative opener, 'Maybe . . .?' can be quashed by the one-word response 'No', if necessary, reinforced by 'Come on Imelda Marcos!' Similarly, routine 'planning' of, for instance, what to buy on the way home from work can be dealt with by a response consisting of a list of one-worders: 'milk' (I know I only buy skimmed, so no need to specify); 'korma' (standing for all the ingredients of chicken korma and implicitly for tonight's dinner); 'fairy' (washing-up liquid, noted as nearly empty this morning); 'stamps' (picture of check-out where they are sold). On the other hand, there are reflexive tasks where the appropriate adjectives for the corresponding internal conversations are the exact opposites of those listed in the quotation from Tomlinson, intended to establish a parallel with Bernstein's restricted code.

One of the most important reflexive tasks, in the view of the majority of those interviewed, is 'rehearsing', as in practising for a job interview. They reported considerable internal elaboration, including working out fully-fledged sentences and trying out verbal formulae to do very different jobs, such as covering up some sticky biographical patch, packing in as much relevant experience as possible and hitting the right note between self-confidence and willingness to learn. Social class made no difference to whether or not subjects engaged in this process (effectiveness is a different issue). Of course, these are instances of internal conversational rehearsal for external exchanges and thus remain part of the linguists' bailiwick. Conversely, the reflexive activity of 'clarification' (sorting out what you think about some issue, problem or person) is performed internally for and to the subject's own satisfaction. This is the aspect of reflexivity where Blachowicz's argument comes into its own, namely that the careful internal articulation of our initial notions is a logical requirement for self-understanding. It is also a task where the corresponding internal conversation would (aim to) be extended, crystal clear and fully explicit, yet might be highly abstract, non-descriptive and deductive rather than narrative in form – contra Tomlinson.

Thus, to Blachowicz, the 'demand for articulated thought is one I am quite capable of imposing on myself for myself. *It is a logical, not a social demand* . . . this articulation in fact occurs *within* myself and not just (or even principally for others) . . . My conversation with the person I know best – myself – does not and cannot remain at the level of abbreviated speech, for I must, even at mundane levels of experience, explain and articulate my experience for myself.'[54] Where academic writing is concerned, Blachowicz maintains that he expands on preliminary notes '*for myself*, so that I might be satisfied with the extent to which I have clarified and articulated my original ideas'.[55] He argues that the same need for clarification also pertains to everyday experiences. Sometimes that may be the case, as in trying to clarify 'What did his look really mean?', but not always, as my shopping example tried to illustrate, nor as the sole or principal function of internal conversation. Nevertheless, even if the force of his argument is greatest in relation to the reflexive task of clarification, what is appealing is his plea for voluntarism: that we reflexively determine *what* we ourselves want to clarify through internal deliberative extension, independent of any need or pressure for external communication.

Not only do I believe that he is correct in this, but the same two points about voluntarism and extension could be made about another of the reflexive tasks investigated in the present study, namely holding 'imaginary conversations'. Presumably Blachowicz would agree, since his thesis is general, but rather more surprisingly, so does Sokolov,[56] who maintains that inner speech is not always abbreviated, especially when we reason or argue with ourselves. When doing so, some of us find that we engage with an imagined opponent (as in: 'What would the social constructionist say about that?') and discover that our provisional formulations have to be re-articulated to anticipate a potential riposte or expanded to cover a weak spot. This is not an academic preserve. For example, some interviewees volunteered, wryly or regretfully, that they could spend hours fine-tuning vitriolic repartee designed to slight imagined interlocutors whom they were never likely to encounter again. Whilst sticking to the argument that the use of syntactic extension and semantic exactitude do characterise internal conversation in relation to certain reflexive tasks, in other reflexive activities Tomlinson undoubtedly makes his point: if we used the public voice for all our thinking, we would never have time to think at all. Thus, abbreviation and extension work like an accordion within the internal conversation, in relation to the functions of reflexivity and the preoccupations of the reflexive subject.

---

[54] Blachowicz, 'The Dialogue of the Soul with Itself', p. 190.   [55] Ibid.
[56] Sokolov, *Inner Speech*, p. 115.

Personalisation and uniqueness

Internal conversation is rich in personalised meanings, ones deriving from an individual's history. There are blatantly idiosyncratic usages of common words in our inner dialogue because of their semantic embedding in our biographies. Sometimes when students are describing their unsatisfactory accommodation, I mentally docket this as 'light bulbs', invoking a grasping Cambridge landlord of forty years ago who insisted we each inserted our own bulb when using the bathroom. Equally, we can coin or recycle words to capture a complex concatenation of experiences that we find distinctive. To me, 'a Casaubon' (borrowed from *Middlemarch*) stands for someone who devotes more time to cross-referencing his bibliography, book-marking and blogging than to getting down and writing something. In such cases and '[u]nlike our public voice, which has to share many features with other public voices in order for it to be understood, our inner voice is private, personal and unique. It is our own voice, which we can use and develop in any way we wish.'[57]

Personalisation leads directly to uniqueness in the form and content of internal conversation and this is reinforced by the fact that even the common usage of common terms may regularly carry personal emotional loadings, individual associations or ineluctable imagery. In the dictionaries that we all carry around in our own heads, these are the meanings of those words to us. Why do I find the word 'gristle' one of the most off-putting in the English language? Because it is never dissociated from the visceral revulsion, the sight and the smell of the school stew I was admonished to finish. As Wiley states, when words gain their meaning from events peculiar to us, circumscribed by our own intra-subjectivity and completely meaningless in inter-personal conversation, we are in the house of egocentric vocabulary. These packed-with-meaning expressions give our inner speech its emotional flexibility and lightning speed. They also show that some things, which are easily handled in inner speech, cannot be introduced in outer speech at all. This is our own private little world. It is nobody's business but our own, and it does tasks for us that could not be accomplished in any other way.[58]

Two of the reflexive tasks most marked by this semantic personalisation are 'reliving' (some episode or relationship) and 'imagining' (as in 'what would happen if . . .'). Memory, which played such an important role in Augustine's concept of the private inner self,[59] far from being a social

---

[57] Tomlinson, 'Talking to Yourself', p. 124.
[58] Wiley, 'The Sociology of Inner Speech', p. 9.
[59] Philip Cary, *Augustine's Invention of the Inner Self*, Oxford, Oxford University Press, 2000.

construct that has received public authorisation,[60] is too personalised for anything but summary external recall. When each new primary school year began, it was routine to be set an essay on 'My Summer Holidays'. All of us knew the ropes: a page and a bit of 'went there and did that', showing basic competence in using adjectives and adverbs. The standardisation of these products would have warmed the heart of a constructionist. Except, that is, for the fact that part of knowing the ropes was knowledge of what to keep incommunicado, what to protect from defilement by chalk dust and chaffing. I can still relive a long afternoon, alone on a cliff top, simply 'entering into' the sea but, even as a ten year old, recognising full well that this neither could nor should figure in that page and a bit.

When we relive, what we are reliving is a personal *anamnesis* – the felt particularity of an experience which remains with us. Although he used the term with flexibility, in his coining of 'inscape', Gerard Manley Hopkins comes closest to capturing personalised reliving as distinct from public recall. By it, he meant grasping the kernel of a thing (being or episode), as expressed in outer pattern or design – and thus as beauty or evil. Hopkins was fully aware that the effort to convey 'inscape' would ring oddly rather than communicating directly, despite his semantic innovations in poetic language. As he wrote to Robert Bridges, 'No doubt my poetry errs on the side of oddness . . . what I am in the habit of calling "inscape" is above all what I aim at in poetry. Now it is the virtue of design, pattern, or inscape to be distinctive and it is the vice of distinctiveness to become queer. This vice I cannot have escaped.'[61]

That was the self-judgement of a virtuoso who *sought* to communicate his own 'inscapes' publicly. Most of the time, most of us do not. Regardless of whether we do or don't, all of our internal conversations are characterised by personalisation *plus* privacy. In turn, that formula has radical implications. To begin with, it underscores the fact that internal conversation is ineluctably a first-person phenomenon: 'It might be incoherent to an eavesdropper but it is coherent to ourselves.'[62] Wiley draws out both the logical and the methodological implications of the formula. Even if someone invented a mind-reading machine, they would be unable to understand another's inner dialogue, without having access to that person's whole life, and thus their code, and hence becoming another 'him'. In practical terms, someone's internal dialogue would be 'inaccessible in its meaning even were it accessible in its signifying forms'.[63] Therefore,

---

[60] See J. Coulter, *The Social Construction of Mind*, London, Macmillan, 1979, pp. 56–61 and Rom Harré, *The Singular Self*, London and Beverly Hills, Sage, 1998, pp. 143f.

[61] Cited in G. F. Lahey, *Gerard Manley Hopkins*, London, Oxford University Press, 1930, p. 22.   [62] Tomlinson, 'Talking to Yourself', p. 131.

[63] Wiley, 'The Sociology of Inner Speech', p. 26.

[i]n this case the linguistic code is not fully inter-subjective in the third-person. Rather it is intra-subjective and a mixture of first and third person points of view. Some semantic elements are ordinary words and therefore could be third person. But others are so self-styled that they can be understood only in the first person and from within, their cognitive accessibility being exclusively interior to someone's consciousness. And by their nature as first person qualia they cannot be understood by another, cannot become inter-subjective and cannot be transformed into the third person.[64]

Methodological consequences follow directly. The first is to reinforce the injunction, reiterated many times in this text: never substitute a third-person interpretation for a first-person meaning, on pain of getting it completely wrong. When an investigator imputes his own meanings to a subject, it has been found empirically 'that people are sometimes surprised to learn that observers are attributing higher-order motives to their behavior than they are attributing themselves'.[65] Does this then mean that the formula 'personalisation + privacy' makes internal conversation intransigent to investigation? Does it follow that since there are no can-openers to other people's heads, the only inner dialogue to which we have access is our own, yet we cannot generalise from ours to other people's without committing the third-person fallacy? Wiley argues that methodological intransigence is not entailed and I agree with him that 'semantic privacy does not prevent one from describing one's own inner speech to another, at least to a substantial extent'.[66] Much that is valuable will be lost – the personal affect, individual imagery and biographical embedding – but it is possible 'to communicate the gist of it, in other words to transform first to third person meanings'.[67] The subject alone can do this. But one does not have to be a poet of Hopkins' stature to accomplish it, as the Coventry interviewees generously illustrate in the following parts of this book.

Context dependency

All of our internal conversations are context dependent, which is closely related to two of their other features, personalisation and elliptical contraction, although these relationships are imperfect. Sometimes the proximate context is externally supplied, but in such cases a double contextual dependency is involved. Take those subjects, mentioned earlier, who were 'rehearsing' through inner dialogue for a forthcoming job interview. Let us

---

[64] Ibid., p. 25.
[65] Michael F. Scheier and Charles S. Carver, 'A Model of Behavioral Self-Regulation: Translating Intention into Action', in L. Berkowitz (ed.), *Advances in Experimental Social Psychology*, Vol. XXI, New York, Academic Press, 1988.
[66] Wiley, 'The Sociology of Inner Speech', p. 26.   [67] Ibid., p. 28.

suppose that a higher-level position has become available at a subject's place of work and that for whatever personal reasons he has applied and is keen to succeed. Obviously, he would not be going through his 'rehearsals' had the opportunity not presented itself; it is the change in his occupational context which, in conjunction with his response to it, has focused his mind on this matter. However, from then onwards, the subject's preparations display exactly the same *generic* contextual dependency as does any other internal conversation (even though its form will be extended rather than displaying more the usual feature of contraction).

What is meant by context dependency can best be explained by considering what this subject might do in his preparatory internal conversations and what he cannot do. Not only does he have the formal job description in front of him, but he has worked with the previous incumbent, believes he was well regarded and can ponder about presenting himself as potentially possessing the same qualities. He also knows quite a lot about the environment in which the institution operates and can mull over what best to say about meeting its challenges and so forth. In other words, he packages his skills and marshals his contextual knowledge, putting them together to the best of his ability during his 'rehearsals'. But there are some things he cannot know. One of them is that the management is toying with the idea of relocating this post at its base in the next large town and, in case they decide to go ahead, they insert a question in the interview about the subject's willingness to move. He is unprepared, thrown and blurts out something about having to think it over because his young children have only just settled in school. Nearly all the interviewees regarded 'rehearsal' as useful, but most were savvy enough to say that they 'couldn't cover all the bases'.

This is the main difference from the spontaneous internal conversation, where subjects do take their contexts for granted and 'unthinkingly' assume their knowledge to be perfectly adequate even though imperfectly complete. This presumption about their contexts enables a fast, truncated and effective response. When driving home I say to myself 'Shop – bread', but do not conduct an inner review of all the possible shops on this journey where potentially I could, but in fact never have picked up a loaf. In short, we take our incomplete contextual knowledge for granted, but we could not get by (or home) if we did not – at some point.

We get by through increasing contraction and by presumptuously taking our context for granted. As Vygotsky maintained, inner speech is characterised by 'omitting the subject of the sentence and all words connected with it, while preserving the predicate'.[68] In fact, both Vygotsky

[68] Vygotsky, *Thought and Language*, p. 139.

and Sokolov argue that, as life goes by, the contextual dependence of inner speech greatly intensifies. Internal conversation 'must become more contextual and idiomatic and include not only the objective meaning of words but all of the intellectual and affective content connected with it; this must lead to the dominance, in inner speech, *of the contextual meaning of words over their objective meaning*'.[69] In that final assertion, Sokolov breaks completely with the notion that our self-talk mirrors even the most abbreviated form of natural language. Certainly, inner dialogue still depends on the use of (contracted) words, yet the meaning of those words is not found in a dictionary or the pronouncement of an Academy, but resides in their contextual dependency, which is a personal matter.

The interface between external and internal conversation was the major preoccupation of these two thinkers, with inner speech being accorded the role of decoding public speech addressed to the subject and encoding the subject's responses, yet to be made to his interlocutor(s). However, now that inner speech has been endowed with a full quotient of the four features discussed in this section (privacy, ellipsis, personalisation and context dependency), it follows that the enterprise of expanding our inner speech into external conversational contributions has become vastly more arduous. As Tomlinson notes, we have to do much more for others than we need do for ourselves: 'when translating into a public voice we have to consider addressee factors and we have to modify our utterances to take into account the status, roles, interest, knowledge, goals, norms and age of the addressees and our relationships with them'.[70] The last phrase is the key one for my concern with reflexivity because it raises the question: 'Can we perform such translations for anybody?'

Tomlinson, whose main interest is second language learning, doubts that this is the case. He is sceptical both when the relationship is that of a language learner communicating with a mother-tongue speaker and also when conversation takes place between strangers: 'the expansion and elaboration required is extensive if, for example, we are attempting to communicate complex ideas to people we do not know at all. This is an extremely difficult task for native speakers and many of us fail to translate what we can say effectively to ourselves with the inner voice into what we want to say to others in the public voice.'[71] Not only is he entirely correct, but also, in relation to reflexivity, he seems to be pointing to the most crucial factor – namely, 'contextual continuity' or 'contextual discontinuity' – determining whether our reflexive deliberations are shared with others or remain autonomous.

[69] Sokolov, *Inner Speech*, p. 48 (my italics).   [70] Tomlinson, 'Talking to Yourself', p. 131.
[71] Ibid., p. 126.

This theme is central to the present book in which human reflexivity is regarded *not* as being homogeneous but as assuming different modes that are *differentially dependent upon internal conversation being shared in external conversation.* Therefore, it is useful to pursue congruent insights about the contextual dependency of internal conversation and how this relates to the ease or difficulty of conveying it externally to others. Tomlinson signals something of great importance when he notes that 'if we are communicating with intimates, the expansion required is minimal as we share referenced contexts with each other'.[72] This would be the case in the 'Darby and Joan' relationship, where the long-married couple apparently communicates with mutual understanding in monosyllables. But its applicability extends to other 'intimates' (family, friends or school fellows) who share the same continuity of social context.

In such cases, the internal conversations of these subjects are context dependent, as are everyone's, but with the hugely important difference that much of their respective dependency has *the same contextual referents.* So many factors are shared by them – common acquaintances, history and biography, unchanging geography, familiarity with the same schools, hospitals, churches, factories, employers, pubs, buildings, and a common fund of anecdotes, idioms and local knowledge. These furnish a mental landscape with the same topographical features. Provided that people retain and sustain this 'contextual continuity', their communality of landmarks together with their experiential overlap facilitates the sharing of their internal conversations. To use Piaget's term, 'de-centring', or the cognitive ability to assume the perspective of each other in external speech, is rendered much easier. Someone's conversational extensions (the translations of their internal conversations) may be unintentionally 'egocentric', as is usual, but the difference here is that their egocentricity also happens to be very similar to that of their interlocutors.

In general, communicative competence entails de-centring the self by adapting to the listener's perspective. It is 'to discriminate those role attributes of L [listener] which appear to be pertinent to the L [listener's] ability to decide communicative input regarding X [message]'.[73] Stated in this way, it is a wonder that any of us ever communicate anything beyond the bus timetable, such is the sociological expertise required to go further. Yet, the crucial point is that the question of developing such expertise

---

[72] Ibid., p. 126.
[73] J. Flavell, *The Development of Role-taking and Communication Skills in Children*, New York, Robert E. Krieger, 1968, p. 9.

simply does not arise for those who share the same 'contextual continuity' *because they already possess it*. Their relatives, neighbours and peers are 'similars and familiars': they speak in the same way, share the same word meanings, draw upon a commonwealth of references and a common fund of relevant experiences. Because of this, to share one's inner world by voicing one's inner dialogue is not the arduous enterprise just represented. It becomes commonplace to do so, for there is little discouragement deriving from misunderstanding, and it becomes common practice by virtue of its functionality.

For a young subject confronted with new decisions (such as school leaving) and seeking to clarify her concerns in life (such as the choice of her first job), her 'contextual continuity' represents a major resource. As she internally fumbles through the infinite variations upon those ineluctable questions ('What matters?' and 'What to do about it?'), she receives two gifts if she shares her incomplete reflections with her 'similars and familiars'. These gifts are external 'confirmation' and 'completion' of her internal conversation. Regular acceptance of them makes for what I have called a 'communicative reflexive':[74] someone whose reflexivity is initiated through internal conversation, but is not finished until nascent conclusions have been confirmed and completed through external dialogue. This is regarded as a distinct mode of reflexivity with distinctive consequences for how its bearers make their way through the world.

Conversely, the experience of 'contextual discontinuity' has exactly the opposite effect. For whatever reasons discontinuity came about in any individual case (some of the macroscopic trends that promote its increase were discussed in the last chapter), the subject in question lacks 'similars and familiars'. Because these subjects have undergone particularistic experiences and also confront novel situations, their reflexive deliberations become more difficult to communicate. They are not only context dependent but this dependency is also specific to each of them. Their problems with competent communication can be expressed in terms of their confronting a much more intransigent problem of 'de-centring' than was the case for the group discussed above:

As we assume the cognitive perspective of the listener(s) we make choices concerning what words, illustrations, narratives, and syntactical and organizational structures to use to help the listener(s) to understand our expressive spoken language. Even if we are capable of assuming the listeners' perspective we face the natural tendency to regress and express our symbolic thoughts using words and syntax *that make sense only to ourselves*.[75]

---

[74] See Archer, *Structure, Agency and the Internal Conversation*, ch. 6.
[75] Johnson, 'Intrapersonal Spoken Language', p. 186 (my italics).

Johnson presents this state of communicative affairs as universal. Although there is some truth in his statement, it lacks the social dimension, namely the recognition that certain sections of the population (probably now in the majority) systematically undergo this experience, whilst others do so to only a minor degree.

For those people who gradually learn that their internal conversations do indeed 'make sense only to themselves', this discovery has far-reaching consequences. Attempts at spoken interchange about one's internal deliberations are rebuffed by incomprehension or misunderstanding. Since renewed efforts to make oneself clear usually involve greater self-revelation, continued failure is doubly hurtful and self-defence consists in withdrawal. I recall a hiking weekend with a diverse group of my sixteen-year-old school peers and the start of a conversation about how many children each would like to have. Internally, I rebelled against the premise and declared that I wasn't at all sure I wanted any. Equally, I felt at a complete loss about what to respond to their question, 'How can you say that?' Being 'lean and fast' my internal conversation reviewed and discarded various ripostes (which queried their social conformity or raised the importance of a career and the need for a like-minded partner), but I also remember the sinking feeling that none of these would 'get through'.

That feeling was one of many such experiences and their cumulative effect was simply to stop trying. And to stop (or possibly never to begin) throws one back on one's own mental resources. In turn, that makes significant tracts of a person's internal conversation self-contained and knowingly not for traffic in spoken conversation. This response is shared by those I have called both 'autonomous reflexives' and 'meta-reflexives' (the differences between them are taken up later on).

As far as the functions of reflexivity are concerned, the differences in its modes of practice – deriving from 'contextual continuity' and 'contextual discontinuity' respectively – profoundly affect two of its central tasks: 'prioritising' and 'decision-making'. These are accorded centrality because of their role in answering those generic questions: 'What matters?' and 'What to do about it?' The responses given have a direct influence upon the positions a subject desires to occupy in society. In turn, the acquisition of any social position entails a relationship to social mobility – be it immobility, upward or downward mobility or socio-occupational volatility. The overall aim of this book is to vindicate the claim that there is a relationship between patterns of social mobility and the different modes of reflexivity practised by various groups of subjects. However, a little more has to be said about these two elements and the relationship between them before the substantive argument can be presented in the rest of the book.

Internal conversation and social mobility

As the 'little gods' of our own inner dialogues, we dictate their agendas, which may be as trivial or as profound as we please and, in the course of a single day, may oscillate repeatedly between triviality and profundity. Colapietro[76] is right to warn that internal conversation becomes unrecognisable to Everyman if its 'heavy' aspects alone receive attention. Instead, old men can dream dreams, young children invent their fantasy friends and we can all imagine ourselves on silver beaches, mountain summits or driving a Ferrari, just as we can revisit our childhood's secret garden, relive an accident or simply count sheep to fall asleep. However, regardless of the proportion of time devoted to it, the reflexive portion of internal conversation shoulders responsibilities for all normal people. As Wiley concisely puts it, 'inner speech does have a job to do, it has to steer us through the world'.[77]

Part of making our way through the world concerns the positions we assume in society and the particular trajectory of social mobility that each of us describes over his or her life course. This reflexive task of navigation was pared down earlier to the two tasks of *prioritising* our concerns and *decision-making* about their realisation in practice. Although I have discussed the connection between the two in previous books,[78] it seems necessary to give the briefest summary in order to highlight the role played by reflexive internal conversation in each task and thus in shaping the trajectories of social mobility taken by individuals. Only then will it be possible to enter the last leg of the journey and to introduce the role played by different modes of reflexivity in generating distinctive trajectories.

The goal of defining and ordering our concerns, through what is effectively a life-long internal conversation, is to arrive at a satisfying and sustainable *modus vivendi*. Through *prioritisation*, conducted by means of inner dialogue, '[i]t is these acts of ordering and of rejection – integration and separation – that create a self out of the raw materials of inner life'.[79] Because we are social beings and because we are discussing attempts to position ourselves within the social order, it is unsurprising that many of our concerns are social in nature. However, in dedicating oneself to a cluster of concerns, one takes responsibility for them and makes them one's own. The subject constitutes her identity as the being-with-this-constellation-of-concerns. Thus, through her internal

---

[76] Vincent Colapietro, 'Cartesian Privacy and Peircean Interiority', draft manuscript, coutesy of the author.   [77] Wiley, 'The Sociology of Inner Speech', p. 18.

[78] Archer, *Being Human* and *Structure, Agency and the Internal Conversation*.

[79] Harry G. Frankfurt, 'Identification and Wholeheartedness', in his *The Importance of What We Care About*, Cambridge, Cambridge University Press, 1988, p. 170.

conversation, the subject reflexively *attains a strict personal identity by virtue of her unique pattern of commitments.*

Any subject who arrives at this position, be it in preliminary form (as with a young person) or as the result of a series of revisions (as for many older people), has then to confront the second generic question and *decide* 'How do I go about it?' In other words, what course(s) of action should this subject adopt in order for the concerns she cares about most to be realised in an appropriate *modus vivendi*? Elsewhere, I have discussed this as a matter of completing the sequence

<Concerns → Projects → Practices>

and presented the definition of a *modus vivendi* as a major preoccupation of internal conversation[80] (summarised in Figure 3). That is to say, we talk to ourselves *about* society in relation to ourselves and about ourselves in relation to society, under our own descriptions. What we seek to do is reflexively defined by reference to the concerns that we wish to realise. Ultimately, that realisation means becoming who we want to be within the social order by personifying selected social roles in a manner expressive of our personal concerns. That means establishing practices, ones which are both satisfying to and sustainable by the subject, in an appropriate social environment. Through such a *modus vivendi* a subject's personal identity is aligned with her social identity. Arriving at this alignment is a dialectical process, generally requiring adjustment and accommodation between the personal and the social. It is rarely optimal, it is frequently revisable, but it is always reflexive in nature.

Nevertheless, within their internal conversations, subjects cannot subjectively conceive of any course of action they please and they cannot assume any social role they wish. There are objective structural factors which must be confronted: life chances, the distribution of resources, the availability of positions, the extant role array, institutional configurations and so forth. There are also equally objective cultural equivalents to confront. However, there are two kinds of arguments that would deny any role to human reflexivity in the determination of the outcome. Both are versions of the Two-Stage Model, presented in the Introduction. In fact they stand for the structural and cultural versions of it – for third-person accounts which either deny a role to subjectivity altogether or regard subjectivity itself as being socially determined and hence beyond the control of the individual.

The structural or 'hydraulic' argument maintains that objective factors – summarised as 'life chances' – work *directly* upon subjects. They exert their pushes and pulls by endowing some people with advantages

---

[80] See Archer, *Being Human*, chs. 7 and 9.

Defining and dovetailing one's **CONCERNS** ▶▶▶ (Internal goods)	Developing concrete courses of action **PROJECTS** ▶▶▶ (Micro-politics)	Establishing satisfying sustainable **PRACTICES** (*Modus vivendi*)

Figure 3 Internal conversation and pursuit of the good life

and others with disadvantages, which are directly manifested as differences in outcomes. Note that there is no question of subjective mediation here: an objective advantage is an objective bonus leading to an objectively better outcome, and an objective disadvantage is an objective penalty resulting in an objectively worse outcome. In contradistinction, the argument for reflexivity is not talking about 'independent influences' or 'direct effects' at all. It is an argument about *mediation* and it is as a mediating process that reflexivity is held to be *indispensable*. The crucial difference is that the very causal efficacy of 'objective factors' *is held to depend upon their reflexive mediation*. In other words, objective advantages have to be found subjectively advantageous, objective bonuses have to be considered subjectively worthwhile, and objective advancement has to be deemed subjectively desirable. Without all of this, the 'direct effects' of objective factors upon human subjects are inexplicable, unless all humanity is taken out of the subject and he or she is reduced to mere throughput – the ultimate 'passive agent'. Conversely, the argument 'for reflexivity' in no way denies the importance of objective structural and cultural factors; it only insists that they are reliant upon 'active agents' for their *activation* and consequent *efficacy*. Since activation and non-activation are themselves reflexively determined and because reflexive powers vary between people, no form of constant conjuncture can be expected.

Where culture is concerned, the equivalent 'hydraulic argument', which also denies reflexivity a role in charting an individual's social mobility (or lack of it), is 'dispositional determinism' – as already encountered in chapter 1. If 'structural hydraulics' had social structure overriding human subjectivity, the 'dispositional' approach has cultural factors invading and pre-empting people's subjective space. Because the cultural argument rests upon assigning an exaggerated influence to socialisation, reflexivity is marginalised by the *prior* 'occupation' of the life of the mind by dispositions deriving from a subject's social background. Bluntly, dispositional socialisation gets in first and thus reflexivity gets no look in. Thereafter, third-person accounts (of attitudes, expectations and aspirations) are substituted for the investigation of the conception and conduct of action as reflexively designed in the first person.

However, the development of our dispositions and reflexivity need not be seen as sequential, such that one (effectively) precedes the other during maturation. Another way of putting this is that the 'active agent' does not have a passive childhood or adolescence, which allows 'society to get at them first'. Once self-consciousness has emerged, we each engage in active interplay with all orders of reality, including the social. This interaction cannot but be reflexive, because surviving depends upon exercising powers of reflexivity – particularly those of self-monitoring. But our thriving entails the use of a larger array of these powers, especially reflexive self-evaluation and self-regulation, which inform us of what to seek and to shun in the outer world, including the social domain. Certainly, socialisation differentially exposes different collectivities of young people to different experiences, but it cannot enforce endorsement of their natal context or suspend the power of observation and the ability to conclude that there is better to be had elsewhere in society. The very course of acquiring dispositions like 'acceptance' is intimately intertwined with the development of a particular mode of reflexivity. In short, dispositionality and reflexivity are not separate or sequential developmental characteristics; they emerge contemporaneously and interact with one another.

As the dominant mode of reflexivity is consolidated, it comes to play the *same role of reflexive mediation vis-à-vis culture as it does towards structure*. We *activate* cultural powers by making these properties our own. Because we are 'strong evaluators', with first-person knowledge of our dispositions, these possess no immunity from our evaluations. The only way of preventing that from being the case is to grant dispositions asylum deep within the unconscious – from where they cannot figure in internal conversation if they are held, in principle, to be inaccessible to consciousness.[81] All else apart, that would undercut understanding of the meta-reflexives, subjects who have in some sense surveyed the cultural system and found there an 'ideal' which they seek to live out as their vocation in society.

Investigating internal conversation

All normal people are reflexive and the exercise of reflexivity is essential to their normality. Moreover, they are aware of being reflexive, which follows from reflexivity being a self-conscious process. However, there is a

---

[81] See John R. Searle, *The Rediscovery of the Mind*, Cambridge, Mass., MIT Press, 1999. Searle finds the above assumption strange – to have a disposition which influences what we do, without the ability to know it. I concur with Searle's argument in defence of the proposition that, 'The notion of an unconscious mental state implies accessibility to consciousness' (p. 152).

methodological problem[82] about ascertaining this awareness, which is wholly semantic: words and concepts such as 'reflexivity' itself or 'internal conversation', its many synonyms and cognate terms, are not part of everyday vocabulary. To circumvent that problem, the following question was used during the pilot investigation: 'Some of us are aware that we are having a conversation with ourselves, silently in our heads. We might just call this "thinking things over". Is this the case for you?' Since all subjects answered 'yes' and no subject in the pilot study expressed difficulties with the substance of the question or its formulation, it was retained unchanged in the main investigation. (Details about the conduct of the study, sampling and selection of interviewees are found in the Methodological Appendix.)

To begin exploring the nature and extent of their reflexive processes, ten mental activities were put to all subjects, the same ten that had proved so fruitful in *Structure, Agency and the Internal Conversation*: 'mulling over' (a problem, situation or relationship . . .), 'planning' (the day, the week or further ahead . . .), 'Imagining' (as in 'What would happen if . . .?'), 'deciding' (debating what to do or what's for the best . . .), 'rehearsing' (practising what to say or do . . .), 'reliving' (some event, episode or relationship . . .), 'prioritising' (working out what matters to you most . . .), 'imaginary conversations' (with people you know, have known or know about . . .), 'budgeting' (working out if you can afford to buy or to do something, in terms of money, time or effort . . .) and 'clarifying' (sorting out what you think about some issue, person or problem . . .). Subjects were assured that far from everyone engaged in all of these inner activities and that people differed greatly in how much time, importance and value they attached to engaging in any of them. They were questioned on each of the ten in turn and, every time their response was positive, they were invited to provide an everyday illustration from their own experience.

Quantitatively, the vast majority of the forty-six subjects[83] interviewed during the main investigation agreed that they engaged in at least half of these activities, with a minority illustrating that they regularly spent time on all of the ten. Three points are significant. Firstly and qualitatively, it was clear that those who did practise any of these activities were reflexively involved, which is not necessarily the case, at least for some of the ten. For instance, it would be quite possible for anyone with a skilled trade

---

[82] The general methodological problems surrounding investigation of internal conversations are discussed in Archer, *Structure, Agency and the Internal Conversation*, pp. 153-7.

[83] Interviewees consisted of ten communicative reflexives, twelve autonomous reflexives, twelve meta-reflexives and twelve fractured reflexives. The last sub-group will be analysed in the volume that follows this.

or professional qualification to agree about spending time on 'clarification' of a problem, but for the issues that regularly exercised them to be entirely technical. Instead, almost all the examples volunteered showed subjects considering themselves in the light of their circumstances and vice versa. Secondly, many (though not all) of the circumstances mentioned as illustrations were unequivocally social in nature. People undoubtedly do deliberate – under their own descriptions – about themselves in relation to society and about the social in relation to themselves. Thirdly, there were already evidences of patterning, ones reinforced qualitatively by subjects' attitudes towards certain of these ten potential manifestations of reflexivity. For example, some who did not engage in 'imagining' or holding 'imaginary conversations' would say dismissively that they wouldn't waste their time on those, whilst others would say ruefully of 'budgeting' that no, they were utterly incapable of it. In other words, they supplied early confirmation of the expectation, derived from the previous study, that the practice of reflexivity was not a homogeneous phenomenon.

Because it is normal to be reflexive, the fact that reflexivity is found to be a heterogeneous process is highly consequential. It means that if the aim is to explore its relationship with any other factor whatsoever, let alone the life-long task of making our way through the world, it is necessary to come to grips with its common and its variable features. There is a ready parallel in psychology: we may all be said to have a 'personality', but that is not useful unless we know something about the differences between personalities. From the small group of twenty subjects, explored in depth for *Structure, Agency and the Internal Conversation*, it was ventured that there were four distinctive modes of reflexivity. These also constituted four distinctive stances towards society and consequences for it. On such a frail basis, all findings were tentative and, in particular, the following questions could not be answered:

1 Were these four modes general to the (British) population?
2 Were they exhaustive or did further modes of reflexivity remain to be detected?
3 Were these four modes mutually exclusive or overlapping?
4 Were the differences in the modalities practised causally related to subjects' social origins or to social outcomes?
5 How stable or mutable were these modes of reflexivity over the life course?

The present study was designed to furnish additional, but far from conclusive evidence in answer to the first four questions. The fifth requires time-series data and will have to await the findings from the three-year

Table 1: Modes of reflexivity

Communicative reflexives:	Those whose internal conversations require completion and confirmation by others before resulting in courses of action.
Autonomous reflexives:	Those who sustain self-contained internal conversations, leading directly to action.
Meta-reflexives:	Those who are critically reflexive about their own internal conversations and critical about effective action in society.
Fractured reflexives:	Those whose internal conversations intensify their distress and disorientation rather than leading to purposeful courses of action.

longitudinal study of undergraduates.[84] Through the construction of ICONI (Internal Conversation Indicator)[85] it is possible to provide quantitative responses to the first four questions, although it cannot be overemphasised that the contribution of this study is held to reside in the qualitative data garnered in the long and generous follow-up interviews. No attempt will be made to summarise these latter findings here, precisely because I want the reader to become immersed in the lived reality of real people, their concerns, deliberations, courses of action and consequent *modi vivendi*. Only by immersion in these concrete particularities can we avoid abstracted empiricism. Nevertheless, as an introductory backcloth, the following quantitative indications can be given in response to the four questions.

In brief, and with the caveat that the sample was not even completely representative of Coventry itself, let alone the rest of the country, it does appear that the four modes of reflexivity, as originally ventured and as now measured, did apply to 93 per cent of the 128 Coventry subjects investigated. Table 1 provides a quick summary of these modes, but they will only be fully understandable – and I would hope recognisable – when they are unpacked in later chapters.

For twenty-seven subjects (21.1 per cent), communicative reflexivity was their dominant mode; for thirty-five (27.3 per cent), autonomous reflexivity; for twenty-nine (22.7 per cent), meta-reflexivity; whilst twenty-eight subjects (21.9 per cent) registered fractured reflexivity, thus accounting for 93 per cent of those investigated.

---

[84] The aim of this study is to escape from the limitations of data collected at one point in time and to be able to say something about the formation and mutation of modes of reflexivity. It will be published as a companion to the present volume once data collection is complete and this cohort of students, studied from their first week in university, have graduated and taken up their first posts or enrolled for further training.

[85] For details of its construction, please consult the Methodological Appendix.

The development of ICONI provided information unavailable from the previous exploratory study. To begin with, the existence of only nine respondents who could not be classified provides some assurance that there are not additional, undetected modes of reflexivity being practised among the population – in answer to question (2) above. This conclusion seems justified because the majority of these 'unclassifiables' were people who gained the same score on two modes of reflexivity and thus can be presumed to be exercising both equally rather than practising some unknown mode. Just as importantly, because each subject could now be measured in terms of the *relative strength* of each modality in his or her case, an overall profile of every respondent's reflexivity was obtained. The significant new finding, derived from inspection of subjects' detailed scores, was *that none registered zero on any mode whatsoever*. In other words, in answer to question (3) above, the four modes do overlap, although to different degrees for different subjects. Therefore, respondents were classified according to the mode which *predominated in their profile*, meaning that particular score was at least one point higher (out of seven) than for any other mode. It follows that every subject practised every mode of reflexivity to some extent, but that the vast majority (93 per cent) showed an inclination towards one modality in particular.

In sum, this indicates that the reflexive process is a multi-faceted activity for everyone. All subjects use all of its facets in some of their mental deliberations, despite the fact that for nearly everybody one facet was dominant. Because the nature of these facets is already known, it is possible to convey the type of contribution each one makes for a reflexive subject. Here, I will give the most spare and bare description of what each different mode quintessentially contributes to the life of the mind.

The communicative mode entails 'thought and talk', that is, internal conversation which is completed and confirmed by external dialogue with others, prior to a course of action being initiated. This is the case for those practising it both as a dominant and as a subordinate mode, although the following consequences will be more marked for the former. Since inner deliberations are open to (selective) public scrutiny, they tend to be cautious because 'second opinions' are introduced and also conventional because interlocutors are given the chance to act as censors. 'Communicativity' implies trust of and concern for those who are regularly consulted (usually significant others) and respect for those acting as consultants on an irregular basis (for their skills, professional expertise or personal characteristics). This does not mean that use of the communicative mode represents an approximation to dialogue with Mead's 'generalised other' and thus exposure to social normativity. On the contrary, although employing the communicative mode does reinforce normative conventionality, it is the norms of the 'particular other' that are privileged in this process – precisely because of their *selection* as interlocutors. In turn, the tendency is for 'localism' to be reinforced amongst its 'dominant' practitioners and for the existing occupational hierarchy to be legitimated by its 'subordinate' practitioners. Of course, semblances of 'communicativity' are not always reflexive in intent: as in asking someone's opinion out of politeness or simply liking to air one's own opinions.

Use of the autonomous mode is the precise opposite in every respect. In it, practitioners display confidence in relying upon their own mental resources and, when these require supplementing, generally prefer expert advice or a search for independent information, such as reference books or the Internet. Obviously, everyone finds themselves in situations where their courses of action have to be autonomously determined. Whilst the subordinate user copes perfectly well with the autonomous mode in everyday situations, only those for whom it is dominant prefer to depend on their own judgement when matters are more problematic or more is at stake. Consequently, the courses of action they adopt are often innovative, risky and sometimes ruthless. When dominant, the autonomous mode is more concerned with self-advantageous action, as individually defined, than with any form of normative conventionalism – whether geo-local or macro-social. The other side of the coin is that in being self-motivated and self-reliant, the dominant autonomous reflexives will volunteer to devote more time and effort to their self-defined projects. Conversely, those using it as a subordinate form will either go no further than they must (communicatives) or require additional moral justification for continuing on such a course (meta-reflexives).

Meta-reflexivity entails reflecting upon one's own acts of reflexivity. Everyone engages in it to some degree, if only because there is a plethora of everyday tasks (such as crossing the road and holding an external conversation) which cannot be accomplished satisfactorily without self-monitoring. Subordinate usage, therefore, tends to be task oriented and confined to specific situations. Conversely, when meta-reflexivity predominates, subjects consistently engage in self-evaluation (about being the person they seek to be) and display social awareness (about circumstances advancing or hindering the realisation of their ideals). Because of this, pronounced meta-reflexives have greater difficulties in defining a satisfying and sustainable *modus vivendi* for themselves than do markedly communicative or autonomous reflexives. They share neither the localised normativity of the former nor the self-confident individualism of the latter. Whereas subordinate users circumscribe the areas where the self-critique typical of meta-reflexivity is appropriate – and largely refrain from it outside them – when this is the dominant modality, its practitioners generalise the process throughout their life worlds since they aim to live up to an ideal and to find a social context which helps them to do so.

The examination of fractured reflexivity is reserved for the next volume because, when dominant, it produces the 'passive agent' whose internal conversation serves only to intensify their personal distress and social disorientation, without enabling them to determine upon a purposeful course of action to alleviate or resolve their problems. Yet, everyone experiences periods, problems and instances in their lives when their reflexive deliberations go round in circles without issue, other than to make them feel ever more impotent and helpless. This can be limited, as in the case of having a particular student with whom one simply does not know what to do, or be general, such as literally having become a displaced person. It should be noted that none of the subjects presented in this book scored four (the mean) or over for 'fracturedness', otherwise they would have been assigned to that category. Nevertheless, more than a few scored just under the limit. Depending upon what contingencies they meet, these subjects (and others) could be pushed over it. The continuous exercise of our reflexive powers, which is what makes us 'active agents' – those who can exercise some governance in and over their own lives – is always a fragile property, ever liable to suspension. However, the present study is devoted to those who *pro tem* do employ their reflexivity to make their way through the world.

The guiding hypothesis behind this study is that the interplay between people's nascent 'concerns' (the importance of what they care about) and their 'context' (the continuity or discontinuity of their social environment) shapes the mode of reflexivity they regularly practise. However, in connection with question (4) above, about the relationship between the endorsement of a dominant mode of reflexivity and its social origins or consequences, it is crucial to be theoretically consistent. The assumption is that we are dealing with 'active agents' who are responsible, through the projects they pursue, for activating the causal powers of emergent social properties. In other words, they are not 'passive agents' subject to the pushes and pulls of social hydraulics. Consequently, as far as social origins are concerned, the expectation is that, even as young agents, they will have interacted in an evaluative way with their natal backgrounds and have actively contributed to the perpetuation of their 'contextual continuity' or to the exacerbation of their 'contextual discontinuity'. In other words, it was unsurprising that no significant correlations were found between the dominant mode of reflexivity and such variables as social class background, gender and various objective indicators of contextual stability, such as absence of geographical mobility or changes of school.[86] Conversely, substantial qualitative data is later presented in support of the formula 'concerns + context', as capturing how reflexive modalities are shaped. This appears to be the case *provided that* active agential interventions are incorporated – ones that accentuated or diminished the impact of social background upon a subject.

The present study makes its contribution less in relation to the social origins than to the social consequences of endorsing a particular mode of reflexivity as the dominant one, particularly in defining subjects' trajectories of social mobility. If reflexivity is indeed a personal emergent property, it will operate as a generative mechanism whose causal consequences are both internal and external. Internal effects arise for the subject because anyone who tries to make his or her own way through the world is also attempting to regulate the relationship between the personal and the social in conformity with their concerns. Obviously, it is easier to change oneself than to change society. Hence, in the attempt to align the self and the social, more effort is put into self-monitoring than into seeking social transformation.

The internal causal efficacy of reflexivity derives directly from the fact that reasons are causes. When a subject converts her life 'concerns' into practical 'projects', she has found good reason for giving her conscious assent to their pursuit because she has (fallibly) examined herself, surveyed the social contexts accessible to her and decided upon a feasible combination. She commits herself to her project in the belief that she can realise her definition of the good life (or at least an approximation to it) in a particular kind of social context, providing she works at it. The work involved is mainly self-work, entailing very different forms of self-monitoring – depending upon the dominant mode of reflexivity practised: for the communicative reflexive, self-sacrifice; for the autonomous reflexive, self-discipline; for the meta-reflexive, self-transcendence. Under their own descriptions, these are the forms of subjective dispositions that underwrite the objective trajectories of social stability, mobility and volatility described over their life courses by different types of reflexive subjects. That is Hypothesis 1.

However, to accentuate the effort devoted to self-monitoring over that invested in social transformation does not free the subject from having to deal with structural and cultural properties. These are necessarily

---

[86] The only significant correlation concerned education. Those subjects with university degrees or equivalent professional qualifications tended to endorse the autonomous or meta-modes of reflexivity. On the contrary, subjects with lower qualifications or none tended to practise the communicative or fractured modes. Although this result was significant at the 5 per cent level, this chi-squared test failed to meet the validity criterion and should be treated hesitantly at most.

confronted when attempting to pursue a project in a social environment and the fact that the individual is doing a great deal of self-work cannot obviate it. However, the nature of this confrontation is held to vary with each dominant mode of reflexivity: the key responses being 'evasive', 'strategic' and 'subversive' in kind. These represent different stances towards social properties and powers as summarised below. In consequence, a distinctive pattern of social mobility – stability, upwards mobility or volatility – is associated with practitioners of each respective form of internal conversation. A full understanding of how actors reflexively make their way through the world, dealing as they must with at least some of its social properties and powers, requires an exploration of their life and work histories. That is what the rest of the book supplies. What is being done at the moment is to signpost where we are going.

> *Communicative reflexives* remain deeply embedded in (extensions of) their natal social context. By *evading* both the objective costs that would be incurred in resisting constraints and also refusing the objective bonuses associated with enablements, the combined results of their actions make them socially immobile. This is Hypothesis 2.

> *Autonomous reflexives* actively endorse 'contextual discontinuity'. By adopting a *strategic stance* towards constraints and enablements, they seek to avoid society's 'snakes' and to climb its 'ladders'. They thus aim to improve upon their social positioning and, if successful, become upwardly socially mobile. This is Hypothesis 3.

> *Meta-reflexives* are 'contextually incongruous' and also contextually unsettled. They are *subversive* towards social constraints and enablements, because of their willingness to pay the price of the former and to forfeit the benefits of the latter in the attempt to live out their ideal. Their difficulty in locating a suitable context together with their willingness to foot the bill in searching for a better one tends to generate a pattern of social volatility. This is Hypothesis 4.

External causal consequences are not confined to the individual level because they also constitute aggregate effects for social reproduction and social transformation. In other words, the micro-life politics of individual subjects contribute to the macroscopic structuring and restructuring of society. This is Hypothesis 5. It states that the combined unit acts of communicative reflexives will serve to reproduce the structure of social stratification. More generally, the practice of communicative reflexivity represents the cement of society. Cumulatively, autonomous reflexives foster social development because its practitioners inject considerable dynamism into the new positions they come to occupy. Generically, the practice of autonomous reflexivity is the source of society's productivity. Collectively, meta-reflexives function as the well-spring of society's self-criticism. Fundamentally, meta-reflexivity ensures that the fund of socially transformative ideals is constantly renewed – that the *Wertrationalität*, or value rationality, always remains alive and well.

3   Reflexivity and working at social positioning

This chapter acts as master of ceremonies, making the introductions and inviting various guests to take the floor. The proposition introduced is that regular conduct of each kind of internal conversation generates a patterning of social mobility over the life courses of its practitioners.[1] Making that connection entails: (1) defining the three modes of reflexivity to be examined; (2) detailing their linkages to different combinations of 'social contexts and personal concerns'; (3) delineating how differently the three kinds of internal conversationalists conduct their encounters with constraints and enablements, both structural and cultural; and (4) describing the distinctive trajectories of social mobility characterising their work biographies. Instead of working through these points formally, we will meet a communicative, an autonomous and a meta-reflexive and let their narratives cover the ground.

To engage in one form of internal conversation more than any other is to have a particular life of the mind, which thinks about the self in relation to society and vice versa in a particular way. Folk psychology does not endorse this. On the contrary, most people assume that how they talk to themselves is similar to everybody else's self-talk. This is not the case.[2] Therefore, each reader is intimate with his or her own form of inner dialogue but cannot justifiably presume it to be universal or necessarily common even to their friends and colleagues. Instead, to understand other modes of reflexivity we have to enter into the subjective landscapes[3] of others. This means becoming familiar with their internal topography and processes of inner

---

[1] This is not a Humean constant conjunction, which can be detected as a correlation coefficient. During any given period it will not necessarily be empirically manifest because overlaid by contingent interventions, such as illness or involuntary redundancy.

[2] Both the folk assumption and the evidence running counter to it were discussed in Margaret S. Archer, *Structure, Agency and the Internal Conversation*, Cambridge, Cambridge University Press, 2003, pp. 157f; ch. 5, 'Investigating Internal Conversations,' deals with the methodological problems involved and the arguments are not repeated here.

[3] This term is borrowed from Douglas V. Porpora, *Landscapes of the Soul: the Loss of Moral Meaning in American Life*, Oxford, Oxford University Press, 2001.

navigation, which choreograph how they also move around our common social world and seek to position themselves within it.

The likelihood is that most readers will find one of these landscapes to be closer to their own than the other two, although they will differ over which one. With the other modes, they may well feel like strangers in strange lands and begin to think that the phrase 'to be lost in thought' should be taken literally. Of course these unfamiliar others are not 'lost' at all; it is we who would be at a loss were their internal conversations suddenly to be broadcast. 'A penny for your thoughts' cannot buy them. These are free gifts from three generous people who have tried to share the lives of their minds with us in this chapter and invite us to see how their life histories require such sharing if they are to be understood.

Communicative reflexivity and social immobility

Communicative reflexives are those who complete their thoughts about themselves in relation to their circumstances by talking them through with other people. This makes us all 'communicatives' to some degree. When we visit the doctor or car mechanic, thinking that something is wrong but unsure either what it is or what to do about it, then we necessarily engage in communicative reflexivity. In such cases we acknowledge our lack of expertise to solve these physical or mechanical problems. Equally, we accept that it is inadequate simply to present our ailing bodies or vehicles to the expert as objects. Acts of inter-subjectivity are indispensable for bridging the gap between our putatively objective symptoms and the expert reaching a solution which is defensibly objective.

Inter-subjectivity is necessary even if the agent's inter-subjective contribution is as spare as 'I don't know what's wrong with me/it . . .', because there is always a 'but' after the ellipsis. The 'but' can be amplified uncertainly and unhelpfully – 'I just don't feel myself' or 'Somehow it's not running properly.' Alternatively, it can be expatiated upon at length and with great assurance. Both contributions are, of course, fallible, as will be the eventual diagnosis. Nevertheless, the volunteering of some reflexive statement is necessary for the process to engage at all. They are necessary but rarely sufficient, because they usually usher in a lengthier inter-subjective exchange, intended to home in on or at least towards a diagnosis of the problem. (There can be simple exceptions, often reinforced by ostension, 'I've got something in this eye' or 'My exhaust bracket's loose', but even these may not be the end of the exchange.) At times – and sometimes with reluctance – we all engage in acts of communicative reflexivity, at least in certain tracts of our lives. Moreover, many people, whose dominant mode of reflexivity is other than the communicative, willingly tell self-aggrandising anecdotes or jokes against themselves, where approval or approving laughter is what is sought. This is substantiated by the finding that none of the 128 Coventry subjects registered a zero 'C' score, however strong their dominant, but non-communicative, mode of reflexivity happened to be.

Yet, these common examples of practical exigencies, knowledge deficits or psychological promptings, which lead all normal people to engage in some degree of communicative reflexivity, do not begin to capture the communicative reflexive. What they fail to portray is the *routine nature of the 'thought and talk' pattern* to them. In describing this mode of reflexivity, it must be emphasised that communicative reflexives are not people who are incapable of initiating a train of reflexive thought when alone; indeed these subjects recount that they regularly do so under their showers, at the steering wheel or ironing-board, and very frequently when dropping off to sleep. However, what is distinctive about their pattern of internal conversation is a need *to share these thoughts with others in order to conclude their deliberations*. 'Conclusion' means receiving confirmation from another before a subject deems that a train of thought constitutes a satisfactory basis for action. The need of the communicative reflexive to supplement intra-subjectivity with inter-subjectivity (or internal with external conversation) is vastly more general than in those common but discrete instances, mentioned above. In those cases, the necessity arises from some particular requirement that cannot be met by the subject drawing upon his or her own mental resources.

Here is how some of the ten communicative reflexives, interviewed at length and to be properly introduced later, express and explain this need for sharing their thoughts with others in order to feel that their ideas are complete. For Jeanette (a 36-year-old unemployed horticulturalist), 'thought and talk' seems to be a matter of boosting her own confidence: 'Mostly [I'm] looking for assurance I would say, to sort of see if – I'm not a very confident person and I think I constantly need assurance off other people . . . I suppose it's a back-up, just to see if somebody else agrees with what I'm thinking, and also to get input for other ideas that perhaps I haven't thought of.' To her, consultation is 'across the board, I wouldn't say there's anything I particularly hold back on'. Jon (a 30-year-old automotive design engineer) reiterates this need for confirmation and, in particular, reassurance that he has taken all considerations into account: 'I'll come up in my own head with what I think I want and then I will speak to my parents or sister or friends and see what they think as well. And then I'll weigh it up in the end and decide which is the best way to go . . . I like to feel I'm getting it from all angles before I finally make the decision.' Assurance that he has covered all the options, which implies respecting his own limitations, also means that the 'thought and talk' pattern comes into play in his work as a designer: 'You could get given a brief and it might not be something that I was one hundred per cent familiar with. So, if that was the case, I'd come up in my head with what I thought would be the best route of action and then I would try and find someone else who knew a bit more about it and maybe get their opinion as well before I went ahead with it.'

Similar references to requiring confirmation, completion and enhanced self-confidence recur with other subjects. Thus, Sheila (aged fifty-seven and retired because of ill-health) again picks up on how she and her long-term friend and interlocutor reciprocally provide an independent angle on one another's problems: 'I can be worried about things and I can ring her and she'll put it all into perspective and I do the same with her – like her daughter's going away travelling for three months . . . She's straight round here and I'm straight round there if there's a problem – yes, I do talk it through with her.' In addition, Sheila is underlining another facet of how communicative reflexivity works; in general, face-to-face contact has to be possible, which highlights the geo-local nature of 'contextual continuity'.

Alf (a 69-year-old retired miner) emphasises the same theme, but also brings out how the dangerous nature of mine-working reinforced the practice of always seeking a second opinion. He is thus reiterating Jon, but in a context where ensuring that one has covered 'all angles' is even more crucial for safety. 'When I went down the pit I did every job there was to be done, except for shot-firing and, of course, managerial jobs. What I used to do [on] a strange job – I used to sit and look round for maybe ten minutes, just looking – planning in my head what I was going to do, where I was going to start.' Mining forces his own internal conversation to engage constantly, but the process is not completed intra-personally. Even several years later, when he became the charge-hand responsible for decision-making, Alf would seek second opinions and talk through how to crack problems with his workmates, despite the fact that 'nine times out of ten they'd agree with me . . . I wasn't bombastic in forcing my will on them, I did used to listen to people and see what they had to say if I had a problem of any sort – oh yeah, I would listen – and if I thought it would work, I'd do what they say.' Here, he brings out another facet of communicative reflexivity, namely the ineluctability of deliberation because routine action can rarely suffice in his type of employment. When it does not, then *both* 'thought and talk' engage. This harks back to the point made in chapter 1, namely the paucity of situations in which a non-reflexive response is an adequate guide to action because the solution is a completely routine one. Since subjects like Alf are aware of this, their awareness means that they have evaluated some routine course(s) of action and found it wanting – and thus resort to the exercise of self-conscious reflexivity. Nor is this practice of reflexivity confined to the special exigencies that Alf and Jon confront in their work; when young daughters first go back-packing, what is the routine response? By definition, it cannot be part of one's own repertoire, so the response of communicatives is to resort to their friends, even if this means no more than putting their heads together when neither party shares the relevant experience.

The constitution, the consolidation and the consequences of communicative reflexivity are the topics explored in preliminary form during this chapter. Exploration entailed the identification of seemingly clear practitioners of the communicative mode from ICONI; that is, those whose 'C' score was 5 or over (out of a maximum of 7), who appeared to be non-fractured (an 'F' score less than the mean of 4), and for whom the dominance of the 'C' mode of reflexivity was clearly differentiated on the indicator in relation to other modes (by a difference of at least one point). Such scores were used for convenience; they were not held to guarantee that the subjects so identified were communicative reflexives, but only to increase the probability of this being the case and thus narrowing the group targeted for interview. Lengthy interviews were conducted with ten subjects who conformed to the above criteria and also were confirmed as being communicative reflexives on *qualitative* grounds. It is the rich, long and generous contents of these interchanges which form the qualitative basis for attempting to answer my three core questions – about the constitution, consolidation and consequences of communicative reflexivity.

As an introduction to the lived experience of being a communicative reflexive, we are going to make the acquaintance of a very vibrant practitioner. Joan's life history has been composed by somewhat rearranging the material she supplied to provide a clear biographical sequence. Maximum use is made of her own words because paraphrasing would have leeched their colour. The key themes will be touched upon: acquiring a trusted interlocutor from amongst her 'similars and familiars'; embracing and extending 'contextual continuity'; working through the sequence of <concerns → projects → practices>; encountering social constraints and enablements; and, finally, reducing her aspirations and confirming her social immobility. However, these will not be laboured or heavily labelled at this stage. It is much more important to listen to her in order to grasp the out-workings of the life of her mind and to understand that *pathos* is just as crucial as is *logos* in this, as in all other kinds of internal conversations.

Joan's story

Joan is sixty-four years old, partially disabled after two hip replacements, widowed, and now technically retired. She is the eldest of four children, brought up in a small town outside Coventry by her mother (a housewife) and her father (a builder), who remained together until their deaths. Joan married Tom (1964) and had three children, Simon (1965), Jessica (1968) and John (1970). Simon's wife is Claire, and their two children, Emma (aged fourteen) and Ben (aged twelve), now live with Joan in Coventry. When invited to list the three most important areas of her life at the moment, ones about which she cares deeply, Joan filled in only 'my family'. Her ICONI 'C' score is a high 6.33 and she recorded a low 2.00 for 'fracturedness'.

Retrospectively, Joan paints a sunny picture of growing up, accentuating the cloudless golden and blue days and presenting her parents as responsible for the good weather. 'I had a very happy childhood, my mum and dad were wonderful and I've got two brothers and a sister . . . Oh yes, we had a lovely family, wonderful Christmases and two weeks' holiday in the summer and at Easter, I can still see it as if it were yesterday. My mum and dad always made it happy for us – you do get your tensions but not all the time. I mean everybody has tensions in the family, but without it you'd have nothing.' Yet, close to the start of the story, these inter-personal tensions seem to be ensnaring Joan and to be at war with her idyllic portrayal. Her self-reminder that without the family one 'would have nothing' appears to be an attempt to resolve this contradiction.

On the one hand, 'Dad was the old school. He was good to my mum, but he was a hard man sometimes, but when I was a very little girl it was always him I went to.' When she became a teenager, wanting to fly the nest rather than climb on his knee, her desire to realise her concerns collided directly with his 'hardness'. On the other hand, Joan admits, 'I didn't really get on with my mum until I got married. Mother suffered with her nerves really badly and worried about everything.' Joan seems to have distanced herself from such anxiety, by defining herself as a non-worrier, one who accepts that what will be, will be. 'I always think, "Well, whatever's going to happen is going to happen, there's damn all you can do about it."' This acceptant attitude, developed in contradistinction to her mother, would later lend itself to propitiating her father's 'hardness'.

Such a tendency was reinforced by the negative self-image which was instilled in Joan by adverse comparisons with her younger sister. 'My sister's really beautiful and people used to say, "Oh isn't Rosemary beautiful, but whatever happened to Joan?" And you know what kids are like, they used to say, "Ugh, you're ugly" and I've always grown up to believe that. It doesn't make any difference to me, it doesn't matter. I got to a stage in my life where I thought nobody can hurt me any more; I will do my best for everyone and do a good turn – and by being like that then I don't think [anyone] can complain, and so that's what I did.' In determining to repay bad with good, to be uncomplaining rather than assertive, Joan also signals her desire to please people and thus to avert their censure. Simultaneously, she is telling us that she has undergone a lot of pain within the family, without being able to identify a single member to whom she related with trust and confidence. Nevertheless, she continues to idealise this unit. 'We were a very close family – compared to other people we had a good life, we had a good family background. My brothers and sisters, we're still in contact with each other. We did, we had a good start in life, a wonderful start.'

Conflict was released precisely because Joan formulated her own project about her future employment whilst still at school: 'I desperately wanted to be a nurse and my father wouldn't let me. He said I'd be a servant to other people. He was really, really naughty like that . . . He said, "You're not going, you're staying at school till you're sixteen," so I did but it was an utter waste of time because all I did was fool about. So then I left school and he said, "You're not going anywhere, you're going to learn how to keep a house." So, I learned how to clean, knit, sew, cook (my mother was a brilliant cook), and the general things that he said a girl should learn. And then I got fed up and said, "I really want to go out to work and I really do want to go and be a nurse." And he said, "You're not going, you'll do as you're told till you're twenty-one, you're not going." ' Joan had confronted an extremely domineering man with deep-set gender prejudices and little to restrain their expression in the 1950s; her response was to capitulate and attempt to propitiate.

She went to work on a local farm, but even this was an independent step too far for her father. 'I worked for six months with poultry. I didn't like poultry because I was scared of them, but that was another thing dad interfered with. He said to the boss, "Make her work with the poultry, I'll cure this fear," and I had to do that.' I asked if it had ever crossed her mind then that she could stand up to him or get round him. Joan responded, 'It is weird, but it was just that he thought he could rule us, but he always ruled me more than the others. It's like when my brother was courting and he had to be in by eleven o'clock. It was ridiculous – he was coming up to twenty and had to be in by eleven – and he never was. I used to go downstairs and turn the clock back so he wouldn't get into trouble when he came in. It's terrible, but that's how it was in those days – and dad never did find out!' Tricking father in his patriarchal role was fine; confronting him in it was a different matter. For four years, Joan moved laterally, working in the kennels of the local hunt and enjoying it until her development of asthma put an end to that job. She then confronted her father with her continuing desire to become a nurse, and once again he vetoed her project.

I asked Joan if she had later come to understand his opposition to nursing; 'I don't know; I think what he really wanted was for me to stop at home and look after them – just so that he could see where I was.' By appealing to her mother, who now offered to act as intermediary, Joan finally succeeded in negotiating a scaled-down version of her aspirations and went to train as a nanny rather than a nurse. Why her father should have regarded this as a less servile role remains a mystery to Joan, since it entailed washing and ironing for the newborn's family rather than skilled work on the wards. Perhaps one can surmise that it approximated more closely to his stereotyped notion of an appropriate woman's role. Although she was happy in her various placements, Joan had actively revised her aspirations downwards in the light of the domestic politics of the possible.

By the time she was nineteen Joan had met Tom, thirty-three years her elder, living in the same road, and in need of child-care because of his marital difficulties and his working in London. Initially, Tom had asked Joan's mother to care for his son, until he returned in the evenings, but mum soon passed the task on to her well-qualified daughter. Gradually, Joan and Tom drew together, although she continued taking placements as a nanny for two more years, invariably enjoying her month's work with each family. However, by the time she was twenty-one, Joan wished her relationship to become a married one, as Tom was now divorced.

When marriage was broached, Tom revealed reservations, which were based not upon their age difference *per se* but on a sensitive recognition of Joan's ultimate concern – to which children were central, having realised her 'second-best' plan and become a nanny. It seems as though he may have had greater doubts about his own fertility than about becoming a somewhat elderly father. The following exchange is also significant because it again reveals Joan's willing self-sacrifice, reconciling herself to the absence of her own children and to the care of other people's. 'Tom said he didn't want to ruin my life. He said, "What happens if we can't have a family, because kids are your life?" And I said, "I don't care, I'd rather have ten or fifteen years with you."' He was not convinced and called off the wedding the day before it was to take place. This cast Joan back upon her domineering parents, who sought to make the break final. 'My mum said she didn't want him in the house again, and I could see my father sitting there grinning, thinking he's got his way. But I thought to myself, you haven't – no way.' For three more years, Joan and Tom continued to see one another and at twenty-five she presented him with an ultimatum; she needed 'security', commitment and to move forward – not to be trapped between domination and flirtation. They were married the next day and Simon was born nine months later. The details of the negotiations that took place between them and Joan's parents over the next three years are crucial to how Joan eventually worked through the sequence < concerns → projects → practices >. This coincided with her communicative mode of reflexivity being fully realised because she had acquired a dialogical partner.

Firstly, Joan demonstrates her commitment to realising her concerns: although her precise project remains fuzzy, she knows that any satisfactory realisation of it is predicated upon her acquiring greater independence. Simultaneously, she (and Tom) positively embraced and endorsed their context and its continuity through their reactions to their first – and last – local home. Both elements are clear in her description of events immediately after her marriage. 'The first thing my mum said was "You've made your bed, now you lie on it!" And I said I never intended to get married without I stuck with him. No matter what would have happened I would never have left him, never ever would I have left him or deserted him. I married him and I was determined to stay married. It's the same with this house you know, I'd never leave here, even if I won a million pounds tomorrow, I wouldn't leave here – I love this house. When we first came to see it, Tom hated it because he'd had his own home and he had to come into rented property which upset him. But then, when you start a new life at fifty-eight, fifty-nine, you don't expect to have everything, do you? I mean his wife took him for everything she possibly could. As I stood looking at [the house] from the pavement, it was just as if it was saying "come in", and I knew, as soon as I walked in through the door, that I'd never leave until I go out in my coffin. Ever such a weird feeling and I've always been happy here. Tom died here, he died in my arms. All he said was "I want to see our twenty-fifth wedding anniversary" and someone said something about hospital, and he said, "Oh no, I'll never go to hospital. I'll die in here and go out in my coffin." And he did, that's exactly how he went.'

Secondly, Joan and Tom are now left to construct their own *modus vivendi*, which is still nebulous in terms of its guiding project and the practices to be established, apart from the arrival of their three children. Then it became clear that Joan might have escaped paternal domination, but that henceforth she could expect no family assistance. In fact, Joan and Tom were being propelled into constituting their own 'micro-world' and its contours would be shaped between them. Tough as the beginning sounds, Joan had acquired more degrees of agential freedom than ever before to define her own projects. Although her mother had somewhat relented with the arrival of the grandchildren, she had also developed heart problems. 'She looked after Simon and Jessica while I went into hospital to have John, because when I had him I was sterilised, so I was in hospital a bit longer. My father fetched me because Tom was at work, he brought me home. Mum was just rinsing some stuff out to put on the line and my father walked in and looked and said, "Get your coat," and she said, "No, I'm staying." And he said, "No, you're not; she wanted the kids, she can look after them – we're going." And I was just left on my own till Tom came in – and that was how it was.'

Thirdly, with the couple now being thrown in upon themselves, Tom assumed the role of Joan's dialogical partner in her 'thought and talk' and, at least to begin with, her mentor. He tried to wean her off her desire to please and to propitiate others, with some success in relation to her parents, but Joan's need to be needed was ineradicable. Some of this need Tom came to learn and to accept. 'He used to say, "Stand up to other people" because I was very much, "Well, should I or shouldn't I?", and he used to say, "Don't let people walk all over you for the rest of your life." I used to get into situations where I'd say, "Yes, I'll do this, you have that," and then regret it afterwards. He used to say, "Count up to ten before you answer anything." I started this with my mum and dad and then I found it was quite easy.' This is nicely illustrated by the following vignette of how she mediated between her father and young son, child-rearing not being a province in which Tom ever tried to pay Svengali. 'If my father was there and Simon wanted to show me something, he'd say, "Excuse me mummy," and dad'd turn round and say, "Be quiet, kids should be seen and not heard." And I used to say, "Don't speak to him like that, he only wants to ask a question." And dad'd say, "Oh go on, make a rod for your own back then," and that sort of attitude. So I was determined that although they would be brought up fairly strict, there would be a lot of love in it; and if I was there and if they wanted to know something, I'd drop everything. You can go and do potatoes four times a day, but you can't pick up what that little soul wanted to say to you – and that's how I worked.'

In Tom, Joan had found a trustworthy interlocutor for her communicative reflexivity: 'He was such a knowledgeable man and such a clever man, but he wasn't bossy with it, he was gentle and kind.' Although the age difference may have made him more influential at the start of their marriage, it did not prevent Joan from continuing to ruminate about transforming her concerns into concrete projects – in which Tom gradually became an active participant as well as a dialogical partner. This began to evolve, not as a grand plan with any long-term strategy, when their youngest child started school at four, which also coincided with Tom's retirement. It entailed yet a further cut-back on Joan's initial project. She had begun as a teenager, wanting to be a nurse, had settled as a young woman for working as a nanny, and now, for her remaining twenty years with Tom, she again reduced her socio-occupational status and became a childminder.

Given few restrictions, other than occasional inspections, Joan and Tom were soon taking in up to twelve children, besides their own, and she was deriving enormous fulfilment from this 'extended family'. 'I had such a wonderful career, I really did, it was fantastic, because I used to take them from six weeks to five years, and then when they were five they were supposed to go, but the mothers didn't want them to go, so I started taking them to school and fetching them. So in the end they didn't leave even until they went to the comprehensive school.' Since I had my doubts about Joan being paid *pro rata*, I queried what satisfaction she derived, and received an unhesitating answer: 'Oh, the love; the love they give you is fantastic.' Still, I wondered quite how Tom felt about an additional twelve children crammed into their small house and lunch for fourteen being served every weekday. Joan assured me that this was a joint under-taking, thought and talked out between them. But, at first, she too had clearly wondered about his commitment: 'he never got fed up. It used to astound me because I would have thought he would have been browned off. I used to say to him, "Do you want me to cut down?" and he'd say, "No, I don't, they're fine."' By now, Joan had settled for 'third best' as a childminder, but here she is again offering to cut down on what clearly gives her huge satisfaction.

It seems that Tom meant what he said, since his words were well matched by deeds. 'Sometimes I'd go out shopping and perhaps wouldn't take them with me, if it was a wet day, and he'd say, "Off you go, leave them with me, I'm fine." And when I came back the house was like a pigsty, but at least they'd all be happy and laughing – he was absolutely fine. He used to take them to the toilet and I'd say, "Really, you're fantas-tic the way you do this," and he'd say, "Oh, it's no sweat, it gives me some-thing to do."' Living this life for twenty years, Joan and Tom confirmed and consolidated their social immobility.

Simultaneously, their *modus vivendi* entrenched them even more deeply in the local context, expanding their social network in the district and winning neighbourhood approval, as they actively constituted their own 'contextual continuity'. Joan encapsulates it: 'I used to take them all up to [the precinct] shopping, some walking and some in trolleys, and we'd go round and I made loads and loads of friends because I'd got so many chil-dren and they couldn't believe how good these children were. I got to know the girls on the checkouts and I'd go in of a weekend and they'd say, "So-and-so came in with their parents – you'd never believe they were the same child because of the way they behaved!" So, she said, "You must do something right."' Joan still hears from parents whose children she once minded, is in touch with many of them herself, one of whom visits most weekends.

Joan insists upon her contentment during this period, although she was fully aware that her work was sub-optimal in its modesty, compared with being a nurse. Nevertheless, she did not regard her *modus vivendi* as one of self-sacrifice: 'Well, you do make sacrifices, but it was only because I wanted to, I wouldn't do anything I didn't want to do. I'm just the sort of person that likes to care for other people. And the way I did that in my early years was to look after other people's children and to try to give them what the parents – well, sometimes it was better than what the parents gave them. That was my philosophy, really; just to do what I can for people and help them out and look after them.' I suggested that perhaps she had to relinquish other activities she could have done or would have liked to do, but Joan insisted, 'I didn't really want to, there wasn't really anything.' Yet, Joan is candid and self-aware about her need to be needed, which probably underlay the contentment she derived from childminding and offset her enduring regrets about not becoming a nurse.

Very openly and against herself she tells a revealing story about Tom's stroke and hospitalisation, precipitated by Simon being in a coma at the age of ten because of undiagnosed diabetes, whilst she herself was just recovering from a hip replacement. Joan found Tom in a dishevelled state on the ward and negotiated his discharge from hospital. 'I looked after him, got him up and washed him and dressed him and then as he got over his stroke, I used to make him do the potatoes and hoover the floor to make his hands more supple. And then one day he'd got himself up and had got himself washed and dressed – and do you know, that really hurt, the fact he didn't need me to help him any more, that really hurt.' Although Tom did not die for nearly another decade, Joan's very self-awareness raises two questions: how does a communicative reflexive cope when they do lose their dialogical partner and how does someone who acknowledges that she needs to be needed re-establish a different *modus vivendi* for herself?

The answers to the two are closely related. Fundamentally, Joan has pre-served her practice of 'thought and talk' with Tom. 'I still talk to Tom every night and I always ask him to look after me and not to fetch me until the [grand]children are grown up, until I'm not needed any more.' She thinks of Tom as an abiding and accessible presence, a view shared by Jessica and John, by Emma, Simon's daughter, who both sees and chatters to him as he smokes his pipe at the top of the stairs, and by Sandra, one of their charges, who comes in and talks about her day at school with him. Thus, Tom is not an absence but a presence, projected into the next generation, and it is that generation of grandchildren which founds Joan's current *modus vivendi*.

Simon's wife has suffered from depression since the birth of her children and it is their care, beginning when Ben was two days old, which has progressively become Joan's main concern. Relations with Claire have always been fraught and Joan reports a serious dispute with her over Ben's nursery schooling as well as, she believes, Claire's unwarranted attempts to have Simon charged with domestic violence. Joan's main aim has been to 'keep the family together'; the grandchildren now live with her, Simon visits daily, but Joan praises him for and supports him in continuing to live with his wife, whilst trying to ensure that Claire remains part of the family circle. She recounts the following story after the three adults had been to watch Emma in her school nativity play: 'when we came to go home, she [Claire] hadn't seen the children since March, and of course they're very, I suppose, cold towards her, you can't expect anybody to sort of jump in. And she said goodbye to the children and stood back, and I went across to her and I said, "I shall see you soon Claire," and put my arms round her and just held her tight and she burst into tears. The next morning, Simon came in and said that Claire cried all the way home. I said, "Why?" And he said, "Mum, it's the first time anyone's cuddled her, it's the first time anybody's held her really tight." I grieved for her because I loved her, well I still do love her really.' There is, of course, a serious question mark over what Claire's interpretation might be, especially when she was told that, as far as the children are concerned, she and Simon 'don't have to worry about anything – about the hairdresser's, the dentist, the doctor's. Everything's done, the washing, the ironing, cleaning the shoes, packing the lunches up.' Is Claire being unduly marginalised by Joan's need to be needed, or is disabled Joan working at full stretch to provide a stable home life for her grandchildren, or is there something of both?

Whatever the case may be, this 'third-generational' family performs the same role of embedding Joan firmly in her neighbourhood context and protracting its continuity, rather than allowing loneliness or withdrawal to become the results of bereavement and disablement: 'usually I've got visitors in and out all day, most days, not every day but most days there is. I've got real good friends and a lot of acquaintances. When we go up to [the precinct] the first thing Emma says is "Oh gran, can't you walk through anywhere without someone knowing you?" But it's lovely, it's absolutely lovely they get to know you.' The frequency of visitors was immediately confirmed by the interruption of Vickie, a young mother of twins from across the road, who benefits from Joan's baby-sitting; and the two of them proceeded to arrange their next visit.

Such is the density of this 'micro-world', which began to be constructed with Tom, more than quarter of a century ago, that Joan feels no need for organised activities: 'I don't need to go to clubs and that. I go and see my sister, perhaps once a fortnight. But no, I'm not one for that – we take the kids to the park or go swimming, but not to be with groups of other people, that doesn't interest me. I don't want to go. We go and have a drink with my daughter, sometimes on a Sunday, the kids go with us and they play in the garden, and if she's not working we go for dinner. But I don't want anything like that, I've never needed anything like that.' As far as church attendance is concerned, Joan claims not to be religious: 'None of our immediate family were religious, but they still taught us a prayer to say before we went to bed. And my father used to say, you don't need to go to church to be religious. If you're good all your life and you can do some-body a good turn, then that to me is religion.' Politics is given much shorter shrift: 'I do vote but I don't take an interest in it.' Joan's views on society immediately reduce to the effects of educational pressures upon individual children, and her overall message to Simon about the grand-children is: 'as long as they're happy and they're content, that's all that matters – they'll get by in the end, I did.'

How Joan 'got by' was through settling for 'third best', by embracing social immobility and immersing herself in the family and the contextual continuity that she actively developed and maintained after her marriage. Without doubting her life-long contentment, one can nevertheless ask whether or not her *modus vivendi* for 'getting by' was free from regrets, particularly about the frustration of the first project she entertained. The answer is 'no', meaning that the agent who has been an active collaborator in their social immobility, as well as the subject of structurally constrained opportunities and culturally enforced gender norms, is also a person with the self-awareness that she has worked hard to obtain her half-loaf – pre-cisely because the full one was withheld from her.

'No, I've never stopped regretting [nursing] even now. I have to go to hospital for blood tests quite regularly and even now the adrenalin gets cracking. I know it's a terrible thing to say, but I'm ever so happy when I'm in there. I've been in to have both hips replaced and when I was there I was so happy. They used to say, for God's sake stop interfering, you're always trying to do something you shouldn't. It's just something I like to do – I like to be there and on the scene – and I really regret it so much. Oh, it's awful and of course when I was – I finished childminding when I was sixty and there was a thing on the TV about wanting nurses. And I rang up and the chap said, ' "Oh yes, we'll send you a pack, and by the way how old are you?" And I said sixty and he burst out laughing and said you're too old. I thought, at least if I could have done a bit . . .'

Autonomous reflexivity and upward social mobility

Autonomous reflexives are subjects whose internal conversations about themselves in relation to their circumstances are self-contained mental activities. The courses of action that they determine upon are the products of such lone inner dialogue. When this is the dominant mode of reflexivity, subjects rarely feel a need to share their internal conversations because they are not seeking completion of their ideas, confirmation that they have considered all angles or enhancement of their self-confidence to act upon their ratiocinations. Of course, this does not mean that they never engage in communicative reflexivity because there are many more reasons for doing so than those three – such as consideration for other people affected by their decision-making, lack of requisite technical expertise in a given area, the need to justify their proposed actions in situations of accountability, or simply being dragged into conversations where some degree of reciprocal exchange is expected or hard to avoid. Whilst the autonomous subject may respond readily, articulately and take interest in the reactions of others, none of these interchanges is driven by need.

Equally, every functioning human being exercises some degree of autonomous reflexivity or they would not have been able to get through the past twenty-four hours. Even were one to subscribe to the pragmatist conviction that large tracts of life are governed by routine action and that deliberation is mainly prompted by encountering problems, each day supplies its quota of these and a decision, however trivial, has to be made. The contingencies that can and do arise also necessarily out-strip the repertoire of coping routines that have been developed. Otherwise, no car would speed so fast as to defeat the pedestrian's safety procedures for crossing the road, thus precipitating an autonomous decision about retreating or advancing; no item would be misplaced, enforcing a decision to make a search or do without it; and no one would make a request, observation or enquiry that called for an unscripted response. Indeed, when people refer to having been 'put on the spot', this is a colloquial way of saying that they have had to exercise autonomous reflexivity – quickly and often with discomfort or embarrassment. Nevertheless, everyone can 'think on their feet', even if they would prefer not to do so. This is unsurprising because, as was seen in chapter 2, none of the Coventry subjects obtained a zero 'A' score on ICONI.[4]

What is distinctive about those who practise autonomous reflexivity, as their dominant mode of internal conversation, is that they initiate their own inner dialogues, conduct lone deliberations and come to conclusions for which they are solely responsible. Subjects express this sometimes as a straightforward lack of need for input from others (except when they are

---

[4] The lowest score was 1.33 (out of 7) and the only subjects scoring less than 2 were fractured reflexives.

out of their depth technically), sometimes as a desire to maintain their privacy and sometimes both. The following self-observation, offered by Rachel (a 25-year-old hairdressing salon manager), covers all of the above: 'I don't particularly need other people's opinions; I'm happy with my own opinions in things . . . I don't discuss my private life with anybody really . . . I don't tend to share a lot really, I just make my own decisions.'

Instead, Nick (twenty-nine and a self-employed builder) places prime emphasis on privacy and a desire to keep his thoughts to himself: 'I do tend to bottle things up quite a bit and don't give a lot away to people. Secrecy is the wrong word, but I don't like people knowing my business . . . I don't enjoy talking about problems or anything like that. I'd much rather think about problems myself and try to deal with them myself than have a second or third party involved.' Additionally, he stresses the importance of lack of distraction when dwelling upon something in order to clarify it: 'The mulling over thing, I'd do something like that when I'm on my own rather than when I'm out with people. It's not heavy thinking but pretty strenuous thinking. If you're out with friends, having a drink or something, there's too much going on to sort of think about it.' Thus, the presence of other people is a hindrance rather than a help, and far from seeking out interlocutors, Nick prefers to be alone: 'mulling over, that sort of thing, would be if I was on my own, like driving or doing something a bit tedious – maybe having a bit of a think instead of having the radio on'.

Logically, if a subject feels no need for an interlocutor then it follows that there are far fewer restrictions upon *when* the autonomous internal conversation can take place. Thus, most of the interviewees describe themselves as engaging in it 'all the time'. One of these is Martin (a 30-year-old dispensing optician), but he also tries to pinpoint regularities in his pattern: 'I do it a lot, all the time I think. I reflect on things through my mind quite a lot; I tend to ponder things quite a lot. I suppose most often it's at night when you try to get your head to sleep. With me, I have a big problem sleeping and that would tend to be the time when I'm doing exactly that and mulling through quite a lot of things [that happened] during the day or things for the future in my head – mainly then, but pretty much all the time I'd be kind of – it's just a thought process all the time in your head.' Another is Damian (a 33-year-old manager of two shops), who agrees with 'all the time' and adds 'about everything', including what he is going to have for dinner. This is because, in the exercise of autonomous reflexivity, there is no interlocutor who can place restrictions upon the agenda for internal dialogue. However, Damian sees his most intense deliberations as being work-related: 'If I've got a lot of things going on in my mind, particularly at work, I kind of mull it over in my mind, what do I need to do first, prioritise it. That's when I do it most, when I've got lots of things and both shops are on my mind the whole time. I'm thinking is the [first] shop OK, they're going to have a delivery [at the second shop], I need to be over there, so I'm kind of thinking all the time what I'm doing, I'm quite conscious that I'm thinking about it.'

Such self-monitoring is a common theme amongst these interviewees, but Ralph (a 56-year-old car salesman) is currently unemployed and, because he has no work preoccupations, his internal conversation is much more wide-ranging than Damian's focused concerns. Thus he engages in inner dialogue, '[c]onstantly really. I'm a prolific observer; I watch everything that goes on . . . Even when I don't have a particular subject to consider, something specific that's sitting there waiting to be done, the grey matter's still there considering options.' To Tony (a 36-year-old freelance researcher), the frequency of inner dialogue is something he attributes to his personality. Internal conversations are times when 'You tend to come to terms with where you are, what you're doing, who you are, where you will be . . . I sometimes think I may be overindulging in these conversations. I'm less likely to be in a group of people, having a conversation in a group; I'm much more of a loner kind of character so these conversations tend to take place more frequently than if I was more social. I think my life is lived less with others and more with myself.' Precisely because they are reflexive beings, subjects will have a concept of what they are doing and a notion about why, under their own descriptions. However, the present concern is to describe this mode of reflexivity rather than to explore self-understandings about it.

To return to its distinctive features, autonomous reflexivity is associated with the ability to arrive at quick decisions, uncomplicated by second thoughts. This is not a necessary connection and it is open to the psychological claim that 'decisive people' would be prone to adopt this mode of reflexivity. However, that would not be the case unless this modality accommodated rapid decision-making, to the satisfaction of its practitioners – thus encouraging them to persist in it. One of the main reasons why it does so is because there is no need to await the availability of interlocutors before subjects review their options and reach conclusions about them. Moreover, precisely because subjects 'do it all the time' their deliberations can be more complex, long drawn-out and far-reaching, covering any number of considerations and reviewing the likelihood of different outcomes. In other words, the process is not truncated or diverted by subjects precipitously sharing their initial 'gut reactions'. Furthermore, by *not* sharing their preliminary responses with others, these subjects (unintentionally) protect themselves against the conventionality of 'similars and familiars', which reinforces normal custom and practice and tends to discountenance innovative conclusions. Lone internal conversation facilitates a thorough examination of any issue and, even though information will necessarily be incomplete, it can be supplemented by reference materials rather than being confined to the experience of a few interlocutors.

The decisions reached will tend to be sub-optimal if compared with a situation of perfect information, but deliberations can be concluded within the necessary time-frame and according to a procedure that subjects deem appropriate. Clive's account of his autonomous internal conversations (that of a 34-year-old business manager) is significant because, effectively, it incorporates a comparison with communicative reflexivity, which he volunteered without prompting at the start of the interview. Self-talk is something in which he engages 'all the time. Often it's just a progression of – well, I use a lot of logic, I'm mathematically based in my mind – everything tends to be working through a structure . . . to come out with the answer that I think is the most reasonable.' He adds that he does not need this to be supplemented by anyone else, but also admits that 'I don't mind if somebody comes back and says, "I don't think that's necessarily the right way," because it almost adds to the equation.' Communication and discussion are subsequent to deliberating and deciding; if relevant, they represent additional considerations needing cross-checking rather than sources of confirmation or completion.

Indeed, Clive finds these external conversations more tasking than his internal ones: 'explaining to people how I came to the decision is much more difficult than the way I come to the decision. Quite often it's finding people [with] the same intuitive way of comprehending. To me everything ends up being very black and white, even the greys tend to resolve one way or the other . . . If I feel I've got to explain it to somebody, it's very much as a list of positives and negatives.' In the exercise of autonomous reflexivity, the conclusions reached are the subjects' own; Clive's final comment is that he is fully prepared to take responsibility for them: 'It sounds very grand or like I've put the world on my shoulders, but at the end of the day it's my decision and it all comes back on me how I make the decision. And I don't want to say, well, somebody else gave me advice because that would suggest it's their fault. At the end of the day it's my fault. And that's the easiest way to do it. You can always take information on board but . . . it's always my decision.'

To the autonomous reflexive, inner dialogue is about matching 'options' with 'information' and is light years away from canvassing opinions or enhancing one's self-confidence. Here is Liz (a 55-year-old primary school head) trying to determine the reasons for her self-talk: 'having a conversation with yourself, it's the conditional isn't it? It's mulling really because there are options open and then you pull out the one that eventually you decide is the best.' Donna (a 22-year-old bank service adviser) emphasises exactly the same theme but is as emphatic as Clive that this is an autonomous and not a consultative exercise: 'I'd tend to make the decision by myself. I would keep it to myself for a while until I'd considered all areas and then not necessarily make a decision but sort of distil the information. It would possibly be the case that I'd have ten options and I'd try to narrow it down to two options and then it would be the case that I'm sixty/forty to fifty/fifty . . . I don't think I'd let anybody sway me in any way with a personal decision.'

Those subjects who have already been introduced are from a group of twelve interviewees, identified on ICONI as seemingly clear practitioners of the autonomous mode; respondents whose 'A' score was 5 or over (out of the maximum of 7), who appeared to be non-fractured (an 'F' score less than the mean of 4) and whose dominant mode of reflexivity was clearly differentiated from other modes and qualitatively confirmed as such. It was unfortunate that the twelve who constituted the final group of interviewees comprised eight males and four females because no association was found within the sample as a whole between gender and those for whom the autonomous mode was predominant. This imbalance arose solely from the availability of those approached and their willingness to be interviewed.

Before beginning data analysis it is important to gain a feel for autonomous reflexivity. The following narrative attempts to enter into how a young subject has tried reflexively to steer his life in society to date. Again, the main themes will be covered but not laboured: the causes bringing about 'contextual discontinuity'; the development of lone deliberations; the investment of self in the practical order; the importance of lighting up occupationally; the attempt to cope strategically with constraints and enablements encountered in the world of work; and the resulting trajectory of upward social mobility.

Martin's story

Martin is thirty years old, divorced with two children aged nine and twelve. He was adopted when he was eleven and brought up in the northern Shires. His adoptive father is a joiner and his adoptive mother an office manager. He now lives in Coventry where he works as a managing dispensing optician. His ICONI 'A' score is 6.00, one of the lowest for interviewees in this sub-group, and he recorded a low 1.50 for 'fracturedness'.

Except for being well maintained and the grounds landscaped, these alienating blocks of flats with their impenetrable numbering system could have been found anywhere in Eastern Europe instead of on the outskirts of Coventry. A black jogger materialised under the street lamp and offered his services as guide to the right staircase of the right block, with suitable asides about Kafka. Succinctly he conveyed that this complex was a 'very safe' way-station for young middle-class professionals. The inside of Martin's neat flat was remarkable for the number of detailed black and white drawings, some unfinished, but all executed with confident draughtsmanship and for photographs of two young schoolgirls at various ages since babyhood. So much of Martin's biography was on view.

Martin himself, with his quiet articulacy, was equally direct in his self-characterisation: 'I think I'm quite a realistic person; I don't sort of ignore the facts and think, well, that's just going to go away and this is going to happen – that isn't going to be the case. I don't tend to fluff around things. I try to look at what's there, what's real and if I can do something about it – and if some of it's left to chance, then that's just how it's going to have to be.' This seems a very fair summary of his life too, marked by circumstances and contingencies beyond his control, which he confronts before trying to steer a path around and beyond them. In this context, he presents himself as decisive: 'it tends to be, that's out of the way and finished, next problem please!' Yet, his story did not begin easily nor does it run smoothly and, as we settle into the sofas for what becomes a long evening, some of the pain of this journey starts soaking through the circumspection bandaging his narrative.

During the first ten years of his life, Martin and his younger brother were moved seven times from one form of care to another. What he accentuates from his memories of this period is his complete dependency upon others: 'I was having to sort of take someone else's word quite a lot that this is the right thing, this is the wrong thing, and I had to be quite accepting of that.' Moved around at other people's say-so spelt his complete dependence upon the social order, yet without him enjoying close or lasting inter-personal relationships. Thrown back upon his own resources, Martin resorted early on to the more dependable practical order, which has remained his redoubt ever since: 'I draw and I paint and I play the piano. That's something I've always done from a very young age, no matter what, I've always liked my drawing. So my main interest was my art, my music has sort of come on since I got older, but when I was younger I would always paint and draw. It's focusing your mind on something and keeping it off things you may not want to think about at the time. So it kept me very focused and I got a lot of enjoyment out of it.'

'I was adopted – I went to them when I was eleven, so the time up to then I was in care homes and [with] foster parents and that tended to be quite a journey.' Although stability followed his adoption, affection and involvement did not develop within his new family: 'I think they got a shock when they adopted us to be quite honest . . . a lot of people when they're adopting, they tend to get this rosy family ideal – which you don't get at all. Certainly at our age, ten- and eleven-year-old boys who have been passed from pillar to post and had to trust lots of people, the relationship side of it never came really. Certainly, you tend to find the mother–son relationship that never happened! Not that we've not been close to them, we get on very well with the parents and I've always been able to talk to them to a degree, but there's something that isn't there. I can't even say what it is, but it just isn't. I've seen as I've grown up, my friends, my male friends, with their parents, especially their mothers, and I've thought no, it's not the same for me and I don't know why it is. It just didn't happen.'

Mainly, what seems not to have happened was the growth of closeness and concern. There is no hint that these adoptive parents ever proffered themselves as interlocutors, whether or not by then Martin would or could have availed himself of a dialogical partner. As he moved into his teens he seems to have been increasingly aware of their affable disinterest and of the negative consequences of their non-involvement: 'They were always like, yes, you can do that, that's good, but that's kind of where it stopped . . . I think if I'd been leaned on a bit and had a bit more encouragement on certain things, I might actually have been better at certain things. My parents didn't really go one way or the other. If I said I wanted to do something, I didn't really get "OK, let's give it a try." I tended to be put off for whatever reason.' In consequence, Martin continued with his lone pursuits, taking up cross-country running and continuing to immerse himself in painting and drawing. However, it is clear that his satisfaction came from the practice of art, from the lone honing of his skills, but that he lacked the backing and motivation to harness these to the school curriculum – to doing art in the social order – despite gaining school prizes. 'I even disappointed myself at school because I really did flunk my exams big time, even the art one I didn't do very well in, purely because I didn't apply myself to the course side of it. I think I got a C in Art and the teacher went mental . . . he said, "There's no way you should be walking out of here with anything but an A*" – he was mad. It was purely because I didn't apply myself. I did the pictures, but they wanted a bit of the explanation behind the pictures and the work behind that – I just didn't do it. I put together a very nice portfolio, which scraped me a C, and the rest of it was history, unfortunately.' Most of his subsequent history is strongly marked by the theme of 'contextual discontinuity', one which, in Martin's case, is quantitatively measurable but also qualitatively moving in kind.

At home, Martin was not encouraged to make the connections between his artistic concerns, the school curriculum and his future career, an essential part of beginning to fit together parts of the sequence <concerns → projects → practices>. Instead, he was driven to treat his art reclusively and to rely upon the standards intrinsic to its practice. This was because social approval was entirely lacking in the family and Martin tries to analyse why this was so: 'This sounds a bit daft, but I actually found that my dad, because of his character, was a bit jealous . . . if I did a particularly good drawing, he was like "Oh yes, that's all right," but he wouldn't be over the top. Whereas, if my children bring something to me, I'm like "Oh that's really good" and try to build them up and make them feel like they've done something really amazing, which is what you want when you're a kid. It's certainly what I wanted and I didn't always get that reaction.' Martin's initial comment upon this sad lack of support for his artistic prowess was to say tersely: 'But it hasn't stopped me doing it.' Towards the end of the interview, he was more willing to ruminate on the painfulness of these relational absences: 'I try not to get too down. Certain things in my past I have not been happy with at all and it's really bothered me. But I've had counselling for that kind of issue and I've been through various points in my life and personal things that happened – I think it's just acceptance of what's done is done, and it's getting on and trying to make sure that sort of thing doesn't happen again to someone else, that being my kids at the moment.'

As a sixteen-year-old school leaver, Martin himself determined to 'get on' by turning his artistic concern into a career. The following statement already provides evidence of strategic thinking, of how to balance his intrinsic interest with his extrinsic interest in earning a living, of how to translate skills rooted in the practical order into a job within the social order. 'When I was younger, I was going to do some sort of fine art or computer-aided design. I like doing fine art but career-wise I thought the money, the financial side of it, would be in the design process and the computer side of it I knew was starting to form at that time – and I thought that's probably a really good area to get into for the future because everything's going into computers. So I went to do computer-aided design, started to do a diploma at college in basic art and design rather than fine art – and it just bored me to tears to be honest.' Such false starts are quite common amongst young autonomous reflexives; they attempt to act strategically but necessarily lack the self-knowledge and societal knowledge to do so effectively and to begin forging a *modus vivendi* with which they could live.

Usually, this is the point at which they return to the internal conversation and regroup their resources around a redefined project. Martin was deprived of a breathing space in which to replan his future by the intervention of what he quite rightly sees as contingency: 'it's kind of been quite haphazard for me. I certainly didn't plan to get married, I didn't plan to have children, the whole process just happened, it unravelled . . . My girlfriend, who then turned out to be my wife, fell pregnant with our first one when I was seventeen – a bit young. So, basically, I had to pull myself out of college anyway and get a job, simple as that.' Martin immediately enrolled on a Youth Training Scheme and gained employment as a salesman in a large chain of electronics shops. As he puts it unassumingly, after a couple of years 'I worked my way up a little bit there until I was assistant manager.' The tendency to become upwardly mobile was already manifesting itself when Martin was still less than twenty and following an unplanned occupational track.

However, contingency again intervened to derail him, this time in the form of twelve to fifteen employees in the retail chain being sacked for 'gross misconduct', which in Martin's case amounted to giving away a small promotional item to a customer making an expensive purchase. That, as he puts it, 'left me stuck because of the little one – and my wife was basically working part time. She upped her hours and went full time and left me back at home with the nipper, which was great. It was circumstantial; I had taken one route and ended up taking another.' Yet, above all, this period as a housefather was a time of stock-taking for Martin. He consolidated his relationship, married his girlfriend and they had a second child before he was twenty-one. He returned to his solitary consolation – the art, which had seen him through previous bad times – and he was sufficiently good to be invited to exhibit as a local artist. 'As much as being at home was OK, I did a lot of drawing and painting then because that was the only thing that I could do that would keep my mind occupied, because I'm quite active.'

But he was also thinking about and working towards a goal that seems almost irresistible to autonomous reflexives – self-employment. 'I was looking after the kids, taking them to school, but I was doing a business and finance course at night because I thought – I was fairly miffed that I could be dismissed out of a big company so easily, so, I thought I want to find something I can do and set up my own business, and then I went on to this business and finance degree.' Although Martin did not finish this particular course he was already displaying the start of the pattern, typical amongst autonomous reflexives, of progressively adding to his qualifications. His aim at the time was to open his own computer shop 'or something along that line'. Since he was clearly not fully committed to the product, I queried his motivation for the venture in the hope of understanding the appeal of sole-trader status amongst this sub-group. Martin replies, 'It's a control thing. I think what happened to me wasn't fair and I didn't have any control over that. Obviously, I shouldn't have done what I did at the time, but it seemed quite a menial thing. I didn't see it as a big issue and certainly not a reason to sack people. So, it would be in my control, what I say goes and if things go wrong for me then it will have been through my own fault. If I get it wrong then it's my problem and my fault, but at least I'd have given it a shot. I was quite willing to give that a go because I thought, yes, I've got the ambition to do that.'

Simultaneously, Martin is presented with an alternative option, an opening to become an optical technician, proposed by a friend's wife who works in optics. He now has to weigh 'being in control', at the price of considerable risk-taking, against the opportunities of a new career and the benefits of it dovetailing well with his concern for his family and ethic of responsibility towards its members. Strategic thinking comes immediately into play and the two considerations that prompt his final decision are the circumvention of constraints and the availability of enablements. In his own terms, he thinks of this more as being on a 'snakes and ladders' board: on his next throw he could take a crashing fall or be back on the way up. But this is not a game of chance, and Martin reveals how he weighed the two prospects against one another and decided to circumvent the snake-pit. What is not yet revealed in his following explanation is the full role that enablements played in reaching his final decision.

'It was either starting your own business, which really was the harder decision, or take the easy option, which I think I did . . . [having] weighed up the pros and cons. I thought if I was on my own and it was only me that was going to be affected by my decisions at the time, then I would have gone and have a computer shop by now, but the risk of falling flat on my face again, having to go back to not working, I thought no, I'll just take something that's there – that I know is stable and balanced and looks like it's still going to open up a good lot of opportunities, which I suppose it has. It seemed to be a good career move and that was the decision. That was probably one of the biggest decisions I've made actually. I don't ever regret doing it . . . this is not the self-employed age at all, it's not a good situation to be in . . . there's too much left to chance and being in the right place at the right time. Everyone's scrapping for what's left over from people that have already had businesses established and are able to do silly prices like the Internet.'

Equally important was the fact that entering optics presented Martin with a new opportunity for harnessing his practical skills to work in the social order, which computer retailing would have failed to supply. His friend's wife was perspicacious enough to put the proposal to Martin *as an enablement* that would advance his concern in the practical order and he interpreted it in precisely that way. 'She said, "Why don't you go for it

– you've got the design and you're good with your hands; it's quite a manual job, but you've got to have quite an eye for detail." So the art thing came in quite handy because that's exactly what I had. I tried it for a little while and I was actually quite good at it as well – and carried on from there. My wife went back down to part time and I got myself back on the ladder with the optics career.'

Not only did Martin view entering optics in terms of upward social mobility, he immediately enrolled for the qualifications necessary to secure it. In the process of taking a vocational diploma in optics, he discovered that subjects he had switched off from at school were perfectly manageable now that they were coupled with a skill he sought to develop. 'When I went on the optics course, they said maths was important, you should have A-level maths, and I haven't even got GCSE! So, I took a basic maths course alongside the technical course that I did, and did quite well at it. I started to find that I did quite enjoy proving to myself that I could do things that previously I'd not had an interest in doing.' Martin agrees that he is very self-motivated, 'if I want to do something', but also sees the strength and weakness of so being. 'If I don't want to do it then I won't. But if I want to do something then I will get off my backside and do it – which is good and bad because there are times when I should apply myself to certain things. If it's something that I want or I can see a benefit for me or someone else that I want the benefit for, then I'll certainly not stop until I've got it.' And once he has got it, he insists he will go with it 'as far as I can take it'.

At first, the challenge of novelty, of putting his existing practical skills to a new use in an unfamiliar setting, of exploring their flexibility and adding to their range was sufficient to sustain Martin. But boredom is the bogeyman of the autonomous reflexive and it set in as soon as he had gained mastery. 'When you first start the job, everything's new, so learning all the new procedures and the routines and how things work, that's challenging. But then, once you know all that, there's nothing else coming in that's any different from what you already know . . . over time I started to get bored, I think everyone does after a while. I don't like routine very much, so that probably is what it is. It's just the same kind of situation day in, day out, whereas with certain jobs you can say you've experienced something different every week. I started off as a technician just making specs up, that's basically the path you take, you start off as a technician and then go on to maybe an optical assistant, and then you go on to a dispensing optician and you go up and up and up.'

Martin was then in his mid-twenties, a qualified optical technician who was not content to remain as such and was bored with his present employment. His marriage was also breaking up, despite his great love of his children, and he had begun a new relationship. Just as his girlfriend was applying for higher degrees in the area, Martin was offered a much better post with greater prospects through a friend who already worked in Coventry. As he puts it, 'the whole thing just clicked . . . I made quite a bold move from [further north] and coming down here, which again was sort of promotion work wise, it was a step up.' It was bold because it constituted making another substantial increment in his 'contextual discontinuity', a significant geographical distancing from the two people he cares about most and an acceptance that paying child support would preclude his acquiring a mortgage.

The new relationship did not work out but the new job did; the two were not unrelated. After only a few months in post, the most important thing for an autonomous reflexive happened to Martin: he began to light up. 'I started this new job, got a little bit hooked by it, and then I could sort of see that I need to do this, go on this course, go on that course and build up' – to becoming a dispensing optician. Rather dryly, for someone who is not at all cavalier about his relationships, he remarks that neither he nor his girlfriend had a lot of time to give one another and that the demands of work won out. Predictably, these latter were treated in supererogatory fashion. Martin has now completed three years of training towards qualifying as a dispensing optician and has only three exams to go, which 'I can plod through at my own pace and try to do a good job of them . . . just to say, that's it, I've finished, it would be nice . . . That is my next challenge.'

Adding further qualifications and 'making a good job of it' in general are characteristics and attitudes prevalent amongst autonomous reflexives, but it is clear that Martin's superiors were also impressed since he was promoted to managing dispensing optician before finishing his course. Reflecting upon this he says, 'I'm lucky to be where I am now really without the qualification because you don't really become manager of a practice until you've done a dispensing course and completed it. But I've got the position anyway, so I'm lucky – I kind of jumped the gun a bit, jumped the ladder.' His trajectory of upward social mobility is indubitable, but at the age of thirty, how does Martin look back upon it and forward from it? Retrospectively, he admits, 'with me it wasn't my first line of work and it wasn't ideally what I wanted to do. I've just sort of grown into it and still had the enthusiasm to get as high as I can – I'm still not there yet.'

This is an ambivalent statement; does it mean that Martin has made his pact with the social order, will continue to move still higher and establish his *modus vivendi* within it – or does he continue to hanker after his initial ideal of investing himself in the practical order? When this question is put to him directly, his response reveals self-knowledge, frankly faced: 'I still would like to do fine art or be able to make a partial living off doing fine art, but again applying myself. I tend to have stints of being able to concentrate on something for hours and hours and hours to get it finished – or I have an hour's stint and then bin it, get bored, and then come back in two weeks' time and do a bit more. If I'm honest with myself, I'm glad I'm in the position I'm in because if I'd gone down the fine art side of it, I probably wouldn't have been able to do stuff on demand, that isn't how it works for me . . . I just do it in stints.' There is also a hint that perhaps Martin thinks he has reached his ceiling with art when he says that he now spends more time playing the piano: 'the art is something I can just do now and get a result, and still get satisfaction with the end result, but with music, because I'm still learning, I find I get more satisfaction.'

Conversely, Martin has achieved a relatively smooth dovetailing of his concerns and this is the linchpin of a sustainable *modus vivendi*. Yet, dovetailing can slip and sustainability requires someone who wants to sustain it. On the plus side, his job requirements and the children's visits fit together harmoniously: 'the work side has been pretty flexible, so I've not had to choose between going to work or having the kids – it's tended to fit quite well'. Equally, he maintains that in terms of the relationships which matter to him, 'at the moment . . . I'm quite happy. I've got a girlfriend and we get on really well and I can confide in her. We don't see each other too much but we don't see each other not enough, it's just a nice balance. And the relationship with the children is better than it ever was I think. The time we do have together, we have a really good time and I know that they like to come and see me and like me going to see them. That's important.' On the minus side seems to stand the unlikelihood of further upward social mobility itself. This emerges as I seek to discover what he would want to be doing occupationally a few years hence: 'the work side of it – that's the area I wouldn't know what's going to happen in ten years' time because I probably will get bored with this job and move on . . . I wouldn't mind if there was a further position I could go to in this company. If I could get higher, then I would, but really the two people above me are the two directors, so either I take over the company from them or stop where I am.'

Yet, until he has his full qualifications, the chances of moving to a bigger company as, say, area manager, are remote. Moreover, in the three years it will take for him to become qualified his daughters will become teenagers and their relationship will be reshaped. As a typical autonomous reflexive, Martin is also typically an individualist: drawing little upon organised activities (preferring his solitary pursuits), having minimal involvement with social institutions (regarding their overall impact as damaging) and having few significant others (anchoring him to this context). Being highly self-motivated, he is not moored in place by entanglements at the micro-, meso- or macro- levels and is thus unrestrained from making further contributions to his already high level of 'contextual discontinuity'. Martin supplies his own motto for his life politics: 'if I'm doing something and I believe in it, for me that's good enough and I shouldn't have to try and get it justified by anyone. If that's my opinion, then go with it – if it turns out to be wrong, then learn from it.' He is still only thirty; his current dovetailing may slip even if he works hard to make it stick, or the signposts reading 'boredom' and 'challenge' may lead him to slip anchor and attempt to establish a new *modus vivendi* in a new social context that he feels could provide better scope for his ultimate concerns.

Pulling away from the kerb, I start wondering what Martin will do with the remnants of his evening. Nothing seems more evanescent than the image of this young man hunched solitary over his piano at the top of a convenience block of flats on the darkened outskirts of Coventry.

Meta-reflexives and social volatility

Meta-reflexivity, namely reflecting upon our own reflections, tends to sound an abstruse activity. Alternatively, it strikes some as indulgently narcissistic in its self-preoccupation. Its ruminative nature attracts opprobrium from certain social psychologists because it is viewed as an impediment to the swiftness of routine action.[5] Despite the negative attitudes, excited more by this mode of reflexivity than by the other two, every subject in the present study was found to practise it to some extent: none of the 128 respondents gained a zero 'meta' score on ICONI.[6] That is unsurprising because every act of self-monitoring is meta-reflexive in kind and every day is full of such acts.

Meta-reflexivity takes the standard form of questioning and answering ourselves within internal conversations. One of the most common instances to provoke meta-reflexivity is self-puzzlement: 'Why didn't I come out with what I'd planned?', 'Why can't I ever get my say in?' or 'Why am I always putting my foot in it?' Its 'partners' are self-diagnosis followed by corrective injunctions, which constitute the answers: 'Just don't let her rile you this time'; 'Calm down, deep breaths, panic makes exams

---

[5] E.g. T. D. Wilson and J. W. Schooler, 'Thinking Too Much: Introspection Can Reduce the Quality of Preferences and Decisions', *Journal of Personality and Social Psychology*, 60, 2, 1991, 181–92.

[6] The two lowest 'M' scores recorded were 1.33 and 1.67, both by respondents whose scores for autonomous reflexivity were highly dominant and whose 'F' scores were low.

worse'; 'Watch your speed – you can't afford another endorsement.' These inner responses can also serve to illustrate how someone obeys popular external exhortations, such as 'Pull yourself together' or 'Get your act sorted out.' But these commands do not have to be external in origin; ordinary people internally administer their own 'kicks up the backside'.

Those for whom meta-reflexivity is their dominant mode are considerably more expansive in their self-talk and the lives of their minds embrace all of the ten mental activities examined. As a group, they appear conversant with their own reflexivity. Two subjects avow that (contra Piaget) they continue their childhood practice of conducting some of their inner speech out loud. Here is Maurice (aged sixty-nine and retired) at the start of the interview: 'As a kid I used to talk to myself so much . . . Actually I do it very often when I'm taking the dog for a walk down the field because it's just me and the dog in the field and I can think and I can talk aloud to myself and answer myself in a way and come up with some ideas – and remember what I've said.'

In practising their reflexivity 'all the time', about which this sub-group is unanimous, they resemble the autonomous subjects. However, as Geraldine (a 34-year-old adult basic skills tutor) makes her first response in the interview, she indicates a different texture of inner dialogue and a self-awareness that her self-talk interweaves both imagery and affect. As is common, her internal conversation takes place 'Everywhere! In the car I do it a lot . . . I go through things I've got to do in the day, what am I going to do next.' As she continues, she imperceptibly shifts gear: 'what am I doing here, where am I going? All of the time, it's like your brain's working overtime – when I'm relaxing as well. I don't know whether I consciously talk, whether its words that come to my mind or just images, things that have happened in the day – not necessarily that I can see people, but feelings.' The constancy of self-talk is always underlined, with some meta-reflexives hinting at its burdensomeness, as in Jonathan's (a 31-year-old information technology team manager) immediate reaction: 'Oh God, all the time. I find it hard to switch my mind off so I'm analysing everything all of the time, analysing everything I'm doing and saying – thinking "Should I have said that or done that?" It's a constant thing for me.'

Despite its constancy, these subjects – some of whom apply the term 'loner' to themselves – do actively seek to be alone for some of their deliberations. The reasons they give for this make them the polar opposites of those for whom communicative reflexivity is the dominant mode because they reveal a conscious wariness about external influences. As Bernadette (a 56-year-old social development officer) puts it: 'When I try to think things through in a logical way, it's when I'm quiet, when I'm on my own. And I do try to do that because I know that outside events can take over.' Equally,

Anouar (a 24-year-old pharmacist), growing up as a first-generation British Asian, recognised early on the importance of retreating into his own world in order to insulate himself against the local norms: 'Round where I was living, it was basically people who didn't really have any ambition or drive – going on the wrong tracks with alcohol or drugs. To stay strong in that period, you have to go into your own head or you'll follow everybody else. In a way, you have to be inside your own head to survive that.' Gina (a 37-year-old university tutor) makes the same point about deliberately *avoiding* interlocutors since they would not understand or because to share would be to overburden them: 'I will keep a lot of what I'm thinking to myself, partly because I always feel it's very complicated and it would be too much for other people to have that kind of conversation. I suppose I try to rein back on that.'

In other words, precisely those factors that draw communicative reflexives into the 'thought and talk pattern', with the unintended consequence of reinforcing their normative conventionality, are recognised and resisted by meta-reflexives. The latter do not expect to be readily understood, do not seek confirmation of their 'first reactions' but prefer to explore their implications thoroughly, and they do not regard local norms and conventions uncritically. Their withdrawal into 'aloneness' strengthens the boundary between the public and private domains for these subjects. This does not mean that they shun all elements of communicative reflexivity, as we know from their ICONI scores. Indeed, many of the twelve interviewees sustained warm and continuous relationships with their families and early friends, but without sharing everything with them. Their subordinate use of the communicative mode is for purposes other than having interlocutors to complete their deliberations: for the self-clarification gained from fully articulating one's ideas in the 'longhand' of external conversation; for ascertaining the needs of significant others, which meta-reflexives take particularly seriously; and often from an interest in hearing others' views, which also constitutes a respite from their own internal conversations.

Does this mean that they are much closer to the autonomous reflexives, those firmly avowing themselves to be 'lone thinkers', confidently arriving at their own conclusions, decidedly in subjective control of their own courses of action and seeking objective social positions of control? Qualitatively, meta-reflexives reveal a more self-interrogative warp and a weft of tentativeness about how to act for the best in the circumstances that weave a different fabric for their life of the mind.

One of the features most clearly distinguishing between the two subgroups is that the meta-reflexives allow considerable free play to their imaginations: most are self-confessed, unapologetic daydreamers, they tell themselves stories, invent improbable scenarios, envisage themselves in unknown places, compose letters that are never intended to be written and script imaginary conversations in the knowledge they will never be staged. Conversely, the autonomous reflexive clamps down hard, in Protestant ethic vein, upon such an 'unproductive' licensing of the imagination. Like everyone else, he may be unable to exorcise his nocturnal terrors but he can discipline his diurnal mind-wanderings. Ironically, in exercising this self-disciplined repression he is, of course, making use of his subordinate capacity for meta-reflexivity.

However, this qualitative difference in internal conversational texture forms a prelude to the substantive difference between these two modes of reflexivity. As we have seen, the inner dialogue of the autonomous reflexive is single-mindedly *task-oriented*. He may thoroughly enjoy his music, sport, family activities, do-it-yourself or, indeed, external conversation, but none of these is allowed to engross his self-talk. In contradistinction, the meta-reflexive is *value-oriented*. She is preoccupied by moral issues, about which she feels an obligation to come to some conclusion; she has embraced an ideal towards which she feels a duty to conform herself as closely as possible; and she has a sense of social injustice in relation to which she wants to make some difference, however small.

This substantive distinction is accentuated by the fact that these two dominant modes of reflexivity are both exercised alone and thus the internal conversations of their practitioners are unconstrained in length and uncontrolled in content. Meta-reflexives are aware of devoting long tracts of time to their deliberations, although there is no way of measuring whether or not they devote more time to internal conversation than do autonomous reflexives. They are also conscious that in their inner dialogues they can behave like a dog with a bone. As Eunice (a 57-year-old Anglican vicar) describes her own self-talk: 'If there's something going on then yes, that will come back and back until I've come to a conclusion, done something about it or moved on.' Her ability not only to answer the question but immediately to reel off three different conditions which would cause her to terminate that strand of thought is indicative of the greater self-awareness displayed by this sub-group about their reflexivity itself.

This seems to be a straightforward consequence of the different purposes with which the two sets of interviewees conduct their lengthy deliberations. The *task-oriented* autonomous practitioners are relatively unconcerned about their own contributions to the deliberative process; what preoccupies them is becoming as sure as possible that they have factored in all necessary considerations and examined the matter from all relevant angles. Because meta-reflexives are *value-oriented*, they cannot divorce questions of doing and being from one another. If they are to 'make a difference', in line with their values, they also have to become the kinds of people who exemplify their commitments – otherwise they will be incapable of realising anything of what they care about most.

Thus, whilst the problems upon which the autonomous reflexive dwells are about technical proficiency and the adequacy of personal qualifications, meta-reflexives are concerned with the moral worth of their undertakings and their own worthiness to undertake them. Self-examination thus becomes an intrinsic part of the life of the mind when meta-reflexivity is dominant. Yet, its practitioners know that self-awareness is not auto-veridical and that there is no unvarnished news about themselves. They readily acknowledge that they are just as affected as anyone by subjective bias, wish-fulfilment and distorted perception. Equally, many acknowledge that they have been academically trained to recognise this and to work at counteracting it. This combination can readily lead to an over-scrupulousness of which several subjects are acutely (meta-)aware. Geraldine provides her own self-diagnosis of the two sides of this unwieldy coin and the resulting difficulties in handling it: 'I suppose [mulling over] is a way of gaining clarity, but I think there's a danger as well that you take away with you things that have happened, and things that you think have happened, and then blowing them out of proportion because you haven't got all the information . . . you can get it wrong because you've got your own biased opinion of what's actually happening.' Conversely, she is also aware that, from her school days onwards, 'you're trained to think about both sides of a situation. There isn't a right or a wrong but there is a bias and you try . . . to look at both sides and work out why the bias is there.' Then she draws the personal consequences, ones which are not confined to her alone: 'because I've been trained like that in my academic life you put it on your own life as well. But it's not terribly healthy because you find it hard to find your own way – because you're too busy concentrating on what the two sides of the story are.'

Such self-criticism is part and parcel of meta-reflexivity. Jonathan says in the simplest of terms that 'sometimes if you think too deeply you can just end up getting a bit tangled up in knots'. However, the process pre-occupied him to such a degree that he wrote two hundred pages of a novel about a character who became so absorbed with the life of his mind that it obliterated awareness of anything beyond it. Before going to university he concluded that the unfinished manuscript was completely 'egotistical and threw it away'. Having just completed her PhD, Gina voices the same self-criticism that in trying to think her way forward, she deliberates 'to an excessive level where I almost feel that I'm setting up scenarios I don't even need to be worrying about'. But

Siobhan (a 25-year-old environmental economist), who is fully in accord
with this self-diagnosis, gives the reason why meta-reflexives must nevertheless engage with their scrupulousness – one that can stand for her
fellow interviewees even though some do not share her articulacy. In
coming to a decision, 'I think about permutations and combinations of
things and rehash them probably more than is good for me because
sometimes I just end up going round and round in circles and spending a
lot of time on a decision that's probably fairly straightforward. I do think
through all the "ifs" – if I did this and then that happened and if that then
happened as well, with tiny probabilities . . . But, with every option
there's a choice that you don't make!'

Morally, meta-reflexives take responsibility for the consequences of
their inaction just as much as for their actions. In contrast, autonomous
reflexives are people of action and what they seek are personally desired
outcomes rather than right action despite one's imperfections. Of the
latter, meta-reflexives are acutely aware and attribute the shortcomings in
their self-talk to personal deficiencies: to worry, anxiety and frustration,
to fear of the unknown, to a need to give internal vent to censored feelings
and to being unsuccessful and unhappy with how one is. Yet, self-critical
as they are, meta-reflexives do not take all the blame and all the responsibility upon themselves. Much of their pondering over right action is about
how to act so as to make some difference in a social world that is far from
being right – or just, or fair or caring.

Those whose voices have been heard so far come from a group of twelve
interviewees, identified on ICONI as seemingly clear cases of people for
whom meta-reflexivity was their dominant mode. The lowest 'M' score
was 5.67 (out of a maximum of 7) and all had scores for 'fractured reflexivity' below the mean of 4. As usual, these were subjects whose scores were
clearly differentiated from other modes and whose dominant mode was
confirmed during the long interviews. Their high mean 'M' score of 6.4,
contrasted with the lowest mean 'C' score (2.6) recorded, supplies some
justification for regarding these as polar modalities.

Again, prior to analysis, let us make the acquaintance of a meta-
reflexive whose biographical narrative spans half a century. The key
points to be covered are: her experience of 'contextual incongruity'; the
emergence of a value-commitment as her ultimate concern; her unwillingness to compromise her values when she encounters occupational
constraints and enablements, but rather her resistance to their influence
by paying the price of moving on; the repeated clashes between her value-
commitment and her working contexts; resulting in renewed contextual
critique followed by lateral mobility, which weaves the pattern of social
volatility into her work history.

Bernadette's story

Bernadette is fifty-six years old, married with four children, all of whom have been to or are at university. She grew up in the north of England, in a family of seven children, all but one of whom entered the 'caring' professions. Her father, a secondary school head, died when her mother was thirty-five. The latter became a school secretary when the children were older. Bernadette lives in Coventry where she has recently taken a new job on a social development project. Her ICONI 'M' score is a high 6.67 and she recorded a low 1.75 for 'fracturedness'.

Modes of reflexivity are not personality types, so it is contingent that Bernadette happens not to be very outgoing. As she says of herself: 'I think I've always been a fairly quiet person and a thoughtful person, quite a shy person too.' (Indeed, she has one of the very lowest 'C' scores.) Unlike a handful of meta-reflexives, who respond with a torrent of reconstructed deliberations, and others, who are still seeking the ideal articulation of their thoughts whilst being recorded, Bernadette's responses are forthcoming but seem to aim for functional adequacy, with each sentence being pared to the bone. Consequently, it was all the more important to be attentive to each word and its connotations, for the words were carefully chosen and sometimes proffered handles to be turned if they were grasped. Accepting such words as quotidian encouraged her to employ more of the personal shorthand in which she reflects on her own reflections.[7]

Significantly, the examples she provides about each of the ten reflexive activities – and she practises all of them – almost uniformly revolved around the new development project (outreach work with prostitutes) on which she has been working for less than a year. For instance, 'mulling over' is exemplified by 'the work I'm doing currently. We work via a management committee and I'm the proactive person pushing the project forwards and there's a certain resistance amongst people to moving forward. Possibly it's a question of pace rather than anything else, I'm not sure. I have to come home and think about that resistance and the reasons for it. So, yes, a lot of that goes on, trying to look at things from the other person's view as well.' This response includes most of the themes running through Bernadette's occupational history: commitment to a project involving the underprivileged, striving to make a real if small difference,

---

[7] I see interviewing (of this kind) as an inter-personal exchange and do not try to assume the role of a cipher-with-a-recorder. Since there were enough cues on her pre-interview biographical data sheet to indicate that she was a practising Roman Catholic, we shared Catholic references just as with other subjects we discussed having children and dogs, DIY projects, Val McDermid's three female detectives and so forth.

encountering resistance, attempting to understand it and weather it, but often becoming frustrated by and critical of obstacles to making progress.

Her dedication to this project is so manifest that I enquire directly if she would call it a 'vocation'. Bernadette's response is: 'I suppose anything you do is a vocation,' and she specifies that this covers her past forms of employment and also her future activities. Ten years down the track, she envisages being 'retired but doing something similar in a voluntary capacity'. I press her on what underlies this sense of vocation by questioning whether her expectation of a 'working retirement' turns on a need to keep busy or a need to feel useful. Her reaction is revealing because of the speed with which it covers those meta-reflexive characteristics of self-awareness, motivation by an ideal rather than by the approval of others, self-monitoring and self-criticism. 'That's a good question. A bit of both really. I don't know whether you've ever done the Enneagram[8] – I'm definitely a "Two" on there. I definitely need to do this [project] and I hope it's no longer for anybody's appreciation. There is something in me that has a need to be helping people, which you've got to be careful of as well . . . Anything I'm involved in does tend to take over! . . . It's something that I'll have to learn to discipline myself a bit more about.'

In an explicitly Christian text of the Enneagram – of the kind Bernadette most likely encountered – 'Type Two', called 'The Need to be Needed', is described as follows: 'TWOs employ their gifts for the needs of others and care for their health, nourishment, education and welfare. They impart a measure of acceptance and appreciation that can help others to believe in their own value. TWOs can share generously and . . . stand by others when they have to endure suffering, pain or conflict, and in this way they give them the feeling that someone . . . accepts them.'[9] Bernadette does appear to endorse this characterisation of her value orientation. However, what I want to bring out is the emergence of 'contextual incongruity' between her adoption of these values and her natal context. This incongruence was between her ultimate concern, as reflected in the formation of her first nascent project, and her mother's needs and views, with which it clashed.

Bernadette's early childhood has the same objective features of 'contextual discontinuity' that have been presented as typical of autonomous

---

[8] Opinions differ about the origins of the Enneagram, with the majority attributing it to medieval (Sufi) Islamic sources, but others, like the authors in note 9, tracing it back to fourth-century Christian origins. It purports to differentiate nine cognitive types on a socio-psychological basis. It became popular in Catholic spiritual direction in the early 1990s, since which time secular versions have proliferated for management training, etc.

[9] Cited from one of the earlier (Protestant) texts, Richard Rohr and Andreas Ebert, *The Enneagram: a Christian Perspective 1989*, New York, Crossroad Publishing, 2004, p. 63.

reflexives and she herself held these to have been 'very disruptive'. Born in the north-east of England, at the age of seven she moved and changed schools when her father gained a headship in the north-west. Two years later he died, leaving seven children under the age of ten in the care of their 35-year-old mother. Interestingly, Bernadette also has the highest 'A' score in this sub-group of interviewees as well as having invested much of herself in the practical order when growing up by becoming a proficient pianist. One difference that distinguishes her from the autonomous reflexives is that she never considered making any kind of career out of music, though she and her children continue to be instrumentalists. So, what did the teenage Bernadette come to value more than her playing and why did it represent a source of 'contextual incongruity'?

She was brought up as a cradle Catholic and gained a place at a direct grant convent, which she describes as being a very happy secondary education. However, around the age of fourteen or fifteen her faith, which today she lists as her ultimate concern, began to assume an importance disproportionate to her upbringing. Not long afterwards Bernadette conceived of her first project, which was encouraged by the school but rebuffed and vetoed by her mother: 'there was one particular Sister at school that I got on extremely well with, so at the age of fifteen to eighteen I also wanted to join the religious order. But my mother would have nothing of it at all and so I didn't. She thought I was too young and I think at the time my oldest sister went over to France. My mother was quite close to me, as the second child in the family, and she depended on me rather than my older sister who was more flighty than I was. I certainly did try to make my case from the age of fifteen. She said, "Wait until you're eighteen," and when I was eighteen she had to go into hospital because she had a lump on her breast and she said, "Wait until that's all over," which I did. Then it turned out to be non-malignant, so I thought, "Great, I'll be able to go now," but when I brought it up again she still wouldn't have it.'

This account of how her dream had been quashed was given flatly and factually, so I query whether this had been or remains a source of great regret. For the first time there is a flash of emotion and Bernadette becomes quite heated as she continues: 'It has, yes, and certainly with my children I said when they're eighteen they will do whatever they want to do because you are old enough. Even if you make a mistake, it's better to let them make a mistake than force them into doing something that they don't want to do.' She is so emphatic because she does not believe that she herself was mistaken about her vocation at that age. She had been trapped in 'contextual incongruity' between her own vision, backed by her school, and her mother's opposition, which was hard to resist when expressed as a need for support. The latter prevailed. Thus, bowing to her mother and responding to the need to feel needed – because in those days entering the novitiate effectively severed one from any contact with one's family – Bernadette went to university to read French. The flatness with which she describes becoming an undergraduate and then proceeding to a diploma in education indicates the tepid, almost somnolent, manner in which she took this course of action: 'so I ended up going to the university that my father went to. I suppose I probably modelled what I thought I wanted on memories of my father.'

Of course, had Bernadette entered the particular religious order she desired, she would anyway have become a teacher and appeared happy with that prospect. So, in preparing to teach French, was she not acting like Joan who, as a communicative reflexive, seized half a loaf rather than no bread? There is an important difference. By making their constrained choices and scaling down their aspirations other communicative subjects also became materially worse off – as with Joan working as a childminder rather than a nurse. This was not the case for Bernadette. As a qualified secondary school teacher, she was objectively much better off than she would have been as a young Sister living on a tiny personal stipend. However, at fifteen and at eighteen she had been willing to pay this price – by taking the vow of poverty – in order to live out her vocation. Its incongruity with family demands and its consequent abandonment set the pattern for the rest of her volatile occupational life.

In the new context of her first teaching post Bernadette shelved her disappointment, began with enthusiasm ('I loved teaching when I started') and appeared to be constructing an alternative *modus vivendi* for herself by marrying a fellow teacher during this five-year period. Seemingly, by her marriage she had closed the door on her broken dream and had embraced her new occupational context. However, this dovetailing was imperfect – always a problem for meta-reflexives who seek organic integration between their concerns[10] – and the proposed *modus vivendi* did not stick. Initially, she diagnosed the discordant factor as her subject specialism: 'My first teaching job was in [a northern city] and at the end of that I remember thinking I will not go back into teaching French in this country because people are so insular and they can't understand the reason for learning another language. So there was this disenchantment, not with teaching but with teaching French.'

This is the point at which the socially unsettled pattern of the meta-reflexive was unambiguously revealed, if in miniature. It consisted firstly in contextual critique (of attempting to teach French in that northern

[10] See Archer, *Structure, Agency and the Internal Conversation*, pp. 278–88.

city), followed by a determination to undertake different work in a different context, entailing alternative training and, most distinctively of all, at a cost paid for by the subject. Bernadette and her husband undertook Voluntary Service Overseas, went to North Africa as teachers of English, lived on a pittance but found the two-year experience very rewarding. This period of VSO had not been intended to be indefinite and when the couple returned to England, with Bernadette expecting their first child, the underlying need to establish a lasting way of life re-confronted her.

The couple changed context, moving to Coventry where David obtained a post in a Catholic secondary school. They decided to go ahead with the large family they wanted and this signalled a fourteen-year break from paid employment for Bernadette. Although she viewed it as 'a real luxury to be able to stop at home with the children', she soon began voluntary work in their new parish church and was up to her eyes in it before her fourth child was born: she became the church organist and a member of the liturgy group; she founded a youth club and another for children with disabilities, meeting at weekends; she became involved in catechetics, and after five years was serious enough to take the certificate and was then appointed as parish catechist.[11] For approximately six years it sounds as though Bernadette achieved a satisfying and smooth dovetailing between her three main concerns: her faith, her family, and working for the disadvantaged in a Catholic context: 'I was very happy in that work, really enjoying being a lay person who was involved in what was happening in the parish as my children grew up.'

Financially it was not easy going for the family living on one teacher's salary. When her youngest child was six, Bernadette decided to take a half-time post but showed her uncertainty about resuming teaching by applying for administrative work in the local university: 'I wasn't thoroughly convinced I wanted to get back into teaching, and having got back in I found it pretty difficult.' Simultaneously, she continued as parish catechist, and with her other church activities was, effectively, working full time. However, within a couple of years Bernadette found herself equally critical of both her paid and her voluntary work contexts.

Although she did not have great expectations when taking up teaching again, even in a Catholic comprehensive, she found that job satisfaction had completely evaporated. I ask her to pinpoint what had deteriorated and instead of a list of discontents receive an analysis of the destructive interplay between educational institutions which perpetuates social

---

[11] Usually, as in this case, an unpaid position whose main duties are preparing children for First Communion and sometimes for Confirmation.

inequalities in Britain: all children do not 'achieve what they're capable of . . . I feel very strongly about private education because I feel that it deprives a whole lot of people of the education they deserve. Taking the better teachers and taking the better-motivated children away from the classroom, I think has a real negative effect on comprehensives.'

Her full critique is so damning that Bernadette could not reconcile herself to attempting to 'make a difference' within her own comprehensive school – to her, the structural context was too strongly opposed. Obviously, given her educational views, teaching in the private sector was not an option. Confronted with these structural and cultural constraints, I wondered whether, after seven years of accumulating discontent, she was ready to quit – forfeiting both the convenience and the salary – or whether her voluntary church work provided sufficient compensation.

As she remarked earlier, she sees all work as part of a vocation. Therefore a 'trade-off' in personal satisfaction between the two forms of work did not seem very probable. However, it was not even possible given the attitudes of her new parish priest. 'He would not entertain me at all as a woman who'd been working, who'd been making some positive contribution in the parish. He really would not speak to me . . . I was still the organist at the church and he wouldn't have the fact that we had a liturgy group that organised the hymns and the rest if it. He didn't like that, he came in with his list of hymns which we had to have and we could make no contribution at all. So things were not looking good but I clung on for five years . . . I gave up playing the organ because he wanted someone to do what he wanted – there was no compromise at all in his approach – very authoritarian, totally uncompromising. So in the end I had to give up and move away from the church for my own sanity because I was actually feeling very angry about it. That was something I was very happy in and had to give up – that cost me dearly.'

Eventually she left the two contexts in which she felt unable to realise her values by 'making some difference'. Doing so entailed a price she was willing to pay, emotionally, financially, and in terms of job security and socio-occupational status. To begin with, when much of her time ceased being invested in her home parish, she became an unpaid volunteer worker in Birmingham, alongside a couple of Sisters, doing 'outreach' work amongst prostitutes. She enjoyed it from the start and I asked whether she could put her finger on what gave her such satisfaction: 'I think it's dealing with, relating to a group of women who despite the crushing difficulties in their lives remain very resilient and very upbeat and able to enjoy the present minute without worrying about what's going to happen in the future . . . which is really quite inspiring given the deprivation they have undergone in their earlier years.' Soon, as well as acquiring a counselling certificate, Bernadette assembled a group of co-workers in Coventry to launch a parallel project with the help of the Birmingham Sisters.

This ran for five years on a voluntary basis with Bernadette's role being to organise the local group of volunteers. Towards the end of that period, 'I was spending so much time doing it I then felt there had to be a paid worker.' To cut a long story short, Bernadette pressed for the designation of a post whose occupancy was to represent her own downward social mobility (financially) or, at best, lateral mobility (in terms of status). She footed the bill herself, thus acting subversively towards structural constraints in order to advance her value-commitment: 'working with women who are marginalised, who are very vulnerable, who've had very difficult backgrounds of neglect and abuse . . . That troubles me and that's really why I do this job.'

Bernadette finds her new work extremely worthwhile but is far from being blind about the objective costs it has entailed: 'Oh, I'm loving it, really enjoying it. It was a good decision in the end, it makes me wonder why I didn't leave teaching long ago. But it wasn't easy either to leave the safety of teaching; that was an established job which I knew I had until I retired. To leave at the age of fifty-six was a daunting thing because we've only got funding for a year. If our future bids for funding aren't successful, I'm going to find myself at fifty-seven out of a job and no safety net at all. But I don't regret having left teaching . . . I'm currently working forty-six hours and being paid for twenty-eight! I'm hoping that next year it will be full time and that there will be funding. I'm an optimist! I really enjoy that work . . . I'm convinced the need will be there and we'll apply for funding and just hope we will get it. If we don't I'll be searching through the [local paper] for jobs!'

Thus, a cut in salary, a big increase in working hours and a complete lack of job security have been the prices paid in the attempt to live out her vocation. The rewards have been in terms of 'internal goods'. When pressed about the satisfaction Bernadette derives from her involvement, she returns to the theme of ministering to a manifest need of specific individuals at a particular place and time: 'We're getting them to develop – well, to build up their own confidence first of all, their assertiveness.' This signals a readiness to work in terms of intangible goods, without objective returns even in the form of 'success stories'. Without questioning that each of these inter-personal encounters is important, it remains to clarify why Bernadette herself has chosen this hands-on work amongst the marginalised in preference to 'making more of a difference' through involvement in national or local politics.

Her responses are revealing because they show that the typical meta-reflexive has not abandoned either type of political action, unlike the vast majority of the communicative and autonomous reflexives interviewed. It is not that Bernadette is any less critical about the lack of integrity of government leaders or of her own constituency MP, or any less disaffected from national politics than many of the subjects examined in later chapters. It is rather that she sees 'politics as a vocation' too, one where the decision to participate is unrelated to the probability of achieving a desired outcome. Because of her own disaffection from parliamentary politics, her political activities are focused on social movements. These range from her early involvement in the Campaign for Nuclear Disarmament to her most recent participation in the Stop the War in Iraq movement, the latter being of signal importance because of her own experience of working in Algeria: 'I do feel very sensitive to questions that involve Muslims, having known them as a very peace-loving people, peaceful in a way that we aren't really.'

I ask her how effective she feels these and other peace movements in which she has been involved have been, still hoping to gauge where she believes one can make 'more of a difference'. Her initial response fits in neatly enough with my intentions when she asserts that the Stop the War campaign had not been efficacious because national politicians tended 'to use it for all sorts of political ends which had nothing to do with the war'. However, as she continues to think out loud, Bernadette produces a pure statement of 'politics as a vocation' and one that she herself links directly to the nature and outcomes of her own vocation: 'I'm not sure that's what's important. Actually, I think you do it because you know that it's right. And what comes of that – I don't expect the questions to be solved really, in the same way that I don't expect prostitution will come to an end. You just do what you can to fight what you see is an injustice.'

Does this mean that Bernadette is reconciled to the fact that any form of social movement is nothing more than expressive action – without impact? In that case, her work amongst a small number of prostitutes would reflect a realistic investment in the practical politics of the possible. Her views are more complex than that dichotomy, as became clear when we started to talk about local political action. She is conversant with three on-going urban development schemes in the vicinity and approves of their 'giving ordinary people a voice', improving police liaison with the public, providing community centres and funding other resources, but also regards their dynamics as damaging to those who are socially marginal: 'from our own point of view it means that the women involved in prostitution are just further marginalised. These schemes very much work for the residents – and the interests of the residents are certainly not to have women working on their street corner. It is double-edged.'

Therefore, in terms of her own analysis, Bernadette is engaging directly in practical politics by working with one of the most marginalised groups whose members are not served by government or opposition and who suffer the perverse effects of social movements in the community. It is not simply that her *stance towards society* represents a generalised form of sub-version because of her manifest indifference to social constraints and enablements. Instead, Bernadette is concretely subversive in seeking to empower a pariah group and to include them in the local *demos*. By working for the values that she has culturally endorsed, which are in opposition to the prevailing social structure, her vocation is literally transformational. She is amongst society's critics, as is the case for meta-reflexives in general. Having embraced a vocation, Bernadette wishes it to be synonymous with her full-time employment in society, precisely in order to 'make a difference' to the social order. In the process, her biography has revealed contextual unsettlement, institutional unease and occupational volatility. Right now, whilst I am finishing her story, she may be consulting the adverts for 'posts vacant'.

Part II

Introduction to Part II: how 'contexts' and 'concerns' shape internal conversations

Being reflexive is part of being human and plays a crucial role for humans as social beings, but it is a quality that varies in kind. Since the kinds of internal conversations we hold about ourselves in relation to society and vice versa are maintained to have far-reaching consequences for both, what accounts for such variations in the practice of reflexivity? The theoretical intuition, derived from my previous exploratory investigation,[1] was that all modes of reflexivity were forged from the interplay between subjects' natal social contexts and their ultimate personal concerns. This introduction examines the formula 'context + concern', in the light of current findings.[2] The aim is to discover whether distinctive combinations of the two are related to the practices of communicative, autonomous and meta-reflexivity respectively.

It was tentatively advanced that the combination fostering the emergence of the communicative mode as dominant was represented by the following three conditions: firstly, by a dense and continuous natal 'context', characterised by geographical stability and resulting in continuity of schooling with the same peers and a continuous social network maintained in the locality; secondly, by stable family relationships, free from marital breakdown, bereavement or repartnering; and thirdly, by the availability of occupational outlets in the vicinity, acceptable to the subject. Next, it was provisionally argued that only if subjects could fulfil their personal 'concerns', particularly those of partnership and work, within the boundaries of the natal context would they endorse and thus reproduce this context through the practices they established as their own *modus vivendi*.

Such 'contextual continuity' in the lives of subjects was hypothesised as weakening the public/private boundary for them by creating a group of 'similars and familiars' with whom they could and would share 'thought and talk'. On the one hand, this group was made up of people

[1] Margaret S. Archer, *Structure, Agency and the Internal Conversation*, Cambridge, Cambridge University Press, 2003. See Conclusion for a summary.
[2] For details about the conduct of the present study please consult the Methodological Appendix.

who were qualified to comment knowledgeably upon the exigencies faced by subjects, by virtue of their own similar experiences in much the same context. On the other hand, they were also those whose relationship with the subject entailed a reciprocal acknowledgement that they knew one another through and through, because of the frequency of their interaction. This combination appeared propitious for nurturing and sustaining the 'thought and talk' pattern of communicative reflexivity. In turn, the re-endorsement of their contextual backgrounds in conjunction with modest projects for employment, to be realised within their confines, meant that the constraints and enablements deriving from the occupational structure would not be activated by these subjects. The latter could effectively be evaded, because no structural costs were entailed and no structural bonuses accrued to achieving their common aim of founding a family and living within their means in a context spelling social immobility.

In the light of the present study, this notion of a *combination* of 'context' and 'concern' turned out to have been correct in its thrust but in need of refinement. In sum, it was too static. 'Contextual continuity' had been treated as given, as a property bestowed upon certain subjects by the nature of their natal context for the rest of their lives. Yet, the quantitative study of the Coventry sample revealed no significant correlations between any of the measurable aspects of background context and the communicative mode of reflexivity: be it the socio-economic class of the natal household, length of parental residence at the subject's place of birth, whether or not the subjects moved home, whether or not the subjects changed school or attended a selective secondary school, and whether or not their parents separated or one died whilst the subject still lived at home. Moreover, there were not even sufficient tendential findings among the above factors to encourage an attempt to develop some combined index of 'contextual continuity'.

Perhaps the main key to reconceptualisation lay in the quantitative finding that although the dominant mode of reflexivity was not correlated with socio-occupational class background, there was a tendency (chi-squared significant at only the 10 per cent level, rather than the more acceptable 5 per cent level) for the different modes to be associated with the subjects' *current* socio-economic positions. What this prompted was a much more active concept of 'contextual continuity' – not as involuntarily given from birth for the rest of their lives, but as something *actively constituted* by communicative reflexives, woven out of a plethora of agential decisions until it constituted the warp and weft of their everyday living. In the last chapter, we have already seen what 'contextual continuity' meant to Joan, as a lived reality, and how hard she worked to sustain it.

Similarly, the notion of people's 'concerns' could not merely be taken nominally, otherwise the 'family' represented the first concern listed by the majority (78 per cent) of the Coventry population.[3] Interesting as this may be in relation to theories about the 'death of the family' and the new imperatives of 'individualisation',[4] simple listings of nominal concerns were blunt instruments when seeking to understand and explain the precise type of *modus vivendi* established by various subjects. Instead, it became crucial to grasp what, as well as how much, practitioners of different modes of reflexivity invested in their own families and above all the nature of their qualitative relationships with their natal families.

In short, the notion of a *simple and fixed combination of 'context' and 'concern'* required reconceptualisation as a *dialectic between 'contexts' and 'concerns'* – one that abandoned any static element of given-ness in favour of accentuating their active interplay over time. Here, it should be stressed that to place more emphasis upon the qualitative and nuanced nature of relationships does not entail the privileging of agency over structure in any way. This is because such relations, both past and present, are themselves structurally situated. The subject thus has to confront the structural context in which they are embedded and its causal properties and potential powers, in order to endorse and reconstitute a social network as her own.

Obviously, every subject will think about contextual endorsement or rejection under his or her own descriptions, because this is the only way in which anyone can think about anything. Thus, the implication is not that subjects are engaging in their own internal conversations about structural constraints and enablements in sociological terms. Nevertheless, their deliberations and subsequent actions add up to a dialectical process involving the following elements:

1 accepting (or rejecting) dialogical partners from their natal contexts,
2 developing their nascent concerns in (partial) interlocution with them,
3 elaborating upon their social networks in the light of their concerns, and

---

[3] This showed no substantive difference for gender, the percentage for males being 77 per cent and for females 79 per cent. For those currently married or in a partnership of at least two years' duration, the proportion putting the 'family' first rose to 83 per cent. Again, gender differences were small, with males at 85 per cent and females at 81 per cent. For those with children, regardless of their marital or partnership status, it rose again to 84 per cent. Once more this finding is not a heavily engendered one, standing at 81 per cent for men and 87 per cent for women. See Margaret S. Archer, 'Family Concerns and Inter-Generational Solidarity', in Mary Ann Glendon (ed.), *Intergenerational Solidarity, Welfare and Human Ecology*, Vatican City, Vatican City Press, 2004, p. 135.

[4] See Ulrich Beck and Elizabeth Beck-Gernsheim, *Individualization*, London, Sage, 2002. Also see Elizabeth Beck-Gernsheim, *Reinventing the Family: In Search of New Life Styles*, Oxford, Polity Press, 2002.

4 both refining and reinforcing these concerns through on-going exchanges with this elaborated contextual network, until

5 a particular *modus vivendi* is established, which is continuous with the subject's original context.

For the communicative reflexive, it is maintained that the end result of the sequence is social immobility. Moreover, this dialectical process also has repercussions for the social structure, because the aggregate effect of the consolidation of communicative reflexivity represents an agential property that reinforces social stability. However, such large claims call for considerable justification. Substantiation will be supplied in the form of qualitative analysis of the responses furnished in the ten interviews examined in the next chapter. Because the full dialectical sequence can only unfurl in biographical time, the data supplied by the subjects are organised in terms of stages in their life and work histories.

At the outset, the constitution of autonomous reflexivity – as with all modes – was seen as arising from a distinctive interplay between subjects' 'contexts' and 'concerns'. However, the initial hypothesis again turned out to be far too static. It postulated that various events that took place whilst growing up in the natal home, ones that could be construed as objective experiences of 'contextual discontinuity', would predispose towards development of the autonomous mode of reflexivity. This rested on the assumption that such events would have two effects: firstly, they would represent disjunctions in the continuity of interchanges between potential interlocutors (family members and early friends) and, secondly, subjects would be thrown back to a greater extent upon their own internal resources. For the Coventry sample as a whole, the events considered likely to introduce 'contextual discontinuity' included whether or not the subjects changed school before the age of sixteen; whether or not subjects attended selective secondary schools; and whether or not the subjects' parents were separated, divorced, repartnered, remarried or widowed whilst the subjects were still living at home. For all of the above factors there were slight tendencies for these types of 'disruption' to coincide with endorsement of the autonomous mode rather than any of the other modes, but none of them achieved statistical significance.

Qualitative exploration with the interviewees forcefully underlined two points. The first was that these subjects' testimonies emphasised the heterogeneous impact of such episodes upon them. It was not the factual occurrence of these events *per se* that affected them, but rather what qualitatively transpired from them. In other words, it was not the event in itself (which is what the survey recorded) but rather what was *made of it*, in terms of family relationships, that exerted causal powers. Thus, although six of the interviewees came from 'broken' backgrounds (compared with one-third for all autonomous respondents), these six people interpreted the importance of this 'same' event in entirely different ways, with two scarcely mentioning it, three dwelling upon the severity of its negative effects for them and one explicitly attaching little significance to it.

Consider Rachel (the young hairdressing manager) whose parents divorced when she was ten, seemingly without severe objective consequences. Yet, the very first thing she mentions, when ruminating on the nature of her internal conversation, is the effect of this split-up upon her: 'It just makes me, like, I don't need anybody, I'm very determined and I can manage. I'm one of those people that if someone doesn't like me, I don't really care – I can cope on my own. I've built that resistance up because of how I've been as a child.' What is crucial about 'how she has been' is that after the divorce, Rachel and her mother became locked into a love/hate relationship of unbridled competition, which still impinges heavily upon her present life. Now compare Rachel with Donna (the young team manager in banking), who reflects on her parents' early divorce and remarriage quite positively: 'It didn't necessarily affect me really. I still saw my dad from time to time and carried on living with my stepdad, who's been my stepdad for twenty years – so he's like my dad, I've always had a solid father figure there.'

If it is indeed the qualitative nature of family relations that are influential in increasing the extent of self-dependence and reducing reliance upon the natal context, then the features promoting disjunction should be widened in relation to the list of stock 'events' examined in the survey. For example, Liz (the primary school head) and Billy (a sixty-year-old unemployed van driver) emphasised how being only children gave them significantly more freedom than their peers enjoyed – a freedom Liz used for lone pursuits and Billy to get out of doors. Nick (the self-employed builder) had parents who believed in allowing him a lot of rope, but he appears to have tugged the leash out of their hands as he pedalled off on his bike to cultivate his passion for the countryside – to the extent of accustoming the family to his 'going missing'.

The second key point is that some of the interviewees themselves either courted or caused 'contextual discontinuity' early on in their lives and in ways that the survey entirely failed to capture. In other words, just as 'contextual continuity' was actively built up by the communicative reflexives, so 'contextual discontinuity' was often something that autonomous subjects *had made happen* or at least had exacerbated. Thus, the fact that Martin had been adopted at the age of eleven, after living in a series of care homes, and developed only a rather distant relationship with his adoptive parents may indeed have encouraged his lone absorption in painting and drawing. However, much more important for prompting a radical disjuncture with his background, for projecting him out of college, into unplanned employment and for repositioning him in a different social context was the fact of his becoming a father at the age of eighteen. Very different, yet with the same effect of augmenting 'contextual discontinuity', was the decision of Oliver (a 49-year-old financial adviser) to leave his family and the troubles in Northern Ireland behind when he was seventeen, to go to south London to work; similarly it was Damian (the retail manager) himself who decided to move out of home when he was sixteen in order to live as a gay man. Neither of the latter reported anything negative about inter-personal relationships within their families, but both clearly felt very negatively about other aspects of their natal contexts. In other words, 'contextual discontinuity' can only be fully understood as something that is actively promoted by subjects themselves – at least in part and even from its beginning.

In turning to the dialectic of 'context and concern', one of the most striking findings from the interview data was the life-long importance that autonomous reflexives had attached to the practical order, to achieving virtuosity in performative skills and deriving enduring enjoyment from them.[5] This is significant because very few questions explicitly touched upon practical knowledge or skills unless these were related to training or employment. Therefore it was all the more surprising how much information these interviewees introduced about the importance of the practical order to them. This emerged at three points: when subjects reflected upon their interests and pastimes whilst still living with their parents, when recalling the first careers they had seriously contemplated, including starting training and employment along those lines, and when mentioning their current hobbies and leisure activities. Since these three points of reference cover the subject's biography, it seems reasonable to consider such practical skills to be life-long concerns for members of this sub-group and as particular to it.

In other words, in and through their practical 'concerns' these interviewees had become conversant with the lone mastery of practical skills, whether or not these were acquired alone. Where performative mastery is concerned, the feeling of making progress, of failing to attain some standard or even of having reached the limits of one's ability are realised autonomously – even if they happen to be socially shared or seconded. Thus we have subjects who, from an early age, developed interests as divergent as fine art and hunting, which led them to become schooled in making independent judgements and operating according to practical

[5] See Margaret S. Archer, *Being Human: the Problem of Agency*, Cambridge, Cambridge University Press, 2000, ch. 5.

standards of proficiency. If these 'concerns' were lasting and if such subjects were also situated in a natal 'context' the quality of which was hostile to their becoming embedded in it, then we have the two elements that institute the dialectical process through which autonomous reflexivity emerges.

The interplay between 'contexts' and 'concerns' involves:

1 disengagement from the natal context under a variety of promptings, all of which served to loosen contextual embedding and to accentuate personal freedom,

2 the development of nascent practical concerns, capable of being exercised independently,

3 the attempt to express and realise these concerns in an appropriate social and work context,

4 reinforcement, revision or redefinition of such concerns according to their (new) contextual reception, until

5 a *modus vivendi* is established within a different social context and some accommodation reached with its properties and powers.

For the autonomous reflexive who does succeed in establishing such a *modus vivendi*, and not all do, the result will also tend to constitute upward social mobility. However, as will be seen in chapter 5, this is not a necessary outcome for all individuals, nor is it a linear progression for most – as the examples will show, reverses and reconsiderations go hand in hand.

Crucially, when and where upward social mobility is registered, it can only be explained in full by reference to the doings of active agents. In part, this is underscored by the absence of any statistically significant association between the socio-occupational status of the parents of autonomous reflexives and that of subjects themselves in the Coventry survey. Seemingly, we are not dealing with the inter-generational transmission of social advantages. Even though there is a significant association between the highest educational qualification achieved and the mode of reflexivity practised, this finding should not be assimilated to the effects of social background.[6] The reason for not doing so emerged from the biographies of many of the interviewees; namely that their 'highest' qualifications had been acquired not immediately after leaving school, but later on and cumulatively over the life course. These qualifications were the products of subjects' mature deliberations and exertions rather than the

---

[6] Those subjects holding university degrees or equivalent professional qualifications tended to endorse the autonomous or meta-modes of reflexivity, compared with those with lower qualifications for whom the communicative or fractured modes predominated, $p = 0.015$, chi-squared significant at the 5 per cent level. However, this chi-squared test failed to meet the validity criterion, because in this cross-tabulation, 25 per cent of the expected frequencies (i.e. four cells) had a count of less than the requisite 5.

transfer and exchange of parental cultural capital for educational capital prior to leaving home. In other words, the educational advancement of these subjects has to be attributed largely to their own efforts – only one having gained a degree by proceeding directly from school to university.

In part, their social mobility can only be explained by their own doings because the association[7] (significant at only the 10 per cent level) between mode of reflexivity endorsed and current socio-occupational status relates to subjects themselves and not to their backgrounds. The weakness of the association is to be expected because autonomous reflexivity is a generative mechanism at work in an open system. As such it is at the mercy of two kinds of contingencies counteracting or limiting it, as can be documented retrospectively for particular subjects.

Firstly, although all interviewees had indeed striven to 'get on' strategically, this is in their own terms and is limited by their personal powers. To have a strategy of which the goal can be construed as 'upward social mobility' does not make these subjects master strategists. Some overestimate their personal powers and others engage in illegal manoeuvres in their haste to realise their projects – with both paying an objective price for these miscalculations. Moreover, although what constitutes 'upward social mobility' is objectively defined, how far subjects wish to go is subjectively delimited. It will be shown that some interviewees had very clear notions about where they wanted to stop. The general desire for occupational promotion does not mean that everyone wants to get to the very top of their particular greasy pole.

Secondly, despite subjects usually attempting to act strategically, their employment projects are influenced by the structural constraints and enablements encountered. For example, we will meet one interviewee who again and again improved upon the occupational position he had assumed, only to be made redundant four times over. In this respect, there lies the greatest difference between the autonomous and the communicative subjects. Because the former do aspire to socio-occupational promotion, under their own definitions, such projects activate structural constraints and enablements. There is nothing whatsoever to guarantee that their personal powers as 'strategists' are able to minimise the constraints and maximise the enablements. Conversely, because the communicative reflexives

---

[7] For those who had achieved managerial or professional status in the Coventry sample, 39.3 per cent were autonomous reflexives, and meta-reflexives accounted for exactly the same percentage. The communicative and fractured reflexives made up 14.3 per cent and 7.1 per cent respectively of this socio-economic category. Conversely, for those with routine and manual occupations, 32.3 per cent were communicative reflexives and another 32.3 per cent of them were fractured reflexives. The autonomous reflexives accounted for 25.8 per cent of this sub-group and the meta-reflexives for 9.7 per cent.

entertain life projects whose implications are social immobility or even downward mobility, they encounter little social resistance.

At the start of the study, it was thought that meta-reflexives shared the same 'contextual discontinuity' with their natal contexts as the autonomous reflexives and that this accounted for the development of 'lone inner dialogue' by both sub-groups. What explained the subsequent divergence between practitioners of the two modalities remained obscure, beyond the fact that, at some (indeterminate) point, the concerns of meta-reflexives crystallised into a commitment to a 'vocation' – in the Weberian sense, embracing secular as well as religious forms of self-dedication. The quantitative data analysis yielded no results that helped to differentiate significantly between these two groups. Tendentially, the autonomous and meta-reflexives appeared to be rather more similar to one another than they were to communicative or fractured reflexives: in terms of social class background, current occupational status, objective indices of 'contextual discontinuity' (such as marital breakdown or loss of a parent whilst the subject was living at home) and, finally, in having a university degree or an equivalent professional qualification.

Thus, the trends did not serve to spark off any speculative hypotheses about what differentiated these two groups from one another. If anything, they did the opposite and fostered the initial presumption that they were variants upon some common theme(s). This was consonant with the finding (again, only a tendency) that the proportion of meta-reflexives increased as one moved up through the age cohorts. In other words, it could be that meta-reflexives sprang from autonomous stock, only diverging later on in life after some, as yet unidentified, experience. However, since none of these findings was statistically significant, save the relationship with education which was common to the autonomous and the meta-reflexives, it is not justifiable to regard them as giving any ballast whatsoever to the very tentative initial hypotheses.[8]

Therefore, as with the autonomous reflexives, it is the qualitative interviews that carry all the weight in advancing our understanding of the constitution of a meta-reflexive. The substantially longer duration of discussions with these subjects, because of their ruminative nature, enabled a novel picture to come slowly into focus. What lies at the heart of this

---

[8] Moreover, deficiencies in data collection and coding left us mute about two crucial matters in relation to the social mobility of these two sub-groups: firstly, registration of the 'highest educational qualification obtained' revealed nothing about the variety and spread of alternative qualifications, at the same level, possessed by any given subject (for example, someone possessing diplomas in both teaching and social work); secondly, it was impossible to differentiate between the *stability* of occupational status over subjects' careers and the *amounts* of lateral mobility that had taken place.

picture is a distinctive relationship of 'context + concern', which then leads to a different dialectical relationship engaging between them. In fact, it was only grasping something of this dialectic that served to clarify *what* was crucial about the subjects' relations to their natal contexts.

In getting to know these subjects, the temptation to regard the twelve meta-reflexives as some kind of variant upon or mutation of their autonomous counterparts (to whom 'something happened later') was intensified by the discovery that five of the present group had experienced breakdown in the family whilst living at home: one case of adoption and subsequent divorce of the adoptive parents, two divorces (one shrugged off, the other deemed traumatising), the death of a father when the subject was nine, and the startling case of a respondent with a single mother who had five children by five different men and a father with five offspring from three different mothers. The pull to begin exploring these events as qualitative starting points for 'contextual discontinuity' was irresistible – except for the fact that the subjects themselves resisted it. They did not seek to minimise the pain and misery of their family circumstances (with one exception), but they did refuse to embellish upon a scenario in which they had been 'thrown back upon their own resources' and developed into 'self-reliant' people. Instead, they portrayed their responses as 'withdrawal', 'distancing' themselves, 'daydreaming', 'depression' and 'blotting it out', which were puzzling because these are much closer to the reactions of the fractured reflexives. Yet, these were indubitably very 'active agents' (with low 'F' scores).

The puzzle deepened when turning to the seven interviewees with stable parental backgrounds. In no sense were these upbringings 'permissive' and again the subjects in question balked at the 'autonomous scenario' in which they grabbed at any freedom proffered, stretched it to its limits and soon severed the leading strings. On the contrary, one respondent had lived continuously (and happily) with her parents and still did so, another was travelling long distances to support her recently bereaved mother, the youngest saw himself making a home for his parents when he soon married and the oldest was a grand Irish matriarch of the old school. On the whole, meta-reflexives maintained close, warm, though not usually continuous relationships with members of their natal families. My puzzlement grew because most of these subjects, the concordance of whose family backgrounds I had no reason to doubt, also voiced similar themes to those coming from 'broken homes': as children, they 'lived in a world of their own', were 'withdrawn' or 'daydreamers', got 'lost in books', and one had harboured the idea of being a changeling. Perhaps, after all, the explanation lay one stratum further down and the quest should be left to the personality psychologists – whose potential contribution is not discounted.

However, starting from 'the other side' by exploring subjects' 'ultimate concerns' provided an interpretative key that no amount of tweaking with their narratives of family life could have revealed. The latter approach would necessarily have failed because the crucial aspect of 'context' was not a factor proper to it, but rather the relationship in which it stood vis-à-vis subjects' nascent 'concerns'. At its simplest, these interviewees had a 'dream'. For many, it was clearly etched, for others, it was still coming into focus; for some, it had arrived early (the age of two being the record), for a number, it had crystallised before the end of their teens, and for the rest, it steadily grew upon them until they fully embraced it. For some, the first vision had been displaced and replaced, but for all, it represented their ultimate concern.

What is 'ultimate' about an 'ultimate concern' is that it is architechtonic: it forms the organising principle around which all else should be integrated. This is why there is a tense relationship between 'concern' and 'context' – one that will be found to be life long and always problematic for the meta-reflexive. And this is why, within the tension between 'concern' and 'context' that dogs their life courses, the most crucial strain is often that between the first nascent concern and the natal context.

What this means for the constitution of meta-reflexivity is that we are not talking about 'contextual discontinuity', either objectively or under subjects' own descriptions. Instead, what is central to their formation is 'contextual incongruity' – in relation to their dreams. At some point, all twelve subjects encountered an incongruity between what they would become – their aspirant vocation or the preconditions for it – and their social context, which impeded its realisation. In fact, they underwent twelve different experiences of this incongruity, given the differences in their dreams. Some pertained to the family itself (its relationships and resources), others to wider aspects of the natal context (such as the school curriculum), whilst a few made their encounter somewhat later, once launched upon an occupational course *by* their families. The key clash is between the cultural values of the subject and the social context he or she inhabits. In a variety of ways, examined in chapter 6, these subjects encounter values to which they become committed and yet something in their natal context is resistant to such commitments finding a complementary (occupational) outlet.

The effect of the ideals to which these subjects are attracted is the antithesis of the normative conventionality into which the communicative reflexives are drawn. As they lend themselves to the communicative mode through adopting an interlocutor(s), they are unknowingly enmeshing themselves in the web of local norms and values. Conversely, the more a proto-practitioner of meta-reflexivity comes to 'value a value', the more she seeks to know (read, hear and learn) about it and the more knowledgeable she becomes – with an unintended consequence. Such subjects increasingly render themselves incapable of sharing this 'concern' within the natal context. Effectively, they are unknowingly working at disqualifying themselves from the possibility of communicative reflexivity. Some, at least, recognise the futility or embarrassment of attempting to share what now preoccupies them more and more and thus retreat into their inner worlds. Others do attempt to share for a time, but are driven inwards by the incomprehension they meet or the impossibility of communicating freely and fully. Fondness of family may not diminish, but familial relations are decreasingly relationships between 'similars and familiars'.

The gradual crystallisation of a value-commitment is also what later forges the link with a distinctive pattern of socio-occupational volatility. These subjects, busy defining or nurturing a vocation in their youth, are inwardly straining towards self-dedication. Their first encounter with 'contextual incongruity' does not lead them to back down – unless other serious issues are at stake – but rather to battle on. Unlike the communicative reflexive, they do not revise their aims, settling for second or third best in order to propitiate significant others, because that would be a contradiction in terms where a vocation is concerned. Unlike the autonomous reflexives, they do not think strategically about circumvention, about adroitly locating ladders or about circuitous routes to their destinations. Values are not the kinds of ends that can be attained by 'wheeling and dealing', a vocation is not realised by a 'smooth operator' and dedication is the antinomy of 'sharp practice'. Instead, meta-reflexives meet matters head on. They may deeply regret any pain caused to others, but they are fully willing to pay the price themselves even though most do not yet know the full costs involved. In short, 'contextual incongruity' cannot be met by compromise or circumvention, it can only be confronted.

Necessarily, such a confrontation entails a search for a different social context in which the nascent vocation can be lived out. Because the vast majority of people need to earn a living, such a vocation also has to be (or to entail) an occupational role in the social order. Thus, the tyro meta-reflexive distances herself from her old or natal context in the hope of finding a role in which she can live out her values. However, when she accepts a post nothing guarantees that she finds the novel context or the unfamiliar position living up to her expectations. Precisely because what she cherishes is a cultural ideal, whereas occupational roles are always embedded and enmeshed in the social structure (economic, political, bureaucratic), satisfaction is usually far from perfect. Yet being a perfectionist, the response of the meta-reflexive is institutional critique rather than personal compromise. These subjects might spend a decade or more in growing disenchantment before finally avowing the radical imperfection of their current working context and beginning the quest for a lateral shift of context.

This may be the first of many such shifts, which is what is meant by volatility, a term which captures some subjects rather better than others because the sheer number of occupational moves made is variable. What is distinctive about meta-reflexives is that these moves are characteristically voluntary,[9] they display indifference to material loss or gain but entail a cost to the subject herself: retraining, relocation and refamiliarisation – the insecurities of starting all over again. The cycle is repetitive because the structural contexts of work and employment consistently fall short of their value requirements. In brief, 'contextual incongruity' is a recurrent situation in which meta-reflexives find themselves. Since they are ready to pay the price of moving on (laterally), they subvert both the penalties extracted by constraints and the rewards dangled by enablements. In their dedication to values and definition of work as a vocation to express and realise their commitments, meta-reflexives take on the stance of society's critics because of their on-going contextual critiques, which provoke them to move on – often again and again. For them, 'contextual incongruity' tends to be a life-long condition and its long-term effect is a trajectory of social volatility.

---

[9] Meta-reflexives are no more proofed against involuntary redundancy than any other subjects and, like them, this eventuality affects the least qualified most.

4 Communicative reflexives: working at staying put

Dramatis personae

Pseudonym	Age	Current/last occupation
Alf (m)	69	Retired (miner)
Jeanette (f)	36	Unemployed (horticultural worker)
Joan (f)	64	Retired (childminder)
Jon (m)	30	Unemployed (car design engineer)
Luke (m)	18	Unemployed (forklift truck driver)
Olga (f)	63	Retired (secondary school teacher)
Pauline (f)	44	Night care assistant
Robbie (m)	23	Team manager, e-banking
Sheila (f)	57	Retired (caretaker)
Terry (m)	28	Senior scientist

This chapter is devoted to the justification of a single proposition, namely that the practice of communicative reflexivity has the consequence of fostering social immobility amongst its practitioners. The crucial point is that such socio-economic immobility is not seen as resulting from passive agents – people to whom things happen rather than people who make things happen. Nor is it a default option that becomes operative when people fail to do things. Certainly, it would be wrong to regard 'social immobility' as an end which is directly or explicitly sought of and for itself by any of the subjects examined. Nevertheless, it is held to be an objective tendency manifested by those whose subjective reflexivity assumes the communicative mode as their dominant one. Moreover, the production of social immobility as an outcome entails just as much effort and deliberation as does any other pattern of mobility. In short, 'staying put' has to be worked at by an active agent. The remainder of this chapter is devoted to illustrating what kinds of work this involved on the part of our subjects and to showing how this work was entailed by becoming and remaining a practitioner of communicative reflexivity – which is where we begin.

The communicative reflexive must have at least one other particular Thou whom they trust implicitly in order to exercise the 'thought and talk' pattern. That is definitional of communicative reflexivity. Yet it raises legion questions which only its practitioners can answer – are they aware of this need to trust before they place the life of their minds in the custody of another/others? What gives them the confidence that any particular Thou will prove trustworthy? How, where and when do they encounter and adopt these trusted interlocutors? Are these matters of personal idio-syncrasy or manifestations of social tendencies? Finally, do our subjects have enough self-understanding about the workings of their dominant mode of reflexivity to be able to answer such questions – obviously under their own descriptions? The very hope that they are capable of so doing also implies that everyone has a dash of meta-reflexivity, but that has already been established to be the case in chapter 2.

To feel trust is a more wary business than many other feelings, because it requires some kind of warrant; a few may say that they fell in love at first sight, but on first sight most will hedge their bets and say that at best someone seems trustworthy. Our subjects' commentaries highlight the problematic nature of being able to say 'In thee I trust', but they all reveal varying degrees of awareness that trusting relationships are indispensable to them. Otherwise, matters can go seriously wrong, well before the state that has been termed fractured reflexivity occurs. Exploring this funda-mental issue with interviewees provides the opportunity to introduce more of the cast of communicative reflexives.

In thee I trust

Earlier, it was argued that 'similarity and familiarity' were the usual war-ranties for trustworthiness and that this made family and early friends the likeliest candidates as interlocutors for the developing communica-tive reflexive.[1] But if interlocutors are to be adopted from someone's early background there are two provisos. Qualitatively, these family and friendship relations have to satisfy the subject and, equally, the subject has to remain in continuous contact with their natal context and surrounding network. Three cases were found in pure and uncompli-cated form.

Alf, the retired miner, came from the Durham coalfields, made friends with boys from the same village at an early age, this group attending the

---

[1] In this book I am not systematically examining what predisposes someone to become a communicative, or any other type of reflexive. That question will be taken up in *The Reflexive Imperative*, which is or can be read as a companion volume to the present work.

same schools and eventually going down the pit together.[2] When he was twenty-five and that pit closed, he went south with eleven workmates in search of open-cast work. Connections with Durham were sustained: Alf travelled up every fortnight whilst his mother was still alive, two of his sons now live there, some of his mates moved back, and he had just returned from another visit immediately prior to the interview. Alf is blunt about the importance of this network to him: 'Well, if you haven't got friends, what sort of bloody life have you got? Family's all well and good, but you don't want to depend on family all the time. When you've got friends you go out for a change to different places. If they're friends, you'll always remain friends and if they're not, you'll always find the buggers out.' Here, he is referring obliquely to one of the eleven who went back to Durham, taking Alf's first wife with him (and with whom, significantly, Alf still drinks), but more generally he is talking about warranted trust. This he believes is tested and reinforced in the mine: 'When you went down the pit you didn't know whether you were going to come back up or not. Not when I first started anyway – it's improved a lot now. Pitmen are tight-knit. You always depended on somebody else and although we all took the mick out of each other, you still knew in the back of your mind that one day I'll need you or they might need me.' Alf is now sixty-nine, lives a couple of hundred miles away from his natal context, has remarried and added new friends, but he has sustained contextual continuity. Those original mates are still his dialogical partners and, as far as trust is concerned, he has not yet found all 'the buggers out' – as wanting in trustworthiness.

Jon, the young car designer, presents a similarly uncomplicated picture, which illuminates his earlier comment about the partners in his 'thought and talk': 'I'll come up in my own head with what I think I want and then I will speak to parents or sister or friends and see what they think as well . . '. I think that's probably because I trust the other people I would ask, I trust their opinion . . . I'd say I probably consult the same people about most things.' He describes a united and extended family, happy in their activities together (at thirty, Jon and his dad still attend car and air shows together) and intertwined with his friendship network. 'I'm still friends with people I grew up with as a child. My best friend is still the same person I had for as long as I can remember. He lives three doors down from me and is still my best friend – we still go on holiday together and things . . . [My parents] were friends with the parents of the children we were friends with. I suppose that's how we got introduced really,

---

[2]   Alf remarks, 'I'd say there were seven lads who went to school with me and lived in the same area, and only two out of the seven went to other jobs, the rest went to the pit.'

because my parents were friends with their parents and we were sort of brought together through them.'

Thus we have a dense and continuous Coventry background of congenial 'familiars', but this time from the intermediate class. Jon believes that his own current illness (he suffers from severe blood clots) and the cancer from which each of his parents now seems recovered, bonded them more closely together. Experientially, they became 'similars' as well – sharing the life-threatening as well as the life-enhancing. Thus, Jon can say of these interlocutors, 'I respect my parents' opinions on matters because when all is said and done, they're older than me and have more experience of life, so I do value their opinion.' That could be voiced only by someone who valorises these parental experiences, seeing them as relevant to his own because he views his own experience as continuous with theirs. Here Jon gives them the final accolade for trustworthiness; he will follow their advice (he instances house buying) even though it goes against his own inclinations: 'Even when sometimes they haven't given you the answer you really wanted to hear, I trust them enough to know that what they're saying is true.' But that could only be done by someone who believed such truth-telling was in his own best interests and other subjects have not been convinced that this vital ingredient of trustworthiness was to be found in their immediate families.

Robbie, however, a 23-year-old sales and service adviser from a working-class background, has no such doubts, but neither does he share Jon's poignant reasons for close family bonding. His own background exemplifies the density and reproduction of 'contextual continuity' which was initially expected to be found amongst communicative reflexives in general. Robbie stands as an important reminder that reproduction requires both agential activity and self-conscious reflexivity. He too has managed to become a house owner, but has literally re-embedded himself in his natal context after a couple of trial flights at social mobility. Nevertheless, the theme of trust is closely interwoven into his descriptive account of where and how he now lives. 'I come from Cobford [a suburb of Coventry], and basically, where I live, next door to me is my auntie, who I'm really close to as she has no kids, so I'm spoilt rotten. Then, about two minutes' walk away is my mum's, and just round the corner from her is my nan – and the other side of Cobford is my grandma. I've always had my close family near me all the time . . . I've got like a really close relationship with my mum and dad and my grandma, my nan and my auntie. I tend to see at least one of them every day – at least one member of my family a day. It's just something I've always had, so it's very important to me . . . When you're in real trouble, you find out who your friends are, but your family will always be there and will always help. They won't say they don't want to know.' Robbie has also retained friends from school and added on friends from work, but, as he puts it, 'I don't try to get everyone to be my best friend – I know who I've got and who I can trust.'

However, some subjects are much more like Joan in finding that the quality of their parental relationships is inimical to the trust required of a dialogical partner. In such cases, and depending upon domestic circumstances, the tendency is to turn to friends in the immediate context, or, as Joan did, to find her husband and her reflexive partner in the same person. Sheila (fifty-seven and now retired) supplies a narrative which, in all salient points, is a virtual carbon-copy of Joan's – minus the parental idealisation. She is very open about the dysfunctional over-protectiveness of her mother (for which Sheila underwent counselling many years later) and about the wasted five years of occupational vicissitudes before she could realise her project of becoming a nursery nurse. Nevertheless, Sheila immediately encountered her life-long dialogical partner, Judy, during training and she stresses the importance of their similarity, familiarity and the stability of their relationship in underwriting the trust that exists between them: 'We've known each other for so long [that] I think we know everything about each other. And [in] all the ups and downs we've always been there for one another and met up . . . our children are the same age as well, so we met up with the children – we know everything about all the children. Now she's [Judy's] retired, so we do classes together, like parchment and quilting and other things. We see each other three times a week and we're very alike. All the things Judy likes, I like, and that's made a difference to the friendship because we like the same things. So that's a close friendship. A lot of people don't get that friendship from a young age, if they move away – it's stability, isn't it?'

Yet, Jeanette (now thirty-six and recently made redundant) had felt that she must move away from the indifference of her middle-class family. At first she made a fairly dramatic attempt to retain the stability of her early friendships, by getting herself expelled from boarding school in order to rejoin them at the local comprehensive and then to proceed routinely alongside them to college. But their concerns were not her concerns; indeed their enrolment on child-care courses attenuated this network because Jeanette has no desire for children, finding them 'scary', and frankly preferring her cats. Equally, her rather passive acceptance of the catering course in the same college neither helped to sustain her original friendship network nor engaged her interest sufficiently for her to form a new one or to care enough to envisage a career related to her training. Instead, her twenties were largely passed in a drifting quest for a boyfriend who would also be an interlocutor. This involved London squats, itinerant bar-work and becoming a Glastonbury hippy – where at last she met her husband, possibly one of the few people actually working on site. Unlike the previous interviews, nearly all of which took place in well-maintained (ex-)council houses, I met Jeanette in a caravan behind the horticultural centre from which she and her husband (another extremely high communicative reflexive)[3] had just been made redundant. The tent-like awning was a New Age den; the caravan was an immaculate space dominated by large cats of commensurate character. Very open and attractive, though not dressed to make any particular statement, Jeanette pounced on the first question about sharing 'thought and talk' in order to insist on the centrality of trust to the process. She shares 'more or less straight away, it depends who I'm with at the time. Some people I don't open up to at all, but certain people I trust with my life – they're the ones that I'll target and say, "What do you think of this?" ' Above all, this now means her husband, but also her father, a solicitor, to whom she has grown close after his divorce, and her brother, when he is not in thrall to their mother from whom Jeanette remains alienated.

Conversely, for some, the natal context can prove problematic as far as a source of trustworthy interlocutors is concerned. The last two introductions are to subjects who are struggling with different aspects of this problem. The youngest respondent, Luke (an eighteen-year-old forklift truck driver), still lives at home and has the same dense and continuous relationship with the 'mates' amongst whom he grew up. From what he first says, I expect him to continue in the same vein as Alf, Jon and Robbie, with suitable adjustments for age. This is because what he underlined is that in sharing his thoughts with early friends, he feels no need for caution or self-monitoring because their commonalities guarantee that he will be understood. 'With my mates, I don't have to worry about what I say because they love me, man! [laughter] They're friends; they don't pick you up on every little thing. You have fall outs, but by the end of the day we're friends again because we grew up together – we're all best friends so I don't have to worry about things that happen with my friends. But it's people; like you met someone and you class them as a friend, but not as your best friends – then I probably would think what I'm going to say to them.' What he means is that 'contextual continuity' – in the simple form of growing up together – does not automatically underwrite trust.

---

[3] Two assistants were employed to make the preliminary contacts and were instructed not to administer ICONI to both husbands and their wives or partners in order to avoid discussion between them, especially if selected later for interview. However, in this particular case Jeanette was contacted by Assistant A and her husband by Assistant B. It was the only occasion upon which this happened and the husband was deliberately not selected for interview.

At eighteen and having taken a few hard knocks, Luke's problem is that *he* does not consider some of his original friends still to be desirable, and yet, as can be seen from the following reflection, he remains in touch with them. 'One of my friends . . . he started taking drugs . . . and is going to jail now. I told him last night, because we went out for a drink, I was like [saying], "You need to grow up", and he was like, "I know that now." And I said, "You're only saying you know that now because you're going to jail and you're shitting yourself." He's like all gutted because he's going to jail and he's sorry for doing that, but he wouldn't have been if he didn't get caught for it . . . I don't want to be like that. I just don't want to be a deadbeat; everyone else is, but I don't want to be like that. I don't want to be a smackhead and I don't want to be smoking crack or charlie or things like that – things like the rest of the losers without a job. They just mess their life up, and I look at them and I don't want to be like that – in and out of jail for the rest of your life – it's not worth it, because you're not living.'

On the other hand, Luke has another group of friends from school with whom he went on to college at sixteen and still plays football. Since Luke managed to get himself disbarred from college, early on in his computing course, he now feels that such friends are simply leaving him behind. In between these two friendship groups stands his father, an undoubted interlocutor but one who is trying to steer Luke between both sets of friends by insisting that he finds and sticks to a job. His father clearly matters to Luke, but not to the point of being willing to follow in father's footsteps and take a routine job with no prospects. 'I love my dad, my dad's wicked. He's always been a good dad – he's always looked after me and that. He just tends to moan about things . . . He's a moaner and I can't be arsed with it. He says to me, "I'm glad you've turned out the way you are. You look around and they're all druggies and they don't want to work. And there's someone like you who doesn't take drugs and you want to work, but you can't get a job."' Not surprisingly, pulled in these three different directions by his different interlocutors, Luke currently concludes, 'I'm stuck.' He has learned who not to trust but has not yet found anyone with whom he can trustingly complete this thoughts and thus formulate a project.

Terry (twenty-eight years old and a senior research chemist) is also of working-class origins and shares the same generic problem about trust as Luke, but for entirely different reasons. Terry could not formulate a satisfying project within his natal context and thus lent himself to staying on at school and at university until he emerged with both a PhD and a ready-made post as a research chemist. Close as he remains to his parents, he repeatedly returns to their inability to provide dialogical guidance at key points in his past decision-making. Terry dwelt particularly upon his need for this, once his school took it for granted that he would go on to university. 'I kind of said that I wanted to go and that I wanted to do chemistry, and my mum and my dad didn't really have any advice they could give me. I think at the time I was a very naïve child who didn't know what he was doing and probably made bad decisions, well, not that bad but not as informed as they could have been.'

As an undergraduate he made friends through sports, all of them male, but found major problems surrounding his relationships with girlfriends, especially as time went by with those who were successful professionals and probably not communicative reflexives.[4] Terry still felt the need to find an interlocutor for the full gamut of his 'thought and talk', but reckons that he got into difficulties because of the honesty of his disclosures – trusting them to trust him and to reciprocate, which may have meant 'revealing too much of myself, being too open. They see it as an invasion of their privacy almost. I'm not too sure how to put it into words. I think I take it too far and say too much and perhaps they're not ready to or not feeling that way.' In addition, a recent sporting injury, which is not responding to treatment, has 'meant I haven't been able to do any of my usual social activities, so my social group of friends has dwindled massively, so that has been a real problem'. It is such a problem for someone who deliberates through 'thought and talk' to find a suitable interlocutor, that Terry has been explicitly casting around for new activities in order to meet new people.

Trust has to be earned, which is why it seems to emerge naturally from amongst 'familiars', when these are people amongst whom a subject has grown up – the foundations having been laid unobtrusively over the years, like capital accumulating in the bank. The more that has been shared, the easier it is to share more, provided there is mutual recognition of similarities by those involved. Encountering a like-minded friend, early on in one's training, or finding a spouse who is also a dialogical partner, means that these footings can be dug and common experiences then accumulate on that basis. What seems most difficult of all is literally to go out in search of an interlocutor (under a subject's own description) because familiarity and similarity cannot be prefabricated, yet the intimate and implicit trust required by the communicative reflexive means an attempt to build upon sand without them.

Cutting projects down to size

One of the early consequences of the 'thought and talk' pattern for its users is that by precipitously sharing their projects with others, such proposed

---

[4] As has been noted, communicative reflexivity is negatively correlated with years spent in education.

courses of action are reduced to more modest proportions – in conformity with the conventions of the local context. This effect is produced through curtailing internal conversation proper, restricting it to 'gut reactions', eliminating long-term planning in favour of waiting upon contingency, and ultimately leading agents themselves actively to reduce their ambitions.

These steps, which result in the communicative reflexives accepting very early on to aspire lower than they originally intended, can be illustrated by vignettes from our interviewees. We have already seen that young Luke feels 'stuck', caught between his expulsion from college and a range of 'dead-end' jobs. He also vituperates against Coventry and voices his desire to get away from it. Luke continues in this vein, and although his racism will not endear him to the reader, it is necessary to understand his scapegoating in order to comprehend his desire to emigrate. 'Everyone in Coventry's dossers, aren't they? I hate it. Everywhere you look you've just got a dosser and a tramp and a smackhead and a deadbeat – who don't want to do anything with their life, and I hate living around here. I'd rather get away from England, get away from all these frigging immigrants, there's too many of them. I'd probably like to go to somewhere like Canada, where there weren't as many and they speak English – kind of, but some of them are French though, aren't they? All the immigrants are coming over here now, aren't they – got all the Kosovans, all the Iraqis, all the Pakis, all the Indians. Soon this country's going to be overcrowded and I do not want to be there by then. There's going to be no jobs here, there's barely any as it is.'

I question Luke as to what he has done about this scheme of emigrating to Canada and gain three revealing admissions from him. Firstly, he has discussed the plan with a 'mate' and, in the light of this mate's reaction, he did not explore Canadian immigration requirements any further. 'I was thinking about writing away [about Canada], but my mate said that if you want to move abroad, you've got to have a trade, you've got to have a good job to go to. And that's one of the reasons I sent away [applying for] apprenticeships and that, because I don't want to stay here. But, because I haven't got a trade, I've just been thinking, "Well, it's not worth it."' Thus, whether or not he accurately reports what his mate said, this 'guidance' was sufficient to deter Luke from further exploration and effectively led him to abandon the scheme. Secondly, although his mention of pursuing apprenticeships may look like longer-term planning, this too has no follow-through. When he fails to receive replies to his applications, I query how hard he has tried to get a response, but he quickly negatives the idea that he might visit companies to press his case. 'No,' Luke says, 'because they're all like in Leamington and Dudley – too far. And it would just be the same thing anyway – here's some forms, fill them in and send them back and we won't get back in touch with you. There's no point doing it now, I don't think.' Luke's attitudes are not endearing, but neither is his situation enviable, so I press him further on attempting to realise his Canadian project. His final reply indicates that what is holding him back is his attachment to the very context he vilifies: 'I've got to get away from here, that's it. But I wouldn't want to leave my friends and family, that's the downer of it.' Thus, Canada is a castle in the air – a safety valve for airing his grievances. Instead, as Luke puts it, he is 'waiting for a break'.

Like Luke, all of the interviewees confine their planning to the immediate future because they have an identical respect for how contingency rules their lives. This, it was suggested, could be attributed to the dominance of interlocutors as the prime source of information – meaning that their experiential limitations could not encompass much that was indeed regular but appeared to them as random. All concentrate upon planning for the day ahead or at most the week to come. Alf 'lives for today, not tomorrow – taking things as they come'; Sheila says, 'I go with what the day brings'; Pauline just waits 'for the day and see what I'm going to do that day'; and Jeanette admits: 'to be honest, I never really look far ahead, I never do, I think that's part of my problem'. Even those who admit that they confront major problems do not believe that they could design a course of action to circumvent them. Thus, Jon, with his serious illness, mortgage to pay and recent redundancy, simply hopes that 'something will turn up'. Terry, who is adamant that he no longer wishes to be a research chemist, nevertheless has stock options in the company, which may or may not rise in value, but, although he could now cash them in advantageously, his response is that, 'Yeah, I'd like to see my future a bit clearer, but I don't have any control over that at the moment – that's the way I see it.' Robbie alone has turned this into a philosophy of life based on chaos theory: why not take this job or that job, which may not turn out as hoped, but then again he may meet his future wife there! Despite his philosophising, Robbie, like the others, will 'wait for a chance to come up'.

Where the future is concerned, Olga (a 63-year-old migrant to Britain through marriage) oscillates between intercessory prayer and superstition (if a fox comes tonight, then her son will get a job). However, as a teacher of English in an Eastern European school for many years, she confesses her inability to plan lessons even when under inspection: 'they asked us to write plans for every lesson – it was the worst thing for me just to write it so that somebody could look at your papers. I always came to the classroom without any plan of what I will do today . . . I would suddenly have an idea in my head and just try to apply it on the spot – sometimes it failed.' This is interesting because Olga also confides that her school had a circle of teachers of English 'and naturally we used to share our worries – after each lesson you had something interesting to say. We would laugh a lot in the teachers' room, or ask for help. And you could share with colleagues if your lesson was good and it helped a lot. If you had a success you would like to share.' What this may indicate is that Olga did not see her inability to do the requisite planning as a 'worry' or, alternatively, this was seen as a laughing matter to her interlocutors. Thus, neither did Olga resort to internal conversation to ask herself how to crack lesson planning (though retrospectively she knew some sessions could have been better) nor did her dialogical partners offer practical help rather than collegial support. Since this problem was well within their own repertoire, perhaps we should conclude in advance of further data, that for the communicative reflexives, inter-personal support is much more important than a quest for information amongst those with whom they share 'thought and talk.'

Working at social immobility

Finally, through externalising their deliberations, the first occupational project adopted by communicative reflexives represents an active contribution to their own social immobility. There are three different scenarios through which this same result is produced, as will be illustrated from the life histories of different interviewees. The first script is written by subjects who actively refused proffered employment, which would have represented upward mobility, in favour of a humbler job recommended by their interlocutor(s). Alf, the son of a miner and the nephew of a miner, made a straightforward choice of social immobility the weekend after he left school. Whilst he was growing up with his mother, aunt and uncle, his father having died young, Alf dreamed of becoming a jockey. However, his height soon meant that his racing life would be restricted to studying form and regular gambling. His mother and his aunt separately determined that he should not go down the pit and obtained shop work for him. In the following excerpt Alf tells us how he declined to follow in D. H. Lawrence's footsteps.

'So my aunt got me a job in the butcher's shop, and my mother, unbeknownst to her, got me a job in the chemist's shop and I was supposed to start on the Monday. But the day before, a group of lads I went to school with decided they were going over to the pit, about five miles away. And I went with them, just for the ride – and I signed up as well. On the Monday, we had to go back to the pit, but we only had to go in normal clothes because they were only showing you round. So, my aunt thought I was going to the butcher's shop, my mother thought I was going to the chemist's shop – and I came back black because I'd started at the pit. There was hell on.' But regardless of the furore, Alf rode out the domestic storm, continued working there until that particular pit closed, went south with his mates – some of the same lads with whom he had signed on – and resumed mining until he had done twenty-six years in all. The concrete opportunity for white-collar work had been available twice over; it was Alf, along with his mates, who 'thought and talked' himself into social immobility by becoming a miner, like his father. Social reproduction is an active task: staying put requires an agent who does something towards occupational replication and that action may be as simple as sharing one's thinking with one's school mates rather than one's family.

In case Alf's story is too readily assimilated to the community pressures of working-class traditionalism, we should recall Jeanette and how she evaded private boarding school to rejoin her friends at the local comprehensive. Jeanette, daughter of a solicitor and a school secretary, was middle class by background, but because she had chosen her friends over her (dysfunctional) family, she effectively hitched her wagon to their star because she had no guiding ambition of her own: 'everybody else was – I want to be a housewife or an air stewardess or a policewoman, but I never had an idea and still haven't got a clue to this day. I'll just have a go at this, that and the other, and hope that it will find me one day – like I say, no ambition. It would be nice to do something helpful, like with people . . . If I'd been serious, maybe a nurse or a doctor or something, but I haven't got the staying power for that sort of work.' Thus, as we have seen, Jeanette followed her school friends into further education, applying for child-care courses, which 'was totally out of character, but just seemed to be what all the girls were doing', and accepting her second option, catering, in which she had no interest; she never used her qualification. Her first job was happenstance, when someone showed her an advert for a mother's help in London, a post she held for a year, taking a seven-year-old to school, walking the dogs and cooking. Thereafter, Jeanette drifts and at thirty-six has held nothing other than routine manual jobs. Since all she seeks is security and a simple life, she does not look for social advancement, but only for a job which will enable her and her husband to move from their caravan into a house. The similarity with Alf is that again Jeanette's preference for her friends over her family resulted in a downwards social movement in relation to her parents' expectations and indeed their educational investment.

The second scenario is like Joan's, where a subject has no difficulties in deciding upon an occupational project early on, but where structural factors or inter-personal influences lead them to settle for 'second best'. At forty-four, Pauline now works as a night care assistant in a home for the elderly, but her initial project, like Joan's and Sheila's, had been nursing. This interest was sparked by regular visits to hospital, accompanying her mother who had been ill for seventeen years and died when Pauline was just eighteen. In Pauline's case, the opposition came from her school, which clearly deemed routine manual work appropriate for her and, like Joan, she fought back to rescue something of her aspirations. 'My mum started to go into hospital quite a lot as I got into my teenage years. I used to wonder what happened behind the curtains and got interested in nursing. I left school before I took any exams because I really hated school. So, my careers officer was trying to get me to do hairdressing or factory work, and I said, "I'm not doing either of them, I will get into the hospital." He kept saying, "No, you won't," but I did – I spent ten years as an auxiliary.' It is understandable that Pauline's family were too preoccupied with her mother's terminal illness to give her careful support at this time. But why did Pauline herself not subsequently take advantage of the opportunity placed before her to become exactly what she had wished?

She explains that, as an auxiliary, 'You could do an entrance exam to get into being an SEN. But the ward I was on was just great and they let the auxiliaries do practically everything anyway. And I got so stuck in that I didn't move on. But I'm glad now because if you're a trained nurse now, it's all paper work and that's not me. I'm definitely a hands on person. I much prefer to be doing things for people . . . Being an auxiliary was just good fun. The nursing students used to come and ask us for help and advice because we'd been there for years and we knew the routine of the ward and it was nice because you felt quite important.' The slippage into the second-person plural towards the end of this excerpt is significant. Pauline's fellow auxiliaries had become her interlocutors, and she 'got so stuck in and didn't move on' because she found her status quo so enjoyable, even though she had first envisaged becoming a registered nurse. 'But', as she puts it, 'people were so nice and you felt like you were doing a worthwhile job, because people were getting better and going home – and that was great. So I would have stayed for ever.' Pauline's 'half loaf' had proved thoroughly satisfying, her co-workers found it so too, and working as a nursing auxiliary was the highest socio-occupational status she was to achieve. Again, like Joan, her 'second best' was later to be willingly ceded for 'third best'.

The third scenario is the script followed by those who begin by being unable to design an occupational project within their natal context, remain in school *faute de mieux* and may eventually arrive at university, only to ask themselves what on earth they are doing there. Sooner or later, these communicative reflexives wonder how to climb back down the ladder which they had mounted without any plan in mind. Thus, Robbie, now twenty-three, a home owner and team leader at his call centre, has already had two attempts at degree courses and dropped out of two universities. To begin with, he had wanted to become a geneticist and applied to his local university, but did not obtain the entry grades. As he puts it himself: 'If I'd got in, I probably would have gone through with it – because I could have lived at home, because I would have had family support.' As it was, he enrolled at a distant Welsh university on an allied course, and almost immediately he 'started realising that I don't want to do it . . . then by the end of the first year, I didn't want to do it at all, and, to a certain extent, I'm still like that – I don't really know what I want to do, I only know what I want to do "now".' This is the 'presentism' of the short-term planner. Not knowing what he wanted to do, Robbie came home and took a job as a contact agent at a call centre.

Two years later, he entered a new university in a nearby city for an arts course, only to repeat the scenario. 'I realised, four or five months after I was there that, yes, I probably had made the right decision when I applied, but now, it's not the right decision. I've started off on a three-year journey and where I'm going to end up at the end is probably in the same position where I was three years ago . . . People say it was a waste of time, but I think "no", because I know I don't want to go back again.' Robbie has gone out and acquired for himself the experiences which lay outside his interlocutors' repertoire, but he has returned to them and re-embedded himself in his natal context. Yet he is still unable – alone or with their assistance – to see far enough ahead to design a project to which he can commit himself. 'Two years ago, I wanted to be a team manager, but now I don't. Two years ago, I didn't want anything to do with systems and data, whereas now I want to do that. So, if the job comes up, I'll go for it. But I know in two years that I'll probably want to do something completely different – and I'll wait for that opportunity to come up. In the meantime, I'll keep doing [my present job] to the best of my ability, but I wouldn't be dedicated, I'd just be waiting for the next chance to come up.'

Robbie has thus worked through all the stages of the return of the native; he has gone back to his dense natal context in Cobford, at the cost of relinquishing the social mobility which completing his university courses would normally have brought. He has returned to where he feels comfortable and thus voluntarily extends his contextual continuity, but still without any particular occupational project in view. It appears that his reiterated appeals to chaos theory rationalise his lack of longer-term planning and perhaps also mask his choice of social immobility from himself. In other words, the return home is the principal aim, a goal in itself, which entails a willing reduction of realisable aspirations, without it being motivated by any well-defined occupational end. As Terry, the unhappy research chemist, puts it: 'I know I don't really want to stay in this area. I would rather move back nearer my friends near London, and that's sort of my dilemma. I don't really see I can commit to this area and sort of make a life for myself round here.' For the communicative reflexive, the price of 'making a life' seems to mean endorsing social immobility – even when its precise contours remain unclear in definition.

Digging oneself in

Having taken the first active step towards social immobility by a voluntary reduction of occupational horizons, communicative reflexives find themselves in post with new co-workers and, by making friends amongst them, they actively forge the next links in their 'contextual continuity'. This is particularly important in reinforcing their social immobility; the supreme significance that they attach to inter-personal relations means that these new friendships further anchor them within this context because of their *new reluctance* to abandon these new interlocutors. Under their own descriptions, the communicative interviewees express this in terms of human relations being the most important aspect of employment, overriding considerations of pay, promotion or prospects.

Those who, like Luke, are not content with their current or last job, accentuate deficiencies in the inter-personal relationships it supplies/d. In fact this ultimate concern colours their views on the entire occupational panorama. Looking back on his expulsion from college, Luke's regrets are people-centred. 'The only thing I was gutted about really was because all my friends were there, and I was gutted because they were wicked, they were, well, really funny. And the next year when I was working, they were on the next course ahead of me and then the next one . . . I'm thinking, why did I do it, why did I act like a prat? If I hadn't got chucked out, I could be with them now, rather than being a little dole-dosser looking for a job.' Yet, equally, bad personal relations are precisely the reason why Luke has not been able to stick to any post in the past two years. 'Whenever I get a job, none of my friends are there, so I'm a bit gutted. And they're all older than me so they tend to look down on you . . . they've made me do scummy jobs and I don't want to do that. I've got my forklift licence now, but when I'm employed as a forklift driver, then like the forklift driver I've took over from – they'll all get sore and that . . . people get jealous because I'm younger and can do the job they've been doing for thirty years or whatever.'

Conversely, despite all his problems, Jon has remained in continuous contact with his old fellow apprentices and what he misses most, now his firm has closed, is the camaraderie. 'The lads I was an apprentice with . . . were really good, and we still keep in touch even though we're not working for the same company – we still meet up for nights out. I think that was part of it, the environment was really good, I was happy with the people I was working with, I was happy with the work I was getting.' Significantly, Jon recognises himself as a 'team player' and remarks insightfully about himself as a communicative reflexive, 'I think if you work by yourself, it can be very lonely, whereas if you're part of a team, you've got more.' What does he miss most, now that redundancy and ill health have left him unemployed? 'I miss the laugh we used to have in the office. It was the sort of office where we'd all be sat at our own particular computers, but because we were in a group environment, we'd be talking while we were working and we used to have a really good laugh – because we've all known each other for like thirteen years. It was missing that really, going from that group environment and talking all day to people – to being at home.'

Sheila's reflection shows much more pointedly how the durability of the working group outlasts the work itself. She preferred to give up full-time work when her children were born, despite there being no need to do so, but it is important that she did not do this alone. 'Oh, it was lovely, yes, we were all the same. Judy moved to my nursery because it was so friendly, it wasn't a teaching nursery or anything, and we had such fun together and we didn't stop until we'd got the babies . . . We all did, we all finished work, all of us. We could have taken our own child back to nursery and had it with us, because it was day nurseries then. But none of us did and we all needed the money . . . We all met up, I had Andrew first . . . and they all did the same as me, they worked right up to maternity. So we've always had one another like that . . . We come in and we've got our worries, we say, "Come on, who's got the worst worry, the most trouble and trauma?" – once a month, it's a good purge.' So durable has this forty-year-old network become that Sheila and her friend joke half seriously about which care home they will enter together.

Even Robbie and Terry, disenchanted with their present jobs, both confess that the quality of relationships they currently enjoy at work is a major deterrent against moving. Robbie is restless and is thinking about changing firms, but hesitates because 'I'm comfortably off, and I really like the people where I am, which made it difficult to do anything different. I was in that stage where home life is good, earning enough, get to do the things I want to do, work with people I enjoy being with, why do I want to change it?' He has a job offer in his pocket, carrying a substantial rise in income, but it remains uncertain whether or not he will take it. Terry has already said plenty about not wishing to continue as a research chemist in the science park where his PhD supervisor literally placed him. However, although wanting to go home to London, it is not just the stock options that detain him. Terry gained his appointment along with two of his friends from undergraduate days; his main job satisfaction derives from their company and they constitute the real force of inertia: 'me and two of my mates run it [the small firm] pretty much, so there's a lot of banter and we have a lot of fun while we're working . . . To be honest, I think people-interaction is the most important thing in my job. Yes, it makes it more enjoyable – we can get away with a lot of things that we do, and that's part of the appeal of staying . . . So, I suppose the work is OK, but I can see when this ends, which it inevitably will, I won't want to stay in. I don't want to go to a big chemical company, where you become ambiguous and you're not really having those interactions with people in the same way.'

Thus, for communicative reflexives, people make the job. If they can have the post but not the human relations, which are their ultimate concern, then, like Luke, they keep reappearing at the Jobcentre. If it is possible to keep the friends whilst shedding the work, in order to make way for a greater family concern, then, like Sheila, there seem to be few regrets. It is only when giving up an appointment would also mean sacrificing the company of valued co-workers that communicatives like Robbie and Terry look twice before they leap and may postpone their jump. Finally, what Alf shows us is that, for him, the arrival of uncongenial and positively offensive workmates can put paid to three decades of fully satisfying employment. During the miners' strike of 1984–5, Alf was out for a full fifty-one weeks. The Coventry mine was kept going by 'migrants' from all over the country and, as Alf puts it, 'When we went back there, these blacklegs had all stopped at the pit and you just couldn't depend on them, to my way of thinking anyway. Your workmates are the ones you've got to depend on, especially down the pit. To me, a bloke that's come from another place to work because he hasn't got the guts to go to his own pit – to me, they're not people at all, they're gutless people. So I took the redundancy and then I worked on the roads for a few years . . . When you've got a job, I think it's the people that you work with, the good, kind, genuine people – it doesn't matter what job you do because you can always have a laugh and a bit of fun and take things with a bit of snuff. Friends are important, especially my work friends. That was the reason I left the pit at the finish, because the people I was working with, I just couldn't get on with. They weren't people as far as I was concerned – that's the reason why I left.'

Sealing social immobility

Because of the nature of his ultimate concerns, Alf made a sacrifice in taking up roadwork but, as he quickly adds, 'at least the family never suffered'. This is the final *leitmotif* of the communicative reflexives: they will actively seal their social immobility by *voluntarily making a further reduction in their socio-economic status* in the interest of family concerns (or, in Alf's case, providing the family does not suffer). In other words, and for the older respondents, there comes a second stage during which these subjects actively make another cut in their occupational projects in order to satisfy family needs, as they see them. These are objective self-sacrifices in socio-economic standing, willingly taken in the interests of family well-being, because subjectively they are deemed necessary if the ultimate concern is not to be placed in jeopardy. It is in this way that the communicative reflexives report their (three) prime concerns to be smoothly dovetailed; these are prioritised and all else is strictly subordinated to them.

Yet, what they rarely do is to take any personal credit for the acts of self-abnegation by which they have actively engineered this state of affairs. On the contrary, although fully self-aware about what they have objectively forgone (like Joan, still hankering to become a nurse in her retirement), subjectively they will not entertain this as sacrificial action – because they believe that the outcome has been beneficial and resulted in all-round contentment. Nevertheless, this second move on their part serves to confirm their social immobility for the rest of their lives. Without reference to the life of their minds, such actions would remain incomprehensible. It would be simplistic to attribute such deeds to the expectations attaching to gender roles, although many of these action patterns are indeed engendered, because the same sacrificial element pertains to men and to women.

Thus, for Alf, work on the roads was hard with twelve-hour shifts, seven days a week at times, and up to eighteen hours at a stretch when pouring concrete for bridge-building. That was the sacrifice he made to retain the integrity of his friendship network. However, to him, 'as long as I've kept the family right and nobody's wanted for anything – that makes me happy . . . On the whole, so long as the wife and kids are all right, I don't give two jots.' From the start of the interview, Alf made no bones about his love of gambling on the horses and the dogs. However, in the following reflection we can see how carefully he monitors his own behaviour in this respect, precisely so that it does not endanger his family's well-being. 'I've never been one for great expectations. I just like a normal life and as long as the family's happy – they've got enough to live on – then I'm happy. I've never been a one for saving. If I won on the dogs, I always spent it. I would buy a new table and chairs or a new telly – the gambling never went back to the bookie, it went in the house. If I had £20 a week to gamble and I had £50 a week to keep the family on, and £5 for my fags and beer – then as long as that £50 was there for the house, I wouldn't bother about that £20. If I won £100, I wouldn't go to the bookies and put £40 on instead of my original £20 – and the other £80 would be spent on the house or the kids.'

Jon displays a different kind of loyalty. He had been with his firm of car designers for eleven years, thoroughly enjoying his job as we have seen. Then the rumours of a takeover became a reality, with jobs being shed immediately. Instead of getting out or even looking out for alternatives, Jon was so content that he remained where he was for a further two years, until made redundant (the fate of all but two out of two hundred employees). His present notion of contentment is simply to have his old job back: 'I'd like to be in a similar situation as I have been for the last thirteen years, in a group environment with people who I got on well with and could chat to easily – doing the same sort of thing. I think the happy working environment is more important to me because you could end up working a lot more on your own and not have that camaraderie. And in a lot of places as well, there's that "us and them" scenario, with people in the offices upstairs you never see. No, I wouldn't want that kind of thing – being behind an office door.' Yet, given the intervention of Jon's illness, this act of loyalty (which he would simply call the action of a contented man) may mean that he can never re-establish the same socio-economic position for himself.

Olga is rather similar to Alf and Jon because her working friendships accounted as much for her rejection of promotion as did family considerations. In mid-career as a teacher, she had the opportunity to realise her earlier ambition to become a translator, but she turned this down, saying, 'I'm happy I didn't [do it] because working with young people is so rewarding – I like to be among young people.' Somewhat later, she had another opportunity for promotion, this time to become head of a Catholic school. She seems to have had three different reasons for turning it down. Firstly, she reverts to her inability to plan: 'maybe I didn't have enough self-confidence, but I simply didn't want to be on the top. I thought, "No, that's not for me." Because of not being able to plan the day, I thought I'm not suitable for that.' Secondly, she mentions her female cousin who is a head teacher, but whose children have become demanding and difficult because of the additional money available. But the third consideration appears to have weighed most: 'It took me only one day to say no. I didn't contemplate this for a long time because I just knew. I think I was more conscious, not about my children – but

I thought, I have so many good friends among the other teachers, and when you stand on top, you suddenly lose all these contacts – they would-n't consider you a friend any more.'

Pauline and Sheila have more stereotypical stories to tell of women who make sacrifices explicitly for the family, rather than more inclusively – for friends and family and ultimately for contextual continuity. As such, the effect is a shrinking of their already quite restricted social network to the familial micro-world. Pauline and her husband are interesting because they both have taken reductions in occupational status in the interests of the family unit. Throughout her discussion of this latter period, there is no doubt that she was very self-aware about the causes and consequences of her own actions and those of her husband. Retrospectively, she maintains and reiterates, 'My nursing days were definitely my best', and that what she misses most is that 'it was just such a nice crowd to get on with'. Why did she eventually quit as a nursing auxiliary, given there was no necessity to do so when she became pregnant with their first child and that working part time was possible? 'I would have stayed for ever, I think, if I hadn't had the children, but the hospital hours didn't work out [though] they were definitely the best years of my life. I went back part time after I'd had my daughter. But then I had my son and my dad was looking after my daughter, and I thought I can't leave my dad with two – it's not fair. And we worked out if we got a childminder, it would be too expensive; I would have been going to work for a few pounds at the end of it – and I thought, well, it's just not worth it. So, I had a year off and then I went into working nights at care homes.'

Working as a night care assistant involves a strenuous timetable and also represents a reduction in occupational position and pay. But now Pauline compares her earliest aspiration, with her 'best years', and her current position, from which she produces a positive balance sheet: 'At first I thought I'd regret not doing my nurse's training, but when I see it now, they're constantly on your back to keep on training, to keep updating things – and I don't want to be doing that sort of thing. I'm glad I stuck where I was. It's nice to sit with the old folks sometimes, when they can't sleep, and have a good old conversation – and I wouldn't have had that if I'd been a qualified nurse.' Once again, the inter-personal satisfactions are held to counter-balance the objective losses, enabling Pauline to express contentment with her current lot. However, a key factor in the latter is that her husband made parallel 'sacrifices', ones which objectively reduced the family income but were subjectively positive because the couple could spend more time together.

Pauline's husband, Patrick, had experienced 'a rough time with jobs', including multiple redundancies. Looking back, she does not see his best-paid jobs as coinciding with the best times in their relationship: 'I think sometimes we've been happier with less money than having more money, because you just tend to get on with it. When he did have a job, he was having to work a lot of hours to get the money. I'd much rather have him at home, so we can be together.' At this point, when Pauline's father is now living with them and she herself is working nights, Patrick obtained a well-paid job in Manchester, entailing lengthy commuting and a late return home. 'By the time he came in at 8.00 p.m. I was at my wits' end and didn't want to be bothered . . . By the time he'd driven back, all he wanted to do was to have his tea and a quiet time and go to bed. And there were lots of arguments because the kids would be playing up and I would hardly see him. Then I'd go and spend money on things I didn't really need, just to try and make me feel better. Even though we had the money, it wasn't the best time in our marriage.' Thus, Pauline was pleased when Patrick gave up this job and settled for less well-paid and less regular employment. 'So, now, we just plod along. We don't go without and it's nice just having the company.' This is her own definition of contentment, and she adds that the bonus was that Patrick could (and willingly did) look after her father overnight, once dad became seriously ill and Pauline was on night duty at the care home.

Sheila still reproaches her own mother, the school secretary, for having been a 'career woman', and we have seen that she herself resolved to resign from the nursery when she began her family. Immediately, she reduced her occupational status to school cleaner and then to playgroup supervisor, each taking only a few hours a day – what she describes as 'little jobs'. And this seems to have been the pattern followed by her close friends too. 'Whatever job I got then, I got so I could take the children with me . . . we all did the same; Judy got a cleaning job in school at night and Kitty worked nights as a midwife so that she could be at home in the day as well.' Although it appeared that Sheila's determination might be compromised at this stage, because she and her husband separated, she found an ingenious solution, which meant that accommodation also came with her part-time job and its flexible working hours. Thus, Sheila struck her final deal with social immobility, becoming a church caretaker for the last eight years of her working life, before being disabled with arthritis. 'So I got a job as caretaker where they [her two children] could come with me in the pushchair. I was always at home and able to go to all their plays, and if Lisa was poorly I could get her from school. I was there at home time and always used to go and fetch them from school and take them. That's why I did the job, so I was always there for them.' Once again, her verdict upon this sacrificing of work and social position for the sake of her children is 'I think I've had a lovely life.' Moreover, her contentment is redoubled because her son and his wife as well as her daughter have the same intentions when their own families come along. 'They've got the same values. My values are the children and the family – more people than possessions – so I know they are all right. And Lisa says how grateful she is that I used to be here when she came home from school and that's what she wants to do with hers. She said, "I wanted that feeling that when I walked down the road, you were going to be there, no matter what had gone wrong at school." So it's nice to know it's going to continue – that's the main thing.'

But is this sacrificial compact with social immobility going to continue amongst communicative reflexives? After all, with the exceptions of Jeanette and Jon (whose case is complicated by ill health), the subjects examined in this section are aged forty-four and over. Jeanette is interesting, not simply because she is in her mid-thirties, but in view of her doubting that she will ever want children. Does this mean that she will escape the second instalment of self-sacrifice? When she married in Glastonbury, she was about to start an IT training course (free, as part of the jobseekers' allowance), but abandoned this project to live in the caravan at the garden centre for eight years. Now that the couple have been made redundant they plan to move north, where her husband has family connections and he intends to establish himself as an independent repairman. Since they would like to rent a house – which will be a new expense for them – Jeanette knows that she must find work there. I ask her what she would now look for in a job, given that she hates catering, has no pretensions to have picked up any horticultural skills, but is fully acceptant that she must help to meet the bills. They have discussed this at length and her husband has queried whether this is not the moment for her to resume training in IT. In other words, his plans for himself hardly represent social mobility, but he is not imposing the same immobility on his wife.

Therefore, it seems all the more significant that Jeanette not only insists upon employment where human relations come first, but also designates shop work, which would consolidate their social immobility as a couple – and represent another voluntary step down from where a boarding-school girl was destined to be: 'I suppose, most importantly, it would be nice to work with people you get on with – because I have worked at some places where you're really looked down on, and people can be so cliquey . . . I don't like backbiting and all that kind of thing. That to me would be awful – so a nice working environment with nice people . . . But the type of work, yeah, doing something useful, even if it's just on a checkout where you can chat to people, somewhere you can talk! I like talking, as you've noticed . . . Well, the feeling that you've done something good, made someone happy. I think that's probably the most important thing – a smile on someone's face – even if it was just one person in a day, and they said, "Thanks, you've cheered me up" – to me that would be worth a lot of hours. You've only got to sit in the supermarket and you'll get the odd miserable cow on the checkout and you'll get the one that's chatting to all the old dears, and I think, "Yes, I could do that, just make somebody happy." Simple really, simple but effective.' I have made no attempt to conceal that I warmed to Jeanette, as to Jon, but when I tentatively mention access courses and training for social work, for the only time in three hours, she displays an impenetrable far-away gaze, which I hope does not mean she is dreaming of the checkout! What it probably did signal is that she is fully reconciled to social immobility. As was found during the first-year student interviews at the start of the longitudinal study, every single communicative reflexive *anticipated* a career (and often a brief one for the young women) which fell short of the qualifications they were almost certain to obtain.

The micro-world of communicative reflexives: in society but not of it

The paradox of the communicative reflexives is that whilst the density and intensity of their inter-personal support contributes quantities of social cement, their contribution to civil society could not be lower. On the one hand, their *modi vivendi* consist of a set of practices whereby people look after their own, reach out to one another and construct informal networks of conviviality, stretching into the workplace and neighbourhood. Correspondingly, they uphold inter-generational solidarity with more vitality than any other sub-group. Yet, despite some functional similarities, it would be wrong to assimilate the out-workings of their mode of reflexivity to a form of traditional *Gemeinschaft*. They are not the preservers of old-style community because their embeddedness is within a micro-world of their own making. Their 'contextual continuity' is of their own constitution; it may have some geo-local features redolent of the past, but can have its locus in a caravan parked at the edge of a field; it may converge upon the nearest shopping precinct, but can also have tentacles reaching up to the Durham coalfields, back to college or out to a hippy-dom that no longer exists. In short, these micro-worlds are constituted biographically rather than geographically.

On the other hand, whilst it would be nonsense to call these micro-worlds self-subsistent, they do pretend to self-sufficiency in their external social relations, especially their institutional relations. Such self-sufficiency is double sided: it means both the relative autarky of the familial and friendship group for leisure and social interaction, and the relative indifference of communicative reflexives towards the institutions of civil society. What both demarcates this feature and differentiates the communicatives from other sub-groups is their repudiation of interlinking associations – those articulating the individual to the institutional.

As far as clubs, courses or charitable activities are concerned, we have already heard Joan stating that 'I don't want anything like that, I've never needed anything like that.' She may be a little extreme: after all Alf enjoys the racetrack, Jon his country pursuits and Terry his martial arts and golf (before his injury). Various interviewees refer to swimming, and there are frequent mentions of the pub. But 'pubbing' is not 'clubbing'; one can go to meet friends without going out to meet people, and do so by forming a small enclave of privacy within this public space. Equally, an interest in racing, fishing or golf may be more performative than social in nature, and involvement in the practical order may constitute the prime reason for this personal investment of time.[5] Moreover, Joan is not alone in rejecting organised activities, although it may be the case that this characteristic is more accentuated, or at least articulated, by female respondents.

Indeed, Pauline, who looks young, dresses informally and seems very outgoing, gives something of a surprise when she reflects upon how far she wanted her own family to be modelled upon her quiet natal background. It is she herself who begins to speak about her preferred forms of sociability, ones she shares with her husband and that they seek to realise for their children. 'I wanted them to have the kind of upbringing I'd had, because my parents were always around and never went off to pubs and clubs and things like a lot of families do now. My parents never went out at night, except at Christmas, and we've been very much the same with ours.' She explains this by reference to her husband's 'struggled background', as one of thirteen children whose 'mum and dad were never there. The kids really brought each other up.' Subsequently, his preference was for the quiet but intensive domesticity that she values. Hence, Pauline continues, 'my husband doesn't go out very often and neither do I. We still go out for family meals every week and we still think if we're going out to do something, then it's with the family. And even the holiday, we still want to go as a family, even though my daughter's twenty and got a boyfriend. We still do a lot of things as a family, which people find really strange.' Maddeningly, her daughter, now a second-year university

---

[5] For the importance of the distinction between the 'natural', 'practical' and 'social' orders, their associated activities and investments, see Margaret S. Archer, *Being Human: the Problem of Agency*, Cambridge, Cambridge University Press, 2000, ch. 5.

student, chose this moment to enter the room and sit down before Pauline got round to explaining what she meant by 'strangeness'. However, when Pauline picked up the threads again, she summarised her ideas on this theme in the following words, which significantly evoke the idea of living within a microcosm: 'I'd like to think that we were all happy in our own little world – still a very close-knit family.'

Despite her very different past and present life, Jeanette produces surprisingly similar sentiments and is very antipathetic towards organised activities. She begins by reflecting upon the similarities between her brother and her husband, the two people to whom she is closest, both of them being her interlocutors in 'thought and talk'. Each is what she describes as 'reclusive, a typical Virgo man. They don't really need people but they've got certain friends that are solid and they trust wholeheartedly.' From there, she reflects that she and her husband very much 'do their own thing' and that belonging to anything is not part of it: 'I'm a bit anti-clubs and things [like that]. I have done [it] in the past – obviously, as you grow up you join Brownies, tennis clubs and so on. And I wouldn't say I disliked them, but what I did dislike was the people that are so obsessed. I mean, I probably am obsessed in some way myself, but I can't stand obsessions and people that take things too seriously and it's their whole life and everything revolves around this club and that club. I quite dislike organised stuff.' Since Jeanette is clearly very proud of her cats, I query whether or not this includes breeding or showing them. Obviously not: 'I've even been to cat shows and thought what a bunch of horrid people! And people who are in dog clubs, you hear them talking about other people and bitching about them, and you think, why do they do it? It sounds horrible, so competitive. I hate anything like that.' The cats are part of Jeanette's family, not her entrée to social life.

Perhaps it is worth making a tentative aside, if only because of the ubiquitous contributions made by animals to the audio tapes. All the communicative reflexives, who were interviewed at home, rejoiced in at least one pet that manifestly enjoyed a privileged domestic position. Is this a means of making the family circle still more complete, a way of adding yet more cosiness to the micro-world?

It is obviously a valid question to ask whether those who are single, or have become so, share the same stance towards organised activities and forms of association. After separating from her husband, Sheila and her (now widowed) friend Judy holiday together, sing in a choir and attend various evening classes. Thus, at first glance, Sheila does appear to be different, especially as she is the only subject in this sub-group who attended church (until quite recently) and had also assisted the charity MIND for a couple of years. However, as she puts it, 'I used to be with my church, but I have mum on Sundays now for dinner, so I don't tend to go because she has to have her dinner at twelve o'clock.' Similarly, Sheila gave up her voluntary work with MIND, in part because she was not enthusiastic about the permanent staff but, more importantly, in order to care for her son during an illness from which he has now recovered. In other words, the needs of family members have displaced her religious practice and her charity work, both of which were unusual amongst the communicative reflexives. But what of her participation in organised activities with her closest friend and interlocutor? Was this an attempt to fill a gap after both had ceased to live as married women?

Perhaps Terry, the young and single research chemist, can shed some light here, because he is the only other respondent who introduces such activities. He has already mentioned his shoulder injury, lack of improvement in which has seriously depleted his sporting friendships. Terry refers to this group having 'dwindled massively', which now represents 'a real problem for him'. His response to this isolation, which worries him because his long-time friends are grouped in London and most of his undergraduate network has moved on, is the following: 'So that's something that's been bothering me, lack of friends in the local area. Obviously, there's a hundred and one clubs at the university, but everybody's very young – so I'm trying to look outside the university for things to do. I've found a few things, but I've been really unlucky. I tried to do Italian and the course was full, I applied for a wine-tasting course and that was cancelled as well. So, I'm having to look again now.' The implication appears to be that organised social activities do not supplement the sociability enjoyed amongst family and friends, but rather they are a substitute or stop-gap when the personal network of a communicative reflexive becomes too thin. They are a pretext for sociality which is jettisoned if and when authentic sociability is extracted from them and, in any case, take second place to ministering to the needs of family or long-term friendships.

This gels very closely with the generic view of the social, as composed of nothing but individuals and inter-personal relationships, which is common to communicative reflexives. Terry continues to speak on this theme and, unsurprisingly, as by far the most educated person in the sub-group, he struggles to voice a more nuanced view. Indeed, in his first response to being asked whether or not he believes that society is fair, he comes down in favour of that position – in the end: 'I think it's very difficult and there's a lot of imaginary boundaries. They're there in your own head, but they're there nonetheless. I think people have a lot of self-doubt about what they can achieve. I think it's as simple as, "If you want it, you can get it" – to a point.' Terry himself is dissatisfied with that formulation and has another crack at social ontology, this time attempting to reduce it to epistemology, to our baggage of constructs and concepts: 'Imaginary is the wrong word, it's things in your head that you can just let go of if you want – they're not physical boundaries. There's no one else that's going to stop you doing something. I think things happen in your life which strongly affect you and that causes a problem later on if you don't deal with it. Often you won't even realise it's there. I'm not really making much sense I don't think . . .' Nobody could have more sympathy with Terry-the-chemist than I do at that moment as he tussles with the question of whether or not something social can be there without agential awareness of it. Finally, after pondering on his over-protective parents and their fears that he could not cope with university, he comes up with a more robust ontological statement. 'I think because I'd been so protected from society, and what I can and can't do, it made me just think, "Well, I can do that if I want to." They [his parents] were scared that I couldn't, but they never showed that, so perhaps I'd been protected from society and the things I can or can't do. It made me just think: "I can do that if I want to".' Terry had successfully fought through his epistemological illusions about the open society. This discussion has been presented at length because Terry was the only communicative reflexive to battle his way to this conclusion and, it is clear, his struggle was because his first reaction was to endorse individualism and openness.

The others who took up this theme had no doubts that the social could immediately be reduced to the inter-personal. Perhaps these subjects could be called Thatcherites because of their overwhelming tendency to translate any reference to 'society' into a statement about 'individuals and their families'. Pauline's comment can stand for the sub-group as a whole. It is her immediate response to being asked whether she thinks that society is a fair place; is it one in which people can achieve what they wish if they work hard or one where the cards are stacked against some people from the start? Her response reveals what is utterly pervasive amongst communicative reflexives, namely to make a strong assertion about individual responsibility linked to an equally forceful statement about the indispensability of family support. 'I think some people haven't got the family background. One lad I know, his mum's got a new boyfriend and she puts him before her son. He's just been in prison and he's been let out but his mum wouldn't have him home. Some people haven't got the support. He'll probably end up back inside . . . definitely you have to have a good family background and know that they're there for you whatever . . . I know what this lad's done wasn't right, but his mother's just not really bothered about him . . . One of his uncles has taken him in, but whether he wants to make a go of it, it's up to him now.'

Therefore, it follows for the communicative reflexives, especially if they believe that they themselves have had the benefits of a supportive family, that achievement or non-achievement are matters of personal responsibility. Thus Jon, who in all other respects appears to be a very gentle, understanding person, produces the following forthright statement: 'I think a lot of it is down to the individual. If you want something, you've got to be prepared to put in a bit of hard graft to get there, but I think on the whole it's down to the individual to chase what they're after and go and get it for themselves, because I don't believe things are handed to you. I think on the whole you have to go and get it yourself. I think a lot of the time you are able to achieve what you wanted to if you're prepared to work for it.' Thus, it is straightforwardly maintained that if you have family support and put in the personal effort, then there is nothing else in society that can stop you from realising your aspirations. The social is not seen as having any properties and powers of its own kind – it does not distribute preferential opportunities to some and endow others with inferior life chances.

Provided that these two necessary factors – family support and personal effort – are present, communicative reflexives have no difficulty in endorsing the 'open society'. What is significant about the following response to the same question from Robbie is that the 'open society' itself is seen simply as a competition between individuals. Instead of this very notion of 'openness' requiring structural and cultural underpinning, in ways that have been rehearsed since Durkheim first considered the prerequisites of a functional meritocracy, the most that Robbie concedes is the advantage of gaining 'help from other people' – and even then its refusal can result in a stronger individual. 'For those who are ready to go out and help themselves and seize the opportunities there, I think it's the kind of society nowadays where that's rewarded because people see the enthusiasm of somebody and are more likely to give somebody who's enthusiastic about it the chance to do it . . . Others will be there to help you; they won't necessarily go out of their way to help you . . . You've got to go out and ask for the help and some people will give it to you, some people won't, but then you just learn from that. I think it is that kind of society. It's all about if there's an opportunity there – if you don't take it somebody else will.' The only caveat attached to this portrayal of a meritocracy by any respondent is also about 'other people' (as in classical methodological individualism[6]), and consists of the overt racism we have heard from Luke about overseas immigrants.

[6] See J. W. N. Watkins, 'Methodological Individualism and Social Tendencies', in May Brodbeck (ed.), *Readings in the Philosophy of the Social Sciences*, New York, Macmillan, 1968. He 'insists that the social environment by which any particular individual is confronted and frustrated and sometimes manipulated and occasionally destroyed is, if we ignore its physical ingredients, made up of *other people*, their habits, inertia, rivalries and so on' (p. 278n).

However, do those communicative reflexives who had not enjoyed support and encouragement from their families, unlike the speakers above, add any nuances to this picture? Only Terry, and he effectively reinforces it when he openly regrets that his working-class parents lacked the information and confidence to advise him well about university entrance. Unsurprisingly, although we have encountered Sheila, suffering at the hands of her dysfunctional family, and read Joan's long account of enforced gender discrimination by her father, the strong tendency of the communicative reflexives to idealise their family backgrounds does not even allow them to protest about manifest domestic unfairness. The image of the 'happy family' appears as necessary to the subject's assertion of her contentment; even harmful inter-personal relations are acknowledged with difficulty when they pertain to the family background. In other words, we are personally responsible for manufacturing our own contentment, whatever the hand of cards that we have been dealt.

The final ingredient of this social philosophy is that it entails intra-punitiveness for lack of 'success'. Society is held to play no part in this and nor are parents blamed, even by the rare subject who admits that the latter fell far short of perfection. Thus, Jeanette's response to the same question about society's fairness is to blame herself. 'My problem is personally I'm lazy, very, very lazy. And I'm always telling myself, "You could have done better – you could do better," but I can't be arsed. Like not driving, I was too scared really to learn to drive and kept putting it off. I think from my point of view, it's me that's held myself back rather than society. There's a lot of options out there.' Thus, if your family was good and supportive, then the rest is up to you, and if it was not, then it is your fault for not overcoming your background.

We can now draw the strands together and understand why communicative reflexives have so little time for civil society and behave as though their 'micro-worlds' do not interface with its institutions. Throughout this chapter a great deal of space has been devoted to how this sub-group relates to work, but two themes have been of importance – one because of its presence and the other because of its absence. By now, it will not be necessary to re-emphasise the centrality of human relations to employment in the eyes of communicative reflexives, or how work is monitored and regulated to dovetail with family concerns. Conversely, despite references to pit closures, to the takeover of a company and the launch of a new science enterprise, to multiple redundancies, unfavourable working conditions and low pay, there has not been one single mention of the economy, economic policy or political economy. The presences and the absences appear closely related; because work and employment are again conceptualised by reducing them to inter-personal relations, this necessarily forecloses the question of macroscopic economic factors and forces. Even Alf, a life-long unionist, dwelt upon the undesirability of the individual blacklegs he encountered, rather than upon the causes and consequences of the miners' strike.

In other words, institutions are 'personalised' and just as work is reduced to 'other people' in a specific locale doing particular tasks, so too are other parts of the institutional structure of civil society. This is uncomplicated in relation to religion; communicative reflexives talk respectfully of religion, whilst not being church goers. We can now begin to see why and how this is also a matter of personalisation. Nearly all of these respondents maintain that they derive their values from their parents and also that many of their parents had a religious affiliation. It seems as though much of their residual respect for religion mirrors the respect they feel is due to their parents' beliefs, rather than to religious teachings or practices, because hardly any admit that the latter had an impact upon them. Like Alf, they practised when their parents made them do so: 'I'll tell you the truth, I've stopped going to church and if my mother was alive, she'd murder me! That was the first words when I went up to Durham: "have you been to Mass today?" ' Like Sheila, they stop practising for reasons like her old mother wanting her Sunday lunch at twelve o'clock. Everything is personalised, including the disavowals and avowals of faith. Thus, Pauline explains, 'I wouldn't say I don't believe but I'm not really religious. I think because of losing my mum at an early age, it tended to make me think, well, she was a good person, so why did she have to die like that. And my dad, going down with that illness, it's just evil. I'm not a non-believer, but I don't go to church or anything like that.' Jon is exactly the reverse; his enduring faith is also attributed to person-alised reasons. He was brought up as a Roman Catholic and he tells why he keeps the faith. 'I do still believe in these beliefs, because when I had these blood clots and was in hospital – I went into hospital on the Monday after my [practising] grandfather's funeral on the Friday. From that Friday night, all that weekend I'd been getting really out of breath and going downhill, like going up a flight of steps I was completely worn out. And looking back now, I think maybe my granddad was watching over me. And I was able to get in [to hospital] on the Monday, when any one of those days I could have died and that would have been it. So I still do believe in Catholic beliefs, but I don't practise as much as I should do . . . But certain things bring it back, like thinking about my granddad – it is always there, you can always call on it.'

Amongst these interviewees, religious upbringing and attending denominational schools seem to be disproportionate to the population as a whole. Is the outlook upon religion very different for a communicative reflexive who had no such background and for whom the word 'religion' does not evoke Christianity? Here is Jeanette, talking about her hippy days and a mild attraction to (New Age) Buddhism: 'I like the philosophy of it, peace, happiness and flowers round the door, but to actually be among people that really live and breath that is too much, it's not the real world . . . it was interesting, crystals and tarot cards, but they take it too far and start eating cardboard, everyone takes things too far and that annoys me. You get some people who say, "I won't be friends with them because they wear leather and they eat meat; never eat anything with a face." And I think . . . I like all the nice bits but don't get too involved – then it gets fanatical and puts you off.' Although Jeanette's religious referent is entirely different from Jon's, the element of personalisation remains identical.

Reactions to politics are very similar. In other words, the disinclination to participate in the associations of civil society is paralleled by a distancing from political institutions on the part of communicative reflexives. The generalised respect shown towards religion is reserved here for the vote – something it is usually held important to exercise 'because then you can't moan', but without any conviction that it changes anything or that one party is better than another. This attitude towards politics is epitomised in Sheila's advice to her offspring: 'I said to the children, "I don't care what you vote as long as you vote. Whatever happens then, you've got nothing to moan or complain about." I said, "Don't come complaining to me about what the government's doing or what the council's doing, you've been given the vote, now vote." I really believe that; it doesn't matter what you vote, but use your vote.' Despite this generalised approbation of exercising one's democratic rights, voting comes unaccompanied by any conviction that doing so makes a positive difference or by any notion of party loyalty. Jon is fairly typical here as a swing-voter, disenchanted with party politics, but one who persists in voting: 'I haven't really any time for politics because I think they're all as bad as each other – I'm not swayed in any particular direction. I do vote because I think you can't moan about something if you're not voting and having your say, but I just don't consider any party better than another. I don't think any of them are particularly good, they promise you the earth and then it doesn't really materialise.'

· Thus a formal approval of democratic process co-exists with a practical and personal alienation from existing party politics, which are seen as self-interested and dissociated from the interests of these subjects. This view is summarised by Robbie: 'I'm not cynical about politics; I'm cynical about the people who have hijacked it.' He continues, 'last election, I tried to get people to go and spoil their [ballot] papers rather than waste their vote, because if more people spoiled their paper than got nominated through the party then nobody would get elected, it's a big news story and people would have to sit down and think what are we doing wrong.' Terry clearly agrees with the first part of that statement: 'I don't think politics works. They're only worried about public image and getting the next vote . . . Labour have done exactly what they said they wouldn't do; they just haven't really told anyone about it.' In turn, Luke produces the classic statement of political alienation: 'Who's going to want to listen to me? I'm an eighteen-year-old lad with no job. I wouldn't know what to do if I was in an argument with Tony Blair.'

Yet, if national politics are seen as too distanced from our subjects' interests and too geared towards politicians' own interests, participation in social movements is not regarded as having any greater efficacy. Terry's reflection on direct action through public protest is that 'everything's everyone else's problem these days. It seems everyone is just interested in themselves. Protests and things don't achieve anything – the papers and things just turn it round on the protestors and say what a disgrace.' Luke, who could be seen as ripe for recruitment by the BNP, is equally dismissive: 'Marching around like a prat isn't going to change things. That's more the hippies – that isn't me.' But Jeanette, who had her hippy phase, appears at most lukewarm about social movements – being too distressed by anti-vivisection publicity to continue with the league, regarding Greenham Common as full of 'the kind of people that would put you off' and rather embarrassed by her one act of protest. 'I did go on a CND march once, but that was basically because it was a free coach to London for the day. I did go on a bit of the march but people were so horrible. Looking back now I suppose we looked like idiots dying in the road, doing this three-minute warning thing – thousands of us lying in the road and everyone who worked in London was trying to get to work and there's all these idiots doing a protest.'

Thus we are left with the paradox that the communicative reflexives, who do so much inter-personally to support other individuals within their micro-worlds, choose to remain utterly dissociated from the political institutions and activities that shape the macro-context in which they ineluctably live. Another way of putting this is that communicative reflexives remain *primary agents* whose consequences for society are exclusively aggregate ones. They resist mobilisation into *corporate agents*, that is promotive interest groups with articulated interests and an organisation designed for collective action. Thus they go against the flow of late modernity, when more and more groupings achieve these conditions for expressing their interests.[7] Only *corporate agents* are capable of shaping

---

[7] See Margaret S. Archer, *Realist Social Theory: the Morphogenetic Approach*, Cambridge, Cambridge University Press, 1995, pp. 257–74.

and reshaping the societal context, whereas *primary agents* live within it. What the communicative reflexives have been telling us repeatedly throughout this chapter is that they do so contentedly – inside their micro-worlds and within the confines of the contextual continuity that they have both embraced and actively reconstituted.

Conclusion

There is one main point to be made in concluding this section, which must remain incomplete until practitioners of other dominant modes of reflexivity have been introduced and examined. It concerns the relationship between communicative reflexives and structural or cultural constraints and enablements. In other words, are the relations between 'objectivity and subjectivity' or 'structure and agency' such as to produce distinctive consequences for those practising the communicative mode of reflexivity?

It will not have escaped the reader's attention that very little mention has been made of social constraints and enablements in the course of the current chapter devoted to communicative reflexivity. This is true and it is held to be a direct consequence of the predominant exercise of the communicative mode. This chapter is entitled 'Working at staying put' and what has been explored are the ways in which communicative reflexives have been active agents in producing their own lack of social mobility. This activity cannot even be seen as straightforward agential contributions to reproducing their natal positions, as in theories which conceptualise the dispositional as both mirroring and reinforcing the positional. This is because there have been clear cases of subjects (Jeanette) who threw their personal properties and powers into repudiating their natal privileges and also cases (Terry and Robbie) who could have seized upon the enablements represented by the educational elastication of their opportunities, but had turned or were busy turning their backs upon them. In other words, the subjectivity represented by practising the communicative mode of reflexivity appears to make its own independent contribution to the socio-economic position assumed by such subjects in society.

This is reinforced by the large amounts of voluntary activity, contributed by all subjects under their own descriptions, which served to produce social immobility. Their work always pivoted upon the primacy of inter-personal concerns to members of this sub-group. Could this ultimate concern be interpreted as socially induced by cultural influences amongst the subjects examined? Certainly, sociologists have often seen congenial relations with workmates as the subjective compensation that subjects extract from objectively poor occupational positions, the latter being the product of poor life chances acquired at birth. Yet this chapter has biographically tracked precisely the reverse: namely people whose prime concern for human relations led them to an otherwise unnecessary modesty in the jobs they sought and accepted. Although it remains open to the committed social determinist to maintain that the very concern for inter-personal relations is heavily socially conditioned, they would (a) have considerable difficulties in identifying how such conditional influences operate, given that the subjects in question come from different social origins, and (b) they would necessarily have to deny personal powers to decide upon what we care about most, in favour of the effects of social forces upon us – thus rendering human subjectivity entirely epiphenomenal.

In fact, there is only a negative story to tell about the encounter between communicative reflexives and constraints or enablements, precisely because the former systematically *evade* the latter over their life courses. In completing the sequence <concerns → projects → practices>, these subjects conceive of no occupational projects that activate either the constraints or enablements associated with the employment structure. In establishing the life practices constitutive of their *modus vivendi*, their endorsement of modest aspirations, their reluctance to seek occupational advancement, their tendency to scale down their socio-economic positions rather than to scale them up and their absorption in their families and friends attract no social sanctions. In short, if the outcome of practising communicative reflexivity is social immobility, then none of society's emergent properties or powers is activated to resist the personal election of *stasis*. Nevertheless, it is indeed a matter of subjective and deliberative election, meaning the exertion of personal properties and powers. Social immobility is not something that just happens by default; as this chapter has shown, 'staying put' requires a good deal of work on the part of active and reflexive agents.

5   Autonomous reflexives: upward and outward bound

Dramatis personae

Pseudonym	Age	Current/last occupation
Abigail (f)	48	Finance officer
Billy (m)	60	Unemployed (driver/storekeeper)
Clive (m)	34	Business manager
Damian (m)	33	Shop manager
Donna (f)	22	Team manager, e-banking
Liz (f)	55	Primary school head
Martin (m)	30	Managing dispensing optician
Nick (m)	29	Builder (self-employed)
Oliver (m)	49	Senior financial consultant
Rachel (f)	25	Hairdressing salon manager
Ralph (m)	56	Unemployed (sales manager)
Tony (m)	36	Freelance researcher

Once again, this chapter is devoted to establishing and elucidating a single proposition, in this case that the practice of autonomous reflexivity is a personal power, a generative mechanism fostering upward social mobility. Any such mechanism is at the mercy of intervening contingencies when it operates in an open system like society. Since these contingent interventions may suspend, mask or override its powers, the association between autonomous reflexivity and social mobility will be manifest (at best) only as an empirical tendency. Although all the interviewees demonstrated this upward trend over substantial tracts of their life courses, two are currently unemployed and have little to show objectively for their previous exertions. Nevertheless, it is maintained that the generic project of 'getting on' is intimately related to the autonomous mode of reflexivity. However, as the hallmark of how these subjects would like to make their way through the world, upward mobility is only an aim – one which may not be achieved because of individual miscalculation or circumstances beyond a subject's control.

To begin with, work and employment are listed among the ultimate concerns of all twelve interviewees, it being the prime concern for one and 'getting work' being the only concern recorded by another. As people for whom the autonomous mode of reflexivity was extremely dominant,[1] this concern is more marked amongst these interviewees than amongst other autonomous reflexives for whom this mode was less strong. Qualitatively, the interviews revealed how much of their time, thought, effort and, indeed, of themselves these subjects invested in their working lives. In addition, these extremely active agents worked reflexively at dealing with the structural constraints and enablements that they activated in the course of and as a consequence of their doings. Of course, there was no compulsion for this subjective effort to be made by anyone above and beyond their objective exertions. Epistemically, someone could simply believe that 'hard work brings its own rewards', but part and parcel of autonomous reflexivity is to monitor the social context of one's employment rather than merely to engage in self-monitoring on the job. Why is this double aspect the case?

It appears to be intrinsic to the practice of lone internal conversation itself. By definition, any such practitioner stands at some distance from his social context; it is not an environment in which he is embedded so deeply that he unquestioningly accepts 'their ways are my ways' or that established custom and practice are the best ways. Precisely because lone inner dialogue is predicated upon a firm distinction between the private and the public domains, then to reflect upon oneself in relation to one's circumstances is to exercise reflexivity *across* this boundary. The self is seen as discontinuous from its environment, not inseparable from it; one's concrete singularity marks differences from others, not similarity and familiarity; one's potentialities and liabilities are differentiated from the properties and powers of the context confronted, not conflated with them. Without such boundaries, there could be no such thing as lone deliberation about the self in relation to society. There would only be first-personhood *per se*.

Autonomous internal conversation entails much more than the latter: it is selective, evaluative and elective about the world in which a subject finds himself.[2] This is the case despite the fact that these subjects have to utilise the public medium of language *inter alia* in their private deliberations[3] and also despite the fact that they will be subject to misinformation, disinformation and ideological manipulation, as is everyone else. The

---

[1] The mean ICONI 'A' score of the interviewees was 6.19 out of the possible 7.
[2] As the majority of autonomous subjects are men, the male pronoun will be used in this chapter.   [3] See chapter 2.

first question to try to answer in this chapter, by drawing upon our twelve interviewees, is how did they come to distance themselves from their natal contexts sufficiently to be able to hold lone internal conversations within them and at least partially about them?

Whilst the basis of communicative reflexivity was trust in others, the equivalent for autonomous reflexivity is self-reliance. 'Contextual discontinuity' is the most important condition for the emergence of inner dialogue conducted alone and capable of devising courses of action.[4] By definition, the very existence of discontinuity with one's context deprives the subject of those who are similar enough to him to act as his interlocutors – supplying contextual guidance that in turn reproduces the familiar contours of this social setting. Yet, such discontinuity is partly imposed on the subject by circumstances beyond his control, and is partly promoted by him. These are the two faces of 'contextual discontinuity': that which is unsought by the agent and that which agents themselves court. Is it possible to disengage any commonalities between these proactive and reactive aspects in the process of coming to rely upon one's lone deliberations – and thus becoming an autonomous reflexive?

Fundamentally, the subject must somehow find himself acquiring new experiences and confronting novel situations for which his natal context provides no guidelines. Indeed, it may also be precisely this context that presents him with problems but without solutions. He thus has to learn to rely upon his own resources if he is to make out in such situations, because no interlocutor could fully enter into his position.

Furthermore, subjects also need to have developed sufficient self-confidence to marshal their own resources to meet situations for which the natal context provides no scripted responses or normative regulation. The experience of discontinuities and the confidence to handle them are mutually reinforcing; together they generate self-reliance. Indeed, they appear to be dialectically related in the sense that to cope successfully by oneself in unfamiliar situations yields a sense of satisfaction which enhances self-confidence and may then prompt the courting of further lone experiences which lie beyond the natal context.

If these elements, which make for self-reliance, are preconditions of autonomous reflexivity, then we are not dealing with a personal property and power that is psychologically reducible to dispositional terms. There is no *a priori* need to deny that personal psychology may make its contribution, perhaps by a closer specification of what makes for self-

---

[4]   Unlike fractured reflexivity, which may be conducted alone but leads to no definition of purposeful action; instead it merely augments disorientation and distress as it goes round in circles.

confidence. Nevertheless, this mode of reflexivity remains psychologically irreducible because finding oneself in unscripted situations is as much about the structured nature of the new situation as it is about how the individual found himself confronting it. From the biographical accounts given by interviewees, it is possible to venture two scenarios that are propitious to becoming self-reliant, and thus prone to the autonomous mode of reflexivity becoming dominant.

Home alone

On the first scenario, initial 'contextual discontinuity' can arise when the natal context allows the subject freedom to encounter novel situations. If they are relished rather than repudiated, the subject's experiential repertoire becomes progressively discontinuous with that of other family members. This particular and potential source of self-reliance implies nothing negative about inter-personal relations within the family or local environment. It is simply that the young subject has extended his own repertoire of experiences beyond those of 'similars and familiars'. Simultaneously, within his domain of (satisfying or pleasurable) private experience he has acquired an independence leading him to trust his own resources – one that may later develop into full autonomous reflexivity. This is because he has shed the fundamental belief that his natal context is co-extensive with the world and that 'his world' is familiar to family members and similar to theirs.

Alternatively, on the second scenario, 'contextual discontinuity' may be initiated by dysfunctionalities within the natal context. Some of these stem from ineluctable contingencies such as death of a parent or adoption, others from disruptive divorces, yet others from bullying at school, still others from conditions like dyslexia. It is not these events or conditions in themselves that are crucial, but rather how they affect the family dynamics in which the subject is embroiled. Generically, it is when the family and/or local environment fail to supply the subject with familiarity and to embrace him within the fold of similarity that the individual is edged into a realm of 'aloneness'. Whether through simple neglect, the development of intense rivalry with a parent, aggressively competitive sibling relations or hostility at school, the subject's reliance upon his own resources has to enlarge, precisely because the natal context has grown small in relation to supplying his needs – that is, if he is not to go under or to undergo fracturing.[5] Independence is forced upon the individual if he

---

[5] See Margaret S. Archer, *Structure, Agency and the Internal Conversation*, Cambridge, Cambridge University Press, 2003, ch. 9 for a discussion of 'fractured reflexivity'.

is to survive within the domestic context; whether he thrives depends upon his becoming sufficiently self-reliant to develop an autonomous reflexivity that enables him to 'keep his own end up'.

On this second scenario, the natal context has fallen short of the individual by forcing unscripted situations and confrontations upon him; in the previous scenario it had simply given him the freedom to encounter them. *The common denominator is that in both types of cases the similarity and familiarity that underlies communicative reflexivity is absent.* All of these subjects are, to different degrees, 'home alone'. One of the most crucial results – to which the next section is devoted – is what these people do with their aloneness at home. One of the most overt consequences is their marked tendency to leave home, often as soon as possible, and never to return to their natal context except as visitors.

Let us take these two scenarios in turn, although in some cases they overlap. Nick (the self-employed builder) gives the most interesting insight into the 'freedom and independence scenario' because he also volunteers his own interpretation of its enduring effects upon the kind of person he has become and the type of reflexivity which predominates for him.[6] From chapter 3 it will be recalled that Nick treasured his privacy and sought time alone for his inner deliberations. His father is a social worker, as is his sister, and his mother works in the city's register office. On Nick's account, his parents provided a liberal environment with few prohibitions and no curfews, whose ambience was warm and tension-free: 'I was lucky and fortunate that my parents were always around and are still together now. I had quite a lot of freedom when I was younger and I think that's why I'm quite independent now: no curfew, I was never grounded. I think that's one of the big things that has made me independent and quite confident. My mum and dad laugh about it now – I just used to get on my bike and go, go for miles on my bike, probably up to when I was about seventeen. I'm still like that now, if I haven't got the kids and I've got no work, I just go out for a drive somewhere. I find it very hard to stay in – always got to be doing something. My parents gave me quite a free rein through my upbringing . . . Don't get me wrong, they used to worry about me! I was terrible, I just used to go missing from an early age and it got to the stage where they'd still look for me but not be worried because it was normal for me to go off on my bike . . . I've always done a lot of things on my own. I haven't been a complete loner but I can do things on my own. I have friends who ring me up to do things, whereas I can go out and do things on my own – I don't need people around me to

---

[6] Nick is one of the three interviewees to have the maximum score of 7.00 for autonomous reflexivity on ICONI, the others being Rachel and Abigail.

enjoy myself. I don't do any cycling at all now but I like my shooting and my fishing, I like my quality time on my own, time with people not around me. I might not be thinking about anything or I might have something on my mind, but it's nice just to be out. I really enjoy just walking the dog, stop for a pint – makes me quite content.' It also made Nick someone who initiated and then amplified his own 'contextual discontinuity'.

Billy (the unemployed driver) and Liz (the primary school head), both only children, make the same point in lower key and both recall stable and amicable parental backgrounds. For Liz, 'I was an only child, so yes I spent quite a bit of time playing by myself – a lot of time . . . When the weather was good in the summertime, I played a lot with other children, but during the wintertime a lot of time would be spent playing on my own at home.' Although these two subjects do not immediately draw any conclusions about their adult selves from these early experiences of freedom and independence, Donna (the young team manager in banking) volunteers consequences that are very similar to Nick's self-diagnosis. 'I think coming from a large family . . . I wouldn't always have a say with overall decisions. But with personal decisions with my parents, I would say that I had quite a lot of independence and freedom. There'd be areas where there'd be boundaries, but there'd be others where maybe I could push it bit by bit . . . From the way that my parents were with me I was very confident, very dominant. I could do a lot of things that other teenagers my age wouldn't do, I was very self-sufficient. If I was fifteen and wanted to go to a pub or a nightclub I would never lie to my parents . . . possibly friends I've had would lie, whereas I was straight to the point . . . There would be time that I needed to spend by myself, which I still do, just reading and drawing, away from everybody . . . I did like to be with people but I would need time by myself. That's still the case. If I don't get time by myself just to de-stress, de-work, just to read and sit with nobody and nothing, I get quite narky if I don't get it. It wouldn't be every day, it might just be once every couple of weeks I might spend a whole day by myself.' Significantly, Donna had moved out of the parental home and bought her own house by the time she was twenty-one.

Lastly, in this same vein, there is Oliver (the financial consultant), growing up in Northern Ireland where his father, with whom he had a good relationship, received multiple death threats as a member of the Royal Ulster Constabulary: 'I was pretty independent as a younger person. I wouldn't class myself as being a confident person when I was younger, I would have said that I was quite quiet and reserved. Well, now I'm older, wiser, much louder and much more self-confident about myself. It's a bit like buying a suit that's too big, I've grown into it!' Yet, it already fitted sufficiently well for him to leave the family behind when in his early twenties, to go to work in London and to find being the lone 'Man from the Pru' a 'fantastic experience', knocking on doors hoping to sell insurance policies.

Clive (the nursery manager) gives a brief reflection upon his parents' separation, when he was sixteen, which forms a link to the blacker scenario, but also reinforces the point that it is the qualitative manner in which this event took place that matters: 'It was fairly amicable – I think they'd spent a lot of time up to that point staying together for the sake of the family. They came to the decision that I was old enough and therefore they could spend time apart. I'm just thinking about whether it had an effect or not. I suppose – freedom! It gave you the opportunity to get what you always wanted actually . . . At that age it was basically they were more concerned about what they were doing in their lives and less worried what I was doing in mine. It does seem like freedom . . . possibly even a reduction in rules; it was a house that was governed by rules . . . It just felt like I can do whatever I like.' In other words, 'freedom' and 'independence', as given by parents or deriving from parental activities, are what enable subjects to *make for their own 'contextual discontinuity'*.

On the second scenario, other interviewees had contextual discontinuity thrust upon them. Four of them experienced it with great severity. We have already heard Martin's story of being passed from pillar to post seven times whilst in care and then failing to establish any deep relationship with his adoptive parents. For Abigail (the 48-year-old manager of a finance department), the first two decades of her life were so horrendous as to render the notion of 'contextual discontinuity' euphemistic. Also an only child, Abbie was the daughter of what she sees as a social misalliance – a middle-class mother from a professional background who married a factory operative. At the age of six, 'suddenly my secure world fell apart – my mum left. Obviously at that time you aren't aware of the reasons, but I can never remember up to that point being insecure or unloved or anything . . . In those days Social Services didn't get involved or anything, I don't think they knew what was going on. I can remember coming home from school and sometimes I'd be sleeping round next door on a lilo on the floor, sometimes I'd be down at my auntie's who'd got a pub in [a nearby neighbourhood]. I can remember a period of being very, very young and not knowing where I was going next.'

Eighteen months later, Abbie and her father moved in with his working-class parents, which entailed her changing from a good primary school in the better part of Coventry to its opposite. For Abbie, this change deeply undermined her self-confidence. 'If you've had the sort of experiences that I've had, I think you're maybe a little more wary, more nervy, you're not as confident, so I think educationally possibly you suffer. I can remember my dad being told before I took my 11 plus that I should pass it but they didn't think that I would. They said I had the ability to pass it but they didn't think I would and I didn't.' Her father then decided that if Abbie was to attend a secondary modern school, he would try to ensure that it was of a decent standard and thus they moved back to his original marital home.

Her secondary school experience was one of unmitigated bullying: 'kids are cruel, they were cruel about my nose, they were cruel about my bust, they were cruel about a lot of things about me. When you come from a background where you're not as confident as all that, it does knock – so whatever confidence you've got is being chipped at.' At the same time, Abbie and her father had to 'muck in together', which meant she cooked, shopped, went to the launderette, did the housework and controlled the domestic budget, all by the age of eleven or twelve. As Abbie says, 'I suppose I had far too much freedom from that age.' Certainly, with her self-esteem spiralling still downwards, friendless, ashamed of her home and confronted with financial decisions no child should be expected to make, Abigail had no *confidents/es*, no confidence and few resources of her own with which to make anything positive out of her freedom and independence.

When she was fourteen, her father started to work nights and took his widowed mother dancing at weekends. Abbie was literally 'home alone' and took the opportunity to try drumming up the friendship network she lacked: 'when teenagers know you've got the house to yourself – well, as you can imagine, we must have been the family that the neighbours hated. I was bringing half the motorcycle club back and all sorts. I started to get in with some bad influences and I drank a lot from an early age, I was having sex before I should have been having sex, everything – had a go at taking drugs . . . I think again that is maybe from feeling inadequate, you feel inadequate and you make more of your mistakes, you dwell more on the negatives . . . I would say at that stage that my self-esteem was low – you don't aspire to where you should aspire to . . . I suppose I dressed tartily and picked up the lads that liked that sort of woman . . . The first chap I got heavily involved with, Mark, he was a rebel and that's what attracted me to him, he wouldn't conform. He was awful, he treated me like absolute dirt and I let him – he didn't give a damn, he'd turn up and treat me like a sex object when it suited him.' Abigail's 'contextual discontinuity', her aloneness and battered confidence are indisputable and more than enough to have prompted fracturing; how she recruited her inner resources to develop into an autonomous reflexive will be told later.

The circumstances that promote isolation and prompt increasing 'contextual discontinuity' do not have to be horror stories like Abigail's. When growing up, Damian (the manager of two shops) had good relations within his intermediate-class family, but greater problems with his peers. Tersely he recalls that 'from say ten onwards, I was like isolated into my bedroom'. It seems that he himself only slowly recognised his gay orientation and tried to cover it at secondary school by consorting with girlfriends, but the concealment was only partially successful: 'Physical education and games, I absolutely hated the whole thing about it. I hated the taunting . . . I wasn't exactly bullied but I was made to feel that I was different.' When he decided to 'come out' at sixteen, this was also the time that he moved out of his parental home. It was not that he was 'booted out'; nevertheless, his parents showed their intolerance of his difference: 'They did take it bad. I only told my mum and then I told her in a letter, it was never face to face and it was never mentioned. It's never mentioned to this day although they know I live with my partner and have lived with him for nine years . . . Yes, they know him, they come and stay with us, but they never mention gay or anything like that.' Thus, Damian's lack of similarity progressively edged him out of his familiar and familial context by isolation, taunting and intolerance, leaving him little alternative but to embrace 'contextual discontinuity' and to make something of it – as an autonomous reflexive.

The circumstances that may ultimately nudge subjects out of their natal contexts can take the form of an in-house drama, with many acts preceding its finale. Rachel (the young manager of a hairdressing salon) comes from a middle-class family whose internal dysfunctions progressively served to sharpen her self-reliance. At the very beginning of the interview, she perspicaciously highlights two events that she believes made her the successful and independent person she now is at twenty-five. Firstly, Rachel pinpoints being diagnosed as dyslexic when she was eight. Although her mother (a deputy head) understood this condition, she would still broadcast her view that Rachel was destined for housewifery, whilst her sister would become the businesswoman and her brother a professional. As Rachel herself sees it, her capacity to repudiate this characterisation and to resist its internalisation sprang from her condition itself and its propensity to encourage thoughtfulness: 'Just generally, because I'm dyslexic I always double think; if I read something I have to read it out loud as well because in my head I can see it differently than what actually it is . . . so I always think over a lot of things all the time.'

Lone thinking began by trying to avoid being stigmatised in the family as the 'thick one' and was intensified two years later when her parents separated. Her father was lost to her, transformed from the church deacon into the unfaithful/drinking/swearing stranger, and an unhealthy relationship unfolded with her mother: 'I get a lot of flak for mistakes that have happened in her life, she always puts me down. She can't ever compliment me really because she sees me in her, though she doesn't admit it.' Rachel cannot reciprocate, not only because the price would be to become her mother's negative foil, but also because she herself sees no similarity to her mother – the professional educator – beyond a certain physical resemblance. Over the years, a nasty rivalry intensified between the two, in which Rachel felt driven to accentuate their difference in order to bolster her self-esteem, and mother sought to be queen of her own turf and of her daughter's too.

In consequence, Rachel became isolated within this household of 'achievers', where every achievement of her own was denigrated but promptly capped by her mother: 'she went and got a sports car because I had one and didn't want me to have a nicer one. She'll criticise things in my house and then I'll go to her house and she's done things like I have in mine, so it's obvious she does like it really. And she wants to grow her hair to have her hair like mine . . .' Petty competitiveness was all pervasive and their struggle over wedding outfits (mother's imitation driving Rachel to disgruntled innovation) seems to have overshadowed both sets of nuptials. Rather than succumb, Rachel has marshalled all her inner resources to succeed on her own terms in her own field, by establishing her difference: 'None of my family could stand in my way – well, I wouldn't let them anyway. I will do what I want to do.' That meant moving out of the family home, buying her own house and thinking about her own future independently.

Hands-on satisfaction

It might be thought that these various forms of 'aloneness' would foster a rich fantasy life, with Nick pedalling along towards his own *Grand Meaulnes* adventure, Rachel contemplating some life-style her mother could not outdo, or Billy dreaming of his castle in Spain. On the contrary, autonomous reflexives are not daydreamers, quite simply because they cannot afford to be. As Donna puts it, 'I wouldn't say I'm a daydreamer,' since, if she makes a mistake, an ideal outcome is only dwelt upon momentarily and with practical intent: 'it would be a case of, oh if I'd done it this way maybe that could have happened – but that to me is a split second thing . . . If I have made a mistake, it will just be, right, this has happened, what am I going to do to rectify it?' Autonomous reflexives are committed to the reality principle and they have to be. Because they have broken with contextual guidelines – relayed by the normative conventionality of interlocutors – in favour of making their own way through the world, they can only navigate by monitoring their actual circumstances closely.

Fantasy is a luxury that they cannot afford and they are aware of this. They know that there is a goodly quota of unforeseeable contingencies over which they have no control. Thus, their task is to master the controllable, to minimise the uncontrollable and to live with the unavoidable. As Ralph puts it forcefully, 'I like real things and, if I get to the stage of fantasising, I blot it out straightaway because it's not going to happen – it might but you have no control over it, so if it happens it's just going to come along and bowl you over.' Things have indeed intervened and bowled over Ralph's best laid plans, as will be seen, but this is not necessary in order for subjects to respect the *bouleversements* that contingency may introduce into their lives. They do so rather than retreating into escapist fantasy and replacing the need for practical mastery with wish fulfilment. As Nick explains his outlook, 'I'm not really a daydreamer. I suppose the word's a realist. Like I say with the thinking side of it – I think about stuff that's actually going on in my life, but I don't really daydream, like, oh I'd like to win the lottery and stuff like that. If things like that happen along the way then they happen.' As 'realistic' people, three themes are regularly reiterated by these autonomous reflexives: keep your mind on your job (which means your feet on the ground); learn from your own mistakes (including means of rectification); and plan intensively for that which is foreseeable – in tiny brushstrokes for tomorrow and in broad, bold outline for the months and years ahead.

If this 'realistic' orientation is not a psychological disposition, what prompted its development in our autonomous subjects? The sequence appears to be that, firstly, because of their aloneness at home when young, these interviewees immersed themselves in practical activities requiring little, if any, social interaction. Through this they learned the discipline of practice, entailing and ingraining self-monitoring, as intrinsic to task achievement, and displacing fantasy as inimical to it. Predictably, the twelve interviewees focused upon very different activities when young. For Martin, Tony and Donna, it was art and drawing; for Oliver and Liz, it was sports; for Nick, Ralph and Billy, it was countryside pursuits; for Clive and Abigail, it was personal extensions of school subjects, computing and maths respectively; and for Rachel and Damian, it was an interest in cooking.

Secondly, a positive reinforcement loop engages between deriving satisfaction from an activity and intensified efforts to become proficient at it, meaning that more of one's time and one's self are invested in it. Subsequently, some subjects appropriate this talent for practical activities as part of their self-definition. Thus, as Nick says tersely, he is for 'the practicalities, not the academic'. More expansively, Rachel explains her old anxieties about not being 'academic' like her siblings. 'I used to say, why have you [the deity?] made me thick? Those two are dead bright and I'm going to end up stacking shelves in Tesco's.' Gradually she came to define herself, in opposition to them, as 'practical'. 'I'm good at practical things, I'm good at cooking . . . My Mum's always encouraged me in that area.' Although this may have been nurturing what mother saw as second best or *faute de mieux* for Rachel, her practical skills enabled her to hold up her own end within the family by accentuating these strengths. Thus, she relishes the memory of herself and her sister enrolling on a short course as teenagers: 'It was lovely when we both did beauty because I'm really good at doing make-up and my sister hasn't got a clue and I was the best – I beat my sister! . . . It was just nice that there was something I'm better at . . . she used to say I was thick all the time.'

Others immediately decided that the youthful hobbies, on which most had lavished much time and effort, obviously signposted their future careers. This is another aspect of the positive feedback loop, namely hands-on satisfaction nurtures a desire for more of it to the point of making a career out of it. Often, as will be seen in a moment, this transition represented a false start but, given their state of knowledge about self and society, it was a very understandable one. Thus Martin, Donna and Tony all enrolled on degree courses centred upon art. Tony, for whom this entailed extricating himself from his working-class background and routine factory job, demonstrates how much commitment he envisaged devoting to his hands-on artistic activities: 'I started doing life drawing, a life drawing class with a bit of painting, and I kind of eventually came to the realisation that this is what I want to do all day. I want to spend my life – I don't want to come to the factory and spend two hours at night doing this, I want to do this all the time.'

For Damian, hating the school taunting he received for his 'difference' and retreating for much of the time to his bedroom, it was amidst ordinary domestic activities that he discerned his *métier*. It came from 'the day to day chores – cleaning and cooking, that's why I decided to go into cooking I think . . . I used to do my fair share around the house, not because I was made to, I enjoyed it. After I left school I chose to do catering.' Very differently with Abigail, the one bright, redemptive point through all her vicissitudes as a young woman was her ability to acquire jobs that called upon her mathematical skills, extended their applications and eventually enabled her to gain professional qualifications in accountancy.

If 'A puppy is not only for Christmas . . .', then it seems, too, that a practical interest is also for life. As was seen in chapter 3, Martin was still enjoying art and as rather more than a Sunday painter. The same is true of Tony as well as of Donna, who is currently enrolled on a life drawing class at the city's university. Oliver and Liz have kept up their sporting lives, and Nick, who was a young hunt foot-follower, continues with his field sports. Ralph, now at rock bottom with his luck and confined to a small rented flat, plans his return to countryside activities: 'having lived in this area when it was greenfield, I'm very much a country guy [with] certain pursuits I like to follow. Animals are one, and you can't do that from where I am at the moment. I have to find a property where I've got at least a small portion of land, even if it comes down to only keeping chickens in a run or ducks in a little pond or whatever it may be, and get a dog.' The hands-on source of satisfaction continues and it represents a continuing involvement with the practical order rather than the kind of leisure activities that are openings to or dependent upon the social order.

False starts and lighting up

The successful translation of these practical interests and skills into an absorbing job or career is necessarily a hit and miss affair. As Clive puts it, 'how do you decide what you want to do in life if you've never done that particular job? And even if you liked it for a week, do you want to do that for the rest of your life? So really it's a case of you try something out and if it's not any good, then you'd look to see if there's something else out there to do.' Given lack of knowledge about self and society, it is unsurprising that mistakes are made because subjects are following their noses and sniffing out what appeals most amongst options that are readily accessible to them in society. If these do not satisfy, then rectification(s) follows until the predilections of the subject are well matched to a particular job description. However, we must be careful not to think of 'matching' as if there were fixed personal properties and an equally fixed array of available occupational outlets, the only question being how long it takes for the two to get together.

Instead, we are talking about two sets of properties and powers, the micro- (the individual's nascent proclivities and skills) and the macro- (the social distribution of occupational openings). To speak of 'matching' the two not only implies that both are static but also denies interaction between them. Effectively, it denies the fact that micro-properties can be modified by learning and experience and, also, that other micro-powers can intervene to rupture 'good matches'. Equally, it neglects the fact that macro-occupational enablements foster the projects of some people, whilst the structural distributions of occupational opportunities are major obstacles to others in achieving their projects. *All of these are matters of interplay between the working individual and the employment structure of society, in which both undergo modification.* The following sections will track variations in the kinds of interplay involved for the interviewees and demonstrate how, despite this variety, the tendency towards upward social mobility remains marked.

Personal powers: getting it right and getting it wrong

Let us begin with the simpler cluster of cases, those subjects who got it right first time and those who got it wrong initially but were successful in making rapid rectifications. Those whose first jobs and careers led them to 'light up' took posts that were broadly commensurate with their socio-economic backgrounds. However, this is rarely a simple matter of social reproduction. There is always a story about active agents to be told and sometimes their personal properties seriously disrupt any reproductive story-line. Nevertheless, what is true of this cluster is that structural factors play a relatively small part in their occupational biographies, above and beyond establishing individuals' starting positions.

The simplest case of being right first time is that of Liz. Coming from an intermediate family and attending a grammar school, the only job she considered (apart from a brief flirtation with air hostessing) was teaching: 'Always teaching from the beginning – playing schools . . . that stuck with me. I can remember playing school with my blackboard and easel when I was about seven or eight.' During her secondary education Liz seems to have lit up immediately and unerringly: 'what gives me the buzz is when people learn – that's what's given me the buzz since I've become a teacher and probably before then too. You know when you see a penny drop if you've explained something to somebody and suddenly it's become crystal clear to them, that's what gives me a buzz.' Liz went straight on from school to gain a teaching certificate and a post as a primary teacher and, eventually, became a school head.

The only other subject who approximates to this ease of transition is Rachel. From the age of seven she had wanted to be a hairdresser – a project that she confirmed in her own mind by becoming a 'Saturday girl', working in a salon from the age of fourteen until leaving school at sixteen. She immediately went on to full-time employment, whilst working for her National Vocational Qualifications in hairdressing and, later, in beauty care: 'I really wanted to do something and I was good at what I did.' Yet, sub-textually, this career also enabled Rachel to establish herself as different but successful in relation to her more academically inclined family. Her lighting up came immediately: 'when I was in my first year I won a competition for my hairdressing and again when I was in my second year and I was only training then! It was like "I've done something and I'm the best"! And like, with my brother and my sister, I'd never been the best at anything. I was better at cooking and stuff but I'd never won anything and I cried when I had it. I was like "Mum, I'm the best of a hundred people!" I was so proud going off and winning.' This is far from simple social reproduction and entailed Rachel coining her own cultural capital. Her only problem was with the social order, with the bitchiness she had anticipated in these greenhouses-of-good-looks. For this reason, Rachel tried and quit seven salons in five years before finding an acceptable working environment. After three years in the latter, she was promoted to salon manager at twenty-four and is already planning for further advancement. It should be noted that Rachel has become socially mobile in relation to her own starting point, but that upward mobility would not be registered compared with her socio-economic background.

Damian is of particular interest amongst those getting it right first time, because two of his other personal concerns later intervened to disrupt this 'match' and provoked occupational reorientation, despite the significant upward social mobility he had already achieved. 'Catering was always what I wanted to do,' but, soon after starting training, he placed a personal restriction on his prospects. 'When I left school I did a catering course, a two-year City and Guilds. I became vegetarian during that [time] so that niched my market. I wouldn't have wanted to touch meat and fish. It would have to be like a vegetarian restaurant or vegetarian bed and breakfast . . . It's something I wanted to do and when I did it – after the City and Guilds I went on to a management course, an HND, and that's when we were sent on a placement for six months. They sent me to London and that's when I worked at the big veggie restaurant and that's when I thought, great, this is what I want.' Damian had undoubtedly lit up, but he realised the limited opportunities outside London, the need for considerable capital to set up his own vegetarian restaurant and that, fifteen years ago, 'I certainly couldn't set up in Coventry.' Despite these nagging doubts, Damian found an acceptable hotel post in East Anglia and, over four years, 'worked myself up . . . I wasn't exactly their licensee manager but I was covering management.'

Towards the end of this period, Damian met his long-term partner and a second personal consideration came into play, namely the incompatibility between his partnership and catering career. 'Well, the anti-social hours . . . would I still have time with [partner]? So time was a big thing . . . And I thought management will stand me in good stead whatever I do. So that was something [I had] under my belt and I thought, well, if I don't proceed with catering I'll go and do management . . . retail is usually nine to five, so I think that's why I chose what I did . . . It wasn't a decision I made lightly.' Reorientation was neither light nor easy because Damian had not got it wrong the first time. Indeed, he still thinks of running a bed and breakfast by the sea, but twenty years further down the track. Various experiences in retail (a record shop and working for a high-street chemist) proved unsatisfying apart from a short spell with Oxfam, which 'was great'. Damian decided to make his second career on this basis and applied to become manager of a different charity shop. After a year in post, which he found very enjoyable, he was doing so well that he was offered a second shop to run. Eighteen months after that he is now looking further ahead: 'In the future, yes, I'd like to have my boss's job. She looks after ten shops, so that's my next phase, that's what – I intend to stay with the charity, in the charity business.' Lighting up for a second time is perfectly possible and quite congruent with a continued thrust towards upward occupational mobility.

This serves as a link to another cluster of interviewees,[7] ones who simply got it wrong the first time but succeeded in putting it right. Donna's is a short story, not because she is only twenty-two but because rectification was almost immediate. Early on at school, 'I decided I wanted to be a graphic designer and I was really set on it. Art was always one of my best subjects, I knew I was good at it and thought I'd stay in that area. As the years went on, it may have changed a bit but it was always the same sector, always art . . . then I came to [the city's university] and started the art and design foundation course, to see which area of art I'd like to specialise in. After doing six months I thought I wasn't – because I was almost being forced to do art, I wasn't motivated and started not to enjoy it. So I decided to stop and decided to get a job.' Being one of six children, 'I knew I had to get a job straightaway until I decided what I was going to do. And by a stroke of luck I suppose I got into the job and followed the path I'm doing.' Electronic banking was intended as a stop-gap but acted as an ignition key: 'I really enjoy it and want to put so much more time and effort into it . . . at school I wasn't a very well-developed individual, I was just a very average sort of kid whereas there were so many academic types, but now I find I can shine.' Having lit up, Donna quickly got to NVQ (level 3) and began extending her portfolio with short management courses at the university. Meanwhile, in the three years she has been with her current employer she has been promoted annually: from customer service agent, to team co-ordinator and then to team manager. Good luck may have initiated Donna's quick rise, but she has grasped the opportunity with both hands and, as she sees it, 'this job I'm doing now is building me up for something much bigger'.

Initial mistakes come in many forms, but Oliver is ironic about his own: 'I drifted into the Inland Revenue really and I suppose it was the comfort

---

[7] Nick's story tracks Martin's quite closely, but he ends up taking the self-employment option.

zone,' as far away as he could get from Northern Ireland's troubles and his own father's death threats. In Ulster, it failed to satisfy; yet he found that it still failed to give fulfilment once he had moved to London: 'as I developed as a person I felt a bit trapped really within it . . . It was very much the lack of opportunity there.' Rather than doing a *volte face*, Oliver remarshalled his resources and decided to enter financial services, working semi-independently in south London, where he lit up immediately: 'Brixton was very cosmopolitan, lots of West Indian people lived there – it was a fantastic experience, a real learning curve . . . but it was fantastic, I really enjoyed it.' He agrees 'it was a massive risk because I'd never sold anything in my life . . . it was effectively running my own franchise.' Gradually, Oliver advanced from selling insurance and dealing with claims, to personal taxation planner (having gained the extra qualification), to being a financial consultant who now wins national prizes for his performance.

Social powers: structural constraints/enablements and personal projects

So far, these have all been stories about how personal powers meshed with the structured distribution of available occupations or clashed with it. When things went wrong, it was because the individual got it wrong to begin with or through a later change in personal priorities. However, there is a very different cluster of cases where both 'lighting up' and social mobility depended upon a battle between personal projects and structural constraints, or upon structural enablements facilitating projects that might not even have been conceived without them.

Billy's chequered occupational biography provides the most severe and protracted struggle between structural constraints and an unflagging personal determination to overcome them in order to get on. It represents a stark confrontation between structural and personal powers because there is only a single point at which Billy could have done otherwise and, probably, made a difference to his trajectory and its outcome. With that one exception, he has contended with both his disadvantageous natal placement and multiple redundancies stemming from the national slump in manufacturing industry, without his personal concerns deflecting him from his avowed goal of upward social mobility or, as he puts it, 'working myself up'.

As the son of a miner, who had no intention of going down the pit himself, Billy left school at fifteen and immediately became a baker's delivery boy on a bicycle. The attraction was 'being outdoors – I've been outdoors nearly all my life'. Once he passed his driving test, thus acquiring the sole formal qualification he ever possessed, Billy was on the look-out for better prospects. He soon moved to become driver for a wholesale grocer's warehouse and was quickly 'promoted up to the supervisor of the warehouse'. This is significant because it is the beginning of Billy's informal expertise in stock control. This and his (diversifying) driving ability were the two skills with which Billy took on the occupational structure of the Midlands.

Retrospectively, he considers the vocational preparation he received at school to have been inadequate: 'in them days they didn't seem to give you the right guidance. I wish I'd gone into, like, an electrician or a plumber or something like that . . . where there was a trade. I think that's the one mistake I did make. That's the one regret I think I have got [especially] if you're made redundant . . . My friend who was an electrician was lucky because the firm he went for were doing apprenticeships at the time. I suppose I could have gone there and pushed there – whereas I was silly and went for a job that I wanted to do and liked doing at the time and you can't go back.' When he was first made redundant, in his early twenties, was it really too late to gain a trade?

On the one hand, he quickly gained re-employment: 'I thought I could better myself again and went to an engineering company. They made all the blades for turbine engines – that was quite interesting.' There was some possibility that Billy could have undergone training as a machine setter within this firm. On the other hand, Billy was then courting and this new personal concern seems to have led to the one mistake for which he reproaches himself. 'I did think about it all through until I was married – going for an apprenticeship – till twenty-four, because in them days it wasn't very late in life. It is today, but in them days they would have took people older. Then I thought, "Well, this job seems pretty good." After that I didn't bother with any apprenticeship, I just went for the jobs where I could use my skills and progress in the company.' He certainly did, but he also ensured that his own son became a skilled mechanic: 'I made him go into something where he's got a trade. I said, don't do what I've done.'

Once again he enjoyed the job for its variety, gained additional licences, and gradually escaped from monotony into a supervisory position. Looking back Billy comments: 'I think most of the jobs I've done have been what I've been interested in because you wouldn't go for the job if you weren't. It's like the forklift job . . . there's nothing there to do, is there? You can't think, well, I've got to do this today, I've got to sort this out – there's nothing there, you're just driving a forklift – no motivation.' Conversely, what he seeks is 'the challenge, the variety' and, as he put it, 'what I can achieve by doing particular projects'. However, after he had been with the engineering company for ten years, demand fell off and he was made redundant again. Once more, and for another ten-year period, the same scenario was played out when he was employed by a wholesale stationers: 'I started off as a driver and then I worked myself up again,' but the company became short of orders and, for the fourth time, Billy was looking for new employment.

By the age of fifty he had developed a strategy: 'If you're going to do driving, go somewhere where you know you can advance yourself . . . go to an agency and do driving for the agency and then say, "Look, I've experience doing so and so." ' In this way he got a job at the local freight airport: 'the reason I went for the job at the airport [was] it had got driver/storeman, so when I wasn't driving I was actually in the stores, so that's where I learned all about the stores, the procedures'. At this juncture, Billy was approached by his previous employers and asked to return to his old job. It was the urge for promotion that proved to be the fulcrum in this dilemma: 'So there was two jobs that I liked and I thought where I am I can progress more than going back to that job – if there were two jobs and one was progressing, I'd go for that and be doing more.' His judgement was good, not only because the previous concern shortly went bankrupt, but also because the airport finally allowed him the responsibility he sought. 'I took over running the stores myself – the chap who was running it before didn't make a very good job, and I brought it all round and everyone said: "What a good job you made." ' Billy clearly enjoyed this immensely and supplied extraordinary detail about the inspection of aircraft parts and assigning shelf-life to components according to the Civil Aviation Authority's regulations. What he particularly relished was assuming responsibility: 'I like to think for myself, not as a team player – I'd rather think on my own and do it myself.'

For nine years he found the work thoroughly satisfying: 'I did enjoy going there, I looked forward to going . . . it's half the battle, isn't it, if you can go to work and there's something there that interests me.' Unfortunately, sixty was the retirement age and although it was agreed that Billy could stay on, the airport was taken over and the new management presented him with the choice between accepting severance pay or becoming a baggage handler. Reluctantly, he took the former and has now been unemployed for two years. Equally, he is unready to collect his benefits meekly and to concede victory to the powers of structural constraints because he has another project in mind.

Who did win in this work history of a socially and educationally disadvantaged man, with only a couple of skills in his armoury, confronting the decline in manufacturing industry and being repeatedly returned to square one through redundancy? In Billy's view, he did: 'I think I did, yes, because in at least three jobs I have progressed from where I started, so

I've done well.' That is objectively the case and not merely Billy's subjective opinion. Yet, on any empiricist study of social mobility, he would not be considered as upwardly mobile at this point in time, either in relation to his social background or in relation to his first job. However, this brief narrative has shown the thrust towards upward mobility to be as strong, or stronger, in Billy's occupational projects than in most others, including those of some autonomous reflexives. Nevertheless, it remains the case that the struggle was always unequal, with the stringency of constraints stacking the cards heavily against Billy.

Taking place two generations later, Tony's story of extricating himself from unskilled work in a chocolate factory shows two major differences. Firstly, the availability of grants for a return to education – and then for a first degree and later a higher degree – introduced a new source of enablements for those with Billy's type of motivation. These allowed Tony to light up at a much higher wattage than was ever permitted to Billy. Secondly, however, it also illustrates the utter indispensability of agential projects if overcoming structural constraints is to usher in upward social mobility. Although Tony now has a PhD, he cannot (as yet) use his personal powers to design an occupational project in which he is willing to invest himself. Thus, in his late thirties he maintains himself through non-committing, temporary jobs and freelance research. Despite the distance that now removes him from the chocolate factory, Tony too would not empirically register upward occupational mobility.

Enablements, as it cannot be repeated too often, require a human project to enable. Such projects may have been nurtured by the subject quite independently from his later encounter with a structural property enabling its accomplishment. Alternatively, the very prominence of an enablement making a certain course(s) of action appear easy and profitable to accomplish, may itself encourage the adoption of cognate projects. What follows is a brief examination of two subjects who approximate respectively to each scenario.

Clive took a couple of years out as a driver after his A-levels in order to think seriously about his future career and then, he says, 'basically through my interest, being a very practical person, I moved into being an engineer and repairing machines'. This was the co-product of an early interest in hardware and an enablement to realise it easily in a particular direction: 'Actually, the company I was working for, their necessities changed. The industry was changing slightly and it was a case of "Can you just help out and do this?" And then I took courses on different machines and the education went through the engineering side.' Although the work began well – 'it started off as always a challenge to overcome a problem' – the interest soon petered out: 'the problems always tended to be the same, the faults were always the same, the things you had to do were always the same . . . And I was thinking, "Now where can I go from here?" '

By then, Clive had been married for two years and their first child was born. His son's growth proved to be an unexpected source of fascination to Clive, a new practical interest that he had never suspected he possessed: 'watching him develop, seeing how he developed and my input into his development was so fantastic and I thought, how can I get over there, how can I do this job?' The answer to that could not have been easier. It was enabled by the fact that his mother owned and ran a small string of children's nurseries. But she had been doing this since Clive left school and thus he could have worked in the family business immediately had he been interested. Therefore, it was only when involvement with his son led to the germination of this project that the existence of the business literally became an enablement to Clive. Certainly it was as available and attractive as they ever come: 'This is actually our fourth business, and she's [mother] developed new ones. It's meant that she's wanted to spend less time here in this particular one and she said, "Well, do you fancy coming over here and helping out?" Actually, we've always been helping out on the maintenance side of the building . . . but it was more hands on, more working with the children and working within the business. Obviously, I then took the courses and here I am.'

If structural factors handed Clive the fulfilment of his new dreams on a platter, leaving him a happy man with plenty of scope for his expansionist ambitions, they played havoc with Ralph and his working life. From first to last Ralph describes himself as a 'country guy'. However, soon after leaving school and prompted by his desire to own a car, he was easily seduced into misrecognising his practical concerns by the boom in automobile manufacturing and sales in the Midlands: 'So I then followed my interest in motor cars, which really started from Day One – this was Motown, UK in that day and age.' At the start he undoubtedly benefited from this structural enablement as he joined the leading car rental agency who were 'great trainers, they would identify your weak spots and strengths and build upon them. They would only ever promote from within and were one hundred per cent supportive of anyone who worked for them. If you gave them a hundred per cent they would give one hundred and ten per cent back . . . I knew that even if I wasn't planning what was going to happen to me, they were.'

Within a very few years he moved from 'rental rep', to branch manager and had the area managership in his sights. Retrospectively, Ralph was to look at this rental agency with considerable ambiguity because of how it had remoulded both him and his projects: 'I laud it for what they've given me and sometimes I hate it – I think overall I would put it down to some of the training I got with them. I was a green kid from Coventry and they turned me into something else. My mum often said to me, especially when I was earning lots of money, "I wish you'd get yourself a proper job," and I look back now and think Mother was right . . . They instigated in me the need to drive forward.' When he did not gain the expected promotion, Ralph was angry but undismayed: 'I was confident that I could transfer my skills to another rental company,' so he approached competitors and became second in charge of a smaller car rental organisation.

By now, his horizons had undergone considerable elastication and the car trade continued to be buoyant in the early 1970s. Then, two factors came into play simultaneously. On the one hand, Ralph had moved over to sales, fast becoming sales manager as the foreign car franchises began to move in upon the Midlands. On the other hand, he became super-confident about his employability, resigning after rows about commission rates and one-off deals, entering numerous law suits against his employers, but able to move without difficulty between ten different dealerships – moving sideways and then upwards to brand manager. However, after the last row and parting of the ways, Ralph concluded that 'I'd rather steer the ship . . . I wanted to work for somebody who wasn't going to knife me in the back, and I decided in my wisdom that the only person who wasn't going to do that to me was me, so I decided to work for myself, which I then did for about ten years.'

Ralph moved to sole trader status, having identified how much money was to be made through directly importing cars from abroad. As the enterprise grew, Ralph took on staff and offices in Coventry, partly prompted by complaints from neighbours about the six new Mercedes parked in his driveway! After a period of loving the travel, the challenge of learning German 'and making lots of money in the process', the structural enablements that had made this possible gradually turned into their reverse – stringent constraints: 'the biggest killer was price increases at the factories . . . it crept up on us slowly, it's a very dangerous market to deal in and the exchange rate eventually killed us'. As his bank manager told him when he sought to raise money on the back of another business plan, '"You're an entrepreneur" and I suppose in retrospect he's probably right, and what an entrepreneur should do is to recognise an opportunity when it occurs, but pre-empt the demise of that opportunity and go on to the next thing.' Unfortunately, Ralph did not get out fast enough and the 'next thing' paved the way to disaster.

He joined forces with a previous supplier and firstly went into a venture involving importing foreign designer clothes 'at a silly rate' and selling them under a 'site label', until this company went 'up in a ball of flames'.

Then followed an equally dubious enterprise in car leasing based upon offsetting the tax liability on capital gains from property sales, until the bank foreclosed on them. After a final foray into importing fitted car mats from Germany and 'doing body kits and other things', Ralph eventually concluded that they had 'all died of the same plague', the exchange rate, which meant that in his early fifties he finally became unemployed.

Looking back upon his period of upward mobility, Ralph reflects that 'the driving force increased as my family [of four children] grew. I actually became more adventurous in what I did . . . looking at having greater earning power. So it was the growth of my family that said go forward. I pretty well always lived without fear of failure.' Now that he has been unemployed for two years, his outlook has changed. He was first lured upwards by structural enablements and then knocked back down by structural constraints. His aspirations had initially been elasticated but Ralph eventually lost his elasticity. 'I suppose the big change is that to a certain extent you lose direction and you lose the ability to have confidence in your own skills, and then you can convince yourself, if you're not careful, that you're not worthy of anything – that's the danger. I can no longer convince myself specifically what I can do, but I know that I can do something.' That 'something' about which he now dreams is no longer about thrusting upwards occupationally, but is rather about a smallholding, and thus spells a return to his earliest concern with country living – one that had been displaced when 'Motown's' streets seemed paved with gold.

Playing snakes and ladders strategically

The last section demonstrated the impossibility of recounting people's work histories and how they were conditioned by social constraints and enablements without regularly introducing strategic action on the part of these agents. These strategies can now be examined systematically because the employment biographies of most interviewees have been brought up to date. Thus, the present section focuses upon the extent to which these autonomous reflexives now approach their occupational futures in a strategic manner. Generically, such an orientation entails two elements: a self-conscious delineation of the next stage(s) in a subject's desired work project and an awareness of the social conditions likely to promote or hinder its achievement. However, these subjects should not be expected to be master strategists, if only because of their imperfect information and human fallibility.

Nevertheless, there is a quantum difference between being a faulty strategist, as we all must be because of living in an open system, and refusing strategic action altogether in favour of 'gut reactions', 'going with the flow' or 'waiting to see what turns up'. Ralph neatly encapsulated the strategic orientation in his dictum 'recognise an opportunity when it occurs but pre-empt its demise', though he was sadly unable to carry it out himself. He is correct to point out that a strategy is a course of action planned on the basis of *searching for opportunities* (since enablements impinge on people as situations that make desired actions easy to accomplish), but also upon *anticipating and circumventing obstacles* (because constraints are confronted as situations that frustrate the achievement of desired outcomes). Thus the formula for good strategy is to keep a careful weather eye upon both and then to weigh them judiciously against one another.[8]

The opportunities and the obstacles need to be taken into account reflexively in conjunction with each other. 'Defective' strategists are those who are riveted by one alone. Thus, there are 'opportunists', people like Ralph himself, so bent upon never missing a chance for advancement that they are oblivious to circumstances that simultaneously threaten to jeopardise their projects. Equally, there are the 'prudentials', those people who are so hyper-conscious about the constraints their projects could encounter that they temporise, unaware that as time passes they are damaging if not forfeiting the opportunities available to them. There is an example of each amongst the interviewees. Both, like Ralph, provide a salutary warning as to the eventual outcome, despite the fact that, again like Ralph, significant upward mobility characterises large tracts of their occupational trajectories. These two cases are worth a brief preliminary consideration, if only to dispel any notion that autonomous reflexives approximate to rational supermen in their *attempts* to act strategically.

Nick is a clear exemplar of an 'opportunist'. Hating the confines of the school classroom, his vocational aim was to become a gamekeeper, in line with his practical outdoor concerns. He was discouraged from this by the absence of an accessible training course and settled instead for a three-year stint in landscape gardening. When made redundant, his parents encouraged him to enrol on a college course in surveying, but he declined on the grounds of detesting paperwork and enclosure indoors. His decision was also partly motivated by the need to make money, given his marriage, his mortgage and the arrival of his first child. He thus entered factory work for five years, many times clocking up an eighty-four-hour week. In both of his jobs he complained about the monotony and lack of challenge ('a bit mind-numbing at times, really repetitive'), although he

---

[8] This would not make for 'rational man' because that which is subjectively deemed to constitute 'judicious action' is not synonymous with 'instrumental rationality'.

was approaching supervisory status at the factory. Matters came to a head when the breakdown of his marriage coincided with his dismissal from work after being prosecuted for the illicit sale of company products. Nick explains the latter in a telling choice of words: 'I saw the opportunity to make some more money . . .' This phrase is the *leitmotif* of his subsequent career, a reckless grasping of opportunities with almost complete disregard to the obstacles endangering his projects.

Immediately prior to his discharge, Nick had started to take on weekend 'cash jobs' in minor domestic construction and he recalls rather surprisedly: 'I got really busy when people knew I'd lost my job and it really took off.' He saw the chance of becoming self-employed and began working as an unqualified builder erecting home extensions. Certainly, he became a happier man, relishing his outdoor work, its variety, challenges and flexibility, and he is equally certain about 'wanting to get on'. To what extent does this very likeable 'cowboy' temper his opportunism by a wariness that his lack of qualifications in construction work plus his police record mean that there are jobs he should not tackle? In other words, does he show strategic sensitivity about the constraints within which he can safely operate?

Here is his own 'give it a go' philosophy, which presumes that he alone can absorb the costs of his mistakes without further repercussions: 'If I do something once like an extension, something might go disastrously wrong and it might cost me, but the thing is I'll know next time where I went wrong, I'll always learn by my mistakes . . . it won't be as worrying the next time. I don't know whether it comes with experience, but I'd literally have a go with anything and not a lot of things faze me. Where some people will see things and think "No," I shrug it off and say I'll give it a go.' The second enterprise that Nick could not resist acquiring somewhat moderated his approach because this work requires few skills and is unlikely to involve safety issues: 'I've got another business as well, a driveways business. My friend started that up but he's got too busy for it now and I'm with a partner that's doing it. I bought the company off him so I'm doing that as well. I took that on board not knowing much about it but that ticks along and does all right as well. I didn't know nothing about it to start off but my friend offered it to me and he'd done all right at it and you sort of learn as you go along, it's not rocket science!'

One can grant his last point but still wonder whether Nick had determined on a strategy of diversification or simply could not resist another opportunity. To clarify this I press him on how he would react to a proposition to build something more demanding than a conservatory or kitchen extension: 'Yeah, I'd absolutely jump at the chance. If someone offered me work I hadn't done before, because I know quite a circle of friends who are in the building trade, I'd always say, "No problem we can sort that out," but I'd get someone else to run the job and I'd take a back seat. That's what I say, nothing fazes me really. If the opportunity's there I'll always have a go at something. There's always a way round things, there's always an answer to everything.' This is an ambivalent response because 'always having a go' is at variance with 'taking a back seat', unless the two are very judiciously balanced.

Nick's response, when pressed further on risk-taking and whether or not he is bothered by it, is 'No, I don't really worry about things . . . Even on jobs I'm not really sure of or where I know I'll hit problems – they might hit [the] mains or something and I might have someone flapping – I don't panic and sort it out. It's funny because some people do. My mum and dad say about me that I'm that laid back I'm horizontal!' If Nick (over)confidently relies on his ability to 'sort it out', where major issues like damaging public utilities are concerned, it seems fair to conclude that the avoidance of constraints plays little part in his thinking. Instead, if opportunity knocks, Nick simply finds it irresistible. The similarity to Ralph points to an uncomfortable prognosis, for he, too, seized on enablements alone, giving cognisance to constraints only when they had done their worst to his current project.

The exact obverse of 'opportunism' is 'prudentialism' and Tony appears to be preoccupied by anticipating constraints to the extent that every obvious opportunity is inspected and found wanting because of its constraining downside. We have already seen how he extricated himself from unskilled work in a chocolate factory, obtained a first degree in art and then a diploma, MA and PhD in philosophy. At each crucial juncture he resisted the instrumental rationality pressed by family and friends because he viewed each employment opportunity as entailing a performative contradiction from him. By the time he gained his art degree, Tony recalls, 'I started to question whether I wanted to carry on painting or making films. At that point a lot of problems had raised themselves . . . a lot of critical questions in terms of the culture in which you find yourself working – whether I can justify producing more of this cultural stuff and I found it very difficult for me to do that.' It was so insuperably difficult that, rather than countenancing 'cultural production', Tony took two years out doing landscape gardening before embarking on philosophy, which he regarded as 'the same activity in a way' as art.

He loved each stage of his postgraduate studies, viewing them, in his words, as 'an opportunity to constantly indulge yourself in your existential concerns'. Yet again, when awarded his PhD, he experienced the same impossibility of translating his intrinsic interests into any extrinsic job description that he would not find unacceptably constraining: 'at that point I'd started to seriously question the relationship between philosophy and academia, the whole academic situation, so that is now one of the central issues. I'm finding it quite difficult to situate the two together . . . it's the recognition, to put it simplistically, philosophy is not equal to a critical discourse about philosophers and their problems. And all too often you do get a sense that that is what philosophy is taken to be.'

When questioned as to whether he thinks there is any way of avoiding the constraints of academic institutionalisation, say by freelance writing, Tony is realistic: 'I don't think so, I don't think there is any outside to the institution, you're always going to be institutionalised to some extent. But it's an issue for me – it's something I'm trying to work through.' Meanwhile he temporises with routine, non-committal, hourly work and is equally realistic about this: 'I need to eat, I need to pay rent like we all do, so certain decisions have to be taken that I regard as provisional. They're just taken strategically, but in the bigger scheme of things . . . that's not the life plan.' It is Tony himself who introduced the notion of strategic action in relation to a life plan, so it seemed fair to press him on his temporisation strategy and what in his view could bring it to a satisfactory end.

Candidly, he states, 'I don't know to be honest what I'm waiting for . . . All I can say is what I'm responding to . . . certain opportunities present themselves that I can recognise as these are the right ones and these are not. It's a matter of recognising certain possibilities . . . An opportunity comes along and I'm absolutely certain that this is what I want to do, and not to spend – get into a situation where energies are being wasted.' When does temporising become immobilisation? Perhaps not at thirty-six but, with every year that passes, Tony's age will increasingly represent an objective constraint, restricting the opportunities open to him – even were he to find them subjectively attractive.

Conversely, all the other subjects displayed a high degree of self-awareness that they were attempting to devise strategies that would simultaneously circumvent obstacles whilst allowing them to capitalise on opportunities. Clive and Liz demonstrate this in the private and public sectors respectively. Once Clive had entered the family business, he was immediately 'open for another challenge' and became the driving force behind growth and diversification: 'it's a business where I'm now looking for expansion . . . and we're currently looking at opening out-of-school clubs around the area, so that side of the planning's being done. And there's always the opportunity to take on another nursery.' Both of these have been done incrementally, but Clive wants to go much further and believes that there is a growing market for various forms of out-sourced child-care.

The opportunity is there, but he appreciates that the very formula that has made their nursery chain successful could be threatened by careless, rapid expansion: 'I don't feel that the corporate image and child-care necessarily go together as the same thing, it's not possible. One of the things we advocate here is a very homely environment for the children, almost like a house, but able to offer the whole range of development and education . . . now if I could create hundreds of nice homely looking environments but at the same time make it a production line – but obviously it doesn't work.' Because of this constraining contradiction, Clive has concluded strategically that 'I want to get fairly large', but has drawn his own line through 'getting really huge'. Instead, he endorses continued incremental expansion of the nurseries, providing that the staffing and ambience can be ensured every time (thus respecting the constraint), together with rapid diversification (to seize on the enablement presented by market demand).

Hence, his strategy is much bolder in the establishment of out-of-school and holiday clubs, which has increased business by two-thirds on one nursery site, and he is now seriously considering a foray into private education. Again, he shows the same strategic balancing of opportunity against the obstacles to be faced: 'It would take a lot more research to work out whether the finance and the benefits are there but obviously, if we could convince the parents that they've had this wonderful start in life, let's carry it on – ideal! It's still a pipe dream though. There's a lot of snobbery so, even if we try to offer that, they'd be saying: "Well, I need to go to St X's" or wherever because "that's the place to be", rather than necessarily the best place for their child.'

Working in the public sector of education, Liz could not think in such entrepreneurial terms. This does not mean that strategic action was denied her, as she shows in mid-career. Once her own children were established at school, she was unwilling to remain 'just a standard classroom teacher'. At the time she also confronted a major constraint in the job market, which she neatly circumvented: 'I decided I could look for some sort of promotion, but there were no jobs – it was the seventies.' She eventually got promotion because she 'did a spell at another school on an exchange'. Strategically, she out-manoeuvred the constraint: after the exchange she returned to her school as deputy head.

Although it was promotion, Liz found she was coping with the worst of both worlds: rising class sizes, National Curriculum and performance indicators on the one hand, and on the other, an inability to put her own stamp on the school against a rather ineffectual head. 'As deputy you never feel you do anything well.' The only way to circumvent this constraint was to become more ambitious than she had previously been.

When the headship became vacant, she decided to go for further promotion, which may have been facilitated by her recent divorce. 'I did go for promotion but it wasn't planned from the beginning. It was about being in a situation and thinking I want to do more of this, I want to have more influence in how things happen. That's what pushed me into promotion I suppose, feeling that I could make a difference or have some influence.' Liz successfully grasped her opportunity, became head and, instead of envisaging retirement at sixty, she has 'got a new lease of life'. Strategic career planning does not have to be the unfurling of some initial design. It can be a series of deliberative responses to the obstacles and opportunities that shape the situations in which people find themselves – the usual manner by which constraints and enablements are transmitted to us.

Strategic career planning, whether for the next, proximate foray into the job market or for a decade ahead, is strongly influenced by the degrees of freedom available to an agent and the stringency of constraints that agents confront. In general, long-term planning is facilitated by high degrees of freedom, whereas stringent constraints foster short-term plans – although ingenious agents may still come up with strategic projects for their circumvention. These two types of structured situations confronted Donna and Billy, respectively. They thus permit an examination of how strong autonomous reflexives respond strategically to the social distribution of occupational opportunities which were not of their making.

As we have seen, at nineteen Donna gained her present job in electronic banking by contingency (having got it wrong first time), and was promoted to team manager within three years. In the process she has 'lit up' and identified precisely what aspects of work she wishes to invest herself in: 'it's people management and project management, being given something small and being able to really build on it, and in the end saying: "this is what I have done or improved".' Donna has considerable degrees of freedom to plan her future career and, given that she both knows what she wants from employment and also makes this her top priority, it is unsurprising to find her thinking in the long term and also considering various options: 'I plan to be in a certain type of job by the time I'm twenty-seven; children-wise – I haven't really thought about that. Obviously, for me my career comes first, so I'd like to be in the job by the time I'm twenty-seven . . . I've got two career paths at the moment: one would be going off and run my own business, and the second would be to stay with a large organisation within the financial sector and build on that.' Significantly, Donna has named the two pathways to upward mobility that autonomous reflexives favour equally: rapid corporate promotion or self-employment. Given her broad degrees of freedom, how is she going to choose between them?

Her approach is strategically based rather than concerned with the maximisation of her current preferences: 'I can never see myself with a long-term future with [present bank] for ten or fifteen years . . . it's a case of looking at areas I might go into next . . . This job is building me up for something much bigger . . . I do really enjoy it, but I have started looking at other areas . . . I want to keep my options open.' Donna is much bolder in seizing opportunities in the job market with both hands, but she is not yet prepared to commit herself to her self-employed option, out of respect for her present financial constraints: 'I do have a lot to lose, like my house . . . I am prepared to take a risk within jobs . . . I think if there are opportunities out there and I think one hundred per cent I could do that then I'm going to go for it.' Importantly, Donna is not only on the look-out for enablements, but is preparing herself to be qualified to take advantage of them. Her reason for continuing to add short training courses to her portfolio is, she specifies, 'To make sure I know what everybody else is doing and I can bring something to it', because she recognises that her present company is 'in a way futuristic' and may not commend her to more traditional employers.

Thus, Donna's strategy is to spend some of the next ten years expanding her experience and expertise through job moves within the financial sector, though always moving on when she feels she has reached saturation point: 'I've got to have job satisfaction, it's got to be somewhere I know I can develop in, I know I've always got areas to go if I reach my peak in one.' After that she feels she will be sufficiently qualified and confident to open her own business: 'I think long term I'd like to do something along these lines . . . go into a sort of bar/restaurant, open one and then possibly a chain.' This, Donna believes, would give her 'the best of both worlds, being able to go out and chat to people and see the good side of management, and then manage my own finances, my own time and the business as a whole'. This is the type of career planning possible with wide degrees of freedom and personal clarity about one's concerns, which can then be translated into concrete projects.

Matters are very different for those who have to deal with stringent constraints. These have been Billy's lot all his life, given his multiple redundancies. As he puts it: 'You're made redundant and you can't get a job in what you want to do, and you try to go into something else where you think: "Well, I can make this work." ' Even there, he exploited his meagre degree of freedom by making applications only for jobs that promised not to confine him to being a driver. Now that he is over sixty and, despite his exertions, still unemployed after two years, does the increasing stringency of constraints fundamentally deny strategic action to him? 'Yes', he has concluded, if he confines himself to the regional job market, but 'no' if he makes a bolder circumventory manoeuvre and relocates in southern Spain – which 'is like Eldorado'. He has now visited the area, costed out housing, established that his pension could be paid there and, above all, ascertained that 'there's plenty of jobs, you've just got to make your money in the season and make it through the winter'. He has investigated the project sufficiently to feel certain that his wife could obtain hotel work and that he could utilise his driving skill, yet again, by providing an airport transfer service.

It is impossible to tell whether or not he will do it because contingency could intervene in the form of unexpectedly finding a reasonable job. Failing that, Billy says, 'I've pushed myself a lot through life to do things I wouldn't have wanted to do. I think this needs just that bit extra but it needs a bit more thought as well. I want to get all the tax and figures and write down . . . I like to think things over, I don't like to rush into things, I like to think, well, I can do that or I can't do it, that's how I've always thought.' In other words, though being careful, Billy is unlike the 'prudentials' because he is well aware that this opportunity for strategic action can evaporate unless he finds 'that bit extra' to see it through soon.

The strategies examined so far are those of people for whom work is their chief concern and who are willing to subordinate their social concerns to it or feel these can be accommodated to their career plans. Donna says 'obviously' her career comes first, and has to be established before even thinking about marriage and potential family; Billy is sure that his wife, daughter and grandchild will happily accompany him to Spain; Clive chivvies other members in the family business into endorsing his expansion plans; and Liz no longer has to consider her ex-husband or the needs of her grown-up sons. However, there is a final cluster of autonomous reflexives whose less ambitious forms of strategic action are governed by two factors: a desire to retain control over their work, which does not differentiate them from the subjects just discussed, and a more accommodative approach to the requirements or the demands of their families.

These are the subjects who 'know when to stop' in their personal pursuit of upward mobility. They are people who recognise the opportunities before them, who will take some of them but not all because they believe that to go beyond a certain point would be damaging to their other concerns, especially inter-personal ones. Oliver recognises that he would have a good chance of becoming area manager, responsible for twelve or more units like his own, but he has reflexively declined this because of the loss of autonomy that would be involved: 'I had an extremely good year last year so I could put myself forward for management and I'm sure they would put me on a course. But my view is I can control my day-to-day working here, I can control my working environment.' Yet, of equal importance to him is that such promotion would also entail geographical mobility, which he sees as an obstacle to discharging his responsibilities towards his family and particularly his disabled son. Since considerable efforts have been devoted to dovetailing the location of house, schools and the jobs of both partners, Oliver is loath to damage these arrangements, especially as there would be no countervailing increase in job satisfaction. At forty-nine he has strategically determined to go no further because he anticipates that promotion would entail conditions that he does not desire and could circumvent only with an overall loss of well-being.

Damian is much younger and, as we have seen, he wants his boss's job – the management of ten shops. Yet, reflexively he restricts his ambitions to that level and does not seek a higher post in the same or another charity. His reasons are identical to Oliver's. He too fears that greater promotion would entail moving to another area, which might be disadvantageous to his partner's career, and also would strip him of the hands-on control and variety he most enjoys in his work: 'I wouldn't want to sit behind a computer for eight hours a day – that would really bore me. So no, not right to the top, but I would like to go higher than I am.' Unlike the communicative reflexives, Oliver and Damian are not *lowering* their occupational aspirations for the sake of their families, they are rather placing an upper limit on the extent of their occupational mobility, such that none of their concerns is jeopardised.

Keeping the social in its place

Dovetailing the practical and the social orders is a problem that arises most persistently between work and the family, although it is not necessarily confined to that area. Successful dovetailing is the predicate of effective strategic action in relation to constraints and enablements. This is because upward mobility is not an end in itself but is sought for specific internal goods[9] highly valued by subjects, such as the triad of desiderata autonomous reflexives unanimously seek from their employment: challenge, control and variety. Overarching these is a still more comprehensive end, the desire to consolidate a *modus vivendi* that is both satisfying and sustainable: a set of established practices that constitute a desirable way of life as defined by the subject in the light of his ultimate concerns. This entails reaching an accommodation with the social order, one which we have already seen is impossible to Tony as yet, and thus leaves him

---

[9] Andrew Sayer, *The Moral Significance of Class*, Cambridge, Cambridge University Press, 2005, pp. 111–38.

unable even to conceptualise a *modus vivendi*. Fundamentally, accommodation has to be such that, whilst the social realm is given its due, dovetailing ensures that inter-personal relations do not usurp the subject's intrinsic satisfaction deriving from work. It is common for accommodation to involve selective subordination as the following vignette illustrates.

Rachel wants to run her own salon but does not aspire to opening a chain of hairdressers, some of her considerations being the same as those of others who 'know where to stop'. However, her further reasons introduce something distinctive about how autonomous reflexives monitor both the self and others in relation to upward mobility. On the one hand, she and her husband-to-be wish to combine their shared business with shared child-care, which limits the time they can jointly envisage contributing over the first few years. However, there is a slight equivocation in what she says at the end of her explanation: 'I'd like children, I would like a salon, I'd like to focus on one really. You can't really say until it settles.' It transpires that this is indeed part of strategic action. It is such because, on the other hand, both partners fear loss of control to other family members were their plan to be any bigger and to proceed any faster. Firstly, Rachel knows that her future in-laws would finance the venture, 'but they're the sort of people who you feel would want something back and I don't want that. I don't want her [mother-in-law] just to walk into the salon making coffee and helping herself and she would do that if she'd put money in.' Secondly, her sister has already suggested that, were the couple to open a second salon, she would willingly run one of them. Rachel dreads this interference and her fiancé is of the same mind: 'he doesn't want to do it for the extended family – he wants it to be ours'. In other words, inter-personal considerations can be matters of self-defence, the precise reverse of the self-sacrifice that characterises the communicative reflexives examined in chapter 4.

Most of the interviewees had succeeded in dovetailing work and home life by negotiation with their partners over boundaries, division of labour and shared versus separate activities. Frequently, they stressed the ethical importance of adhering to their family responsibilities, as these had been defined, something strongly emphasised by Martin and Nick as divorced men in relation to their children. Dovetailing does not correspond to an abstract notion of fairness, it merely reflects the terms struck between the parties involved. These terms can be generous, as in Oliver's description of how he accommodates his son who has special needs: 'yes, stress at work and stress at home, it's not the normal quiet family life where you get home and read the paper. He's there and wants help, constantly demanding of us but you just do it.' Oliver does because he and his wife are 'singing from the same sheet' and have elaborated their coping techniques over a twelve-year period.

Younger subjects may sound much tougher when they stress the importance of selecting partners *for* their accommodativeness. Thus, Donna, whose fiancé is at university in a different town, often clashes with him over her working a twelve-hour day, but she is quite clear that 'we'll have to try and come to some sort of compromise . . . if you put in a short-term fix that's just a mistake from the start, we need to be thinking long term'. Although she sweetens this to him by the prospect that in the 'long term we'll get to spend more time together', she is bluntly honest that her career will remain a permanently protected area: 'I think that's one thing that is never going to change. Partners may come and go but having a career is what makes my personality.' Her social identity is vested in the occupational role that she personifies and her determination to keep the social order in its place is what empowers the clear sightedness of her strategic planning.

That dovetailing is indispensable to strategic action is illustrated by Abbie who, at forty-eight, has only just achieved it and begun to assume governance over her occupational trajectory. Prior to that, her undoubted upward mobility was attributable to a combination of contingency and natural ability. Though no one could begrudge her a generous quota of good luck after the horror of her early years, the latter led her repeatedly to sabotage career gains in response to failing relationships or to shore up a good one.

During her brief first marriage to a 'crook, a compulsive liar', Abbie worked as a trainee wages clerk, gained promotion and lit up: 'I got a kind of hunger as I was doing this manual payroll and my confidence did build up,' sufficiently so for her to master the techniques of computerised payrolls and ledger work. When this marriage soon broke down, she turned back to Mark, her earlier nemesis, seemingly drawn by the warmth and welcome extended by his adoptive, Christian parents. Abbie's marriage to Mark gradually deteriorated and her job was a casualty of their marital stress. Whilst drinking a bottle of whisky each night, they thrashed out an agreement that, since they wanted entirely different things, 'we'd split our salaries and go our own way' – separate spending and separate rooms. Abbie became employed by a group of garages as an accounts assistant, 'a slight step up', where she received further training and quick promotion in her mid-twenties. When she learned, as the last to do so, about Mark's sexual depravities Abbie reached rock bottom: 'there were redundancies at work and I just wanted to go, so I took redundancy. I didn't know where I was going . . . I was desperate because I just felt I'd failed. I'd failed in two relationships and my esteem went again. And at this point, I got the pills and I got the bottle of wine and I thought I'm going to kill myself because I've nothing to go on for, there's no future, he's right, I can't cope.'

She pulled back from attempting suicide by drawing upon her Christian faith, something relatively uncommon amongst autonomous reflexives, and two days later applied for a temporary vacancy as a cashier with a prestige car manufacturer. 'So I went for the interview and I got it, and it wasn't a cashier's job, it was financial analyst, and they took a gamble as I hadn't got a qualification to my name. Everywhere I'd gone I'd just gone a step up each time. Had I realised what I was taking on I would have run a mile.' Nine months later Abbie was made permanent, loved her work and was promoted to training dealers in the finance system. Yet what contingency had delivered, Abbie forfeited when she later met and married Jim, a policeman and church goer, with whom she had a family: 'something had to give . . . and I got a job as a boring administrative clerk, bottom of the pile again, but it was the hours that suited'.

Finally, with a good marriage, with the children moving through school and a husband ready to share responsibilities, Abbie began to make her own way into the police service by grasping the opportunity to run the finances of several ad hoc operations: 'I got that hunger back, I knew then that I wanted to go back into finance.' This she duly did and her chief superintendent was sufficiently impressed to sponsor her through the course for accounting technicians, her first professional qualification. Looking back, Abbie says, 'it's just amazing where I ended up – from where I was to where I am now. I thought when I did AAT I wouldn't go on any further and become an accountant . . . I thought when I took this role three years ago that that would be it and I wouldn't want to go any further, but I'm getting bored! I've acted for my boss now, I've been business manager of the police station whilst he was on holiday, which is the highest you can go as a civilian, and I'm thinking where do I go?' Jim continues to be supportive, their youngest is about to enter secondary school, so having finally achieved stable dovetailing Abbie can assume governance over her own career for the first time in her life. Work had held her together: 'in every job I've been in I've loved the figures and the finance – its maths'. What are her plans? Realistically, she can 'go one more up and then I'm at the top', but tentatively she admits to her dream of joining the Home Office – a very long way from sleeping on the lilo next-door 'and not knowing where I was going next'.

Minimalist citizens

Although inter-personal relationships matter to autonomous reflexives, both in themselves and because their smooth accommodation is essential to the realisation of the subjects' ultimate concerns, these are largely confined to their partnerships, nuclear families and children. In other words, such relations are not the foundation blocks of the dense 'micro-worlds' inhabited by communicative reflexives. Equally, the strong autonomous reflexives make little contribution to neighbourhood, community or the institutions of civil society, with the major exception of the economy. In short, they keep society in its place and see little place for themselves in the social domain. Indeed, their strategic stance, which has been one of the main themes of this chapter, presumed autonomous action on the part of these individual actors in their attempts to play snakes and ladders with social forces – as best they could. There is nothing obvious, necessary or optimal about such a stance because collective action is a perennial alternative.

Yet the pronounced autonomous reflexive is the antithesis of a collectivist and biographically, it is clear why this is so. Initially, contextual discontinuity served to throw them back upon their own resources, fostering self-reliant people who see it as their task alone to make their own way in the world. In short, the genesis of the autonomous reflexive provides the conditions for the parthenogenesis of the individualist. The following sample of answers, given when interviewees were asked to whom they looked for approval, is indicative of the depth of this individualism:

MARTIN: 'I don't. I don't look for approval because I hope if I'm doing something and I believe in it, for me that's good enough and I shouldn't have to try to get it justified by someone.'

CLIVE: 'My own, probably the most important thing is my own standards.'

OLIVER: 'I don't seek approval from anybody. I'm of an age where I should be self-confident about myself and should be able to make decisions and not be answerable to anyone.'

DAMIAN: 'Nobody's. That sounds really big-headed, but if it's worked before, why should I ask anyone else? I just do it.'

RALPH: 'Yes, me.'

DONNA: 'I think it's not the case that I seek approval. I like to have people's approval but, without sounding arrogant, I just don't think it would necessarily affect me.'

BILLY: 'I think I'm self-motivated.'

TONY: 'To be honest, no, I'm a total loner in that respect. I enjoy approval like anybody does, but I don't need that approval from anyone, I don't seek it out, I don't base what is to be done on any presumed or hoped-for approval . . . I don't look to anybody for any kind of validation, you have to look inside yourself.'

Underpinning this unconcealed individualism is an equally unabashed avowal of the subjects' faith in their own 'standards', of their certainty that they personally know 'right from wrong', and of a moral pragmatism based on their own experience. What this means is that the personalised ethics of autonomous reflexives are radically discontinuous with social normativity. Indicative of this is the number of these interviewees who admitted to having had brushes with the law or having engaged in activities that could have resulted in prosecution. Much more profoundly, their self-distancing from social normativity is intimately related to their minimalistic citizenship.

Since every component of civil society has a normative basis (even when it is contested) and is the source of deontic powers, it is not surprising that pronounced autonomous reflexives would, as robust moral individualists, strongly tend to restrict their participation to the unavoidable minimum. Neither the duties nor the obligations, thrashed out historically for the array of institutions constituting civil society, will correspond sufficiently closely to the 'standards' of these individualists to attract their active support. The one exception, of course, is the economy, yet even there the unanimous quest of autonomous reflexives for 'control' at work is also an attempt to circumvent occupational normativity as far as possible. The magnetic attraction that self-employment exerts on autonomous reflexives is that there alone, they believe, most things can be made to dance to the tune 'I did it my way.'

6   Meta-reflexives: moving on

Intrinsic to each dominant mode of reflexivity are relations between what people care about most and their patterns of social mobility. Meta-reflexivity presents a conundrum. Why should the fact that someone is deeply attached to a set of values be related to a volatile pattern of employment, one in which successive jobs do not constitute improvements upon each other in terms of the objective or subjective benefits derived from them? The simplest way of putting this question is: why should the attempt to live up to an ideal be associated with lateral social mobility? An answer will be sought by following the twelve interviewees through the course of their lives and their work histories.

However, there is no obvious answer to be found in the nature of the subjects or of their values. As a sub-group, these individuals make no claims to be voracious for new experiences or changes of environment; nor, unlike many autonomous reflexives, do they quickly complain of boredom once they have mastered a job. Indeed, they are a little shame-faced when they feel that to be called a 'rolling stone' is a cap that fits.

Equally, there is nothing in the ideals they embrace that enjoins frequent occupational moves or implies that job changes would or should be made sideways. These subjects are not 'travellers', stone age hippies or new age globe-trotters, shifting from one form of temporary work to another. Often, an outside observer could inspect their value-commitments and conclude they would be well served by the subject staying in a given career and acquiring more influence through promotion. However, though the association between the ideals held by meta-reflexives and their lateral mobility is not obvious, neither is it spurious. The present chapter is devoted to understanding this connection as part and parcel of meta-reflexivity itself.

Let us start with what is most distinctive about the meta-reflexives as a sub-group and is even more pronounced amongst the twelve interviewees:[1] the importance that they attach to living up to an ideal. This comes across strikingly in interview, but the majority of these subjects – as extreme[2] exponents of meta-reflexivity – also managed to list a value-commitment amongst their three main concerns in life. Obviously, anything and everything that respondents list as one of their concerns is something that they value highly. What is particular to the meta-reflexive interviewees is that they actually value values. Their value-commitments are not taken for granted, nor are they a tacit part of the subject's mindset, but are identical to every other concern: something to be prioritised, nurtured and promoted.

It is perhaps surprising that so many of the interviewees succeeded in listing their value concerns – on the half line provided for this – because it is often semantically more difficult to do so than it is for a communicative subject to record 'my children' or for an autonomous subject to register 'my work.' It is only as easy as this for meta-reflexives if they can cite a direct counterpart, such as 'my church' or 'my faith'. In fact seven of the twelve did list the above, if 'spirituality' is included. In itself, this is unexpected given the widespread assumptions about the growth of secularisation, made until quite recently. Two further interviewees also managed to log their value-commitments by compressing them into 'the environment' and 'environmental and animal rights', respectively. However, it would be incorrect to conclude that the remaining three subjects, who made no comparable entries on the original questionnaire, were therefore less concerned about values or living up to an ideal. For example, Cameron (a 41-year-old carpenter) enigmatically recorded his first concern as 'happiness', which turned out to mean a wholly secular

---

[1] The mean score of the twelve interviewees on ICONI was 6.4 out of the maximum of 7.

[2] As with all interviewees, these are 'extreme types' of practitioners of a given mode of reflexivity. They are real people, who have been encountered, rather than 'ideal types', which have been constructed.

but almost mystical approach to flying a plane, something he valued above all else. Such instances represent intractable coding problems and again place the burden of the argument on qualitative data.

To value a value (or to prioritise an ideal) has precisely the same effect for meta-reflexives as do their very different concerns for other kinds of subjects. It is not possible to have a genuine concern and to do nothing about it. We would properly be dubious about someone protesting to be greatly concerned about a matter but acting with total indifference towards it. When normal people express concern at all – as opposed to sympathy or empathy, both of which are compatible with remaining a bystander[3] – it is usually accompanied by an attempt to do something about it and often by regrets for not having done more. That response is central to meta-reflexives. They cherish an ideal which is important to them and their reaction is an attempt to live up to it, even though they feel they fall short of what is required of them. In brief, they are idealists whose constant points of reference are their value-commitments. These entail perfectionism on the part of meta-reflexive subjects who strive for a self-transcendence and a social transcendence that would enable them to do more and thus better realise their ideals.

The question that most interviewees (of all kinds) find hardest to answer concerns the origins of their values. The vast majority[4] give an almost autonomic response, immediately citing their parents or one parent in particular as the source. Frequently, they are right to do so. If they now hold values based upon religion and it was family members who first introduced them to their faith and its practice, their response seems valid. If they are now moved by ideals of social justice and were brought up in a left-wing home, the same response seems justified. Nevertheless, are these answers complete?

Bernadette's story has alerted us to this question. She was equally justified in locating the origins of her Catholic-based values in her practising Catholic family. However, we know this is an incomplete account. Something additional induced her to take her faith more seriously than was the case within her family, or she would not have sought to become a nun and have battled (unsuccessfully) against her mother to do so. Bernadette herself appeared to be aware that at least one further influence upon her early value formation was that of the teaching Sisters at her convent school. From them came her desire to join the same religious

---

[3] I feel for my students when they file in to take their final examinations, but am incapable of altering their current trial and unconvinced by the various experiments with alternatives that my department has tried over the years.

[4] This was also the case for the undergraduates in the longitudinal study (2003–6), which overlapped with the present investigation.

order. However, that information was produced quite separately from her description of being brought up as a cradle Catholic. In other words, subjects frequently do not synthesise all that is relevant to answering this question fully, even though they are quite conscious of other influences and perfectly willing to discuss them in interview. Since subjects can and do offer the pieces of information needed, the task of reconstructing the origins of their value-commitments need not call upon depth psychology or detective work but is more like doing a jigsaw.

Gaining values and giving value

Socialisation is not a semi-automatic process for meta-reflexives, if it is for anyone. Firstly, for some interviewees, the most salient values in their family backgrounds may indeed prove highly influential. Yet, if they are to be life-shaping, the agent himself or herself has to be a very active cultural agent in the socialising process: someone who can apply these values to their own present and future circumstances, that is, to contexts which increasingly do not replicate those of the parental generation. Usually, this means examining what subjects selectively accept and accentuate from amongst the values transmitted to them.[5]

Secondly, and more important than parental socialisation for some subjects, are intervening factors – often non-ideational in kind – which have to be woven into accounts of their value acquisition. Such alternative or additional influences may occur in early childhood or after it: for example, striking experiences, illnesses and medical conditions, or geographical relocation. These are usually responsible for slanting the normativity of subjects in a particular direction. Such factors can also initiate a radical selection process within a set of values, one in which some elements are discarded and others are reinterpreted.

Thirdly, there are always cases of defective socialisation. When these are extreme, the subject and his or her cultural encounters outside the family are responsible for what is incorporated into their value conspectus. It is usually only these individuals who do not attribute their values to their parents, or do so with serious qualifications. Examples of all these variations upon the simple model of socialisation-as-osmosis are found amongst the twelve meta-reflexive interviewees and are discussed below in terms of 'Selecting from socialisation' 'Socialisation overridden' and 'Defective socialisation'.

---

[5]   As Alvin Gouldner importantly underlined, to share a value system is perfectly compatible with different groups accentuating different elements within it in line with their interests: 'Reciprocity and Autonomy in Functional Theory', in N. J. Demerath and R. A. Peterson (eds.), *System, Change and Conflict*, New York, Free Press/Collier Macmillan, 1967.

What is crucial for the present argument is that the resulting value-commitments provided the impetus towards those forms of training and employment enabling the values in question to be expressed through work. In short, value-commitments are the source of subjects' first occupational projects or dreams. To call them 'dreams' does not imply unrealistic or fanciful projects for employment; they can be as mundane as becoming a draughtsman or a secretary. However, the encounter between culture and structure that necessarily follows is never mundane because of the emotions each individual invests in his or her project.[6] Here we will concentrate upon how values are acquired – ones that are supremely important to meta-reflexives – and how subjects develop their first conceptions of living them out. Their encounters with the structured distribution and availability of occupations are taken up later in the chapter.

Selecting from socialisation

Although there is no doubt that family background and upbringing are an important source of values, we should be cautious about viewing early socialisation as the exclusive source of an individual's value-commitment for the rest of his or her life. This warning is graphically illustrated by Maeve, the oldest of the interviewees (aged seventy-two and running an agency providing care for the elderly). The values she held and lived by for four decades were taken over *en bloc* from her family, especially her mother, and confirmed by the surrounding community. Maeve grew up in rural Ireland, as one of the eight children of a jobbing builder and a 'traditional housewife'. Until she was forty years old, her biography and her subjectivity were exemplars of successful socialisation.

Retrospectively, she feels that she absorbed social deference and stereotyped gender roles as part and parcel of the 'penny catechism': 'My mum was big on humility and I think either she misinterpreted it or I did . . . that everybody was better than us, rather than humility is a virtue but that doesn't mean you're not as good as anybody else . . . I was always giving in to other people, always being the one to appease.' However, there was no scope for misunderstanding the message about gender roles: 'I was brought up to know that really the mum was the key person in the home and it was up to them to keep the peace. In my mother's home, the girls attended to the men in the family.' Nearly three-quarters of a century ago, there was nothing in Irish country life to contradict or counteract these socialised and (almost) sanctified expectations. Maeve anticipated and

---

[6] See Margaret S. Archer, 'Emotions as Commentaries on our Concerns', in Jonathan H. Turner (ed.), *Theory and Research on Human Emotions*, Amsterdam, Elsevier, 2004.

accepted routine work during the 'waiting decade' prior to her marriage and having children. Acquiring qualifications was irrelevant; her life was on hold. The dream she fostered and was encouraged to adopt was entirely conventional.

However, her life falls into two parts, punctuated by her uprooting from Ireland and relocation in England, where her husband came to find work. In a new context, involving different demands upon her and presenting novel opportunities to her, Maeve began to examine and disentangle the two main strands of her socialisation: Roman Catholic beliefs and Irish folkways. Fundamentally, her values continued to reflect the former but repudiated the latter. In mid-life she fully recognised that her mother's social teaching had little to do with the church's social doctrine: 'My mum was a very strong influence that maybe held me back developmentally.' This was particularly the case in relation to traditional gender roles; when Maeve came to value herself as an equal, then equally she looked at the world of work for living out her revised value-commitment.

Anouar (aged twenty-four, a qualified pharmacist and manager of a high-street chemist's shop) contrasts nicely with Maeve. Although his values are also derived from family socialisation, he actively scrutinised them early on. This resulted in his drawing a very clear distinction – unlike Maeve when his age – between what he considered to be central to his Islamic faith and the accretions deriving from family folkways. As he discusses the centrality of Islam to his life, it becomes clear that he put a good deal of thought into understanding his faith when growing up: 'Initially, you put family first but, as you get older, it becomes faith first and family is second, although family would come under the bracket of faith . . . So really I could put faith as number one [concern] and leave [the rest] blank because it encompasses everything. It's always applicable to everything I do, from eating with only my right hand to sleeping on my right side. You have government law but to me that's my law, my religion. Everything I do has to be within that law.' This is the clearest possible statement about the organic integration sought by a meta-reflexive between his various concerns.

However, Anouar readily agrees that he is not blindly following the faith of his fathers. When he was around fourteen, he put himself through a course of reading, the comparative nature and scientific approach of which were alien to his family: 'I had curiosity for all religions. I sat down and thought about every religion. And because I'm a scientist as well I had to find some sort of reason and logic in it too. Even at a young age I was drawing distinctions like that in a logical way and going through all of them one by one and deciding the one for me . . . There definitely does come a point, I think, where you question your – anything you do, especially religion. It seems to dictate the rest of your life, so you do question it.' What Anouar, a high-flyer and all-rounder at school, realised from his study of Islam was its incorporation and integration of all (legitimate) interests and activities. It constituted an architectonic principle for their organisation: 'You've got to remember that the most superior [concern] is religion, you can't go outside the bounds of that. The religion encompasses everything from science to the arts, so it all fits in.'

It was crucial for Anouar to have recognised that because it rendered his particular artistic bent fully compatible with his faith and removed any guilt about his unconventionality. In short, it enabled him to crystallise his first project. As a young boy, keeping himself apart from the rough element in the neighbourhood, as he has already mentioned, he had spent his spare time drawing: 'I originally wanted to become a fashion designer, so I used to do a lot of art work. I'm not necessarily a typical Asian guy because in an Asian community these kinds of things are not really seen as things for gentlemen to be doing – so it does go away from the norm. I think I've got my own sense of style and try to be an individual, I don't like to follow people.' His style is indisputable: how many times are your pills dispensed by someone wearing an Armani suit and a hand (his own) made silk tie? 'Yes, I've always had that side to me, so not the most conventional Asian you'd ever meet . . . Most Asian people – the interest I've got in the arts, they wouldn't really have that.' But Anouar can insert his unconventional dream of fashion designing into the matrix of being a faithful Muslim and, instead of conflict between them, see it as a legitimate way of living out his faith. Thus, Islam in no sense cancels out his individuality, but supply embraces new expressions that match the new opportunities open to a first-generation British-Asian. As with other subjects, what happens to his dream is taken up later in the chapter.

Anouar has illustrated how young people, already active agents, play an important role in what is received and internalised from their socialisation through their own understandings and interpretations. Variations on Anouar's account are supplied by Maurice (a 69-year-old retired materials engineer) and by Eunice (a 57-year-old Anglican vicar). Maurice, a bright, working-class scholarship boy, was brought up within the Church of England, where he remains active today. Essentially, he synthesised the religion he had encountered through his family with the new educational opportunities that had opened up for him, but had not been available to his parents. Thus, he put together his undoubted intelligence and a commitment to serving those in need – still central to his faith today – and dreamed of becoming a surgeon. Eunice, growing up in a similar family but lacking any interest in school, accentuated the Christian values of justice and fairness. She received secular reinforcement in these from her father, as a member of the Co-operative movement. In other words, she synthesised her two background influences into a modern form of Christian socialism. She expresses her values at that time simply as 'helping to make people's lives better'. As a very down to earth and hands-on person, her project for realising her value-commitment was to become a trade union secretary.

Socialisation also has a developmental dimension to it, one that can result in selection rather than synthesis. As maturity approaches, certain elements advance in importance and others recede, according to a variety of factors that include pure happenstance. For example, the early life of Bryan (a 63-year-old machine-tool engineer) closely tracked that of Maurice until his teens, when this scholarship boy's talents as a footballer were officially recognised. He played for both Coventry and Birmingham as a teenager. Gaining a place on the England youth squad confirmed his dream of making a career in professional football. As Bryan, the one-time altar-boy put it, by eighteen 'I was a lapsed Christian.' His project was to join Bobby Moore on the England team.

Socialisation overridden

Secondly, unpredictable contingencies – always possible because our lives are lived out in the open system that is society – can play havoc with whatever socialisation processes are underway. The importance of these contingent interventions for a subject's subsequent life history – and the values and dreams that dominate it for a meta-reflexive – can significantly modify or completely override family influences. Very occasionally, contingent events can even influence value formation before socialisation has fully engaged.

The latter was the case for Cameron (the 41-year-old carpenter), coming from an intermediate-class background. One childhood experience seems to have eclipsed all else. From that event, his value-commitment and his occupational ideal, if not born apiece, seem to have grown apace. The interview constantly returned to the theme of flying planes, because in his own words: 'If someone asked me what is the key to life, that would be it.' What is it that he finds so moving about this experience? His response resonates more closely with the mystics than with Biggles: 'you're flying above the clouds and see the blue sky on the horizon, and as you look up it goes into the most incredible blue and it's just – the whole deal, flying and looking down on the earth – it's just something I've always wanted to do. When I was very small, about two, I took a plane over to Ireland. I remember the take-off, I know the make of the plane, and I remember looking down on green fields and I just thought it was the most incredible thing ever. I remember the acceleration on the runway, taking off and looking down on the green fields. I suppose it stems from then. I love the shape of aircraft, I love the aerodynamics side, I love what they are and what they do – the ideal of something heavier than air flying through the air, it's almost like a miracle. It's the way it got me anyway . . . It's the first thing I put forward to be happy in life. It's all I wanted to do.'

Cameron's story is obviously exceptional, including the clarity and the durability of the dream to which the experience of a two-year-old gave rise. However, a more common contingency to intervene in shaping the development of values is chronic illness, especially during early years. Its effect is partly to deflect a smooth process of family socialisation and partly to distort or delay the translation of values into a project consonant with their realisation. In this respect, their medical conditions had a major influence upon two subjects, although it was the struggles they underwent that served, in their own view, to increase the value they both attach to helping others.

Geraldine (aged thirty-four and an adult basic skills tutor) listed one of her main concerns in life as 'My ability to be useful'. She comes from a warm and supportive family of intermediate status with whom she still lives happily. Geraldine has a congenital condition (malfunctioning wrist and ankle joints), with which she struggled as a child in order to have an ordinary and useful life. She feels sure that these struggles had the effect of making her very demanding upon herself in order to meet the same expectations that were extended to her peers: 'I don't call it a disability, but it looks like a disability and I'm always trying to find ways of proving to everybody else that I haven't got this disability. I probably wouldn't have admitted that publicly until now! I'm always trying to prove you can do just as well as everybody else, but then you push yourself a bit harder.' Part of proving that she could do 'just as well' entailed accepting teachers' definitions of 'doing well' rather than looking for ways to fulfil her own ideas of being useful. With blunt honesty she says: 'My ideal is somebody else's ideal! I always try to live up to what somebody else would expect me to be, which I think is quite a sad thing really. I always want to do my absolute best . . . I know from recent experience I am very hard on myself . . . But there's nothing I can do about it because I can't see myself changing, and I'm always trying to get there.'

The trouble was that for her secondary school teachers 'getting there' meant only one thing: 'I think at school what they were really focused on wasn't long-term plans but whether you were going to university or not.' At the time, there is no evidence that Geraldine wanted to go away to university at all – either to leave home or to get a degree. Thus, instead of being encouraged to explore the full range of training opportunities and find a match with her values, she again worked hard to live up to the school's goal. She increased her chances of university entry by deliberately applying to a small college – which may also have seemed less intimidating – but for a degree in history and archaeology that bore no obvious relationship to her own values. Yet Geraldine is very clear about what she means by exercising 'an ability to be useful': this relates directly to the jobs she does 'in terms of helping other people'. Thus, her first project seems to have been a compromise with 'somebody else's ideal', one rendered palatable through kinship with her childhood interest in 'rocks and things'.

Siobhan (aged twenty-five and an environmental economist) expresses her values in terms very similar to Geraldine: 'making the most of my abilities – for myself and for others' benefit'. However, Siobhan's early years sound idyllic in contrast to Geraldine's. She grew up on a farm, a 'happy home' in a friendly village – 'middle of the road, middle England'. More significantly, the good fairies had also endowed her with exceptional intelligence: at ten she jumped a class and at thirteen she had two scholarships to choose between, one of them at a public school which she accepted. Siobhan immediately confirmed that she was a high-flyer, began the advance enabling her to take some of her GCSEs early, and conceived her first dream: to become a paediatrician. However, during the following year the evil spell took effect in the form of ME, which meant that 'my schooling from the age of fourteen was a challenge just to be at school'. This illness, which recurred throughout her school days, put Siobhan's aspirations on hold. Her project shrank to one of educational survival as an end in itself.

The disruption of her schooling was drastic: she was ill at home for two terms, resumed the GCSE programme at the local grammar school, returned to the public school where the illness flared up again, came home for more months of recuperation until she was able to attend another local day school for two days a week and complete her A-levels. Yet more daunting was the reception her illness evoked. At its start, when she was fourteen, her housemistress 'said that she thought I was making it all up . . . There were quite a lot of people throughout that period, teachers, friends, medical staff who said that it didn't exist, or that it was depression. And that included some doctors, people you would hope would never say that . . . There was one doctor that said that if I didn't do his little routine that I would not get better – that I would get worse and would be in a wheelchair and would never get out of it. And he was an ME specialist – at the age of sixteen that's probably one of the most frightening things . . .'

Siobhan could take the illness as a challenge and, academically, she buckled down to the business of gaining her GCSEs, aided by being a year ahead of her age cohort in some subjects. Siobhan's reaction to her results is typical of meta-reflexive perfectionism: 'I still was cross that I got four As rather than four A⋆s for four of my GCSEs – I know I was being a bit prima donna-y about only having 6A⋆s and four As. We live and learn; at the time it was like the biggest disappointment.' In fact it was not; another group of teachers had that in store. 'At A-levels I was told there was probably no point in applying to university, but certainly not to Oxford or Cambridge, because I wouldn't get in because I didn't go to school often enough. I was only going to school two days a week and they said you can't get to university without us, which was a bit of a red flag to a bull! I decided I would get to university with them or without them.' That became Siobhan's dream. She didn't look beyond it and still admits she does not plan far ahead.

Retrospectively, the whole gruelling episode had been taken as 'a challenge to me. I've been able to say, like, I will get better from ME, I don't know how long it will take, I don't know how much effort will be required, but I will prove that I can get over it, I will prove that it's not depression . . . you say that I can't do any A-levels because I only come to school two days a week, but I will show you that I can,' and get into university. At that time, under those circumstances, university entrance became an end in itself, one so demanding that academic survival sidelined the question 'to what end?'

Defective socialisation

Finally, this small group of twelve interviewees also contains three subjects whose childhoods were severely disrupted by their dysfunctional families. How were their values acquired, since they could not be the product of continuous and consistent socialisation? Were their dreams overshadowed too, re-routed into escapism or trodden underfoot?

Let us begin with Pete (aged fifty-nine, a turner, unemployed for the first time). When he says, 'I suppose I grew up on my own,' he is not exaggerating: 'I had a very weird upbringing to say the least. I'm a war baby, parents not married, in fact he was married to someone else. He married somebody else whilst she was in hospital having me. The hostels in [an area of Coventry] – my mother squatted in them. They were supposed to be for people coming back from the war, single people, somewhere to live because of the bombing and what have you. It got found out and people just squatted in them and my mother was one of them and just stayed there . . . My father had five children by three different women, my mother had five children by five different men . . . I had a weird upbringing – you sort of bring yourself up.' When they were housed, four years later, Pete's mother was working a twelve-hour day and such care as he received was from the (then) wife of his undeclared father. Moving again, about five years later, Pete's care, as he puts it, 'was just neighbours, I think'.

Pete's one thread of continuity was an eight-year-old classmate from junior school, who became his wife ten years later and whose parents were the most important of the neighbours mentioned above. His father-in-law-to-be was branch secretary for the union at a well-known car production plant, his wife-to-be was always 'very left wing'. From the frequent debates taking place in their house, Pete absorbed the values of the old left. He never viewed himself as clever, despite being highly articulate, because he was so far behind at school – still unable to read or write – once they left the squat in inner-city Coventry. Nevertheless, he came to enjoy maths and technical drawing and conceived the modest ambition of becoming a draughtsman: 'because I could do it as much as anything. I wasn't going to be clever enough to teach or anything like that, but I was good enough to be a draughtsman, probably not a design draughtsman, but a draughtsman all the same.' This project would not have been incompatible with his socialist values, but it is hardly a direct expression of them. As yet he is not thinking in terms of living up to an ideal. He is still working in terms of survival and is honest in stating that he wanted this apprenticeship 'because [he] could do it'.

'Perchance to sleep, perchance to dream' refers to possibilities not to certainties. For the last two interviewees, Gina (aged thirty-seven and a sessional university teacher) and Jonathan (thirty-one and a team co-ordinator in e-banking), their sleeping was unnatural and their dreaming was delayed for many years. Dreams, of the kind under discussion, depend upon values to shape them and a value-commitment entails a self-awareness that does not expend itself in restless displacement activities or in induced oblivion. Neither Gina nor Jonathan conforms to the traditional notion of socialisation, one featuring young subjects imbued with tribal normativity, who proceed to seek their fortunes within these traditional parameters. Gina was assimilating the values of her middle-class family of teachers until her trauma, around the age of seven, almost put her life on hold for the next twenty years. Jonathan, who plunged deeper and darker than Gina, had first to surface and then to begin the work of his own socialisation in his mid-twenties.

Gina attributes her values predominantly to her mother ('she's a very good person – I suppose I've modelled my attitudes a lot on her'), but sees her father's influence in their political inflection. Although she portrays him as a less admirable person, it was he who encouraged her activity in CND and support for Amnesty and Greenpeace. Gina presents her current values as being profoundly humanistic: her definition of a good life entails practical service to others – embracing people, causes and issues outside her immediate circle and her own country.

However, when she was seven years old, Gina's parents split up in an extraordinary manner, involving their repartnering with another couple. She recalls great discomfort at being made party to paternal recriminations that she could not understand. She went through a long period of unsettlement before being diagnosed as suffering from clinical depression, followed by, as she describes it, 'a dark period in my life, from the age of about fourteen. I got through my O-levels and then I left school and mistakenly went to technical college because I felt I was too grown up to stay at school and other friends were doing that. There wasn't much pastoral care there and I just stopped going in . . . whatever was wrong with me took over and I gave up on A-levels. Then I had this long period of – I travelled a lot, and worked, outdoor labour and work abroad so that I could travel. There was a sense of drifting as well. I suppose I dropped out of society too.' Gina stayed on the trail to Kathmandu for nearly ten years.

Looking back, she feels 'quite ashamed of it because it was quite a hedonistic life-style in the sense that', as she reflects upon it, 'I wasn't really doing anything for anybody else at that stage in my life . . . I'm very ashamed that I didn't do my bit and put something into society, I was just looking after myself. I think I've got a religious sort of personality even though I'm not.' Towards the end of her travelling years, when she voiced such feelings in chance encounters, various people suggested that she return and take the degree she had earlier evaded: 'even then I was resisting it. I think that's when it dawned on me: "Why didn't I do something like that?" There's a sense, when you travel, of feeling almost ashamed that I wasn't putting anything into society. But you're also not getting anything out either . . . I realised then that that period of my life had to come to an end.'

Gina returned to England almost immediately. At twenty-eight she enrolled on a literature degree as a mature student, did well, and gradually recognised that 'I really loved doing the research and sort of fairly quickly realised I wanted to stay in academia.' She pursued this through undertaking a PhD and, by the end of it, she had conceived her project of becoming a university teacher: 'Yes, it's a vocation. I feel it's a way of life.' Currently she is teaching sessional classes, has made various applications for university posts, and is now awaiting her next interview.

Much as he sought it and wanted it, Jonathan had no such epiphany. Even towards the end of his story, when its colours have lightened to sepia tones, he remains unlike the Magi: seeing plenty of fields and fountains, moors and mountains, but without any guiding star. The following are the bare facts of Jonathan's background, stripped of the pain accompanying them. He had been adopted, experienced major difficulties with his adoptive family, and felt that the added strain he had put on their relationship accounted, at least in part, for their divorce: 'My parents got divorced when I was fourteen and I'm sure that had a major impact. And all sorts of stuff ensued after that. It felt as though I was the hub of all the problems. That's had a major impact on my life and how I feel about myself.' His schooling provided no positive counter-balance: 'a horrible school and I had problems at home, so I wasn't happy anywhere and that came out at school more. Secondary school wasn't good for me. I wasn't in a good state anyway . . . difficulties in my teenage world mean the way I've learned to cope is to back off from a lot of stuff.'

Specifically, 'backing off' meant that vandalism and shoplifting gave way to blotting out most things through drink and drugs: 'Life's difficult and you can either just give in and drink yourself into oblivion trying to ignore it or sometimes awareness can feel like a curse . . . I think it's something to do with maybe not honouring yourself, it's basically a damaging behaviour based on not liking yourself, you need to cover something up by drinking or whatever . . . I didn't know what to do, so I just avoided doing – to get out of it, as a coping mechanism.'

After leaving grammar school at sixteen, 'I was on the dole for years. I don't think I'm lazy. It was more finding something worth doing, working in McDonald's never seemed worthwhile to me.' It appears possible that during this period Jonathan's reflexivity was in the fractured mode.[7] If so, that was no longer the case by the time of interview. Eventually, what also didn't seem worth doing was continuing as a self-harmer. Jonathan enrolled on 'Twelve-step Fellowships' to give up drink and drugs, which represented 'the big turnaround' for him. As he came up from the lower depths, Jonathan had somehow to slough off his past and gain a sense of direction. What is crucial is that he realised he had to search for a set of values that, in his view, could give worth to his being before he could develop in any direction at all. Thus, he undertook the unusual course of explicitly seeking out a value-commitment, in the hope that it would, in turn, specify a fulfilling way of life.

When twenty-four years old, Jonathan simultaneously enrolled on an access course, without knowing where he wished it to lead, and he cast himself into a lengthy examination of different spiritualities, precisely in order to provide that lead. Four years after resuming his education, he

[7] This is one of the major limitations of working with data confined to T1. I venture this comment in view of the similarities with 'Jason' in Margaret S. Archer, *Structure, Agency and the Internal Conversation*, Cambridge, Cambridge University Press, 2003, see pp. 333–41. In addition, the longitudinal data on fractured reflexives under collection gives indications that the fractured state is not irreversible, at least for some subjects.

gained a first-class degree in philosophy and English, but this furnished no obvious occupational calling. Meanwhile, Jonathan had found the value system for which he had been searching in a derivative of Sikhism: 'I have a spiritual view of life which is really something I had to have because if you look at life without it, you start to think the whole place is crazy. It comes from looking for some reason for things to happen the way they happen, which is maybe what all religion is.' Walking its particular path required him to abstain from smoking and drinking, to become vegetarian and to earn a living. The question remained, doing what job?

This narrative does not come to a satisfactory conclusion with Jonathan conceiving of his dream, but it comes to a very interesting one where he recognises his need to do so. He is perceptive about having reversed the normal sequence of socialisation by going out looking for his values after maturity. More importantly, he accepts that having found his other-worldly orientation provides no dispensation from discerning his this-worldly calling: 'When I left university I was looking more in deeper spiritual territory – I had to do it . . . because I can only act if I believe. Maybe I've done things a funny way round in a sense, but I think I had to do that and stabilise myself on those levels before I could look to the world. And now I think I'm much more looking for what to do in the world to earn a living that's a bit more meaningful. I've got there eventually. I think initially I put spirituality first and thought I could avoid the world, but in fact you can't.'

He intensely dislikes his current job in electronic banking, which merely serves to pay his bills. Sadly, having analysed all he has been through so insightfully, Jonathan now talks almost at random about the kinds of employment he would find desirable, mentioning jobs in alternative technology, for which he is unqualified, and in stock-broking, which sits uncomfortably with his spiritual values. Although he has no serious project as yet, it does not seem that his ability to dream has become a victim of his own past victimisation. Nevertheless, at thirty-one he still has no inkling of his calling.

Contextual incongruence

The last section focused upon interviewees coming to endorse a particular set of values as their ultimate concerns and on their first attempts to conceive of an occupational project (or the training for one), which they considered expressive of their value-commitments. The biographies of the interviewees were traced up to the point when their first 'dreams' had developed, with the exception of Jonathan – who had not yet made the transition from prioritising a 'concern' to developing a complementary 'project.' Having suspended their narratives at that stage, we can now examine how the attempted realisation of a 'dream' necessarily entails an encounter with structural reality, in the form of the social distribution of occupations. These encounters are *always fraught for meta-reflexives* because cultural ideals do not have direct counterparts in the form of occupational outlets. This is the meaning of 'contextual incongruity' for and to these subjects.

In part, this imperfect correspondence may arise because aspirants 'idealise their ideals' and then survey the occupational array with disappointment if not disillusionment. In part, there simply may not be appropriate outlets that are accessible to given subjects and that match their aspirations. Yet available posts are (and have to be) accepted *pro tem* in order to make a living. Thus, the transition from 'project' to 'placement' is never fully satisfactory because the correspondence between them is sub-optimal. What meta-reflexives do when placed in such situations is of the greatest importance for their future occupational trajectories and will be examined in the next section. Here we will concentrate on interviewees' first experiences of their values and jobs being at variance with one another.

Anouar's narrative was interrupted when he had conceived the idea of becoming a fashion designer and assured himself that it could be a valid way of living out his Muslim faith, although an unconventional one. However, his university applications for courses in graphic design were turned down, perhaps because he had concentrated on science at school: 'I didn't get any offers – pharmacy was my back-up and I automatically got a place.' He accepted it and launched on a five-year course for which he had no 'passion'. After his third year, Anouar had to undertake a six-month placement in a London hospital. His early dream had not faded away and, finding that 'London's full of fashion', he applied for a three-year fashion design course and was offered a place. Now he was torn between this offer and having only one full year to go before possessing a highly marketable degree in pharmacy, one whose merits were pressed by his university friends and family alike. Partly, Anouar says, 'I decided to stick it out, thinking I can always go into fashion at a later stage,' and partly, he honestly admits, 'I needed the security more than anything else.'

He has now been a managing pharmacist for a year. On the one hand, he tries to tell himself that his work is fully commensurate with his value-commitment to 'just helping people – I'm helping people all the time and they come from all colours and creeds'. On the other hand, he is restless and already thinking about occupational change: 'my life's too routine and I don't like that at all. I get up, go to work, come home, have something to eat, then I've got to go to bed because I've got to go back to work.'

Anouar is only twenty-four, so it is probably unfair of me to press him to imagine himself ten years on. However, as a meta-reflexive, Anouar has dwelt upon his situation and concluded that he can fulfil his ultimate concern, which he now paraphrases as 'inner peace and doing good things', by continuing to work as a pharmacist. His fulfilment, he hopes, will be entirely spiritual in kind: 'you can have those nagging things still coming at you, but your spiritual side is so strong that those things don't affect you. In ten years time, hopefully my spiritual side will be so developed where such things won't affect me and I'll be able to deal with them with ease because they won't be a burden on me and spiritually I'll be content. That's the level I want to achieve.' It's a saintly agenda he has set himself; I don't want to knock it or his determination to see it through merely because I sense itchy feet and symptoms of incipient volatility.

Three other respondents faced the same barrier of not being able to undertake the training leading to their desired occupation, but in their cases it was largely for financial reasons. Here is Maurice's very plain account of how, at seventeen, he started work as a laboratory assistant rather than training to become a surgeon. 'I grew up in a very working-class family and my father always used to tell me I should be doing this or that, and I felt [I knew] where I wanted to go, but I never got there because my parents never had the money to do that. So, yes, I had these aspirations and dreams which didn't come to fruition . . . I always wanted to go to university and I didn't . . . I did have a little bit of resentment in the early days that I didn't go to university. I had to do my studies the hard way and it was second chance studies, you know.' Maurice is hinting at the alternative route he took to qualify as a metallurgist and a chartered engineer, but even that is far from being the sum total of his occupational biography.

The same scenario can be played out at different levels, as was the case with Pete and his modest goal of becoming an apprentice draughtsman in relation to his utterly impoverished background. He actually left school at fourteen: 'I wanted to stay on but I couldn't because there wasn't enough money. So I just had to get a job, and that's how I ended up in engineering because it was the only trade I could get into . . . I became quite a good engineer, a turner on lathes, computerised lathes now – I've become pretty good at that.' Everything was just too tight: another year at school and he could have taken GCEs and had an educational qualification; another ten shillings a week on apprentices' pay and he could have begun as a draughtsman because that would have equalled his starting wage. As it was, Pete, who enjoyed high precision work, could not even get into the type of company he valued: 'I think it stopped me working for Rolls Royce, I always wanted to work for Rolls Royce or a highly skilled company . . . there were half a dozen twenty years ago – really good companies to work for and I couldn't get into any of them because I hadn't got any qualifications.' If Pete was forced to conclude that his chosen route was blocked off, this did not mean that he ceded his value-commitment to socialism – or its expression at work.

Cameron's story is remarkable because, despite encountering equivalent structural obstructions, he has spent almost forty years in the single-minded pursuit of his dream and does not consider himself beaten yet. Whilst still at school, he recognised the obstacles confronting his training to be a pilot. On the one hand, he had strong objections to joining the RAF, based upon social class and pacifism: 'Hurting people is last on the agenda for me . . . the RAF – get in an aeroplane and shoot people, I couldn't do it. All that "Yes sir, no sir" stuff, I couldn't handle that . . . So the RAF was out and apart from that, it tends to brainwash you anyway.' On the other hand, cadetships with commercial airlines were hard to come by in the early 1980s, given that a major recruitment drive had taken place in the previous two decades: 'the minute I apply they don't want anybody any more – full quotas, full crew, everything'. Most airlines also required A-levels but, as fifteen-year-old Cameron saw it, gaining them would not significantly improve his chances.

Thus he took a high-risk decision in leaving school and becoming an apprentice carpenter: 'I just wanted to get my apprenticeship out of the way, work and save the money to get my flying done . . . I didn't smoke, I had no interest in drinking or nightclubs. I decided that's the only way I'm going to become a pilot.' In other words, Cameron determined to challenge his exclusion from training by using his own resources. Becoming a carpenter was something he only accepted as a temporary means to his own ends. Accomplishment of his ideal had been seriously delayed, but it was not ceded and at no point in his biography to date has Cameron become resigned to remaining a carpenter.

Four vignettes have just been given of men – as it happens – whose values, when translated into first occupational projects, were frustrated by structural constraints. On finding themselves in the same formal position, their responses ranged from Anouar's attempt to become reconciled to something other than his dream to Cameron's determination to beat all the odds and realise his ideal. What will be found to be distinctive about these meta-reflexives is that they retained their values and continued to seek ways to realise them despite current occupational contexts being against them. However, the meta-reflexive interviewees did not uniformly find themselves in a situation of incongruity between their work projects and their first actual job placements simply because they had all aimed too high – in relation to their social origins – and were then structurally brought down to earth. On the contrary, sometimes everything seemed set fair for the realisation of their projects, when malign contingency intervened with equally negative consequences for their first dreams.

This was the case for working-class Bryan, the grammar school boy who aspired to be a professional footballer. Having already played for England, he was not a 'wannabe' but, even so, he had to confront his father's opposition: 'My father kept saying you're not going to be a footballer, you're going to learn a trade . . . I kept hanging on until one day my father said I'll give you a week to get a job or you'll come and work with me.' Bryan resisted this latter threat, but only by leaving school at sixteen, successfully taking the entrance exam for a large engineering company and becoming an apprentice tool maker – but without resigning his dream of football: 'In the meantime I continued to play football and the idea was I'd finish my apprenticeship and, if I was good enough, I'd be a full-time professional and forget engineering.'

Bryan seems to have been quite realistic in his assessment of his chances of becoming a professional during his apprenticeship: 'I know I would have made it . . . there were about five or six professional clubs after my services, good clubs like Arsenal and West Brom.' He also found the Coventry club willing to meet him half way: 'they signed me up as part-time professional at Coventry. But in my last year of the apprenticeship I sustained injury after injury on my shoulder. I kept dislocating it, so my career finished. It was dreadful, that really was my world.' Accident and injury forced him to conclude that his dad had won ('so I suppose my father was right') and that tool-making was henceforth to be his employment ('I never looked at engineering as my forte'). As Bryan describes what follows, he says: 'I suppose you just drift' – where he went will be taken up in the next section.

Contingencies of all kinds can intervene at any time. This is what happened during part two of Maeve's biography. After her initial experiences of compatibility between structure and culture, the alignment between the two slipped under her feet whilst she was contentedly living out her family's values. We have seen that, during the first half of her life, Maeve endorsed the traditional project for a young Catholic woman growing up in the Irish countryside over half a century ago. It was one she more than fulfilled between the ages of thirty and forty, by marrying and giving birth to six sons! At that time, she recalls, 'I really wanted to have a successful family, not in monetary terms or career-wise, but a happy, good family. And it did happen . . . and I loved it – loved being not at work and being at home with the boys.' This came to an abrupt end when her husband was made redundant.

Her husband decided to seek work outside Ireland, although Maeve had no desire to leave: 'there was the question of shall I come to England with my husband and the children or stay where I was? I didn't really want to come to England, but I didn't agonise over that at all . . . that was the subservient wife thing, the way I was brought up.' Maeve was taken out of Ireland but, contrary to the popular saying, rural Ireland and its folkways were also quickly taken out of Maeve. This was not because she sought it and not until she had rethought those aspects of her socialisation she had taken to be the social teachings of the church. She remained a faithful Catholic and mother, but entry into paid employment at the age of forty revised her outlook upon work and gender.

At her husband's insistence she went to work, taking a job in a care home for the elderly. Despite these new demands on her time, Maeve was still expected 'to be the perfect mother and the perfect wife'. The impossibility of being all of these things led her to recognise that 'it was a very sexist life I was in'. Matters came to a head because Maeve's post carried the option of training to become a qualified social worker. To avail herself of this opportunity was to intensify the incongruity with fulfilling her traditional role by piling on the need to study. As she remembers, 'I didn't get the courage to speak up until when I was supposed to be having three roles and doing all three. I was definitely expected by my husband to qualify, I was definitely expected to progress in my career and I was definitely expected to be the model housewife – and I was finding it difficult and I did say enough is enough.' She confronted her husband with an ultimatum that one of these three roles had to go and that, in her view, this was the 'model housewife'.

Looking back, Maeve says: 'I did think that through in detail because he's of the old-fashioned type, expecting the subservient woman. He did actually marry a subservient woman, but he hasn't got one now! I'm still basically the same person, but I'm my own person.' What he had instead was someone who struck a new deal in the domestic division of labour and who now also regarded her employment as a field in which to live out her values. These played an obvious role in the selection of her first post. As she goes on to explain, 'My reasoning for going into Social Services was that I didn't want to work in a shop or an office. I wanted to work with people doing something caring.' That was Maeve's solution to the 'contextual incongruity' she confronted, and she anticipated that her newly defined project of qualifying as a social worker would be the outlet for her values, refined of their traditional social accretions. Her disillusionment will be picked up in the next section.

The experience of 'contextual incongruity' is fundamentally about the subject feeling he or she should be able to realise their value-commitments better than circumstances allow. For the interviewees examined above, this amounted to them encountering frustrations beyond their control – be they structural constraints or contingent interventions. Conversely, there are also subjects who invited incongruity because they themselves were too idealistic about particular occupational outlets being suitable vehicles for the expression of their normative concerns.

We left Siobhan battling on with her schooling and determined to gain university entry. Her determination paid off and the years of having to work around ME were now behind her. Her struggle had almost entailed tunnel vision and, as was noted earlier, meant that she had not been able to go further and conceive of an occupational ideal for the future. However, as she started the application process for specific university courses, she had to shed her preoccupation with simply gaining entry and to identify where she felt her future employment lay. As Siobhan admits, she had difficulty in defining a concrete outlet for her values: 'an ongoing question towards the end of school was to what extent should I use my brain and my energy and me to make a big difference to a small group of people, or a small difference to a big group of people – in the policy field or hands on?'

Siobhan read economics and politics, particularly enjoyed the former, so followed it up by taking an MSc. After brief work experience, she felt fully committed to the field of environmental economics, which she saw as demanding, worthwhile and capable of making a difference. However, she found her first post with a firm of consultants to be the antithesis of all three: 'At the minute, I'm working as an environmental economist in a consultancy and I don't think I will stay there very long, probably another year. What I don't know is what I will do after that, but I do know I'd like to do something I find mentally challenging, that makes a contribution to other people. One of the things I find difficult about my job is that it's very abstract. It's me and my computer a lot of the time, and I can produce a hundred and fifty pages of a report that really makes no difference to anyone, so I know I would like to move into a job where I felt there was more of a concrete impact on people.'

This was exactly what Eunice sought after quitting her job as a trade union secretary after twelve years, once she felt prompted to be of direct service to others by her more insistent religious values. Having considered this for some time, she completed three years of theological training and took up the post of a full-time lay worker in the Church of England. This, she hoped, would be a more practical expression of her religious value-commitment and, at first, she found it to be so: 'there was a lot of satisfaction seeing people's lives change more dramatically because I was involved more person to person – there wasn't a trade union official or a letter between us'.

Whilst she had obviously anticipated that she would work as second fiddle to the vicar – in the days prior to women's ordination – what she had not figured on was the extent of her subordination to the youngest ordinand. Diagnosing the situation, she says: 'you were always the bottom member of the full-time staff, young boys would come in and rise up whereas you would always stay there'. Eunice herself is not in the least concerned about status but, as she is the first to admit, 'I know that I don't handle fools well.' She admits that the need to bite her tongue repeatedly began to sour her satisfaction: 'when you've worked with one or two lads in their twenties, who really didn't know which side was up, and you think I've got to sit and watch you do this and I know you'll make a mess of it and I know I could do it a lot better, yes, it became a frustration'.

Eunice too was trapped in an engendered situation, incongruous with her calling; a situation made worse by her feeling 'absolutely sure', in every other respect, that she had been right in responding to it. It is futile to speculate on what she would have done, though she herself was review-ing alternatives when circumstances changed. The decision was taken that women could become deacons, with ordination on the horizon, pro-vided they put themselves forward for reselection. This was not some-thing that Eunice had sought and, indeed, we can hear her bristling at the process: 'I was frustrated in that we had to go to be reselected again to see if we were "suitable". If they'd said no, I don't think I would have stayed then as a lay worker. I really think I would have packed my bags and gone, though I'm not sure what to.' However, this change of role could preserve her value-commitment as a viable work project.

Thus, 'contextual incongruity' can also be something that the subject brings upon herself precisely through pursuit of her values. In other words, individuals precipitate themselves into contexts where a mismatch between their cultural ideals and the occupational structure is almost inevitable. Interviewees of this kind serve to counter-balance those whose projects were derailed by contingencies or constrained by family circum-stances. What they all had in common was a clear vision (or redefinition) of what they wanted to do and some were very determined about pursu-ing their ideals in the face of incongruence. Such decisiveness and deter-mination do have an affinity with meta-reflexivity or we would not find these subjects paying the costs for correcting their occupational positions in the next section. However, the willingness to make sacrifices for one's values does not preclude some individuals having difficulties – for reasons such as Jonathan's – in defining their first project.

Geraldine, too, showed a chronic uncertainty about what she should do in practice, despite the great clarity of her values. Her normativity entails, as she puts it: 'the ability to be useful, what I mean is, by the jobs I do, helping other people. I'd hate to think that I hadn't made an impact on somebody else.' However, that normative orientation does not tell her what concrete job to seek. Because, as has been seen, Geraldine wants to live up to other people's ideals and expectations, she repeatedly placed herself in situations of contextual incongruity after leaving school. Specifically, she enrolled on courses only to realise that where they were heading, in terms of employment outlets, was not somewhere she was either happy or confident to go.

The first false start was when Geraldine enrolled on her degree course in history and archaeology, from which she withdrew for a mixture of reasons, including job prospects. As she confesses: 'I wasn't brave enough to give it up early. I thought towards the end, this isn't going the way I want it to go. And, being rather scared of the last bit of the course, I thought if I get out now, I can go off and do English somewhere else. I think it's the fear of finishing, the fear of not getting exactly what you should get . . . I did kind of love my time there, but I just didn't feel it was getting me anywhere. I couldn't see a job at the end of it.' What Geraldine means is an appropriate job because her fellow undergraduates were taking civil service or administrative posts. Returning home, she took what was intended to be temporary employment with the probation office whilst working on an Open University degree in humanities. Towards the end of that course she recalls: 'I did a module on Shakespeare and it just grew from there because it reminded me what I had at school and those teachers that were very important to me.' Once again their expectations came to the surface and they spelt teaching.

Meanwhile, her work experience in the probation service, where she was a self-taught computing assistant, reinforced this vocational ideal: 'Probation is incredibly backward when it comes to technology, so I was "queen".' She says: 'I did feel very useful there because people kept asking me questions. I think that's why I went into the training side of things, which is what kicked off my idea that, yes, I would be quite good as a teacher.' Her problem was that she was ineligible for a PGCE, because her Open University degree was a mixed one. Therefore Geraldine decided to reverse matters, that is, to take a part-time MA in English, thus overriding her first degree and opening the way to teacher training. Again, she withdrew before completing, this time because she found one of the compulsory courses difficult to the point of incomprehensibility. She explains: 'this was part of my long-term plan which had completely crashed and it felt awful. It's still quite scary in a way because I had this ideal that this was going to be the start of moving on into a career.' Thus, she returned to working full time for the probation office, but she continued to think that somehow her vocation lay in teaching and that her old teachers would have seconded this. As she comments rather sadly, 'I'd love someone to wave a magic wand and say, "You'd be good at this job. Go and do it." '

The dialectics of discontent

This section examines how the pattern of occupational volatility is established because subjects regularly move on in quest of a better job match with their values. The standardised trajectory of lateral mobility that ensues appears inexplicable in terms of individual psychology. Meta-reflexives are not simply an assortment of people sharing a low threshold of personal dissatisfaction (or a collection of 'whinging gits', as one autonomous subject dubbed them). They are not psychologically reducible because systemic features are involved in 'contextual incongruity', namely an imperfect correspondence between subjects' cultural values and their occupational contexts, neither of which were (entirely) of their own making. As has been seen above, it is 'contextual incongruity' that generates unease, discomfort and restlessness and, as will now be shown, it is its repeated occurrence that produces occupational unsettlement and social critique.

To detect a distinctive pattern of lateral job mobility over the life course necessarily means concentrating upon the older subjects – those who have had time to weave it. Nevertheless, it is significant that the two youngest interviewees, Anouar (aged twenty-four) and Siobhan (aged twenty-five), are already manifesting dissatisfaction with their first appointments after only a year in post. Although their initial reactions were very different, with Anouar intent upon spiritually enduring his work as a pharmacist and Siobhan thinking she would not outstay another year with her firm of environmental consultants, examination of older subjects with lengthier work histories (unlike Jonathan and Gina who have barely started their careers) have occupational trajectories characterised by recurrent themes, despite large variations in the nature of their employment.

The four main themes can be illustrated from the work history of Maurice who, at sixty-nine, is one of the two oldest interviewees. They will be found to echo similar *leitmotifs* in Bernadette's story, presented in chapter 3, and to be repeated in the employment histories of other subjects, when allowances are made for age and stage. The first theme is that of *recurrent 'contextual incongruity'*, which dogs the working lives of meta-reflexives from beginning to end. So far, only its coincidence with their first posts has been examined. As will be shown it is recurrent for meta-reflexives rather than corrigible through later occupational shifts – whereas corrigibility was frequently the case for autonomous reflexives who got it wrong the first time. The second theme is the *frequency of requalification*, once more for purposes of alternative employment rather than for upward mobility within a particular job or career structure. The third striking tendency is the willingness of meta-reflexives to *pay the price* for their own occupational volatility: in terms of funding their retraining, refusing promotion as an incentive offered for remaining *in situ*, accepting wage cuts and other sacrifices as the costs of a new start, and taking early retirement from one job in order still to have time to begin yet another. In turn, these three themes are largely what generate the *pattern of sideways mobility*, held to be distinctive of meta-reflexivity. However, there is a final and important tendency for these subjects to *gravitate towards working in the third sector* (known variously as the voluntary, charitable, independent or 'social private' sector) over the life course and particularly towards its end. The significance of this last theme will be taken up in the final section.

Resigning himself to the impossibility of qualifying as a surgeon, given his working-class background, Maurice regretfully left school at seventeen and started work as a laboratory assistant. Simultaneously, he began the long haul through evening courses at local technical colleges to become a metallurgist and eventually a chartered engineer. The progressive augmentation of his qualifications was matched by promotion: from head of a production laboratory to chief metallurgist of the company. At that point, he was approached by the city's polytechnic (later university) to undertake some part-time teaching, which he did for three years. During it, he confides: 'I discovered that I was getting a lot more satisfaction than I was in my industrial job. The industrial job was pressure from the time I went in to the time I came home, so I decided to make a sideways move if it was at all possible, and when it came about, I was very thankful for that.'

Maurice's new-found satisfaction, he elaborates, involved much more than having shed corporate stress: 'I found it very encouraging to me personally, helping students. I think the greatest satisfaction was, I'd say, helping: you were helping people to achieve. They'd got a goal they wanted to achieve and I felt very privileged to be in a position to be able to help them to achieve it. That was tremendous job satisfaction.' The privilege was being able to undertake work that was much more compatible with the expression of his Christian values than the application of his technical expertise to industrial production could ever have been. Consequently, when a vacancy came up for a lectureship, Maurice applied, was appointed, and gradually made his way up to becoming deputy head of the department. However, his increasing success was paralleled by diminishing job satisfaction because his tasks progressively diverged from his values. He comments: 'The paperwork became a problem in the latter years for me. The students were far more important than the paperwork as far as I was concerned. And the paperwork would get done, but the problem was that it was your own time you were filling in – in order to be able to give time to your students . . . And you may not be as patient with people as you should have been because of the constraints that are being put on you in other areas, particularly as you go up to the top. It's OK saying your teaching load is reduced, but your admin load has gone up – it's not very easy.' What was so difficult for Maurice was that he now felt he was failing people's needs on two fronts: those of his students and those of his own young children.

Both were a source of reproach to his values and represented a new version of 'contextual incongruity'. These issues constituted a problem for dovetailing two of Maurice's major concerns – his immediate family and working with the disadvantaged – a point which, it was anticipated, would eventually prompt further lateral mobility. His fairly dramatic decision, taken in his early fifties, serves to illustrate the last two themes associated with meta-reflexivity. Firstly, Maurice was undeterred by having to pay the price for his reorientation. As he puts it, 'Yes, the paperwork involved came to the point where I said enough is enough. I was doing part time at another college as well, so I told them I was packing up and packed them both up at the same time. And the [city] university said to me, there's a degree starting in September and I said well, you can forget me.' Instead, he took (very) early retirement, helped to maintain his family on ten hours part-time lecturing for the next eight years, accepted a serious cut in salary and also turned his back upon the status of academia – despite once having longed for it.

Maurice was already involved with an inner-city family centre and for eight or nine years he dedicated himself to this particular community development project 'in a place that, on the Social Services scale, had got a figure of zero as a deprived area'. Recapping his involvement, Maurice says: 'I was on the management committee. I volunteered unpaid, daytime and evening. And I volunteered when the [same] thing came to [a different neighbourhood], when I was asked if I would look at this. So I took on this development. This one started from a derelict building, the other one was a running concern when I went in.' Reflecting upon his move into the third sector, Maurice concludes: 'I got tremendous satisfaction, especially setting up the [new] one. I was very enthusiastic, it was very satisfying, particularly when we got the building ready and were able to launch it and get people coming in.'

Five years on, and substantial project developments later, Maurice remains dedicated to his work, despite the fact that, as he admits, 'You get frustrated by people's actions or lack of action . . . there's a period when it's really tough and you're feeling really frustrated that you're getting nowhere and hammering your head against a brick wall.' I press him on what kept or keeps him going through such periods. His response confirms that it is the (rare) opportunity to respond to his calling and to realise his value-commitment in practice: 'Determination that you have a plan that you want to bring to fruition. You will do all sorts of things in order to achieve it if you feel it's the right thing to do.' Looking back over his occupational trajectory, he summarises it in the following words: 'early on in my career there was the career structure and then later on, yes, the vocation came in – the importance of it being a vocation came in for me'.

A very similar picture is painted by Maeve as she describes her thirty-two years of work history after she resumed paid employment at the age of forty, with six young sons living at home. Her story makes her the female counterpart of Maurice. Also these are the only two occupational biographies that seem unlikely to have further instalments – given the age of these subjects. Maeve was crystal clear about the nature of her value-commitment when she re-entered the world of work; it is one that has not changed to this day and, at seventy-two, she continues in full-time employment and says: 'I know if I worked in a shop or an office or any other type of organisation rather than caring or helping vulnerable people, I would feel I was wasting my life. I think I'd feel I would rather be at home and would want to retire and have more time off. With this type of work I've never felt there was any waste in it. I don't think my family have felt at all hard done by through it.'

Disillusionment, dissatisfaction and systematic retraining are prominent themes underlying the three main job moves that punctuated her first twenty years of re-employment. Maeve joined Social Services, working with the elderly in residential care, where she admits: 'I got an awful shock, it was very much just like any other organisation, in my view not even a good organisation, that's terrible to say really.' Nevertheless, she backs up her judgement by the following examples: she was warned against revealing her Catholicism, the source of her values, because it would be disliked; she encountered rigid bureaucratic procedures, over matters such as incontinence, rather than client care or staff collaboration; and she tells a revealing story about a disfigured and underprivileged old lady whose love of her cat was manipulated to induce her behavioural conformity by threats to remove the pet. Besides cruelty, she describes finding apathy amongst her co-workers antithetic to her own values: 'I went into the work thinking I'd be caring for people and working with caring people and I didn't find that at all . . . These particular people I was working with in the homes environment and the community care environment, I don't know why they'd come into the work a lot of them. A lot of them had husbands and wives, so it was their accommodation, their food and everything . . . It wasn't that they'd come in with any real wish to make the homes a great place to be or better than they were . . . So I was very disillusioned.'

Maeve decided that only by qualifying as a social worker could she make a difference and within eighteen months she was accepted on to the training course. After qualifying in the 1970s, she took the post of deputy manager in a home 'at a time when there was money in the system and a lot of other people were getting this opportunity . . . so for the next few years there were a lot of very enthusiastic people who really wanted to make a difference and the homes came on tremendously'. Increasingly, however, she became aware of deficiencies in staff training and support, an absence of effective complaints procedures for clients or methods by which staff could introduce innovations, and no means of ensuring that recommendations following inspections were implemented. After mulling this over she decided: 'I still want to stay in this work, I want it to be different but I want to stay in it, and the only way I can make a difference is by being in management . . . If you were in management, you had an opportunity; if you were a good manager, then you could do it; but if you weren't management, you just weren't listened to, it was as simple as that.' After studying for NVQs in management during her free time, Maeve gained the post of service group manager which, as she puts it: 'I used to think would be a great job because I wouldn't just be having influence in one place.'

Instead of that, she recalls her encounter with bureaucratic anomie: 'I remember being asked to present some papers on whether day care or residential care was best for people with dementia, and I put a lot of effort into that, and I think it got lost; I remember being on working parties that were lost and then re-erected two years later with another working party on the same thing, so all our time would have been wasted; some new person gets into a job and says, "I think we'll look at that again," and then they move on and it's dropped . . . it was always on my mind when I was managing for Social Services that the problems with their home care were definitely able to be solved. I knew the problems within Social Services could be done away with and that community care could be an awful lot better . . . a lot more accountable, more quality and a lot more individualised.' Gradually, Maeve says, 'it grew on me and I didn't want to let it go – I wanted to do it myself.'

She has been working for over twenty years with Social Services and, although her employment has been fairly volatile, so far her trajectory has been one of consistent upward mobility. However, her disillusionment moved up with her. Once she was decidedly 'management', she was also in a position to conclude that the attempt to introduce care from the 'inside', promoting the independence of those with dementia, was an exercise in futility. As a founder member of the city branch of the

Alzheimer's Society, Maeve already had experience of innovating through the voluntary sector in the form of day and residential care. Her sideways move into becoming a private care provider was born out of discontent with Social Services and, as she puts it: 'My aim is always to do it better than how it was when I worked for Social Services . . . it was always more expensive than private care anyway.' She now has 80 staff members and 160 clients, Social Services is her biggest user group (for whom she also provides training) and, at seventy-two, Maeve reckons she clocks up a longer working day than at any time in her career. Although her lateral mobility has been a successful venture in risk-taking, Maeve maintains she is not financially motivated, can hardly be said to be business-like, since she leaves her unqualified daughter-in-law to do the books, and is still upgrading her own skills by completing the Level 4 NVQ registered manager's examination. As a summative reference, she cites the comments of her tutor on her reflective paper about work practices in her organisation: 'my NVQ tutor said that most people, when they analysed companies, analyse from the financial perspective, they are sort of finance led. And when I evaluated my company, it was totally devoid of financial analysis . . . It was all about how we managed quality and everything – so that's all about my value system.'

The same themes are illustrated by the rest of this sub-group in the course of their volatile work histories. Underlying all of them is the same fundamental dissatisfaction with (and critique of) successive contexts of employment because of their incongruity with subjects' values. Bryan, whose injuries put paid to his dream of becoming a professional footballer, has a subsequent work biography which is a paler version of Maurice's trajectory. He slowly became reconciled to engineering, helped by continuing 'to do his bit' for years as a volunteer football coach for youngsters. At work, he was a perfectionist and started to derive intrinsic satisfaction from precision-tooling. After a restless shift from tool making into machine-tool fitting, and from there into machine-tool repairs, Bryan eventually found the latter to be, he confesses, his 'little niche': 'it's great to see everything go together like a jigsaw, such pride when it's finished. The achievement is a job well done . . . I would always be thinking, all the time, and I used to like things to be wrong that I couldn't get [immediately] right because it was a challenge . . . we're working to a tenth of a thousandth of an inch – it's mind boggling, isn't it?'

Yet, the *modus vivendi* he had painfully built up was continuously threatened. After eight years with a good engineering company and already a section leader, he was given promotion. This entailed responsibility for more than a hundred men but simultaneously deprived him of his hard-won job satisfaction, as he said with regret: 'my day wasn't about making any more, it was progress chasing . . . the only time my skill would come into being was if the other people couldn't do it'. Bryan decided to pay the price, turned down the extra money and 'saved face' by moving to an aeronautics company. After five years, the identical scenario was repeated. This time he dodged promotion on the pretext that he disliked doing any night work. Again, he rejected upward mobility and again, paid the price for retaining internal goods. The latter were to become still more important to him.

It will be recalled that at eighteen Bryan had described himself as 'a lapsed Christian'. In his forties and prompted by his repartnering, Bryan gradually returned to church attendance – this time with the Baptists. There, he recognised that many of his new friends had something he lacked and eventually, he underwent a conversion experience. As he sees it: 'the difference in me now is that I have a peace where I can think things out, whereas before I was quite volatile.' Paradoxically, this religious renewal was to issue in a final act of occupational volatility. Bryan took partial early retirement, moving to work in an engineering laboratory for three days a week. He now describes one of his major concerns as 'helping those in need', is involved in church charity work, and he and his wife have 'adopted at a distance' a five-year-old West Indian child.

If Bryan could reconcile himself – during that tract of his life when he had drifted away from religious practice – to keeping his eyes down and gaining his quantum of solace from the intricacies of his work, Geraldine's value-commitment placed stronger demands upon her. After abandoning her MA, she continued to be driven by a desire to work for the rectification of social injustice: 'like giving people a chance even if they've not exactly been on the straight and narrow to start with. Really giving people a fair hearing whatever their background is, whether they've had a drug-related background, drink or offending, or whether they've come from another country.' Hence, she was ready to return to the proba-tion service, this time working for the newly established victim unit. The initial satisfaction derived was soon vitiated by targets and performance indicators. She realised: 'you could see the benefits you were giving [clients] in the sense of reassurance and so on. It's an amazing job, but the bureaucratic side of that is pants – to put it bluntly. If they'd left it to old-style working values, rather than we must meet this target at this point and looking at numbers rather than people – I was quite heavily involved in the statistical side of it as well, and I could see the people behind the figures and you could see the managers just seeing the figures and manip-ulating them in a way to make the government happy, which is crazy really. That does annoy me, which is why, when it was suggested I went on to be a probation officer, I said: "No, I can't."'

Out of her disillusionment, Geraldine took a leap in the dark and a substantial salary cut to become an adult skills tutor, teaching basic literacy and numeracy to what she sees as 'still the same client group'. She finds that 'there are moments of absolute gold' in her new post, such as getting a reluctant primary-level learner to light up over his first Shakespeare sonnet. Conversely, there are simultaneously twelve other adult learners to keep occupied, there are some whose attendance is irregular at best, thus nullifying the best-laid learning plans, and, yet again, there is a different set of performance indicators to meet. At the age of thirty-four, it seems as though Geraldine's pattern of lateral mobility and retraining is far from over. As she openly puts it: 'I can't see myself being here too long. But I'm starting to get a reputation as somebody who hops from place to place now: although I was in probation for thirteen years I did go from place to place within it . . . And then the fact that I've yo-yoed from course to course as well – it probably doesn't look too good, but it's finding *the* thing.'

For a meta-reflexive, that is the major problem. But it is one that can present itself in various guises at different levels. With the worst start in life and without qualifications, Pete undoubtedly sets the record for volatility by having held more than thirty jobs. Although about half of these moves can be attributed to redundancies, because unqualified workers bore the first brunt of manufacturing's decline in the Midlands, that is not the full story. Pete was driven by two concerns throughout his working life: to implement his socialist values and to find a satisfyingly tasking job, as opposed to ones 'where you push a button at eight o'clock and don't do anything else till half eleven, just watch it'. The conjoint pursuit of these values has intensified his mobility: moving up to chargehand or foreman and back down to shopfloor work again; shifting from one employer to another, sometimes pushed out because of his over-zealous unionism and sometimes attempting to get out when he saw the writing on the wall. At nineteen, he was a setter, a chargehand and shop steward as well, but part of his time was spent working on a track and, as he realises: 'that drove me crazy, so I had to pack that up; you're just a number in there . . . you could be a week just fitting bumpers'.

His last job, which he held for ten years, provided the challenge of making one-off aircraft parts. However, Pete probably courted fate when he secretly brought in the union and successfully unionised the shop after a management takeover. He himself remains unsure how great a role this played in the decision to move the plant to another city; what he is sure about is that his resulting unemployment at the age of fifty-nine means he will probably not work again, unless he accepts a current offer to make van deliveries. Pete's main regret, as at the start of his working life, continues to be his lack of training. The need to provide for his family prevented him from qualifying as a union rep. As he concludes: 'I'm too old now, it would be a couple of years' training and I'd be sixty-two then. It wouldn't be worth it.' This is not because Pete's socialist values have dimmed, but because of the unlikelihood of his finding a position in which to use such skills, given the continuing decline of manufacturing.

The same themes are repeated by other interviewees at different stages of their working lives. As meta-reflexives, they are fully aware that the pursuit of their value rationality has entailed considerable costs in terms of their employment trajectories and where these have ended. Here is one example, as Eunice sums up the prices paid along the way to her semi-detached vicarage: 'Giving up a well-paid job, to my father's disgust; I could have married and had a family – we're not banned from doing it, but I don't think I would have done the same sort of job if I'd had a family. Financially, yes, and having a home – this is a home, but it's not mine and I'll have to move. But they haven't really felt like sacrifices because there've been compensations, they've been for a purpose.'

However, there are no guarantees of even such a qualified 'happy ending.' Geraldine now earns half a teacher's salary and is chided by some of her friends for 'not being higher up', for resigning from the probation service when she had reached the grade of senior administrative officer. Looking back, she says: 'it was quite a big decision to go into basic skills teaching, which some people thought was a step back rather than a step forward because it was less money. But I don't see less money as always being a step backwards, though there are times when I've thought, "What have I done?" because I was in a very secure job, more or less another family because everyone knew who I was.' Yet, unlike Eunice, her occupational mobility is still incomplete.

Cameron has paid even more, in a variety of currencies. He has sacrificed relationships, friendship networks and home ownership, as well as laying out his own money for flight training on both sides of the Atlantic. Cameron estimates that his pilot's licence has cost him more than £100,000, saved from working as a carpenter, a skill that, unlike the jobs made accessible by his degree, he can practise when and where he pleases. At forty-one, he knows that his age is against him, he is living with his mother and, once more, working as a carpenter. Recently he was interviewed by a new company planning to provide cheap domestic flights. He keeps his mobile in view and waits for them to ring, saying: 'all the decisions I've ever made have been for this'. I ask him whether he feels his struggle has been unfair and his response is: 'only if I ended up as a carpenter and never flew for an airline . . . Right now, though, that hasn't happened and I haven't got to that stage yet – not for a few years.'

Siobhan, now at the start of her working life, does not anticipate remaining long in her first post. She rails against having to supply superficial two-page reports on complex issues and thus being associated with 'all the things that give consultants a bad reputation – coming in and telling people what they already know and charging them lots of money'. Significantly, since she wants to use her 'brain for more than lining [her] pocket', she too is beginning to look beyond the market towards the voluntary sector. Currently, Siobhan is 'trying to run uphill', attempting to persuade the consultancy to start an employee volunteer programme (*pro bono* work), and is also considering working as policy manager for a charity. What is important about her meta-reflexivity – as for the other interviewees – is that she seeks organic integration between her concerns. Consequently, Siobhan rejects having her life divided into work time, governed by instrumental rationality, and spare time, devoted to voluntary activities, in which she can express her value rationality. The idea of moving on is, as she herself puts it: 'in the hope that I would spend more time doing things that I feel make some kind of difference – and to be able to do that as part of my job rather than looking for that outside my job'.

Politics of a tentative third kind

Meta-reflexives are disenchanted with national party politics, but in this they are no different from the other sub-groups examined: some continue to vote without conviction, whilst others feel they have had abstention thrust upon them. However, their critique is distinctive in three ways, which have further ramifications. Firstly, many – including Pete, Gina and Eunice, who have been life-long socialists – accentuate the fact that government and opposition are increasingly indistinguishable as the cause of their political alienation. In Pete's words, 'I'm not happy about it now. It's not Labour, is it? Like the Tories aren't Tories any more – what's the difference between any of them?' As Gina puts it, 'where does the left in this country go now? There's no viable left wing party in Britain at the moment.' Secondly, British government support for the non-mandated invasion of Iraq is regularly cited as the final straw, and not just by Anouar 'who would say that'. Not only is it relatively new for foreign policy to count as the major source of political discontent, but this indicates an approach to politics on the part of meta-reflexive subjects that is very different from those of other sub-groups. It is equally distinct from the interest-based involvement of autonomous reflexives and from the long-standing grievance of communicative reflexives about the abyss dividing the politicians from the people. Thirdly, the failure of national politics is closely allied to parallel criticisms of local government and of social

services. In short, major failures in international relations are seen to be of
a piece with the defects of governance in general.

Because political discontents are viewed as being intertwined rather
than discrete, meta-reflexives are struggling to articulate a new approach
to representative democracy, to civil society and, ultimately, to the relations between them. As yet, this is inchoate but it is already crystallising
around two forms of activism. On the one hand, this sub-group furnishes
active protagonists for and vocal supporters of reinventing community. On
the other hand, it supplies exactly the same for new global social movements. As yet, these two strands – the local and the global – are linked only
by the elective affinity they possess for meta-reflexive subjects.

Where local activism is concerned, what remains indefinite are the
meanings of 'community' and its 're-creation': reanimation of a neighbourhood through popular involvement, the practical incorporation of
marginalised groups in a broader area, local associations addressing
single issues, *pro bono* initiatives directed at particular problems, schemes
targeting the young, the old, the isolated, the newcomers and so forth.
The only common denominator is the constant reiteration of two words:
'voluntary' and 'charity'. The latter is shorn of any philanthropic denota-
tion and is best defined as standing in opposition to 'governmental
agency'. The significance of these two words to meta-reflexives is considerable. Not a single interviewee failed to mention their involvement – to
varying degrees – in a body that could be described by one of the two.
Their significance is also profound, in terms of the potential self-
investment that these subjects entertain. Part and parcel of the dialectics
of occupational discontent were references by the majority to considering
employment with some form of charitable, non-governmental and non-
profit organisation – that is, by those who did not already work for such.

This meta-reflexive concern for 'community', despite its varied meanings, is light years removed from both the communicative reflexives' preoccupation with their own micro-life worlds and the autonomous
reflexives' use of the locality as a place for out-sourcing and paid access to
selected facilities. Members of both of the latter groups may have mentioned loneliness and lawlessness as local social problems, but it is hard to
imagine any of them resigning their jobs – as Maurice did, in an attempt
to reverse community decline – or voicing his following sentiments: 'I
think community projects are an essential part of the social development
of this country. We are in grave danger of becoming isolated in our own
homes. People go out to work and don't see any neighbours, and there is
no neighbouring – that's gone. In a wealthy area, that may not be too bad
because people know they'll be going out to dinner with somebody they
work with or something, but in an inner city that doesn't happen. So I see

it as very important that communities come together to help each other.' Other meta-reflexives invest their energies in different kinds of projects; what unites them is not a burgeoning communitarianism, but rather a common belief that social problems will not yield to individualistic incentives or to centralised political interventions. They are radically disenchanted with 'lib/lab' solutions, although they have yet to articulate and to coalesce around an alternative.

Where 'charity', the second strand, is concerned, meta-reflexives are unanimous that they themselves should do more to alleviate social injustices. However, what are volunteered as examples of 'injustice' are surprising because they are uniformly global in kind. Gina's partial summary can stand for the whole group: 'I suppose poverty and mal-distribution of wealth, I suppose the negative effects of globalisation – although I think there are some positive effects – those are the big social injustices at the moment, with all the issues about the war.' To this list should be added racism – explicitly mentioned and unanimously condemned by the meta-reflexives – and their united concern about the environment, expressed in its most sophisticated form by Jonathan: 'we try to persuade ourselves that we're in charge of everything, which is what the twentieth century was all about really, wasn't it? Like the environment, everything is chaos because we thought we knew everything. I think maybe this century's about understanding our place in things and having more respect again . . . It doesn't always look good, does it, for planet earth? I'm very frustrated at the lack of progress in governments actually waking up to the realities of what we've done to the planet, chasing after oil instead of investing in alternatives, which are all there.'

The pervasive meta-reflexive response to these global concerns is to lend their support to the build up of new trans-national social movements. The most frequently mentioned are Greenpeace, Amnesty International, 'Stop the War', the Campaign for Nuclear Disarmament, Peace and Justice, Oxfam, debt remission, fair trade and Trade Craft. These movements, whose emergence is facilitated by information technology, tend towards the 'post-organisational' in form. This is simultaneously their strength – the speed with which worldwide protest can be mobilised – and also their weakness – the absence of sustained critique and co-ordinated follow-through. As subjects who, by definition, regularly engage in self-monitoring, the interviewees display some nascent awareness about the limitations of these forms of collective action, born of their participation in them.

Given the reliance of such movements upon media attention and their lack of formal insertion into decision-making agencies, their impact is often ephemeral and their protests ignored. The war in Iraq appears to be something of a watershed for the meta-reflexives, several of whom had a history of campaigning for nuclear disarmament. Anouar speaks for several others when he talks about 'the whole fiasco of the war . . . where's the democracy in that? The millions of people who went to London to march and they still decided – just the might of the government over the people. We put them in power to represent us and the majority don't want something and yet they do it.' Geraldine echoes the same reservation: the Stop the War march was 'very visual, but I can't see that it actually does anything really. It does tell how people feel, but whether they do anything about it is another matter.'

In general, meta-reflexives have not resigned themselves to mass demonstration being merely expressive action, without an impact on policy, to which Bernadette alone has become reconciled when she says: 'I'm not sure that's what's important actually, I think you do it because you know it's right, and what comes of that – I don't expect the questions to be solved really . . . you just do what you can to fight what you see is an injustice.' In short, meta-reflexives are vocal critics of national representative democracy as the structure appropriate for tackling the world's worst problems and have willingly responded to new forms of less-structured social movements *sans frontières*. They are the vanguard of those who feel the need for new and effective organs of global governance, but they lack a blueprint for globalised political participation.

From the initial consideration of the importance of value-commitments to meta-reflexives, a picture has cumulatively emerged of the kind of place they seek for themselves in society and of the type of society they would like to see in place. In relation to their own work and employment patterns, their lateral mobility and tendency towards occupational volatility have been explained in terms of their pursuit of the *Wertrationalität*. Value rationality, as an end in itself, is at variance with the instrumental rationality governing market relations. For meta-reflexives, work is not part of a means–ends relationship, whose rationale is the satisfaction of individual preference schedules, leaving them personally 'better off'. Indeed, to them employment is not a matter of exchange relations at all. Rather, it concerns self-fulfilment through 'making a difference', meaning that the personal expression and the social realisation of their value-commitments are inextricably intertwined *because* they represent two sides of the same coin. Hence, meta-reflexives are resistant to structural bonuses and penalties because they will pay the material costs of pursuing their ideals as best they (fallibly) can do. At rock bottom, their unsettled work histories are produced by the generic incongruity between the importance of the values they care about and the predominance of exchange relations in the world of work. Consequently, there is nothing accidental in them being drawn towards the third sector. However, the tentative manner in which this is understood is underscored by the frequency with which our interviewees mentioned preferring to work for 'charity' – charitable organisations being the main manifestations of work not based upon market relations in Britain today.

If meta-reflexives are tentatively rejecting the 'market' hegemony of exchange relations over human relations, they are even more hesitantly refusing the 'state' and its repressive domination over national, regional and international relations. Temporarily, they have found a haven in global social movements, but they also intimate a hazy recognition that mass protest confines them to expressive action, which does not practically advance their values of social justice on a worldwide basis. Meta-reflexives note, for example, that even the iconic cause of conditional debt remission for the poorest countries is not yet a reality. Significantly, not a single interviewee reverted or resorted to any notion of world government. The global Leviathan is as antipathetic to these subjects as is global capitalism. Meta-reflexives are strong universalists, inclusive humanists and participatory democrats. What they seem to be gesturing towards is a notion of a robust civil society, unconfined to existing national boundaries, yet somehow remaining unfettered by a new global iron cage. The best word we have for this inchoate ideal is 'subsidiarity', but it has not yet entered common parlance, let alone become the goal of collective action on a worldwide scale.

Part III

7   Internal conversations and their outworks

In this concluding part, the narrative form is exchanged for an analytical method of presentation. Narratives are good for conveying life and colour, but there is always a danger of losing the plot. Within fiction that balance is under the author's control: make the plot too evident and the novel becomes 'formulaic'; give narrative a free rein and the book becomes slack. Where the freely given life histories of real people are concerned, control is reduced – or, at least, I think it ought to be relaxed. There is a large debt owing to the respondents, which can only be (partially) discharged by respecting them sufficiently to incorporate their precise formulations, qualifications and reservations – their own takes upon their own narratives. That lengthens subjects' contributions and displaces the burden of keeping track on to the reader. Therefore, this chapter takes a more distanced overview and attempts to synthesise the material presented in a more methodical fashion.

Modes of reflexivity are relational properties deriving from different combinations of the interplay between 'contexts' and 'concerns', but cannot be reduced to either. This type of property has internal and external effects. In other words, practising a particular kind of internal conversation – the one most common to somebody – has consequences for his or her life history. The likelihood is that it will foster a pattern of social mobility, according to the mode of reflexivity that predominates: stability, upward mobility or volatility. The threads patterning these different work histories are systematically disentangled in this part of the book, and the process by which a given trajectory is woven is analysed for each.

Simultaneously, these effects for individuals also produce aggregate consequences for society because the various forms of internal conversation promote, respectively, social stability, social productivity and social transformation. Chapter 1 opened with a consideration of 'reflexivity's biographies' and, after examining these aggregate consequences, it will be possible to return to those considerations and conclude with a brief and speculative glance at 'reflexivity's future'.

Communicative reflexivity and social immobility

Trusting similar others

By definition, communicative reflexivity entails a high degree of *trust* being placed in those assuming the role of a subject's interlocutor(s) within his or her deliberations through 'thought and talk'. Generically, the role of interlocutor will be assigned to and assumed by a person's 'similars and familiars'. This colloquial phrase has two implications. To begin with, the interlocutor needs to be similar enough to the subject in terms of communality of experience, shared points of reference and manifestations of sympathy with the subject's preoccupations, such that *they can be trusted to understand*. Someone who conveyed that they were alien to the type of situation discussed, that they required everything spelling out, rather than volunteering a ready understanding of the context and major (type of) players, and indeed that they could not see why the issue merited discussion, would readily disqualify themselves.

The second implication is that the greatest fund of 'similars' also happens to be one's 'familiars'; the most readily available of these being members of one's natal family. Yet the *quality* of family relations is crucial to whether or not some member(s) is found playing the role of interlocutor(s). Family relationships must neither be romanticised nor homogenised. Not everyone enjoys close, warm and harmonious concourse with parents and siblings, and bad blood with one does not preclude intimacy with another. Furthermore, few of those inherited stereotypes about, for example, the tightly bonded working-class family, snugly embedded in its surrounding neighbourhood, actually survive close qualitative scrutiny.

In other words, the qualitative nature of family relationships may not precipitate the subject towards adopting a family member(s) as their interlocutor(s), but rather predispose them to select dialogical partners from amongst school friends and workmates. These will also be trusted 'similars and familiars' – familiarity being underwritten by 'contextual continuity' and similarity serving to reinforce, reproduce and protract the continuity of context when the subject first moves out of the home.

Interlocution and circumscription

Because the interlocutor in the 'thought and talk' of the communicative reflexive carries half of the burden of the latter's reflexive deliberations, the net effect is *to reduce the amount of prolonged internal conversation* in which the subject engages. As has been stressed, such subjects are perfectly able to initiate their own inner dialogues and to use self-talk to establish their personal agendas of problems and preoccupations. Yet, because for them the boundary between the private and the public is weak, they are not prone to persist in lone inner deliberations. Instead, the process is truncated, with the internal conversation being restricted to the subject ascertaining his or her 'first reactions' to a given issue and doing so quickly. Thereafter, the impulse is to turn to the interlocutor(s), which may mean meeting or phoning them, in order to sound out and check out the 'first' response. In other words, if nothing has been missed out, the subject receives the confirmation sought. Were external conversation to conclude that something had been left out, this would then be factored in dialogically between them and the subject would proceed with enhanced confidence.

The 'thought and talk' of communicative reflexives is not conducive to some mental activities which fall under the rubric of the internal conversation. This is particularly the case for those which Peirce perspicaciously termed 'the power of preparatory meditation'[1] or, more generally, 'musement'[2] – when we uninhibitedly use our mental resources for anything we fancy within the privacy of our own minds, without taboo, unrestrained by the reality principle and unabashed by giving cause for scandal. This is particularly the case for the exercise of imagination, including the holding of imaginary conversations with others, known or unknown to us. Communicative reflexives report such activities to be virtually unknown to them. At most, when prompted as to whether or not they ever imagine the best or the worst that could befall them, their responses are standardised. Routinely, the 'best that could happen' is deemed to be winning the lottery and 'the worst' is envisaging some serious illness or incapacitating accident.

This undoubtedly restricts the scope and functions of their inner dialogues. As Peirce commented, 'People who build castles in the air do not, for the most part accomplish much, it is true; but every man who does accomplish great things is given to building elaborate castles in the air and then playfully copying them on solid ground.'[3] In other words, the uninhibited use of imagination is one way in which many people extend their horizons beyond their quotidian contexts and initiate a process of discernment[4] about endorsing much bolder projects – ones which would

---

[1] *Collected Papers of Charles Sanders Peirce*, ed. C. Hastshorne and P. Weiss, Cambridge, Mass., Belknap Press of Harvard University Press, 1934–9, vol. VI, p. 286.

[2] 'Peirce elaborates on musement, saying that he does not mean by it what we would call reverie – an aimless, imbecilic wandering of the mind. But rather a more or less careful thought, lacking only a *determined* direction or purpose.' William H. Davies, *Peirce's Epistemology*, The Hague, Martinus Nijhoff, 1972, p. 63.

[3] *Collected Papers of Charles Sanders Peirce*, vol. VI, p. 286.

[4] See Margaret S. Archer, *Being Human: the Problem of Agency*, Cambridge, Cambridge University Press, 2000, ch. 7, pp. 230–41.

alter their life courses if they could discount the costs and risks by bring-ing themselves to the point of commitment. Instead, there are very strong reasons why sharing one's flights of fancy or inmost urges with a familiar interlocutor will invariably curtail them. Clearly, if the castle in the air is outside the shared context of the interlocutor, then the dialogical partner has nothing positive to contribute because it is beyond his or her experi-ence. However, they can have plenty that is negative to say, ranging from the 'Don't be daft – get real', to perfunctorily entertaining the attractions of being a famous footballer or pop star, yet quickly concluding, 'It'd be great, but it's not on is it?' The problem of offering up one's dreams (or nightmares) for outside commentary is that they are regularly cut down to size – the size that the shared context can accommodate, which thus serves to reinforce 'contextual continuity'.

Cutting down to size also entails reminders of normative conventional-ity. Share your desire for savage revenge on an unfaithful partner and the likely response would be something like, 'Sure, he's a bastard, but he's not worth swinging for!' Just as importantly, the internal, highly vitriolic out-pouring of our recriminations in an imaginary conversation literally knows no bounds and we can derive considerable satisfaction from honing our insults into the most hurtful prose. Such mental activities may simply prove cathartic or constitute the stocking of one's verbal armoury for possible future use; we can harden ourselves to the shocking nature of vituperation by internal repetition. But to share these phrases and formu-lae with a third party is to introduce an independent 'ear' which has the same effect as does 'the gaze' of inducing shame. People find themselves climbing down, engaging in self-editing or adding modifications to with-draw the public sting – 'After what she's said/done, I'll be glad to see her suffer and wouldn't lift a finger . . . but she's old/has no one else/was good to me once.' 'Thought and talk' happens within the boundaries of contex-tual conventions and it serves to keep the subject within those normative bounds.

Other kinds of mental activities are similarly circumscribed in commu-nicative reflexivity and are reported in interview as being rather minimal. These include 'mulling-over', 'reliving', 'rehearsing' and 'clarifying'. The reason seems to be the same in all these instances and consists in the reci-procity imposed by the dialogical partner(s). Suppose one young woman seeks to complete her mulling over with her closest girlfriend about what went wrong in her latest relationship. Although the person doing the confiding may be willing to recount a whole range of instances of her ex-partner's outrageous behaviour, this confines her *confidente* to the largely passive role of listener. The latter's responses are restricted to supportive banalities, such as, 'Oh, he didn't dare, did he?', or 'But that's terrible!'

and, more importantly, 'Well, I wouldn't have stood for that.' By the latter, the *confidente* signals that there is not just conversational turn-taking but also a conventional taking of turns at the podium in relation to the topic. One revelation deserves another. The *confidente* will thus feel that her patient listening has earned her the right to recount a horror story from her own private life – and at equal length. Together they reinforce what forms of behaviour are mutually acceptable to them and which are not, thus buttressing their contextual conventions – until they tire of reciprocal politeness.

The other way in which the interlocutor can play a full conversational role is even more significant. She can steer the discussion back to a more equal footing through valorising episodes which they shared in common, by saying something like, 'Well, I thought it was a bit off at Ben's party when he kept twitching down that boob-tube Patty was wearing.' In this way, which is the same for 'reliving', 'rehearsing' or 'clarifying', the subject is drawn back to their common ground, the implication being that the detailed dissection of shared experiences can and will reveal all. Of course it will not, because a lot of tenderness as well as exquisite types of abuse are exercised only behind closed doors. Yet, what the practice of communicative reflexivity does is to privilege the public over the private, shared experience over lone experiences, third-person knowledge over first-person knowledge. Through the tendency for every issue to be reduced to the experiential common denominators of its discussants, communicative reflexivity is inhospitable to the innovative, the imaginative or the idiosyncratic. In short, the speculative realm is severely truncated in favour of common sense, common experience and common knowledge. In the process, 'similars and familiars' become still more similar to one another as well as familiar with each other.

Privileging the shared present

One of the most important implications of the above is its impact upon the mental activity of 'planning'. Obviously, to formulate any 'project' involves thinking ahead, but amongst all practitioners of the different modes of reflexivity who were interviewed, it was the communicative reflexives who collectively insisted that they engaged in only short-term planning, often confined to the next day or the week ahead. This seems fully consistent with their dominant mode of reflexivity. The lone part of their internal conversation is confined to ascertaining and establishing their 'first reactions' to some current exigency or eventuality, after which they immediately precipitate themselves into external dialogue in order to reach a conclusion. Thus, they confine themselves to the immediate in a two-fold manner. On the one hand, such 'first' responses are restricted to current events. There is no logical necessity about this, because most of us would have such reactions were we asked to state our immediate attraction or aversion to long-term projects such as training to climb Mount Everest, becoming an MP or learning a foreign language. However, by the very nature of her deliberation, the communicative reflexive forgoes the inner speculative freedom to envisage the mid-term and long-term scenarios which could unfurl from following a single 'first reaction'. She forfeits this under the imperative to seek immediate completion from her interlocutor of her response to the immediate. In so doing, she voluntarily confines her planning to the dictates of immediacy.

On the other hand, were her interlocutors rather different from her, especially in the variety of their experiences, then they might point out that, attractive as it may seem to do 'x' now, doing so would probably close the door upon 'y', which the subject may come to regret, or even be likely to result in 'z', which the subject would agree did represent the undesirable. However, because dialogical partners are 'familiars', even if there is a generational difference between them (as in daughter and mother), then the scenarios that mother could present would tend to be familiar too – thus introducing few novel considerations. Once again, it is what they share in the here and now that enjoys primacy in their exchanges and thus prioritises the short term over the longer term.

Hence, the contextual confines that underwrite 'thought and talk' and make it viable, seriously impede long-term planning. This is because to follow one's internal promptings to do 'x' usually means endorsing a course of action that has multiple ramifications and represents taking one fork in a branching set of options, then making one future more likely than others. But the effect of contextual confinement is that the experiences of both dialogical partners are severely limited, such that they are unaware of repercussions outside their familiar context. Although the likely implications of a particular decision may be fairly well known in the public domain (for example, to choose a degree in social policy over one in sociology increases the probability that job options are related to social work or social administration), this knowledge is not equally distributed over all natal contexts – and neither is knowledge about the means to obtain it. Thus, if an isolated exemplar of this empirical generalisation has been encountered, it will tend to be interpreted as a manifestation of contingency rather than as an example of a regular connection. In this way, vast tracts of human experience and of socially structured opportunity are assigned to the domain of the contingent (to good or bad luck) by those whose experiential repertoire is contextually confined.

This is why communicative reflexives usually display a huge respect for contingency; there is simply so much more lying outside their familiar experiences than within them. What lies outside is unpredictable and fortuitous; and that which is not understood to have a generative mechanism, or even seen to display empirical regularities, cannot be factored into someone's planning. Consequently, the focus when making decisions is upon the short term where outcomes are relatively familiar and seem reasonably predictable. Beyond that, respect for contingency engenders an attitude of 'taking things as they come', 'crossing that bridge when one comes to it' and 'going with the flow'. Thus, communicative reflexives are everyday pragmatists, whose tendency is to confront a problem only when it confronts them. They return to their mental drawing boards only when the *present* becomes problematic because 'thought and talk', within 'contextual continuity', treats so many future possibilities as unforeseeable and therefore intractable to longer-term planning. At times this sounds like fatalism, and indeed '*che sera, sera*' tends to be these respondents' motto for the life course. Many will subscribe retrospectively to the notion that 'it was meant to be', even if few of them explicitly subscribe to the existence of a *deus ex machina* who has made matters so. Still fewer of them accept that longer-term planning on their part could have made the outcome 'otherwise'.

The dialogical reinforcement of 'immobility'

To be short-term planners does not mean that communicative reflexives are 'passive agents',[5] even though their common refusal to engage in long-term planning does increase their tendency be people to whom things happen rather than individuals who make things happen. Nevertheless, it has already been maintained that communicative reflexives are as capable as anyone else of initiating their own 'projects' within their own minds, even though the process of deliberating about them is held open to interlocution. It is here, however, in the externalisation of their deliberations, that the communicative reflexive makes *the first, crucial and active agential contribution to his or her social immobility.*

When young people start considering their first occupations, a process which often seems much more casual than most careers services would have it be, the communicative reflexive does precisely what one expects by now and presents his or her initial inclinations to an interlocutor. Since (for those interviewed) these 'similars and familiars' universally came

---

[5] Martin Hollis, *Models of Man: Philosophical Thoughts on Social Action*, Cambridge, Cambridge University Press, 1977.

from amongst their friends and family, the effect of these external conversations is the recommendation of familiar jobs.

In turn, similarity between the dialogical partners is reinforced – thus fostering social reproduction. As an overall effect, reproduction is generated through the *modesty of occupational choices* which result when the definition of this 'project' is concluded in consultation with one's interlocutor. For practitioners of other modes of reflexivity, dreams can be quietly cherished, subjects remain open to a variety of influences and information that can raise their aspirations, and a high level of success – say, at school – can elasticate their ambitions, without countervailing voices being raised to restrict them.

What is crucial is that the communicative reflexive is an *active contributor* to his or her modest social placement by virtue of the first job they take up. In other words, social immobility is not 'quasi-automatic', or 'semi-unconscious', let alone the product of the 'pushes' of significant others or of social background upon the passive subject. Here, it is important to recall that in the present study we found no statistical association between socio-economic origins and mode of reflexivity. In other words, what is being described for the present sub-group is not 'working-class traditionalism' clothed in new vocabulary. The 'positional' and the 'dispositional' are not so tightly bound together as Bourdieu and his followers have represented them to be.

The *active and reflexive* nature of this process, which is therefore neither automatic nor unconscious, can be illuminated by reference to the variety of forms it may take. Firstly, although it has been emphasised that a communicative reflexive's interlocutor(s) will be drawn from 'similars and familiars' and this (on the evidence of the present study) means from their 'friends and family', the latter two are not homogeneous. Indeed, were both given the opportunity to complete the subject's deliberative sequence about first employment, they might do so in quite different ways. Since by definition, friends and family are in close proximity to any given subject, it is highly likely that both will put in their two pennyworth of advice, whether or not they are consulted in the role of interlocutors. Therefore, it is only if subjects can be adduced who *actively refused proffered employment, representing upward socio-occupational mobility, in favour of the socially immobile job* they concluded upon with their chosen interlocutor(s), that we can substantiate the argument that we play an active role in making our way in the world. Such cases would do so because, despite both the existence and the known existence of objective opportunities for upward mobility, the communicative reflexives had subjectively rejected them in favour of social immobility. We have met clear cases of subjects who had done just that: Alf, Pauline, Jeanette, Olga and Robbie.

Secondly, a subject may have arrived at a very clear definition of the occupation that he or she would like to take up, but both structural factors and/or inter-personal influences may militate effectively against their so doing. Do they passively resign their occupational goals in favour of feasibility or a quiet life? The evidence from the communicative reflexives is that they do not. Instead, they do something considerably more active and deliberative than giving in to the force of circumstances or to forceful personalities. As agents they devise a 'second best'. That is, they come up with an occupation that may be socio-economically (and in other ways) inferior to their desired option, but one which shares many of the latter's attractions, such as place and type of work. This decision will have been concluded through 'thought and talk' with the chosen interlocutor(s) and, although the job is humbler than the subject's first preference, arriving at this compromise would be beyond the wits of a 'passive agent'. Nevertheless, the inter-personal and circumstantial politics of the possible have yet again induced modesty about employment – this time because the subject has deemed half a loaf to be preferable to no bread. Joan and Sheila, who had both wanted to be nurses, exemplify this scenario.

Finally, there are subjects who exemplify the 'paradox of uncertainty'. As was maintained in the preceding book,[6] one of the strongest factors that perpetuated 'contextual continuity' was when a young person could readily identify an occupational role within the natal context that he or she desired to occupy – and promptly did so. Yet, some could not; they simply did not know what work they wanted to do. Providing they were performing fairly well, there was a marked tendency for such young people to remain at school, to transfer to college or even to proceed to university – still in a state of uncertainty. As such, they are relatively passive agents, save for their educational achievement being commensurate with required performance levels. Eventually, the need to work finds them accepting a post which, in all probability, represents upward social mobility in relation to their natal contexts. This occupational uncertainty is far from being the preserve of communicative reflexives, but these are inclined to do something distinctive when they find themselves in this situation. Not only are they restless and discontented with their employment, not uncommon amongst those whose jobs chose them, but they also want to go home. Sometimes their interlocutors have remained part of their natal context and sometimes they have been acquired in the course of these literally aimless educational peregrinations, but the consequence is much the same for the subject – a voluntary renunciation of upward social mobility.

---

[6] Margaret S. Archer, *Structure, Agency and the Internal Conversation*, Cambridge, Cambridge University Press, 2003, pp. 189f.

Their internal conversation about occupational discontents transmutes into dialogical deliberations on the theme of the return of the native. Usually, though not invariably, the subject does not wish to resign all the objective benefits that he or she has by then accrued. Yet, in returning to marry the boyfriend from school or to take up available employment 'back home', these communicative reflexives make a different, but now active compromise. They settle for an occupational status which is objectively more modest than those of their educational peers – as the price they are subjectively willing to pay for the re-establishment of 'contextual continuity'.

It is the combination of these manoeuvres, all of which engineer greater modesty in employment than was structurally conditioned, which explains the association detected in the Coventry study between their socio-economic status and their communicative reflexivity, but not between social background and being a communicative reflexive.

Tied down by human relations

In turn, the consequences of the lower-status jobs accepted[7] interact with the causes that generated these socio-occupational decisions. Once in post, all subjects immediately acquire a new fund of workmates, even if some job entrants obtained their employment through the offices of family or friends. These new workmates constitute a pool of potential new friends and are sometimes the source of the subject's partner-to-be. Moreover, each of these new friends also has his or her family and friendship network, serving to extend the dimensions of the pool still further. Yet, this fund of people is in no sense representative of the general population in that geographical area, much less in the country as a whole.

For whatever biographical reasons, workmates share the same socio-economic status as the subject. Hence, as new friendships are formed or new relationships develop, subjects actively forge extensions to their pre-existing social networks and frequently do so within the same locality. Because, for these subjects, taking up their relatively modest forms of employment often entailed considerable activity, tenacity and sometimes ingenuity, it follows that their own occupational status is not the passive effect of their social background. Similarly, their new co-workers are not the automatic products of their involuntary natal social placements either. In a real sense, the communicative reflexives have chosen to work with people who have also opted for the same socio-economic status. And, from

---

[7] That is, lower in relation to the aspirations of some subjects or to the opportunities available to others.

this occupational position, they make further choices which serve to confirm and consolidate it. By expanding their social networks from amongst their new colleagues, they also actively create the next biographical stage of their context – a context that is now predicated upon their social immobility, although this was not ineluctably the case for most.

The ramifications proliferate still further. Many of the communicative reflexives also reported that *now* their most important interlocutors were people whom they had encountered during training or in the course of their early employment histories. Thus, the friends that they have chosen to complete their 'thought and talk' are individuals from the same context of employment, with corresponding similarities of experience, and probably still resident in the same area. Thus, the active and dialectic constitution of 'contextual continuity' unfurls to enfold the future.

Although not a matter of logical entailment, the ultimate 'concerns' of communicative reflexives tend to be heavily vested in inter-personal relationships. This could not be established quantitatively for two reasons: firstly, such a high proportion of the whole sample listed 'the family' as one of their three major 'concerns' (92 per cent),[8] and, secondly, roughly similar proportions of those practising diverse modes of reflexivity also listed 'work'. However, during interview, different sub-groups were found to attach very different meanings to both terms.

Thus, when communicative reflexives are asked what is the most important aspect of their present job or when seeking work, they strongly emphasise human relations – a friendly environment, people with whom they can share a laugh, or the give and take of human warmth. This emphasis overrides considerations of pay, promotion prospects or public usefulness, which preoccupy practitioners of the other two modes of reflexivity. Similarly, the importance of 'the family' is a matter of close companionship and shared activities, whose intensity actually precludes or makes redundant other more public forms of sociality. The well-being of 'the family' is not just an important concern whose compatibility with the achievement of other concerns is internally negotiated. To the communicative reflexive, 'the family', once they have founded their own, occupies *uncontested centre-stage as their ultimate concern*, and, what is also distinctive of this group, it does so *to the exclusion of any other serious form of social involvement*. Both such emphases have further implications for social immobility because 'inter-personal concerns' and 'contextual continuity' intertwine over the life course.

---

[8] The open-ended responses given by subjects were grouped into the following categories and then aggregated: 'family' (81.2 per cent), 'partner/relationship' (singular) (1.6 per cent), and 'family and friends' (9.4 per cent), together totalling 92.2 per cent. In the text, all findings are rounded to whole numbers.

Protection and renunciation

The centrality of inter-personal 'concerns' means that all other consider-ations about work and employment are systematically subordinated by the communicative reflexives. Amongst the young and unpartnered, this frequently manifests itself in a preference for remaining with their famil-iar workmates or work team rather than seeking promotion – a matter about which they are fully self-aware. When they are content at work, for reasons of sociability, they express a desire to remain with the same employer – just as Jon stuck it out, despite rumours about his company folding. Again, it was impossible to document this quantitatively because, as will be seen, the sub-group of communicative reflexives also harbours young people whose unwanted upward social mobility (resulting from the 'paradox of uncertainty') finds them lacking in job satisfaction and casting about for means of restoring their 'contextual continuity' – as Terry was doing. In either case, they represent a considerable contrast with the autonomous reflexives who are extremely knowledgeable about the various rungs on the promotion ladder and have often developed per-sonal targets for the age by which they hope to have scaled each – or the new posts they aim to occupy.

Amongst those with established families, their supreme importance means that all such interviewees willingly make objective occupational sacrifices in order to ensure that family requirements, as subjectively defined, are met and remain unthreatened. This may spell the familiar pattern of women resigning satisfying jobs in order to undertake child-care and then settling for part-time work which can be accommodated with school hours, or subsequently accepting downward mobility in rela-tion to their pre-married post, for later family convenience. But equally, husbands refuse overtime, better-paid late shifts, promotions entailing extensive commuting or geographical relocation if these entail family dis-ruption. They too will accept downward mobility and long, strenuous hours, provided that this is the only means for them to go on providing.

Thus, communicative reflexives are also people who actively endorse socio-economic immobility or voluntarily embrace downward mobility. What it is vital to underline is that for many of these subjects this consti-tutes the second biographical stage during which they have actively trun-cated their own occupational 'projects'. Firstly, as has been seen, this was common practice in relation to their initial posts, either in order to accompany their friends into a lower-status position than the one envis-aged for or by them, or by settling for 'second best' when their initial 'project' met with resistance from the natal family. Later on in the life course, this second renunciation of upward mobility was a common occurrence, which could happen more than once. In combination, these occupational decisions actively served to confirm social immobility on the part of the communicative reflexive.

Reflexively, such actions are not regarded as sacrificial on the part of these subjects. Looking back, far from being consumed by regrets, they usually regard these past decisions as integral to their present contentment. Such contentment is universal amongst subjects who are young middle-aged or more; to them the forgoing of (available) advancement was viewed not as self-sacrifice but as a necessary condition for realising their ultimate concern. If they can achieve that, it is not marred by disgruntlement about the costs involved in so doing. Nevertheless, like Joan, they are aware that their 'internal goods' have come at a price; they can voice objective regret without subjective embitterment.

Perhaps communicative reflexives do appreciate the fragility of the inter-personal relations they value so highly, possibly understanding that these are not readily transferable and not easy to reconstruct. It is significant that amongst practitioners of the three dominant modes of reflexivity, it is the communicatives who are the most prone to fracture. 'fractured reflexivity' is the condition in which the inner conversation merely intensifies distress and disorientation without the subject being able to design a purposeful course of remedial action. In fact the majority of fractured reflexives within the sample and amongst those interviewed originated from the communicatives who were either impeded in practising this mode or displaced from amongst the ranks of its practitioners. Two of the most glaring causes precipitating 'fracturing' were tightly related to the subject's family or work: marital breakdown, particularly when attributable to the infidelity of one party, and the dislocation occasioned by upward occupational mobility, even if it had been welcomed at first. Maybe the communicative reflexive is perfectly correct in diagnosing social immobility as an important ingredient in establishing and sustaining his or her *modus vivendi* in society.

The modus vivendi *as a micro-world*

For the communicative reflexive, the social constitution of this *modus vivendi* is made up of a dense net of inter-personal relations, converging upon the family unit. In a real sense this does represent a familial 'micro-world', with considerably more internal exchanges occurring between its members than with the exterior. As such, it has important and systematic effects for the external social world. However, these consequences must not be confused with theses about the endurance of 'traditionalism', the development of 'privatisation', or 'individualisation'. Instead, their main influence resides in a resistance to organised associations and formalised institutions – a repudiation of *Gesellschaft* which underwrites their very low level of participation in civil society.

On the one hand, the communicative reflexives and their *modus vivendi* cannot be assimilated to the survival of the working-class extended family, as classically described by Young and Willmott.[9] In part, this is because our respondents are not necessarily working class in their socio-economic status or social origins. In part, it is because when they refer to the 'family' as their ultimate concern, the referent is not the historic extended form but, instead, a variety of relatively new and often only semi-institutionalised relationships.[10]

On the other hand, the family relations, which they valorised so highly, did not conform to inherited sociological notions of 'privatisation': life centred round the house, the private acquisition of consumption goods and celebration of new-found affluence. Equally, there is no commonality between the privileging of inter-personal relations in the life-styles adopted by communicative reflexives and the imperatives to 'individualisation' that Beck derives from and detects in the second wave of modernity.

Instead, what they share is a repudiation of secondary organisations which also manifests itself in a deep indifference towards the institutions of civil society. At the local level, this is signalled by a conscious unwillingness to participate in clubs, community organisations, charitable activities or churches. Only the pub, as an ambiguous ground where the private can be inserted non-committally into the public domain, is an exception for some. This indifference on the part of the communicative reflexives seems to be grounded in a perceived lack of need for organised association and a generalised conviction that it has little to offer them. These are the *leitmotifs* as far as the institutions of civil society are concerned.

Thus, in relation to religion, although more of the communicative reflexives who were interviewed reported being baptised and attending denominational schools than would be the case for the population in general, not a single one attended church – even irregularly. All were carefully respectful of religious beliefs and none could be characterised as explicitly secular, but they were uniformly antipathetic to organised

---

[9] M. Young and P. Willmott, *Family and Kinship in East London*, Harmondsworth, Penguin, 1962.

[10] It was clear throughout the Coventry sample that different respondents meant different things by the 'family'. Its referents included 'partnerships of at least two years duration' (incorporating two avowedly gay partnerships); repartnering (which may or may not have involved marriage); having children (regardless of the subject being of widowed, divorced, separated or single-parent status); the amalgamated family, with stepchildren, sometimes from both sides; and having living parents or relatives, when respondents had never married, were not in a partnership or were childless.

religious practice. Their common ground was sometimes articulated in the well-worn statement, 'You don't have to go to church to be a good person,' and more frequently in a syncretism which blended together Christian elements, spiritualism, fatalism and a powdering of New Age references. This could conceivably be called 'implicit religion', but it would still constitute a theological barrier to membership of any given church or denomination. More sub-textually, these respondents seemed to be saying that institutionalised religion had nothing to offer them, which they could not access for themselves, and yet would entail a commitment which they were unwilling to make.

The approach of the communicative reflexives to politics was isomorphic to their religious stance. On the whole, their generalised respect for the right to vote co-existed with a lack of party political support and with swing-voting. Again, with the exception of one life-long unionist, the explanation lay in a conviction that none of their needs could be served by a higher level of political participation – whether in national or local politics or through extra-parliamentary social movements. Instead, political parties were viewed as distant, self-serving, indifferent to the views of the electorate, incapable of changing anything very much and unwilling to listen to ordinary people. In short, the macro-politics of Westminster were not seen as impacting upon or having the capacity to impact on the micro-worlds and concerns of the communicative reflexives.

Their emphasis upon the importance of the inter-personal appears to have the equal and opposite effect of devaluing the institutional for the communicative reflexive. Indeed, when they come to review the social in general, they conceptualise it in reductionist and atomistic terms – thus tending strongly to deny the existence of 'social barriers or obstacles', or that some people are dealt a poor hand of cards at birth, or that anything prevents the determined from achieving their aims. Younger subjects, in particular, have bought the rhetoric of the open society; they are intra-punitive about failure to succeed and they attribute success to 'keenness' and 'hard graft'. They are fundamentalist Thatcherites: strong believers in individuals and their families, but more than agnostic about the existence of society.

As people who attach supreme importance to inter-personal relations, it is probably unsurprising that communicative reflexives see impersonal institutions as lacking the causal powers to serve them; only 'similars and familiars' can minister effectively to their needs. Given their active endorsement of social immobility, they are not prone to seek large-scale institutional change; their principal requirements are ones that can only be furnished in qualitative ways by determinate and well-known people. These implications for civil society appear to be inscribed in communicative reflexivity itself; the necessary intimacy of the 'thought and talk' pattern of this mode of reflexivity is inimical to the impersonality of public life. As such, communicative reflexives are *prima facie* a force for social stability, and that will be their aggregate effect at any given time.

Autonomous reflexivity and upward social mobility

The absent policeman

By its nature, autonomous reflexivity is exercised alone by a subject who, for various biographical reasons, has become accustomed to relying upon his[11] own mental resources. The absence of interlocutors renders this form of internal conversation very different from external conversation – much more so than is the case for the communicative reflexives with their pattern of 'thought and talk'. Several crucial features distinguish the autonomous mode of reflexivity, precisely because, in practising it, no obligations are owed to a third party and no rights can be exercised by one.

Perhaps the most radical difference concerns the sheer amount of time that can be devoted to inner dialogue. Empirically, it was seen early on (chapter 3) that strong autonomous reflexives represent their inner dialogues as going on 'all the time'. There are logical reasons why these internal conversations should indeed be prolonged and ubiquitous. To begin with there is the simple fact that one *cannot be impolite to oneself*; the very notion of displaying good manners *towards* oneself is a contradiction in terms. Unlike injunctions to be 'gentle to yourself', to 'take care of yourself' or even to 'love yourself', manners are other-directed and matters of public rather than private conduct. For example, we do not apologise for interrupting ourselves. Indeed it is questionable whether one can interrupt oneself rather than one's train of thought. Conversely, it constitutes a gross lack of manners to harp on any of our preoccupations to others.[12]

However, in the private space of our own minds we can dwell for as long as we please on any topic, replaying it, examining it from many angles and revisiting it like a dog worrying a bone. Indeed, we too can bury it, knowing that we will dig it up and return to gnawing at it. In the process, we undoubtedly become more familiar with the topic's features, possible causes and likely consequences – and we also become well acquainted with

---

[11] Since amongst the autonomous reflexives the majority of interviewees were men, the male pronoun will be employed in this section, as it was in chapter 5.

[12] Historically, protocols regulated people's unavoidable absorption in events like bereavement or childbirth; today long-term traumatic effects are sequestered by the designation of specialised interlocutors such as psychotherapists or counsellors, who deal with them in semi-privacy.

the process itself. In short, any particular inner dialogue can be as long drawn out and detailed as we allow it to be and it can take place anywhere – when eating, driving, supposedly listening to music and, let's be honest, whilst making love or sitting on the loo. In the privacy of our own minds, we alone are the arbiters. Certainly, we can bore ourselves and shock ourselves, at which point we can act as the censors of our own obsessions, but self-censorship will be more self-indulgent than the dictates of good manners, and self-policing a good deal more lax than external regulation.

Of course, there is no guarantee that the length of time spent dwelling upon a given issue bears any relationship to reaching a more accurate conclusion about it or deciding upon the best course of action in relation to it. Nonetheless, there is a major difference from communicative reflexivity, namely that the process of inner deliberation is neither truncated nor diverted by exposing one's first and unexamined reactions to the scrutiny of another. Instead, the subject can internally examine all the options that he is capable of surveying, whether for the purpose of interpretation or action. He can consider the consequences of endorsing a particular project and the possible consequences of their consequences – until his imagination runs out. He can factor in the likely effects for other people, assigning them precisely the weightings that he attaches to their importance, claims, expectations and so forth. Without infallibility and without becoming an optimiser, maximiser or satisficer, he has still increased in knowledge about the options available and in self-knowledge about his predilections towards them. The internal conversation is not an area where instrumental rationality has hegemony; it is just as much an arena for reviewing the emotional commentaries on our concerns,[13] which are registered internally as we contemplate doing this rather than that.

Perhaps the most important result of these lengthier inner deliberations is that they do not constitute Wittgenstein's notion of 'idle conversation'. The autonomous reflexive does not merely deliberate, he also determines what he will do, although there is no time limit to how long someone may deliberate about something. Husbands can spend years debating about leaving their wives, just as academics can devote decades to one intellectual problem. However, to be unable to conclude (eventually) upon a course of action is much more characteristic of fractured reflexives. The latter do indeed go round in circles, which only serve to augment their disorientation and distress. Conversely, it is typical that sooner or later autonomous reflexives harness their review of themselves in relation to their circumstances to a plan for action.

[13] Margaret S. Archer, 'Emotions as Commentaries on Human Concerns', in Jonathan H. Turner (ed.), *Theory and Research on Human Emotions*, Amsterdam, Elsevier, 2004, pp. 327–56.

Unlike the communicative subjects who took things 'a day at a time' and 'went with the flow', autonomous subjects are planners – for the week ahead, for the next couple of years or longer. Their decision-making process is premeditative and their decisions are premeditated, not spontaneous. The main reason for this difference is that communicative reflexives are great respecters of contingency because their immersion in 'similarity and familiarity' greatly restricts the experiential database upon which they can draw, such that many quite predictable outcomes are regarded as matters of chance. In contradistinction, the mastery of contingency is the main objective of the ruminations in which the autonomous reflexive engages. Although perfect knowledge is impossible in an open system, nevertheless autonomous subjects feel sufficiently confident about having reviewed available options, having surveyed likely outcomes and having evaluated these probable results that they can both plan a course of action and act on it. Events often prove them to have been mistaken but many plans, though not all, can be re-evaluated, revised and replaced. To have got things wrong does not prevent an autonomous reflexive from replanning how to put them right.

Since autonomous reflexivity is practised internally, it is also free from the need to show good manners towards others. Other people are not interlocutors with whom one is striving to share one's innermost ideas and whose reactions one necessarily values, by virtue of having accorded them the role of *confidente*. Therefore, the internal conversations of autonomous reflexives often constitute running commentaries on the external contributions of others. Be these condemnatory or congratulatory, they are necessarily evaluative. Since the views of others have not been solicited, they can be taken into account on their merits because the external source has not been accorded special authority in advance relative to the subject. Instead, the autonomous subject considers nobody to be more authoritative than he himself in matters relating to his own life. For these he takes sole responsibility and exercises it through his private deliberations.

In so doing, his inner dialogue is free from the external limitations that politeness imposes on practitioners of 'thought and talk'. Despite the multifarious forms of socialisation that have sought to inhibit certain types of thoughts (such as vicious, uncharitable or mean) and thoughts on certain topics (such as sadistic or lewd), such internal policemen are never as effective as a face-to-face interlocutor. By not submitting themselves to the latter, autonomous reflexives do not expose their ideas or projects to external policing, especially by 'similars and familiars' who may well be in a position to do more than simply express their disapproval. Free both from such inhibitions and from the remorseless reinforcement of normative conventionality, they can consider and conclude upon projects that are unprecedented in their natal contexts.

Such projects may merely be unusual, innovative or considered to be risky. However, nothing prevents a subject from giving serious consideration to a course of action that flies in the face of convention and/or would satisfy some desire that could attract external opprobrium, censure or prosecution. Nothing precludes subjects from dwelling on thoughts about whether or not they can get away with an action or calculating how best they might do so. And for that they take sole responsibility. As has been seen, autonomous reflexives not only are subjectively in charge of themselves, they also seek positions of such a kind that they are objectively in control.

The primacy of practice

If autonomous reflexives resist the normative pressure of others, if they take social conventions lightly and if they are sceptical towards established custom and practice, what is the source of their standards? Empirically it has been shown that the interviewees do not look for the approval of anyone; instead of supplying the names of individuals or designating a reference group, as did the communicative reflexives, they produce statements such as 'I'm my own man' or 'I'd rather steer my own ship.' When this is put together with their predilection for developing procedural knowledge and enjoying the exercise of practical skills, then it appears that these are not people whose primary investment of themselves is in the social order. On the contrary, their concerns and much of their deepest satisfaction come from their involvement in the practical order. This began with their elected childhood pursuits, was often explored as a vocational outlet, and continues to be a source of enduring pleasure throughout adulthood. The key point is that commitment to practical activities and the development of skilful expertise *also constitutes a source of standards*, but ones that are independent of the social order – even though such activities usually entail a social context for their exercise. However, it is crucial not to collapse the standards that are intrinsic to skilled practice itself into the extrinsic context in which it is exercised (golfing is a skill which is irreducible to being a member of a golf club, even if the latter is a requirement for using the golf course).

The distinctive feature about developing any procedural skill (in contradistinction to acquiring discursive knowledge) is that it is quintessentially a matter of refining subject/object relations.[14] Even though this may

[14] Archer, *Being Human*, ch. 9.

and usually does take place in a social setting (an art class or a clay pigeon shoot), the crucial relationships are not subject/subject ones. Instead, what is central is the gradual mastery that culminates in skilful performance. This is usually captured in phrases such as 'gaining a feel for', 'developing an ear' or 'catching on'. All of these point to the fact that it is in the intimacy of the subjects' exchanges and experiments with their chosen medium, activity and artefact that skills are honed and a practically grounded sense of one's standard of proficiency emerges.[15]

What the subject knows, and only he can know it, is the intimate satisfaction that he derives from *using his skills*, in the ultimate privacy of the subject/object relationship. When a drawing captures something of one's design, when a hair-style exceeds one's expectations and when a recipe yields a taste approximating to the kind of piquancy one intended, these sources of satisfaction are matters of first-person knowledge. Ontologically, they exist only by virtue of the person experiencing them[16] and constitute a deeply intrinsic source of satisfaction experienced by the proficient. He alone knows that it is only by doing just 'so' that he can produce the desired effect. No one gains a sense of exultancy through painting-by-numbers (though they may find it pleasurable), but the inner exultation coming from successfully executing a skilful performance, or the despondency at having botched it, is the private preserve of the skilled practitioner. This is the stuff of their standards. Yet, this independent source of satisfaction, vested in the practical order, has to be extracted via the social order *if* it is to be obtained through paid work and employment.

Getting on the ladder

All (nascent) autonomous reflexives have a difficult decision to make at the point of leaving school. They have already begun to manifest their concerns in the practical order and to develop their rudimentary performative skills. They now have to make the problematic translation between the practical skills they seek to cultivate and the social order in the form of a job or vocational training that will foster the development of skilful practice. As mature subjects, this constitutes their first activation of structural and cultural constraints. Structurally, the natal background may simply not be able to afford the requisite training or the costs associated with

---

[15] Margaret S. Archer, 'Objectivity and the Growth of Knowledge', in Margaret S. Archer and William Outhwaite (eds.), *Defending Objectivity: Essays in Honour of Andrew Collier*, London, Taylor and Francis, 2003, pp. 117–28.

[16] As John Searle argues, 'each of my conscious states exists only as the state it is because it is experienced by me, the subject': *Mind, Language and Society*, London, Weidenfeld and Nicolson, 1999, p. 43.

suitable job placement. Similarly, the locality may not offer appropriate training or posts – and the costs escalate by going further afield. Culturally, schools encourage pupils to pursue their 'best subjects' in training or work and these stereotypical 'best matches' may be incompatible with the type of transition that the school leaver would find satisfactory between the practical and the social order. Furthermore, some of the performative skills towards which pupils have been drawn during adolescence might not even have featured on the curriculum. Parents may be even more dismissive, regarding their children's expressed inclinations as a 'phase' or at best a pastime, and reserving their support for whatever they designate as a 'proper' course or career. As such, these structural and cultural properties constitute different opportunity costs to our young subjects and ones that are differentially distributed across society.

Just as importantly, the personal properties of the school leaver are relatively undeveloped and they usually experience the greatest difficulties in transforming their concerns into concrete vocational projects – largely through lack of self-knowledge and lack of information about society's occupational outlets. Constraints and enablements require something to constrain or to enable, and that something is a project, which their causal powers then impede or advance. The nascent projects of young people express their inchoate practical inclinations and, in consequence, their nebulous projects. These projects succumb to being bent, moulded and refashioned by external causal powers because school leavers themselves lack personal powers to resist or to circumvent them. The result is that these young subjects make 'false starts' more frequently than not: taking jobs that they later quit out of boredom or courses that they abandon or never use for the same reason. Far from young autonomous reflexives being (psychologically) 'decisive people' from the beginning, most are more adrift and at sea than their equivalent age-mates amongst the communicative reflexives.

However, since boredom deriving from lack of performative fulfilment is their collective *bête noire*, young autonomous reflexives are soon casting about for a more satisfying outlet. Their problem at this point is that, although they have acquired negative information, they have not yet accrued much more positive knowledge. For the fortunate ones, the right job or course finds them during this second round; for others their knowledge deficit about self and society may lead to several rounds of corrective action. What is distinctive about autonomous reflexives is that, sooner for some than for others, they recognise when they are well vocationally matched. It is common for them to use the same imagery of 'lighting up': about having found something at which they can shine and about tasks at which they wish to become proficient because they find them absorbing.

Finally, they come to a point in their working lives where they can give a name to the project in which they wish to invest themselves.

Once they have 'lit up', they are impatient to increase their proficiency and become good at what they do. Since they are now committed, they do this very quickly and are immediately on the look out for the next step forward, which is also upward. Partly, this is because they have already mastered a given level of tasks and now know themselves well enough to predict the boredom and frustration that would accompany repetition. In equal part, it is because they welcome the next challenge. They know where they are going and they want to get there. It is the autonomous reflexives who often supply detailed descriptions of the rungs ahead of them on the occupational ladder; it is these interviewees who often announce the number of years they have allocated to themselves for reaching the next rung or the one after that. They are very open about their desires to 'get on', about their willingness to assume responsibility, about their preference for being 'in control' in order to be able to write their own job descriptions. Undoubtedly, this spells a yen for what amounts to upward social mobility, but there is more to this process than individual hard work, good performance, personal aspirations and career planning. One part of that 'more' is what they seek intrinsically from the work process itself.

Autonomy and control

The communicative reflexive, whose ultimate concerns are vested in the social order, and the autonomous reflexive, whose ultimate concerns are invested in the practical order, each seek fundamentally different returns from their working lives. In chapter 4 it was seen that, when considering their job satisfaction, communicative subjects prized the quality of human relations above all else. This was the crucial work factor determining whether or not they stayed or moved on. Retrospectively, their best jobs were considered to be those where they had enjoyed the best working relationships. For the communicative reflexives it was equally clear that even these 'best jobs' would be sacrificed in order to meet the perceived needs of their families. This was precisely what underwrote their social immobility. Everything is the other way around for the autonomous reflexive.

Most important to autonomous subjects is being good at what they do; work tasks themselves must supply substantial intrinsic satisfaction, even though these are not people indifferent to considerations of pay, prospects and promotion. Therefore, monotonous and routine employment, which is readily mastered, is also quickly found wanting. When asked what they looked for first and foremost in a job, the most frequently named attribute was that it should be 'challenging'. The autonomous reflexives seek work that challenges their skills; they want to be engaged by the task itself, to have the experience of progressively honing and extending their skilfulness, and also the prospect that this will continue. Otherwise, what they fear is finding themselves in a cul-de-sac named boredom. If job descriptions do not allow for this practical involvement and self-expression, then neither good human relations nor any other social features of the working environment are adequate extrinsic compensations. That being the case, the autonomous reflexive is not tethered to his post by the camaraderie he enjoys with his workmates and he will not be held back by this from seeking promotion or looking out for a more challenging post. This is the first link between autonomous reflexivity and upward social mobility.

Allied to welcoming a challenge in their work, the other features regularly stressed by interviewees were novelty, variety and flexibility. However, employment is organised within the social order. Thus hierarchies of responsibility, procedures for accountability and job descriptions prescribing and proscribing activities are some of the factors that restrict the desired features from being associated with any particular post. Ideally, the autonomous reflexive would prefer working without restrictions, with the freedom to plan, organise and pace his own activities; he has his own standards of performance and reflexively engages in self-monitoring before, during and after his working day. In brief and in their own words, autonomous reflexives want to 'be in control' of the work process. Since the social organisation of employment conflicts with this desideratum, their problem is how to maximise that feature within social constraints.

Both logically and sociologically there are fundamentally two solutions. Firstly, subjects will seek out jobs whose duties allow them to exercise their own responsibility – in so far as this lies within their powers. Then, quite simply, because they wish to 'be in control' and prefer to be responsible, they will try to become so. Thus, a disproportionate number of interviewees, relative to the general population, had attained managerial positions and done so whilst still very young. Even more strikingly, such positions were usually held within work units that themselves were relatively autonomous, such as shops, salons, nurseries, schools and finance centres. Obviously this represented upward social mobility relative to their starting points, but equally it enabled further mobility to be contemplated. Less obviously, subjects who had pursued the managerial solution were often seriously contemplating adopting the alternative solution.

Secondly, if the aim is to be in control, to assume responsibility and to ensure challenge, variety and flexibility in one's work, then self-employment is attractive. With the exception of two interviewees, all the others were contemplating it, had tried it or were working as sole traders. The risks were well known and one subject (Ralph) had come badly to grief, but only one other (Martin) had been deterred by his risk assessment. This proclivity for owning and running one's own enterprise serves to underline something very important about the relationship between autonomous reflexives and upward social mobility. Although they uniformly seek to 'get on' and manifest a collective tendency to do so in the objective terms of the social investigator, nevertheless, under their own descriptions, what they seek is not synonymous with a single-minded quest to become socially mobile. What motivates them to consider and to undertake self-employment are the desiderata, just discussed, for their working lives. Above all, there is a desire for autonomy at work that parallels their autonomous mental activities and corresponds to the autonomous exercise of their practical concerns.

People very rarely seek social position *per se*. They seek it for something and confusion only arises if the sociologist's description of what they do is allowed to eclipse their own reasons for doing it. To assume otherwise (by illicitly substituting motives imputed by the sociologist for the subjects' own) precludes an understanding of the trajectories described in the occupational biographies of these interviewees. This is because autonomous reflexives frequently have a clear idea about how far they want to go and do indeed stop there – even if conditions were propitious to further social advancement. Such actions remain incomprehensible if agents' reflexively defined aims are not investigated; otherwise their career paths are assumed to be wending ever upwards – because of the motives erroneously imputed to them. Instead, attention to the subjects' subjective desiderata can explain why there will be only a weak and tendential association with their objective pattern of social mobility.

The temptation is to stereotype the autonomous reflexive into a one-dimensional character, burning with social or material ambition, motivated solely by this upward urge, knowing precisely where he is going, ready to climb every mountain and tread everyone else under foot to get there. That projects an image of a thrusting and immoderate entrepreneur, probably untrue even of the early capitalists, and one that would certainly represent a major distortion of the present interviewees.

Strategic mobility

It is once they have 'lit up', wherever this occurs in their personal work histories, that autonomous reflexives make their next important encounters with structural properties and powers. Where enablements are concerned, agents deliberatively (but always fallibly) seek to take advantage of structural properties by deliberately activating their causal powers. On the one hand, they tend to become very active agents in their own career planning. These are the subjects who, above all, busy themselves in adding to their qualifications, supplementing their skills, plugging their gaps and generally ensuring that they have the right piece of paper or satisfactory *curriculum vitae* for the next stage. In this they are quite distinct from the meta-reflexives, who seek *alternative qualifications*, usually in order to facilitate a career change. Yet, as the autonomous reflexives make up their portfolio of short courses or burn the midnight oil acquiring professional qualifications or degrees (and further degrees), they are willingly lending themselves to *elastication*. Not only are their skills broadened and/or deepened, but more importantly, they usually make the discovery that what they once found impenetrable at school is perfectly tractable and even interesting now they are motivated, and that what once sounded a distant and unattainable qualification is well within their reach. In consequence, their horizons expand and their aspirations extend. Simultaneously, they have also rendered themselves objectively more valuable on the job market – even if subjectively that is not how some adopt and absorb their elastication.

On the other hand, as planners who are now conversant with themselves and their part of the employment structure, they survey the latter closely in search of the next 'good match' between them. They are on the look out for new openings, within their existing employment or by moving jobs, they are quick at seizing opportunities for enlarging their businesses and diversifying their enterprises, and they are often ready to repackage their portfolios of skills and redirect them towards new ventures. In all of these, they are fundamentally seeking to take advantage of the structural enablements that come their way – or which they seek out. In a sense, they are niche marketing themselves; elastication has given them the confidence to do so, now they are actively searching for the conditions that will enable them to approach new horizons. All of this implies that autonomous reflexives attempt to become *strategists* in their career planning, but to succeed in this they also have to find a way around being penalised – and thus held back – by structural constraints.

What is distinctive about the response of the autonomous reflexive when his projects encounter structural constraints? Such subjects attempt to cope by anticipating that certain courses of action will activate constraints and then adjusting their actions in order to circumvent this occurrence. Since circumvention depends upon a reflexive judgement by the subject, it is ever stymied by the human capacity for misjudging ourselves, our circumstances and other people if strategic action requires co-operation. Nevertheless, in their career planning, autonomous reflexives attempt to circumvent uncertainty by two basic strategies.

In the first, the subject proceeds with caution and pursues plans that deliberately stop short at the limits of what he believes he can master. These are people who announce that they 'know where to stop', that they do not want their enterprises to outgrow their personal control or that they would like to open their own shop but not run a chain of stores. (This, of course, is another reason why autonomous reflexives should not be seen as people of unbridled ambition.) Many may be correct about this and certainly be more comfortable within these self-imposed limitations, but there are no epistemic guarantees that they will be right about themselves or their environment.[17] However, when he is correct, the autonomous reflexive will already have gone quite a way in socio-occupational terms. That is to say his 'stopping point' represents significant upward social mobility compared with his 'starting point'. Hence, this strategy of circumvention is quite different from the evasions of the communicative reflexives. As was seen in chapter 4, to evade such constraints entirely entails a *reduction* in a subject's ambitions and is tantamount to social immobility.

Conversely, others seek to circumvent constraints by strategic risk-taking. Instead of 'knowing where to stop', they attempt to 'stay ahead': by embracing novelty, exploiting specialisation, discovering loopholes, recognising new trends and venturing first into new fields. The generic aim is circumvention by innovation: if one's market is drying up or one's skills are becoming devalued, then embrace change fast enough in order to have time for corrective manoeuvres before others catch up. There are no guarantees: as was seen in chapter 5, some interviewees have been prosecuted for their strategic creativity and others have indeed got ahead.

It is when faced with the most stringent constraints that the autonomous reflexive proves most dogged and most distinctive, although he remains as fallible as ever. Billy had been made redundant repeatedly, at roughly ten-year intervals. On each occasion he had not only found new employment but succeeded in being promoted to greater responsibilities. However, on the fourth and latest redundancy he was sixty years old and fully aware of the ageist barrier that further reduced his objective chances of finding new work. Nevertheless, he had a strategy worked out for circumventing these constraints – relocation in Spain.

What differentiates and distinguishes the autonomous reflexive from other active agents is not some greater discursive understanding of constraints and enablements. Indeed, meta-reflexives tend to display a more

---

[17] In the previous study we encountered a sole trader whose desire for hands-on control actually precluded him from taking on employees or ceding expensive use of the phone to the impersonal computer. This Luddism means that his business now fails to provide a living. Archer, *Structure, Agency and the Internal Conversation*, pp. 214–20.

developed theoretical attitude towards them. Nor is it an ability to evade their causal powers, since no one does this better than the communicative reflexives because the very modesty of their projects does not activate either kind of structural property. It has probably been overemphasised that autonomous reflexives can never be master strategists (to avoid brotherhood with rational man; busy maximising his preference schedule and always ending up better off in terms of some indeterminate currency). Nevertheless, what justifies calling them strategists is their *attempt* to take advantage of enablements, as they see them and in so far as they detect them, and their *efforts* to circumvent constraints, as they perceive them and in so far as they are aware of them.

Accommodation by subordination

Emergent properties, including personal ones like the dominant mode of reflexivity, exert both internal and external causal powers. The principal external effect is the tendency for autonomous reflexivity to generate upward social mobility amongst its practitioners. When this occurs, and no generative mechanism produces empirical regularities because of the intervention of contingencies, then the external effect interacts with the internal effect. In concrete terms, because most subjects experience some occupational advancement, this serves to reinforce the internal process that helped generate their socio-economic promotion – the autonomous mode of reflexivity itself.

To begin with, subjects volunteer how their deliberations at work affect their inner dialogues in other areas of their lives. Because of their practical concerns, they are all seeking to be 'good at what they do', which entails considerable self-monitoring in relation to their work. All of those in employment report devoting large tracts of their internal conversations to planning their working days, weeks and months, to mulling over work problems and to preparing themselves for future challenges in the work context. They do this to a greater extent than other sub-groups of interviewees. Moreover, as they experience occupational advancement, such deliberations intensify with the increasing demands of their posts and especially as they assume the responsibility they sought – that of being 'in control'. In brief, the end result is that autonomous reflexives engage in internal conversation 'all of the time' and 'about everything'.

However, since these are lone inner dialogues, which expand in scope with increments in social mobility and increasing responsibilities at work, their results are more profound than simply fostering 'better organised people'. If and when autonomous reflexivity intensifies, it also acquires a distinctive and substantive *leitmotif*, manifest most clearly in the most occupationally successful interviewees. At one level, this consists in an attempt to regulate their concerns such that these dovetail together harmoniously. At a deeper level, their overriding aim is to keep the social order in its place, unlike the communicative reflexives, who accord it unquestioned priority. This is evident in two main areas – work and the family – precisely because it is in them and between them that conflict could arise most readily and regularly.

It has already been emphasised that for autonomous reflexives their work involvement is vested in the practical order but that the jobs they hold are also part of the social order. This confronts them with a problem, unlike the communicative reflexives whose job satisfaction derives predominantly from the social features of work, which can be summarised as good human relationships. Conversely, autonomous subjects are task-oriented, so how do they cope with the ineluctable relations with superiors, colleagues and subordinates? As far as superiors, line managers and bosses in general are concerned, it has already been maintained that the main strategy is to rise to their positions as rapidly as possible through promotion. If and when this fails to materialise, then the attractions of self-employment increase or, in some cases, a history of rows and resignations ensues. However, it is in their dealings with colleagues, and even more with subordinates, that the *leitmotif* is most pronounced.

The autonomous reflexive is not a 'people person', which does not mean that he is lacking in social skills; what it does mean is that he is not preoccupied with popularity or camaraderie. On the contrary, these subjects are largely deaf to Saint-Simon's distinction between the government of men and the administration of things. To them, subordinates are another thing to administer, a matter of personnel management, in which pride can be taken, rather than human relationships, from which personal satisfaction is derived. In other words, 'people management' is itself transformed into a practical skill, executed as a form of benevolent manipulation. Although this does not imply callousness or dehumanisation, it is undoubtedly a method of keeping the social order in its place and ensuring that it does not interfere with the subject's ultimate concerns. Not only do human relations at work never hold back the autonomous reflexive from seeking further promotion, but also, such relationships become yet another topic for inner deliberation and lone dialogue.

Similarly, within the family, the requirements and needs of its members have legitimacy but not automatic priority. Although these subjects may be as fond of their families as anyone else, even to the point of listing them as their prime concern, *they do not see family and work as competing in a zero-sum relationship* – unlike communicative reflexives. Instead, they cultivate the dovetailing of the two, such that the question of sacrificing or subordinating the one to the other simply does not arise. What they effectively seek is to establish the positive feedback loop in which job satisfaction and success benefit the family and the family environment is supportive of work involvement. However, the family too is expected to know its place, even though this may be a generous one and one arrived at through negotiation or mutual understanding.

What the autonomous reflexive seeks to do is to *dovetail* his practical concerns with the social concerns represented by different family members. This is not predicated upon sacrificing his work interests if a clash of demands develops. Usually, this also involves his carving out the space for the lone pursuit of his leisure pursuits, which again are practical in orientation. By the strict organisation of his time and their acceptance of his long working hours, by the use of his flexible working pattern to accommodate family activities and, above all, by devoting more hours than most to a planned schedule of commitments and family acquiescence to this timetabling, his dovetailing is achieved. This entails his elaborating a personal ethics of responsibility, because this cannot be derived from contextual custom and practice since he has jettisoned his embedment in his natal context. What he is now attempting to do is precisely to develop new practices that will enable him to establish a *modus vivendi* in the new context to which he has moved.

Successful dovetailing is always something attempted. Its establishment is never a foregone conclusion and its success requires of all concerned a great deal of concerted action, a high degree of organisation, relationships based upon reciprocity rather than direct exchange, plus a lot of hard work all round. In so far as they do succeed, their concerns in the social order are not allowed to usurp their commitments in the practical order. That is the final linkage to upward social mobility. In other words, none of those potent concerns – work relationships, friends or family – is accorded the quasi-automatic right to anticipate accommodative sacrifice of the subject's advancement at work.[18]

Individualists in society

Social mobility generally entails geographical mobility, even within the same area (only four of the interviewees had been born in Coventry and its environs). This means that they have to accommodate to a new context, but it does not spell any strong geo-local attachment. Instead, the home is a base, the site from which radiates out a friendship network that

---

[18] Obviously it remains a crucial question to investigate whether such dovetailing is more likely to be achieved if the autonomous mode is the dominant one practised by both partners.

is also geographically dispersed. Investment in the local community is restricted, largely to the use of its public and purchasable facilities. Autonomous reflexives are the antithesis of communitarians; as individualists their involvements are motivated by their personal concerns rather than by any sense of obligation towards the community. They themselves behave atomistically: out-sourcing to supply their needs,[19] with subscription membership to furnish their leisure activities and considerable usage of educational facilities to further their vocational formation. In other words, the autonomous reflexive picks and mixes discrete and non-overlapping forms of participation in the community on an individualistic basis. This is light years removed from the micro-world constituted by communicative reflexives.

Unsurprisingly, the orientation of this group towards the social is equally individualistic. Society is perceived as constituted by fellow atomistic individuals; it may well have dealt a better hand of cards to some than to others, but everyone's task is to play the cards they hold to the best of their ability. The message is 'get on with it'; sufficient personal determination and hard work are what make for individual success.

The fact that their own collective activities in their new contexts are motivated by individual interests is the key to their participation in civil society. Clubs and courses are elective options where enrolment is often of limited duration and for a particular instrumental purpose. Conversely, church membership or charity work, both of which imply a commitment that is irreducible to instrumental rationality, tend to be shunned by autonomous reflexives. Because of the nexus between personal involvement and individual interests, this sub-group contributes little to making the building blocks of civil society, with a single important exception – the economy. This is the one social institution in which their interests are heavily vested and is thus the beneficiary of their long working hours, propensity to self-fund the upgrading of their vocational skills in their own free time and to develop small enterprises in which all the risks are assumed by the individual.

As individualists who take a fragmented approach to the social, carving out small sectors for their elective and ephemeral participation, rather than embracing their new contexts holistically, their stance towards civil society is paralleled by their limited political involvement. Most express a weary cynicism with politicians, but one that is widely dispersed; much more distinctive are the reasons for their tendency to dismiss political

---

[19] See G. Esping-Andersen, 'Welfare State or Work? The Interaction of Wages, Social Protection and Family Change', in Margaret S. Archer and Edmond Malinvaud (eds.), *The Future of Labour and Labour in the Future*, Vatican City, Vatican City Press, 1998.

parties. Just as they pick and mix from the array of institutions and institutionalised activities making up civil society, so they would like to
express their support or disapproval for particular issues that resonate
with their particular interests in politics. What few can do is to endorse a
party political manifesto in the round. With only slight exaggeration, their
political ideal would resemble a series of referenda, thus enabling them to
vote on single issues, consonant or dissonant with their interests, and to
abstain from voting on the majority of motions.

It might then be presumed that autonomous reflexives would be more
involved in single-issue social movements, which proves only marginally
to be the case. Significantly, the exceptions are those movements (gay
rights and the countryside) which mapped directly on to the ultimate
concerns of particular individuals. Yet, even here, these subjects will
frankly declare themselves to be 'too selfish' for active participation. In
short, the autonomous reflexive is not a very political animal. He would
rather try to circumvent the constraints of his societal environment than
attempt to change the social structure itself – because circumvention is an
individualistic exercise, whereas structural change is a collective enterprise. Autonomous reflexivity is thus the second mode whose practitioners confine themselves to remaining *primary agents* rather than becoming
part of any *corporate agency* pursuing a socio-political agenda.

Meta-reflexivity and lateral social mobility

Meditating on right action

Because the inner dialogues of meta-reflexives are conducted alone they
are not subject to the considerations of accountability (to others) and alter-
nation (with others) that govern external conversation and can, therefore,
be very lengthy indeed. Meta-reflexives, like autonomous subjects, are the
'little gods' of their own internal conversations. However, there are good
reasons for thinking that the self-talk of the meta-reflexives is even lengthier
than that of their autonomous counterparts, despite the fact that this
difference is not measurable.[20] Empirically, interviewees from the present
sub-group placed even greater emphasis upon their inner dialogues 'going
on constantly'. Some subjects found the ubiquity of their self-talk both
oppressive and uncontrollable, whereas none of the autonomous reflexives
voiced the desire for an ability to 'turn it off' at times. Logically, the purposes served by internal conversation for practitioners of the meta- versus

---

[20] This is an empirical statement about the limitations of the present study, rather than an
assertion that these differences are not measurable in principle.

the autonomous mode of reflexivity are also indicative of points at which it would be reasonable for autonomous deliberations to terminate – but ones which are not good reasons for the cessation of meta-reflexive deliberation.

It has already been stressed that a major difference between these two sub-groups is that for autonomous reflexives internal conversation is *task-oriented* whilst for meta-reflexives it is *value-oriented*. Therefore (in chapter 5), it was maintained that the chief concern of autonomous subjects was to feel confident that, in so far as possible, they had factored in all relevant considerations for defining a course of action likely to result in task accomplishment. If this is the case – though the decision made is always fallible – then it constitutes a good reason for terminating that particular sequence of internal conversation. Apart from double checking his data and reasoning, there is nothing further for an autonomous reflexive to gain by dwelling on the matter. This is why, as we have seen earlier, these subjects describe themselves as being 'decisive' – not the kinds of people who indulge in second and third thoughts. In short, having done their sums and checked their calculations they are then prepared to act upon their conclusions and to take responsibility for them.

Conversely, the *value-orientation* of meta-reflexive deliberations does not lend itself to putting full-stops to internal conversations because there is no obvious point at which it is sensible to think that one's deliberations cannot be improved upon. There is no tidiness about terminating one's mental review of moral considerations. Since the aim is to determine upon the course of *right* action, then 'good' is always the enemy of 'best'. Because they seek personally to exemplify their values (religious, humanitarian, aesthetic) as well as to advance them, their deliberations are double-barrelled. Right action consists in more than marshalling the information necessary for conducting an exercise in instrumental rationality. It also entails an internal application of the hermeneutics of suspicion to the self in order to ascertain – again as far as possible – that the subject is using right judgement, rather than self-serving rationalisations.

Right judgement stands in opposition to motivation by self-interest, idleness, self-aggrandisement, convenience and so forth. Attempting to ascertain one's motives is far more difficult than checking one's calculations, because coming up again with the same motivational answer might simply be evidence that one of the above defects is deeply ingrained. Hence, the subject may go over the same terrain many times in her internal conversation, lengthening them because of her scrupulosity. It is these ruminations that attract the disapprobation of certain social psychologists (and the impatience of some autonomous reflexives). Such disapproval implies that right action could dispense with scruples and, instead, be condensed into either routine action or rational action. In turn, that outlook implies there are few moral dilemmas and it reduces morality to the same status as having good manners or making good investments.

'Value rationality' does not lend itself to any form of normative routinisation. Meta-reflexives are committed to particular values which they pursue as ends in themselves. By conducting their internal conversations alone, they *resist* the influence of contextual conventionality – one that is so powerful for communicative reflexives because it is constantly reinforced by their interlocutors. By not sharing many of their (most important) inner deliberations with others, the meta-reflexive is insulated from the running commentaries of those surrounding her and their pressures to conformity. Like autonomous subjects, they thus avoid being caught up in the norms and conventions of any social context in which they may find themselves. However, they are even better proofed against any tendency to take local norms, customs and practices for granted because it is the values that they have endorsed from the cultural system (World Three)[21] which work as both litmus test and filter for what is normatively acceptable to these individuals. It is these values, rather than the opinions of others, which are their sounding boards.

For the same reason, meta-reflexives respond guardedly to objective inducements to action. These have to be sieved for compatibility with their values and resisted if incongruous with them. However great the objective benefit may be, the meta-reflexive is prepared to forfeit it. Consequently, whilst the autonomous reflexive will be readily induced to follow pathways that offer challenging prospects for advancement, the meta-reflexive remains unmoved by such objective social enablements. This difference proves crucial in relation to what work and employment is taken up.

Your ways are not my ways

Wherever young meta-reflexives encounter the values they adopt as their own, these profoundly affect their outlook upon the social order, in general, and their natal social contexts, in particular. As has been seen from Bernadette's story, the source can be as simple as the subject acquiring values and beliefs from their social background and taking them much more seriously than is usual. However, the sources are many and varied, as was explored in chapter 6, including some that only became matters of ultimate concern after subjects have reached their majority.

---

[21] See Margaret S. Archer, *Culture and Agency: the Place of Culture in Social Theory*, Cambridge, Cambridge University Press, 1998, ch. 5 and Karl Popper, *Objective Knowledge*, Oxford, Clarendon Press, 1972, pp. 298f.

What meta-reflexives have in common is that their particular cultural concerns are at variance with their structural contexts. Their aspirations are incongruent with the expectations and outlets found in their local environments. By adopting some ideal of 'otherness', they are effectively saying 'your ways cannot be my ways'.

Ideationally, the meta-reflexive is alienated from her natal context and embattled with its structural limitations. This may or may not be related to the quality of her inter-personal relations in the natal context, but it does induce the subject to begin living a 'hidden life' or, as many interviewees have already said, to 'live in a world of their own'. Two of those taking part in the pilot investigation illustrate these variants. One experienced parental negativity whenever she deviated from their ways. Since both parents were completely secularised, she dreaded real antagonism in her teens when her Christian faith, developed at school and followed up by exploring the local churches, became of increasing importance to her. Deprived of any religious resources, she described foraging through the battered books on a market stall, buying texts for pennies to be read under the bed clothes and hiding her theological acquisitions in the wall cavity behind an air-brick in the loo. The other subject, who has always experienced the warmest relations with her Eastern European family, fell in love with English literature at about the same age and uses an extended bird metaphor to described her mental and then physical withdrawal: 'You realise you've got these bumps on your shoulders and they're wings. You could just go on getting fatter and fatter and end up in the chicken soup, but even a big, golden cage wouldn't make any difference when you look up and see the others flying. You might get singed by the sun or crash to earth, but you have to fly yourself. It breaks their hearts to see you going and your own to go, but you have to move away.' The first interviewee is describing a cultural clash and an institutional embargo (on church attendance); the second, a cultural divergence and structural lack of openings (for becoming fully proficient).

These examples are cited because in neither case were their very different family relations central to the outcome. Instead, both young girls became progressively more absorbed in their unfolding cultural concerns, surpassing the level of knowledge about them current in their natal contexts and finally endorsing them as their ultimate concerns. In so doing, they, as with all meta-reflexives, were seeking to invest themselves not in the social order (unlike the communicative reflexives), or in the practical order (unlike the autonomous reflexives), but in the transcendental order. Instead, they had embraced an ideal and sought to become conformed to it to the extent of personifying it. In turn, this has direct implications, via internal conversation, for both self and society.

On the one hand, endorsement of a transcendental ideal entails an attempt to transcend the self – to overcome one's defects and deficiencies until one approximates more closely to being a personification of that ideal (be it perfect charity or linguistic perfection in the above examples). Consequently, self-criticism is a constant accompaniment of meta-reflexivity because much inner dialogue is devoted to self-examination, self-correction and self-dedication. Obviously, since the aim is self-improvement in relation to an ideal, the meta-reflexive always deems herself to have fallen short and therefore self-criticism is unending. On the other hand, although meta-reflexives are perfectionists, they are far from being entirely intra-punitive. They may indeed deem that they fall short but their response is not self-flagellation. Some of the reasons for their imperfect exemplifications of their ideals are recognised to lie outside themselves in times and circumstances that were not of their making. In other words, the meta-reflexive is also a social critic because another tract of her self-talk is devoted to a diagnosis of the social obstructions that block the realisation of her transcendental ideal – for herself and for others too. Notions of transcendence are universalistic in thrust and therefore it is unsurprising that meta-reflexives are also committed to the elimination of any forms of social injustice or discrimination which hinder others from approaching the ideal. Equally, it follows that no social context can escape critique, if not censure, for long, since by definition structural arrangements are never commensurate with cultural ideals. These considerations have very pointed implications for individual meta-reflexives in relation to their employment.

Vocations and their discontents

The differences between practitioners of the three different modes of reflexivity are nowhere clearer than in their typical definitions of 'a good job'. To communicative reflexives this is a post which is well known, enjoys respect and is also readily available in the natal community; to autonomous reflexives it is a form of employment engaging their skills and promising rapid promotion for manifest ability; for the meta-reflexive it is a vocation in which they wish to invest themselves fully.

However, when it comes to taking up an occupation, meta- and autonomous reflexives face something of the same problem in that both seek to 'translate' ultimate concerns that are vested in a different order of reality into a job, which is necessarily part of the social order. As has already been discussed (chapter 5), autonomous subjects seek personal fulfilment by honing their practical skills in a challenging post that offers prospects of advancement and an environment in which they are in control of their own work activities. Many were seen to 'get it wrong' in relation to their initial training and first posts, largely because they assumed it was unproblematic to transfer their youthful concerns, interests and talents into a course or degree and from there into employment. Because of their lack of knowledge about self and society, a considerable number discovered such training to be too inflexible and the correlative 'first jobs' to be frustrating, stultifying, offering insufficient challenges or over-controlled. Nevertheless, most did succeed in making a successful 'match' on their second or third attempt and, once they had 'lit up', became committed to fast occupational advancement – which was responsible for their trajectory of upward social mobility. Alternatively, many availed themselves of self-employment with the aim of creating a working environment with the desired features.

Conversely, the young meta-reflexive has much greater difficulties and generally has a very different secondary solution to explore as an alternative. What they seek is a social role that they can embrace as a vocation, a position they can personify that will both assist their personal growth and fulfilment and furnish a means for actualising their cultural ideal in at least a small part of society. They are more demanding in what they require of occupational roles, but also place greater demands upon themselves in terms of the self-investment they will make in their work. This is the same if the 'dream' is to become a league footballer, an academic or a care provider. Regardless of differences in their occupational ideals, the subject will give herself or himself rather than so many hours, the basic skills and the lowest acceptable degree of involvement.

However, the dual demands made by meta-reflexives – of positions for people like themselves and of themselves-when-in-post – together serve to stoke the dialectics of dissatisfaction. We have already identified the source of this dialectic in the conjunction between 'self-criticism' and 'social critique', as quintessential elements of meta-reflexivity. On the one hand, the subject throws herself into a role, but then discovers she is frustrated in what she can give, in the full use of her talents, in her personal development – by bureaucracy, organisational procedure, public policy and so forth. On the other hand, the main satisfaction she seeks from employment is the opportunity 'to make a difference' for the better in line with her value-commitment, but suitable roles may not be accessible to her, the subject may meet with resistance or discrimination when working within them, or, more commonly, the role proves deceptive about the occasions it presents for transformative action. Since self-employment is infrequently the solution (although Maeve provided a single exception), this is one reason why meta-reflexives disproportionately gravitate towards the voluntary sector, either on a full-time basis or as part-time compensation for the short-fall between their current employment and their ultimate concern. Working in the 'third sector' is their equivalent to self-employment for autonomous reflexives.

In short, although autonomous reflexives often 'get it wrong' in their choices of first jobs, this is *invariably* the experience of meta-reflexives. The difference goes further, because they show a marked tendency to do no better in their second and third corrected attempts. On each occasion the reason is identical: jobs in the social order do not match up to culturally defined vocations, hence the dialectics of dissatisfaction re-engage. Because the meta-reflexive is a self-critical perfectionist she will not be capricious about resignation. It is more usual to find these subjects remaining in post for a number of years, firstly trying to diagnose where they are going wrong, secondly attempting new approaches and tactics to improve matters – both for their own fulfilment and to show something of the results desired – before finally conceding the futility of going on. Only towards the end of this sequence do they become increasingly articulate – and angry – about the impossibility of realising their value-commitment in a given structural context.

That is the prelude to their quitting and resuming their quest for a better match between their cultural ideal and a new occupational context. It is the point at which they become and remain strident social critics, at least of that institutional sector with which they have been involved. During this period of growing disenchantment with what they had hoped would be their vocation in life, two features are worth noting. Like the communicative reflexives, they prefer working as part of a team and may well form warm and durable relationships with some like-minded people encountered on the job. But, although these friendships may endure, unlike the communicative subjects they will not be deterred from resigning by good human relations alone – those are side-benefits and not the main objective where a vocation is concerned. Secondly, unlike many of the autonomous reflexives, if personal fulfilment is lacking, accompanied by the conviction that one's work makes no significant difference to what one cares about most, then good prospects of promotion associated with improved pay and increased power will be matters of indifference. Again, these will be no deterrent to resignation. Hence, the meta-reflexives' orientation towards work as a vocation, founded upon their value-commitments, is the central link in the chain that makes for their distinctive pattern of lateral social mobility.

The costs of a calling

In general, structural conditioning works by attaching bonuses to certain courses of action and penalties to others. However, because conditioning is not determinism, the other necessary condition for these causal powers to be exercised is that subjects entertain projects involving the particular courses of action in question. In other words, constraints require something to constrain and enablements something to enable – and these things are human projects as defined by subjects in order to realise their concerns. In this connection, we have already seen (chapter 5) how autonomous subjects are reflexively aware of constraints and enablements and seek (fallibly) to anticipate at which points they will impinge – negatively and positively – upon the projects they are pursuing. In consequence, such agents attempt to act *strategically*, their ideal being to capitalise upon enablements and to circumvent constraints. Since their aim is occupational promotion, that is to 'get ahead' in the social order, then autonomous reflexivity promotes a higher level of receptivity to society's inducements and deterrents than do either of the other two modes.

We have also examined the lack of such receptivity amongst communicative reflexives (chapter 4) and explained it in the light of their projects, the modesty of which grants these subjects immunity from the constraints and enablements associated with the occupational structure because they simply do not activate them. That is why their stance towards society was termed *evasive*: not deliberately so, but effectively so, because of their preoccupation with concerns vested in their localised micro-worlds. Towards these daily doings, centred upon family well-being, society could be said (metaphorically) to be indifferent. It neither rewards nor penalises these concerns and the courses of action associated with them, but rather 'allows' the collectivity of communicative subjects to evade penalties and bonuses alike. Society manifests such indifference (again metaphorically) even though it is the net beneficiary of the social cement supplied by communicative reflexives – whose aggregate effect is to reinforce social integration.

If society 'shows' indifference towards practitioners of communicative reflexivity, conversely, it is those practising meta-reflexivity who are indifferent towards social conditioning. In advancing the proposition that meta-reflexives act in this indifferent manner, the last thing that is being asserted is that they are unconcerned about the social order. On the contrary, it is precisely because they cherish an ideal for a better society, based upon their value-commitments, that they are inoculated against any inducements or disincentives that the status quo extends to them or imposes on them. They can neither be 'bought off' nor intimidated into conforming to prevailing values. As such, they are resistant to both the carrots and sticks by which social control is exercised. Short of direct coercion, control in the social order is highly reliant upon manipulating the pliability of courses of action through its structures of incentives and disincentives. This is especially true of individuals and collectivities who explicitly repudiate the prevailing (or dominant or hegemonic) value system in preference for counter-cultural values. Thus, those who demonstrate their immunity to the incentive structure are not merely stubborn, they are positively subversive. They reject the very methods of directional guidance by which the action patterns of members of society are steered and no intensification of the same methods will prove any more effective.

Meta-reflexives demonstrate their subversion in four main ways. Firstly, and underwriting the rest, once the dialectics of dissatisfaction have engaged, the meta-reflexive is prepared to bear the costs of extricating herself from a given occupational position. She will forfeit the benefits associated with her post – such as pay, promotion prospects, social status, eligibility for benefits and job security – and absorb the costs on her own behalf. She does this, for example, by assuming responsibility for obtaining new employment, accepting a pay cut, a reduction in social standing, inconvenience, relocation, retraining and job insecurity. It is emphatically not the case that meta-reflexives court worse terms of employment but, rather, that they are willing to pay this price for shedding work deemed incommensurate with their callings in preference for 'inferior' jobs that promise to be more compatible with their values.

Secondly, their value-commitments provide them with an even broader spectrum immunisation against social inducements. For example, we have seen earlier (chapter 5) that autonomous reflexives are easily prey to boredom at work and champ for greater challenges and more control. However, they are frequently induced to put up with their frustrations for a time, providing the prospects of rapid promotion are real and come their way fast. With promotion and increased control, we have also seen that the initial, lukewarm attitude of some towards their employment can be replaced by an elastication of their occupational aspirations. In other words, the receipt of additional rewards encourages them to seek yet further rewards and, in the process, their commitment to remaining in that form of employment (or self-employment) intensifies considerably.

However, the value-orientation of the meta-reflexive proofs them against this mechanism. If they are both personally dissatisfied with and socially critical of their role as a cog in some organisational wheel, it is not by handing them the wheel (improbable as this would be, given their 'negative' attitudes) that they will become reconciled to their employment. If Bernadette had principled reservations about what she could achieve with her pupils as a classroom teacher, then becoming head would not have improved matters. Indeed, it would have compromised her values still further by making her appear to legitimate a state of affairs that she condemned but could do nothing to change at the level of the school – since her educational critique was pitched at the institutional level, at the relationship between private schools and the state sector.

Thirdly, constancy to their cultural ideal and continued pursuit of a vocational outlet through which it could be realised is what generates contextual unsettlement amongst meta-reflexives over time. They cannot root occupationally if the dialectics of dissatisfaction consistently re-engage, once every change of post has been given a chance. The pattern thus generated, not simply of frequent job changes but of changes in career, is one of lateral mobility – particular to the meta-reflexives. Once again, these subjects pay the price of their unsettlement and not only in terms of the dislocation involved for themselves and their families. A change of career, as opposed to a change of job, entails retraining. This is another price that the subject pays herself. Thus, after her first degree in French followed by a teaching diploma, we have seen Bernadette acquiring supplementary qualifications throughout her working life – a certificate for teaching English as a foreign language, a certificate in catechetics and another in counselling – all of these at her own expense. Some subjects do more and some less, but the key point is that they are paying the price of obtaining *alternative qualifications* precisely in order to try out a different career rather than remaining structurally constrained *in situ*. They pay, without usually becoming any better off, because these are not *additional qualifications* that increase their chances of upward social mobility. On the contrary – they often pay to become qualified for downward or, at best, lateral mobility. What they are paying for is another opportunity to try out another position in which they might be able to live out their callings.

Finally, meta-reflexives are subversive because of the steady source of social criticism they direct towards the institutions employing them or that have employed them. However, the effects of their subversion go beyond these 'patchwork' critiques. By retaining their value-commitments, at the cost of periodic contextual unsettlement, these subjects serve to keep alive not only their personal cultural ideals but alternative sources of values for society as a whole. Of course, once such ideals have been articulated and lodged in the Universal Library of Humankind[22] they can never fade away because they do not need a knowing subject. But what can certainly happen is that they lose social salience, unless they continue to be proclaimed. Continued salience is precisely what meta-reflexives give them and perhaps these counter-cultural commitments are taken more seriously by others when it is seen that the costs of upholding them are

---

[22] Archer, *Culture and Agency*, ch. 5.

not negligible. Be that as it may, the very existence of people practising meta-reflexivity prevents there from being a single homogeneous and hegemonic value system in society at any time. It is always contested, despite the evergreen myth of cultural integration,[23] but that requires that there are always people ready to engage in contestation – and to pay the price.

The demands of the Wertrationalität

Any change of career orientation, let alone more than one, can make a subject vulnerable to the charge of capriciousness. Indeed, autonomous reflexives will often disparage their meta-reflexive counterparts as 'rolling stones'. One way of clearing the latter of caprice would be by furnishing an account of when and why they make their contextual shifts. Such an explanation is also required for reasons of theoretical adequacy. Reference was made earlier to the dialectics of dissatisfaction, but what accounts for the timing of a particular resignation and a subsequent career reorientation? Is this merely a matter of individual differences in tolerance towards occupational discontents, ones that are explicable only in terms of personal psychology?

Alternatively and sociologically, might it be suggested that, far from instancing principled action, this occupational chopping and changing is a self-indulgence that many working people cannot afford even if they are scathing about their jobs? That suggestion would need refining because the meta-reflexives were not found to have a significantly higher occupational status than others and therefore a likelihood of being better off. However, it could be reformulated into the proposition that it is when these subjects are relatively best placed to afford it (relative, perhaps, to overall family income, reduced responsibilities towards their children or to the point of least financial commitments) that they indulge their principles. Such a proposition would entail the commodification of values, which rational choice theorists[24] find no difficulty in supporting, but which must be resisted here because meta-reflexives are presented as exponents of the *Wertrationalität* – that is, people for whom the pursuit of values is an end in itself, regardless of considerations of costs.

In other words, there are many reasons why presenting a theoretically adequate account of the *timing* of lateral occupational moves is needed.

---

[23] Margaret S. Archer, 'The Myth of Cultural Integration', *British Journal of Sociology*, 36, 1985, 333–53.

[24] See Gary Becker, *Accounting for Tastes*, Cambridge, Mass., Harvard University Press, 1996, pp. 229f, and R. Stark and R. Finke, *Acts of Faith: Explaining the Human Side of Religion*, Berkley, University of California Press, 2000.

This is possible if attention is given to the question of how practitioners of the different modes of reflexivity tackle the problem of 'dovetailing' their major concerns. Elsewhere, I have argued that dovetailing is a dilemma confronting everyone because, given our human make up, the way the world is constituted and the fact that the two necessarily interact, we ineluctably have plural concerns: in our physical well-being in the natural order, in our performative competence in the practical order and in our self-worth in the social order.[25] The dilemma generic to any plurality of concerns is that what satisfies one may well be damaging to another or others and vice versa. There is nothing automatically precluding this from happening. Therefore, each agent has to work out his or her solution and practitioners of the three different modes of reflexivity go about this very differently.

Respondents in this study were invited to list the three most important areas of their lives (at the time), in order of importance. Both the communicative and the autonomous reflexives were found to solve the problem of dovetailing by radically subordinating their lesser concerns to their ultimate concern. Hence the findings already discussed: where communicative reflexives drastically subordinate considerations about work to consideration for their families and where autonomous reflexives proceed the other way around, by circumscribing their family obligations so they do not obtrude upon work commitment. Meta-reflexives are quite different in seeking an organic integration between their plural concerns, rather than a principled formula for their accommodation, in hierarchical order. Their difference stems precisely from the value rationality of the meta-reflexive, which is both architectonic in nature and holistic in scope.

The problem for the meta-reflexive is that organic integration is hard to bring about and sustain. Either the plural concerns will not come into alignment with one another or they slip out of alignment. Indeed, these subjects often report that in serving one concern, they are neglecting their others and feel guilty about not working hard enough to restore the ideal balance between them. Yet, this holistic approach is more difficult to make work since intrinsically it is more demanding. This is because something positive is sought of the plurality of concerns and related activities, namely their mutual reinforcement. Conversely, the other two subgroups will accept what is fundamentally a negative principle for the 'accommodation' of their subordinate concerns, that is, non-interference with their prime concern.

Because the integration of their lives around their values is crucial to the meta-reflexives, it is the times at which it proves impossible to bring their plural concerns (and associated activities) back into any semblance or promise of alignment, such that they promote the subject's value-commitment, which prompt a new occurrence of lateral mobility. Thus it was when Bernadette's teaching and her parish work deviated from her values, without hope (as she saw it) of their organic reintegration, that she began her move out of both and into the social development project. Thus, points of occupational volatility are provoked by irremediable mis-alignment between the subject's particular concerns and overarching values. They represent attempts by the meta-reflexives to establish a new *modus vivendi* – commensurate with their value orientations.

Elective affinity with the third sector

The *modi vivendi* established by meta-reflexives are subject to change according to their lateral occupational moves, but these preclude neither active participation in the local community nor involvement in global issues. In other words, the meta-reflexive is unlike the communicative reflexive, immersed in his or her own localised micro-world and voluntarily severed from involvements exterior to it, and is equally dissimilar from the autonomous reflexive who uses both the local and the global for short-term individual purposes, usually on a commercial basis. What the three sub-groups have in common is their disaffection with party politics and their dissociation from parliamentary proceedings. As far as the national polity is concerned, they share the same disenchantment and disaffiliation, with their highest level of participation being its lowest common denominator – the willingness of some to vote in general elections.

However, it is the meta-reflexives alone who display a political engage-ment that exceeds the bounds of national or regional (EU) politics. They are already engaged in a variety of global social movements, whose nature reflects their subversive stance towards the social in general. As was seen in chapter 6, interviewees are unanimous about the unfair nature of con-temporary British society. They do not believe that social outcomes are directly and solely proportionate to individual exertions, although their diagnoses of injustice are not uniform: some accentuate the enduring influence of social class, some emphasise discrimination on grounds of gender, age and ethnicity, whilst others are more preoccupied by the dynamics of exclusion and marginalisation. What is striking is their equal concern about the unjust use of global resources, affecting the welfare of humanity, and about international relations unjustly intensifying existing imbalances of power, wealth and education.

Since meta-reflexives adopt a value-orientation towards the social and endorse the practical aim of 'making a difference', their intrinsically subversive stance transfers directly on to the global canvas. What they hope to mark, if they succeed in doing nothing more, is their advocacy of the restructuring of the global social system. Amongst interviewees, support was signalled for a variety of global social movements: ecological and peace movements (various) – sometimes with Greenpeace as the beneficiary of their combination – feminism and children's rights, debt remission and fair trade, Stop the War and, significantly for making a 'bit' of difference, books for a Muslim university. These particular meta-reflexives varied in their degrees of activism, but with hardly any exceeding some combination of approbation, demonstration and donation. Nonetheless, what this signals is the preparedness on the part of meta-reflexives to undergo the transformation into some (or several) new form of corporate agency[26] – that is, their mobilisation into organised groups with articulate aims on a global scale. Given the difficulties confronted by most contributors to the debate upon how to arrive at global citizenship and, more specifically, who will be the carriers of cosmopolitan citizenship, this finding about meta-reflexivity could potentially be extremely important.

The differences between those practising the three modes of reflexivity are equally pronounced in relation to civil society. Earlier chapters have stressed how communicative reflexives shun institutional involvement and voluntarily organised activities alike, meaning that their key contribution to civil society consists of providing social cement in the form of the dense and supportive inter-personal networks that they sustain in their local contexts. Conversely, autonomous reflexives reserve their contribution to one institution alone, the economy, meaning that their social input is virtually synonymous with the creation of national wealth, economic growth and technical development. Meta-reflexives differ from both other sub-groups. They demonstrate a much higher level of on-going involvement with existing social institutions: schools and further education, churches, social services, sports clubs and community development. They invest more effort, are more proactive, but are commensurately critical.

Increasingly, however, for the group as a whole and over the life course of individuals, the dialectics of dissatisfaction mean that meta-reflexives show a tendency to gravitate towards the 'third sector'. It is through voluntary work (paid or unpaid) in non-profit associations – which can display large variations in institutionalisation[27] – that meta-reflexives

---

[26] See Margaret S. Archer, *Realist Social Theory: the Morphogenetic Approach*, Cambridge, Cambridge University Press, 1995, ch. 8, pp. 247–57.

[27] See P. Donati, 'L'analisi sociologica del terzo settore: introdurre la distinzione relazionale terzo settore/privato sociale', in G. Rossi (ed.), *Terzo settore, stato e mercato nella trasformazione delle politiche sociali in Europa*, Milan, Angeli, 1997, pp. 255–95.

often recognise the best prospects for living out their value-commitments. For example, activities undertaken by interviewees stretched from freely giving football coaching and devoting their skills to community development, through employment on weakly funded projects for marginal groups, to developing 'social private' organisations working for the common good by supplementing social services. In all such cases the satisfactions derived by interviewees consisted in the creation of relational goods – a combination of the intrinsically good, defined by their values, and the 'difference made', through realising something of them. Thus, as an aggregate effect, meta-reflexives are spearheading the reconstitution of civil society on the basis neither of power relations nor of exchange relations but upon 'free giving as the motor of reciprocity'.[28]

[28] P. Donati, 'Giving and Social Relations', *International Review of Sociology*, 13, 2, 2003, 243–72.

Conclusion: reflexivity's future

How we make our way through the world by using the human power of reflexivity also contributes to the remaking of our social world. It is to the latter that this brief conclusion is devoted. When 'Reflexivity's biographies' were discussed, three alternative and incompatible accounts were presented, but they had one feature in common: all three dealt quite simply with *the extent of reflexivity* (seemingly) required in the past, in recent times and – speculatively – in the future. However, if the arguments and evidence presented in the foregoing chapters carry conviction, the discussion can now be refined to deal with the distribution and consequences of *different modes of reflexivity* in modernity and in nascent globalisation.

There seems no compelling reason to conclude that any of the three modes of internal conversation, which have been identified and investigated in this contemporary study, were absent in the past. Both biblical and classical sources yield illustrations indicating that the modes of reflexivity discussed throughout this book were practised and recognised in those times, albeit under different descriptions.[1] It might be objected that such exemplifications include myths, midrash and redactions. At any rate, we can agree they are not interview transcripts. If, for the sake of argument, the entire biblical canon and classical corpus are regarded as 'stories' from times well past – perhaps not from their purported dates – the fact remains that their authors not only conceived of such mental activities but also wrote about them in the belief that they would be understandable to their readers.

Thus, what is being ventured here is that human subjectivity, as a personal property and power, constitutes a fund of potentials, some of which will be more pervasively activated and more clearly accentuated than others at certain times and under different social conditions. This suggestion also has to remain open to the possibility that there may indeed have

---

[1] See Julian Jaynes, *The Origin of Consciousness in the Breakdown of the Bicameral Mind*, Boston, Houghton Mifflin, 1976 for a rare attempt to discuss reflexivity in antiquity. Based on textual sources, my inclination would be to maintain – on the contrary – that subjects were fully aware of their own inner voices.

been other modes of reflexivity that once manifested themselves promi-nently, but have largely reverted to their *in potentia* status because in some way social conditions no longer foster their development.

Such a hypothesis stands in contradistinction to two alternative posi-tions: psychological reductionism and social determinism. Clearly, if 'reflexivity' is viewed as a fixed trait of human subjectivity or as a mental faculty that varies only with factors found at the level of individual psy-chology, social change would make no difference to its incidence, nature and, therefore, distribution. Equally, making the opposite assumption, namely that subjectivity is radically transformed in conformity with soci-etal transformations, means that human reflexivity would be as variable as changes in social forms. The latter implies there may be no recognisable continuities in kind such that one could talk about shifts in their scope, nature and distribution. Instead, it is argued that changes in the social environment are extremely important influences upon the mode of reflex-ivity that preponderates, without their being responsible for the funda-mental human capacity to practise any of these modes – possibly including other modalities that remain *in potentia* during the present period. In contradistinction, the account given here of the different kinds of internal conversation, prevailing at any given time, are *always* held to depend upon various combinations of 'contexts and concerns', neither of which can be reduced to individual terms.

The 'context' confronted by any subject at any time – be it their natal context or subsequent contexts they encounter – is never of their making or of their choosing. The 'concerns' they can adopt as value-commitments are similarly dependent upon the contents lodged in the cultural system – which are not of their making or choosing either. Such structural and cul-tural factors have been introduced into the present account of individual life histories, although they have not been explained during this text.[2] They can be summarised as follows:

(i) Macroscopic structural and cultural factors influence modes of reflex-ivity in conjunction with personal concerns
    contextual continuity → communicative reflexivity
    contextual discontinuity → autonomous reflexivity
    contextual incongruity → meta-reflexivity

Moreover, what individuals make of their structural and cultural con-texts through the mediation of their internal conversations has powerful effects – if not exclusive ones – upon the constitution and reconstitution

---

[2] The main previous works drawn upon in this connection have been Margaret S. Archer, *Culture and Agency: the Place of Culture in Social Theory*, 1998, and *Realist Social Theory: the Morphogenetic Approach*, 1995, both Cambridge, Cambridge University Press.

of the social.[3] This, after all, is the implication of conceptualising social subjects as 'active' rather than 'passive', namely as individuals possessing properties and powers particular to them, the exercise of which has a causal efficacy for them but extending beyond them. Their internal and external effects, which have been the subject of this work, are summarised in the following points:

(ii) Modes of reflexivity affect stances towards constraints or enablements, hindering or helping social mobility
communicative reflexivity → evasive
autonomous reflexivity → strategic
meta-reflexivity → subversive

(iii) through their associated action-orientations
communicative reflexivity → self-sacrifice
autonomous reflexivity → self-discipline
meta-reflexivity → self-transcendence

(iv) with consequences for patterns of mobility
communicative reflexivity → social immobility
autonomous reflexivity → upwards mobility
meta-reflexivity → lateral mobility (volatility)

(v) and aggregate macroscopic consequences
communicative reflexivity → social reproduction
autonomous reflexivity → social productivity
meta-reflexivity → social reorientation

(vi) whose main institutional impact is upon
communicative reflexivity → family
autonomous reflexivity → market
meta-reflexivity → third sector

This book began (chapter 1) with a consideration of large-scale speculative theories about the implications of different kinds of reflexivity for the social and of the import of transformations from early modernity to nascent globalisation for the reflexive processes practised by members of those social formations. In conclusion, it is worth re-engaging in speculation because it can now be informed by the foregoing findings. However, it might be objected, on methodological grounds, that any sensible discussion of tendential changes in reflexivity is impossible on the basis of data collected at one point in time. Detection of any tendency, this argument would go, requires least some longitudinal data from which a trend can be plotted. That would be the case were speculation restricted to extrapolation, but it is not. In the course of this book, three distinctive

---

[3] A complete account would need to incorporate the collective action of corporate agents. What have been examined here are the aggregate effects of individual subjects alone.

complexes of 'contexts and concerns' have been identified; they appear to underlie the development of different modes of reflexivity for differing sub-groups of actors. If this is indeed the case, then it is possible to trace the past and to consider the likely future of such complexes. On that basis, hypotheses about the distribution of the three forms of internal conversation – and their predominance – in the immediate past and the immediate future can be advanced.

The emergence of each mode of reflexivity depended upon distinctive interplays between structural, cultural and agential features. Therefore, societal transformations can be regarded as providing conditions that are more conducive to the development of one potential mode of reflexivity than to others. This is because macroscopic change also induces changes in the microscopic contexts individuals inherit natally and confront experientially. They do so without assuming the macro- and the micro- to be homologous or presuming macro- influences and their micro- contextual consequences to be evenly distributed over the population at any given time. Indeed, I will be arguing the opposite: the macro- can impinge upon micro- life contexts slowly and differentially.

From early to high modernity

The narratives of the founding fathers show a remarkable, if implicit, agreement about the dominant mode of reflexivity fostered by modernity, as deduced from what they have to say about the 'contexts and concerns' central to modernisation. In their very different ways, all accentuated modernity as representing a huge growth in 'contextual discontinuity', manifested first amongst its prime movers. Whether the key transformation was conceptualised in terms of the transition from segmented to co-operative social organisation, from feudalism to capitalism, or from pre-Reformation to post-Reformation, the common denominator was 'contextual discontinuity', represented by new forms of dissimilarity, alienation, aloneness and uncertainty. Correspondingly, similarity, familiarity, solidarity and conviviality were progressively undermined. With them went the conditions propitious to sustaining communicative reflexivity – because the strength of 'contextual continuity' diminished as modernity advanced.

In parallel, the concern promoted by the modernising process amongst its 'beneficiaries' tended to the single end of becoming 'better off', whether this was described in terms of acquiring disproportionate and unmerited quantities of scarce resources, as the extraction of increased and increasing surplus value, or as the accumulation of external signs of inward grace. Human concerns thus underwent commodification, with external goods displacing internal ones, human relationships reducing to exchange relations, and the religious enchantment of the world giving way to its secularised disenchantment – registered first and foremost amongst those most proximately involved. The common denominator of these changes, in relation to human concerns, was the systematic promotion of instrumental rationality over value rationality. The formation of value-commitments, as ends in themselves – expressive of one's personal identity – diminished accordingly, with nineteenth-century secularisation being the most commonly cited index of this process.

Thus, through its impact upon 'contexts and concerns', modernity favoured autonomous reflexivity. This was first manifest amongst its progenitors, but the development of modernisation extended 'contextual discontinuity' and instrumental rationality to ever larger sections of society. Nevertheless, there is no reason to suppose that the other two modes of reflexivity vanished, in part because no social configuration ever universalises those conditions and contexts that appear most distinctive of it, and in part because human subjectivity is impossible to standardise.

The paradox of modernity was that this radical social transformation was nonetheless a slow and patchy process – especially in the first nation to undergo it. Ironically, this slowness allowed 'contextual continuity' to be reconstituted in the new urban-industrial complexes. The 'migratory elite'[4] accurately characterises the captains of industry and, later on, their managerial lieutenants, but the urban relocation of the majority of the population took place gradually throughout most of the eighteenth, the nineteenth and the twentieth century. After this rural uprooting, there was little to discourage urban rerooting on a new geo-local basis: few incentives or enablements in terms of opportunities for upwards mobility and significant constraints in terms of loss of services from and to family members. Most shook down to the novel pattern of urban living, but one still characterised by features conducive to 'contextual continuity', such as: short-distance travel, minimum education, life-long work for one employer, inter-generational solidarity, and knowing, if not loving, their neighbours. In short, the masses inhabited contexts made up of 'similars and familiars'. This side of the 'great divide' was just as propitious for developing and sustaining communicative reflexivity, particularly given the objective importance attached to the family for welfare and well-being among the working classes.

Hence the long-term irony that, whilst the thrusting industrial leaders were, in all probability, extreme autonomous reflexives, it seems equally likely that the majority of the population – some 70 per cent – practised

---

[4] Frank Musgrove, *The Migratory Elite*, London, Heinemann, 1963.

communicative reflexivity. This statement seems plausible because the normative conventionalism, embedded in the 'thought and talk' pattern of reflexivity alone, makes the communicative mode the only one compatible with findings, in the mid-twentieth century, about the endurance of working-class traditionalism[5] and the continuity in patterns of socialisation amongst residual country folk. In turn, the durability of communicative reflexivity amongst large tracts of the population would also explain (and justify) why the notion of 'habitus' was so well received by those who had grown up at that time and why, nostalgically, *Coronation Street*, *The Archers* and *Emmerdale* still enjoy prime broadcasting time in the new millennium.

Were the speculation that communicative reflexivity predominated (numerically) until the late twentieth century correct (and, in principle, this is open to investigation because it is the sole form of internal conversation which directly manifests *itself* in external conversation), it seems unlikely to be the case as the present century unfolds. The reason for its expected decline as a dominant mode of reflexivity is straightforward: there has been a progressive reduction in 'contextual continuity' in response to changing social conditions, which will augment and reinforce one another in the foreseeable future.

Firstly, there is a major increase, intensifying from the 1960s onwards, in the geographical mobility of the entire British population. This is attributable to a variety of intertwined factors: labour mobility, 'pushed' by the decline in extracting and manufacturing industry, 'pulled' by the free movement of workers within the EU, and by multinationals relocating their production sites; foreign travel for nearly all in the form of cheap package deals and flights; the growth of commuting and the separation of work and home, increased by dual-career partners and not offset by the 'virtual office', because that means some can live anywhere; a shortage of homes for first-time buyers, intensified by the diminished stock of public housing, meaning young people buy where they can afford; the sharp reduction in jobs for life; and recreational activities (such as pop concerts, football fixtures, retail centres or theme parks) which assume patrons will drive there for entertainment.

Secondly, there is the increase in university education, from around 4 per cent of the age cohort in the 1960s to some 37 per cent at present, with the government's goal set at 50 per cent. For the majority of undergraduates, this means leaving the natal home earlier – the inverse of the trend in southern Europe[6] – and never returning to live there again. Many are the first

---

[5] M. Young and P. Willmott, *Family and Kinship in East London*, Harmondsworth, Penguin, 1962.
[6] Catherine Hakim, *Models of the Family in Modern Society*, Aldershot, Ashgate, 2003.

from their families to take a degree and are becoming even more culturally discontinuous from their parents than they are geographically removed.

Finally, information technology quintessentially provides a diversity of cultural exposure, in contrast to the standardised offerings of television when it took over the living room in the 1950s. The new possibilities for users to surf the net – to celebrate and augment 'difference' – contrast with the media's early attempts to reinforce normative conventions, from Lord Reith's moral mission for the BBC to the reinforcement of standard pronunciation. Certainly, cell phones, texting and e-mail represent new possibilities of sustaining 'virtual contextual continuity', but the 'phone home' option co-exists with various incentives to 'phone away'.

In sum, these three factors add up to an experiential variety that is hostile to 'contextual continuity'. It is no longer the case that a majority of parents and (teenage) children, let alone neighbours, fellow workers or inhabitants of the same area, have a communality of experiences, the same biographical reference points, a shared history and geography, thus making for a common mental topography with the same structural features and cultural landmarks. *In short, fewer and fewer people actually have 'similars and familiars'*, people who could be trusted to understand them sufficiently to complete their thoughts and to confirm their decisions. As Andrew Sayer recently put the matter, reference groups are not just what we refer to, but also what we live in.[7] Today, deceasing numbers of us live in the situation termed 'contextual continuity', which seems to be the necessary though not sufficient condition for the development of communicative reflexivity. Its decline will have crucial aggregate consequences for the remaking of the social world because communicative reflexivity worked for stability and stable social reproduction in the past.

Nascent globalisation

Since 'contextual discontinuity' is the obverse of reductions in 'contextual continuity' – both inter-generationally and intra-generationally – does this mean that proportional reductions in communicative reflexivity are paralleled by corresponding increases in autonomous reflexivity? Are there reasons, too, for an intensification of 'contextual incongruity' which would swell the proportions of those practising meta-reflexivity? It seems likely that both are the case.

The practice of autonomous reflexivity is certainly expected to rise considerably as globalisation intensifies. The autonomous mode was

---

[7] Andrew Sayer, *The Moral Significance of Class*, Cambridge, Cambridge University Press, 2005, ch. 5.

maintained above to be supremely compatible with early capitalist entre-
preneurship in its practical concerns, self-reliance, instrumental rationality, exchange relations and all those other facets shown in this study to be
conducive to upwards social mobility. Two of the essential motors of
nascent globalisation and its subsequent development are the multinational enterprise and the deregulated international finance market.
Globalisation remains capitalist in nature, but has the nature of capitalism remained unchanged, which is what would be required for it to throw
its weight behind a correlative growth in autonomous reflexivity? Equally,
has the generalisation of business practice to other institutions of civil
society also served to promote and augment autonomous reflexivity?

On the one hand, the number of managerial employees in corpora-
tions, banking, investment and allied positions has increasingly risen and
continues to rise. There is a goodness of fit between the qualities sought
from those employed, the type of rewards offered, the life-style entailed,
and autonomous reflexivity. For those attracted, such occupational contexts appear both objectively rewarding and subjectively self-reinforcing.
The newly mandatory exercises in 'team building' and 'corporate
bonding' could be interpreted as necessary counter-balances to the
unbridled individualism of the competitively upwardly mobile, who must
nevertheless co-operate from day to day.

The multinational firm has become more complex and internally
differentiated. It might be said to have acquired a conscience through
attempting to live up to its own acts of bad faith under the public gaze. To
some extent, self-presentational efforts to appear ecologically friendly, to
be convincing as equal opportunity employers or investors in people, and
to protest concern for the local environment of production have also
had unintended internal consequences. Those now recruited for such
roles do not execute them with invariable cynicism under a veneer of political correctitude, and internal corporate dynamics have become a good
deal more interesting – even though they fall well short of Galbraith's
'revised sequence'.[8] In turn, the implication is that not only will corporate
employment appeal to certain 'extreme' autonomous subjects, but also
many 'moderate' practitioners of this mode will be attracted occupationally – indeed, many internships seem designed for them.

On the other hand, the adoption of business practice in civil society,
particularly by the social services, the traditional and caring professions,
and at all levels of education, opens up new occupational opportunities

---

[8] J. K. Galbraith, *The New Industrial State*, New York, New American Library, 1968. That
is, pursuing the goals of its employees rather than the profit motive – although this
'sequence' requires that companies still remain profitable.

for those with the complex of concerns typical of autonomous reflexivity. Increasing cadres are devoted to the design and monitoring of performance indicators, to quality assurance, research evaluation, to awarding merit, measuring productivity, establishing procedures for transparency and accountability, to quantifying innovation, distilling and instilling 'best practice' and so forth. These activities are regularly anathematised by strong meta-reflexives, as we have seen, but what has not been dwelt upon is that, to *some* autonomous reflexives, this is also a new reason for coming in, staying on, gaining successive promotions and feeling increasingly at home.

There is more than an elective affinity between global capitalism and autonomous reflexivity in high modernity because its cultural protagonists attempt to persuade the world that its features are universal. These are serious attempts to undermine the *Wertrationalität*, to contest the very idea of active agents seeking to direct their life courses in conformity with their value-commitments. The main thrust has come from those positions claiming that all intentional action is instrumental action with the goal of increasing utility: rational choice theory, rational action theory and sociobiology. Intrinsic to these approaches is a flat denial of altruism,[9] of voluntary activities and, underlying both, of free-giving.[10] The strategy is simple. Altruists, volunteers and benefactors can be explained away; they are not what they present themselves to be, but are out to get something in return. Becker has universalised this argument in his assertion that 'the economic approach can explain all aspects of human behaviour'[11] and in his 'demonstration' that instrumental exchange relationships also govern those most persuasive exemplars of the endurance of value-commitment: family life and religious affiliation. This could be called 'the economic theory of everything'.

In short, the very condition of being a meta-reflexive is denied, since their ideals are not true ends but covert forms of instrumental rationality. Consequently, they cannot suffer from 'contextual incongruity' between their ideals and the formal positions from which they try to express and realise them. Therefore they do not exist, instrumental rationality rules and autonomous reflexivity predominates. So it is asserted in the third person. This exaltation of instrumental rationality is erroneous on crucial counts.

[9] Roger Trigg, *The Shaping of Man: Philosophical Aspects of Sociobiology*, Oxford, Basil Blackwell, 1982, pp. 115f.

[10] P. Donati, 'Giving and Social Relations', *International Review of Sociology*, 13, 2, 2003, 243–72.

[11] Gary Becker, *The Economic Approach to Human Behaviour*, Chicago, University of Chicago Press, 1976 and *Accounting for Tastes*, Cambridge, Mass., Harvard University Press, 1996.

To begin with, it seems entirely wrong to stress the colonising potential of instrumental rationality alone and to ignore its equal and opposite effect of stimulating critique from meta-reflexives during globalisation. Intensified morphogenesis places a brand new premium on ideational variety because novel ideas are the motor of technological development. Doubtless, the multinationals still play a revised version of 'industrial espionage', but their investment in research and development is their main access to indispensable novelty. It is not 'home grown', but depends upon research teams drawn from all over the world. To staff these in increasing numbers means promoting the diffusion and development of knowledge everywhere – hence the new global research foundations. In short, ideational innovation is central to the interests of the main 'user groups' of culture. Once articulated, ideas cannot die but are permanently lodged in the Universal Library of Humankind. This has become an electronic library, portable and accessible from home, hotel and in transit, massively augmenting the global diffusion of ideas. Everything ideational is open to being diffused and this includes critical reaction formation. Mass protests – against war, against G8, against poverty – are electronically mobilised. This is the real significance of the new social movements, because commitments to peace, justice, ecological welfare, fair trade, eradicating poverty and discrimination, all represent new forms of value rationality. Whatever immediate and practical consequences they have for the world, they constitute highly visible concerns whose adoption will further promote meta-reflexivity. Why is that so? Why does mass protest represent more than a collective effervescence of expressive idealism?

Because, it is ventured, those who make humanistic value-commitments from amidst this cultural free flow will also find increased occasion on which to experience 'contextual incongruity'. The 'traditional' outlets for meta-reflexives, as detected amongst the interviewees, are becoming incongruous to them. The 'caring' professions, education and welfare services are increasingly dominated by the new metricians and monitors of 'performance'. Welfare, in its broadest sense, is becoming more and more commodified. As paperwork takes precedence over people, impersonal bureaucratic relations over personal relations and cost-effectiveness over human giving and receiving, meta-reflexive workers experience a huge intensification of 'contextual incongruity' with their value-commitments. The consequences are threefold. Firstly, they become the most vitriolic critics of welfare agencies as new iron cages of instrumental rationality. Secondly, when they themselves recognise the impossibility of 'making a difference' through their employment, we have seen that they resign and move on. Finally, when they do so, they show a marked tendency to gravitate towards the third sector.

This 'voluntary' or 'independent' sector is changing rapidly and, one may speculate, this might well be the result of an influx of meta-reflexives in the recent past who increased its scale and scope as well as adding to its diversification. Working for NGOs, for global charities, promoting alternative technologies, seeking to make poverty history, represent new outlets for meta-reflexives abroad and their equivalents proliferate at home.

In sum, as nascent globalisation intensifies, the salience of the *Wertrationalität* actually increases, providing a growing fund of highly visible value-commitments that subjects adopt as their personal concerns. Simultaneously, the occupational outlets provided by the third sector are developing and diversifying. In consequence, meta-reflexivity will be fostered by conditions propitious to it. This does not mean it will become dominant or lead to some humanised utopia, for its agencies are threatened by incursion from both government and market.

Nevertheless, the scenario with which the baby boomers grew up was probably the last in which the social order saw autonomous reflexivity in undoubted ascendancy, communicative reflexivity quietly losing ground, and meta-reflexivity a minority practice. New subjectivities will replace them: meta-reflexives, as has just been argued, but also autonomous reflexives, who are neither the dummy agents of rational choice theory nor humanoids playing at narrative reinvention.

To end with, the ideologues of instrumental rationality also seem to have got autonomous reflexivity wrong. As we have seen, autonomous reflexives have ultimate concerns, heavily vested in the practical order, and dedicated to honing their skills – which have to find occupational outlets in the social order. Their urge to 'get on' is as much about acquiring autonomy at work as about gaining material rewards. Appointments in multinational enterprises and posts in newly bureaucratised 'welfare' institutions might initially prove attractive, in terms of 'being in control', but may come to represent snares and delusions as their regulatory impulse threatens autonomy itself. If this is so, the new small enterprises – hi-tech and computer savvy, niche-orientated, and entirely reliant on intensely specialised skills – can be expected to proliferate because they permit sole control. Given the nature of their ultimate concerns, it follows that the 'flash' and the 'posh' are of as little account to these autonomous subjects as they are to meta-reflexives. Reflexively, some – at least – of the new cosmopolitans have rejected modernity's long obsession with social stratification and social mobility.

New Year 2005/6 was passed in Chamonix. Sitting around the enormous pine table in a chalet – the restoration project of one of my son's school friends – were a group belonging to the new millennium because the gathering could barely have pre-dated it. This was not the new, young, migratory elite because all were seeking to avoid or quit corporate employment, preferring the pursuit of their own concerns. My son and his wife had long ago opted for 'life in a fleece' and their own project of offering adventure courses. Their friends too were busy opting out and fine-tuning new enterprises. These were not 'visitors' but migrants-in-process: two pilots, an ex-SAS officer, a Polish-British policeman and two female accountants, all wanting out and all working out how to do it. Later we were joined by an Australian, currently driving a taxi, whilst he perfects the software for detailed forecasting of local skiing conditions. Those present had no interest in either competition or command. Their concerns were antipathetic to corporate life, their satisfactions internal rather than external. These young professionals were rejecting the organisational contexts in which they were occupationally expected to exercise their skills and were crafting small, new outlets for themselves in the social order.

Towards midnight, as champagne spumed on packed ice, firework showers and snowflakes danced over *l'hôtel de ville*, and glasses were clinked with polyglot strangers, we seemed to be celebrating not only the New Year but also the freedom to pursue one's concerns where one would – following the situational logic of opportunity in order to give due importance to what one cares about most.

Methodological appendix

The Coventry sample

The principal aim of the sampling design was to obtain a cross-section of the local population which maximised its diversity. Financial constraints meant there was no question of designing a sample large enough to be able to extrapolate from it to the English population. Instead, the sample was intended to provide a framework *from which* to select subjects for in-depth interviewing. Thus, from the beginning, this study was conceived of as a contribution to *qualitative research*, which would remain exploratory in nature. Nevertheless, unlike its predecessor, *Structure, Agency and the Internal Conversation*,[1] which used a tiny group of twenty people, selected on an ad hoc basis, the objective this time was to ensure that the major demographic categories were adequately covered. Given the uncharted nature of research on reflexivity, it was impossible to specify in advance any other attributes that should be incorporated into the resulting sample. Beyond age, gender and occupational status, the preliminary interviewers were simply instructed to maximise diversity by, for example, including members of ethnic minorities and avoiding the duplication of people doing the same jobs, working for the same enterprise or living in the same street.

The previous study had tentatively identified four modes of reflexivity – 'communicative', 'autonomous', 'meta-reflexive' and 'fractured'. The aim was not to gain some idea of their proportional distributions – desirable as that would have been – but rather to establish whether or not such modes were measurable, varied in intensity, were exhaustive of the sampled group or left many unclassifiable. In turn, these objectives pointed to selecting a larger sample than those who would eventually be interviewed. Since I was going to conduct all the in-depth interviews myself, and they were rightly foreseen as being lengthy, this indicated a maximum of approximately fifty. With that in mind, a stratified sample of 128 subjects appeared

---

[1] Margaret S. Archer, *Structure, Agency and the Internal Conversation*, Cambridge, Cambridge University Press, 2003.

adequate as a framework for the qualitative work, though clearly not beyond it.

Sample selection

Two preliminary interviewers, female doctoral students from the university, were each allocated one half of the map covering the designated geographical area, relatively close to the campus. The map was drawn to accentuate heterogeneity: in types and costs of housing, in socioeconomic composition, in ethnic composition and, by repute, in terms of being a blend of 'old Coventry' residents, newcomers and transients. The area also had a generous quota of shopping facilities, both precinct and high street, of schools, clubs, pubs, community centres and churches – representing places to make contact – and also a Jobcentre Plus, two colleges of further education, a bus station and two railway stations, a couple of industrial estates and a science park for small IT enterprises.

Students and university employees were excluded in advance, the former because a parallel longitudinal study of undergraduates was taking place over the three years of their first degree and the latter, the employees, because I am known to sit on promotions committees in the university and this seemed to constitute a potential source of distortion if academic personnel were interviewed.

Each interviewer was given a sheet of thirty-two cells, reflecting stratification by gender, age and socio-economic position and asked to obtain two to three respondents for each cell. This exceeded the 128 needed because allowance was made for inadvertent overlap (co-workers and spouses), excess concentration on particular occupations (as it turned out, banking), those too difficult to interview (one severely deaf subject and another with loss of short-term memory), the expectation (incorrect) of acquiring a few 'jokers' and the anticipation (correct) that the interviewers might understandably make errors in the assignment of socio-occupational status to individuals. In total, 174 subjects were interviewed during this phase. This meant all completed the initial sixteen-item questionnaire and also a background data sheet, the process taking approximately ten minutes.

Respondents' ages were divided into four categories, 16–24, 25–39, 40–54 and 55+, which represented tracts of the life course in which people would tend to confront rather different issues. Subjects were assigned to one of four occupational categories, using the National Statistics Socioeconomic Classification (NS-SeC).[2] The simplified and reduced derivation

---

[2] The Standard Occupational Classification 2000 (SOC2000) as downloaded from http://www.statistics.gov.uk/methods_quality/ns_sec/soc2000.asp.

table was used, which collapsed the eight categories of the NS-SeC classification into four, resulting in the following occupational strata: (1) managerial and professional occupations; (2) intermediate occupations; (3) routine and manual occupations; and (4) never worked, voluntarily non-working and unemployed for over two years.

The sample was then refined down to 128 cases. Firstly, those considered unable to be interviewed, as detailed above, were discarded together with two who were going to move out of the area within weeks and a short-term contract worker based in Coventry for a few days only. Secondly, each cell was inspected. If it held exactly four people, these were retained. When more than four occupied each cell, they were inspected for similarity of occupation, and a random choice was made between any who did the same jobs. For whatever reasons, those in banking and teaching were over-numerous. Finally, the remaining eighty cases were determined by using a random number table, until four subjects remained per cell.

There are two major weaknesses of the resulting sample. Firstly, it is a non-random sample because the subjects were selected on the basis of *availability*. In other words, every member of the designated area *did not* have the same chance as every other of being invited to complete the questionnaire. The resulting sample necessarily under-represented those housebound or hospitalised and most likely did the same for those commuting to work outside Coventry, despite evening interviewing being standard practice. The latter may account for the absence of any *exceptionally* highly placed individuals in the managerial and professional category of occupations. The difficulty of reaching this sub-category had been anticipated, but a request to frequent the social facilities of the one private golf club in the area had been rejected. Approaches to parents dropping off or collecting their children from a private school did not solve the problem.

The limited size of the grant would not have stretched to the systematic selection of cases from a sampling frame. The availability method appeared adequate for meeting the prime aim of obtaining a socially diverse group of interviewees. Nonetheless, the major limitation of a non-random sample is that it does not support the use of inferential statistics. Such a sample lacks external validity because its representativeness cannot be assessed and therefore significance testing is inappropriate. In other words, generalisability is necessarily sacrificed. However, given that the aims of the project were qualitative, in conjunction with the fact that a sample comprising 128 subjects is too small in any case to support statistically sophisticated operations, it seemed adequate for the exploratory purposes in view.

The second limitation is that this sample is a disproportionately stratified one and thus does not reflect the demographic characteristics of the population. For example, it seems more than likely that the sample underrepresents the extremely affluent, as already discussed, but also over-represents the unemployed. As far as both are concerned it was not possible to improve the representativeness of the sample by differential weighting. To begin with, it is almost impossible to obtain data on the distribution of socio-economic classes within the population of a geographical zone designated for its heterogeneity rather than because it coincided with politico-administrative boundaries. Moreover, this problem was rendered insoluble by our acceptance of interviewees who commuted into Coventry to work, often from a nearby smaller town which is classified separately in the census. Finally, this particular limitation was compounded by the practice of de-selecting subjects with very similar if not identical occupations in order to increase job diversity.

In short, the sample departs from the ideal in so far as (1) it is non-random, (2) it does not represent the characteristics of the broader population, and (3) it is marked by selection bias. None of that seriously compromises its utility as a framework from which to draw subjects for *qualitative and exploratory* investigation of internal conversation, but that must be considered as its prime function. Conversely, these limitations mean that any significance tests performed are not appropriate for inferential analysis. Consequently, the very few that are reported must also be treated warily as being nothing more than tentative findings.

Developing the internal conversation indicator (ICONI)

This section describes the four main stages through which we[3] worked to arrive at an indicator which was capable of identifying clear practitioners of each dominant mode of reflexivity – these being 'communicative reflexives', 'autonomous reflexives', 'meta-reflexives' and 'fractured reflexives'. Henceforth, these modes as referred to as C, A, M and F.

These theoretical underpinnings meant that we were trying to develop a very different kind of indicator from the array of instruments produced by social psychologists since 1975. Not only was it different in attempting to capture distinctive *modes* of reflexivity, whereas social psychologists have largely treated it as a homogeneous practice, but also there was a second and equally important difference. The various social-psychological instruments developed to measure reflexivity (or cognate

---

[3] The statistical research assistant for Stage 1 was Andrew Timming and for Stages 2–4, Man Wing Yeung.

concepts) were all regarded and employed as 'finished products' and used as 'stand-alone' devices. After their administration, subjects' scores were then related to various experimental prompts and primes, usually under laboratory-type conditions. Conversely, ICONI was never intended to stand alone. At most, its use would be as an economical way of *identifying* consistent practitioners of a dominant mode of reflexivity for interview.

The specific requirements of (the potential) ICONI were, firstly, that it should be able to differentiate clearly between practitioners of the distinctive modes of reflexivity outlined above (assuming the probity of the underlying theory), secondly, that it should be capable of distinguishing 'strong' from 'weak' practitioners of each mode, thirdly, as an identification and screening device, that it should be quick to administer and be readily understandable to those in all walks of life, and, finally, that it be free from any form of referential specificity, which would preclude its use in other countries.

Stage 1: Piloting ICONI

From the start, ICONI was obviously conceived of as a multi-dimensional questionnaire and also each of the above four modes of reflexivity was viewed as being multi-faceted. An initial array of six questions per mode was devised from the mental processes and preoccupations attested by their respective practitioners in the 2003 study. This resulted in a 24-item questionnaire. The ideal was to arrive at the smallest number of questions which discriminated effectively between practitioners of different modes of reflexivity. Since these are seen as *dominant* modes, it was never anticipated that subjects would score highly on one given mode of internal conversation and register zero on all the others.

The preliminary version was pre-piloted on fifty subjects – some working in the Department of Sociology, some employed by a campus building contractor and some resident in my home village. Certain questions were eliminated because they were endorsed by the vast majority. Other questions were reformulated more strongly, emphatically or exclusively. From the above procedures a refined 24-item questionnaire was constructed for piloting proper.

The sampling frame for the pilot study consisted of the 4,053 employees of the University of Warwick in July 2003. The final sample consisted of sixty-four subjects drawn randomly[4] from sub-sets established via

---

[4] Using the random number table in Earl Babbie, *The Basics of Social Research*, Belmont, Wadsworth, 1999, p. 433.

stratification. The intention was to interview thirty-two of the above, which therefore included a 'duplicate' group of the same size and nature as an over-sample. The final sample was stratified on the basis already described for gender, age and socio-occupational status in accord with EPSEM (an equal probability of selection method). To make the study immediately comprehensible to subjects, it was introduced verbally as an investigation of processes of decision-making in everyday life.

Irrespective of gender, age and socio-economic status, and despite the small size of the sample, at the broadest level it appeared that the pilot ICONI had worked. The four modes of reflexivity did appear to discriminate between respondents. (C, A, M and F were each measured by six questions, answered on a four-point scale, and responses were then divided by six to generate an individual score.) Four of the paired t-tests were statistically significant with p-values less than .050. Nevertheless, the failure of the two pairs 'communicative'/'automomous' and 'communicative'/ 'meta-' to achieve significance was disappointing and obviously called for re-examination of these questions. The statistically significant results of ANOVA, comparing subjects' mean scores for the four variables with one another, allowed the broad conclusion that our measures for the dominant modes of reflexivity did in fact discriminate between them – with p-values of .000. However, when the 'fractured' group, whose mean score was well below the others, was excluded, statistical signficance was no longer achieved (p =.187), indicating that the questions for communicative, autonomous and meta-reflexives did not discriminate between these three (theoretically postulated) modes as well as was required.

Four kinds of remedial action were undertaken. Firstly, we sought to increase the overall robustness of results by increasing the amount of variance possible. Thus, the four-point Likert scale, used in the pilot study, was replaced by a seven-point scale. Secondly, it was concluded that both variance and possibly validity might be increased by introducing inverted indicators (all statements had been formulated positively in the pilot questionnaire) in order to encourage respondents to think more carefully and avoid routinised response patterns. Thirdly, questions were simply eliminated if answered in the same way by more than 70 per cent of respondents because of their manifest lack of discriminatory power. Finally, use was made of the extreme values recorded on each variable (mode of reflexivity) to interview subjects who were high scorers and to ask them which of their responses to the six relevant questions they considered to be most characteristic of their own internal conversations – a concept that all understood and acknowledged to be part of their everyday practice.

Stage 2: Refining ICONI

Following the four procedures just described, a revised ICONI of sixteen items was administered to 130 new entrants to sociology degrees in October 2003 and factor analyses were performed on their responses. Obviously, this group is not typical of the population at large, but it was used for two reasons. Firstly, this student cohort was the basis of a concurrent investigation, which follows them through to the completion of their undergraduate degrees.[5] Secondly, there was no intention of finalising ICONI until it had first been administered to a sample drawn from the general population.

Principal axis factoring was chosen as the method of extraction, as is conventional when a study is conducted for exploratory rather than predictive purposes, and in the absence of prior knowledge about the variance of the variables.[6] The latent root criterion was applied to determine the number of factors to be extracted: only those with eigen-values equal to or bigger than one were extracted to facilitate manageability. Results on the Kaier–Meyer–Olkin measure for sampling adequacy and Bartlett's Test of Sphericity indicated that the data collected were suitable for factor analysis.

From these results and close inspection of the correlation matrix, we were able to identify those questions which performed a good discriminatory function for each mode of reflexivity vis-à-vis the others and also to understand *how* it was that other items were being endorsed *across* different modes through tapping into some unwanted commonality. Sufficient evidence had been forthcoming for the retention of eight items, as currently formulated, and for the directions in which to revise the other half. On this basis revision of the unsatisfactory items took place and the resulting sixteen-item questionnaire was administered in spring 2004 to the sample of Coventry residents (N = 128) and re-administered to the original group of first-year undergraduates.

Stage 3: Finalising ICONI

The Coventry population was small and had been constituted as an availability sample, meaning *inter alia* that it was not fully representative (see above). Nevertheless, this was the first cross-section of the local population to whom the revised ICONI had been administered and thus their responses were subjected to careful statistical scrutiny. Three types of

---

[5] This is a companion study, which will follow.
[6] J. Hair, R. Anderson and R. Tatham, *Multivariate Data Analysis with Readings*, New York, Macmillan, 1987, p. 241.

analyses were performed to assess the effectiveness of the revised instrument for the purposes intended.

Firstly, the frequency distributions of the responses to the sixteen items were examined to detect whether any of them were non-discriminatory and therefore should be deleted. The percentage of subjects who agreed with each statement (i.e. answered 5, 6 or 7 on the Likert scale) was calculated for each of the sixteen items. For the majority of C, A and M items, the percentages of such responses were around 40–58 per cent; for F items, the range was 15–28 per cent. However, two items were deemed problematic because affirmed by more than 70 per cent of subjects. Both questions were eliminated as serving no useful purpose.

Next, ANOVA bivariate correlations and factor analysis were applied to the remaining fourteen items to ascertain how far they were producing effective, consistent and theoretically meaningful measurements and factor analysis was again undertaken.

Stage 4: The final ICONI

Following the procedures described above, we arrived at the final thirteen-item questionnaire. The supreme advantage for the present investigation was that respondents' new scores could simply be recalculated from existing data, without the need to re-administer the questionnaire. This represented a considerable saving of time and money because it was unnecessary to contact Coventry subjects again, had that been possible.

The final ICONI accounted for 46.788 per cent of the variance on factor analysis, which compares favourably with percentages attained by well-established instruments devised and employed in social psychology. One of the cognate devices used most frequently is Fenigstein et al.'s 'Self-Consciousness Scale',[7] which accounted for 43 per cent of the variance at its penultimate stage – this being the only published figure. Furthermore, some of the finalised items retained in that scale were endorsed by up to 85 per cent of the population, which is less stringent than our 70 per cent criterion. Next, in relation to the 'Concern Dimension Questionnaire 3', developed by Klinger et al.,[8] it was stated that 'the variable set (represented by 4–6 predictors) probably accounts for about 20 per cent of the variance of thought content frequency'. Continuing with cognate research instruments, Morin et al. developed an 'Inventaire d'auto-verbalisations pour l'auto-

---

[7] A. Fenigstein, M. F. Scheier and A. H. Buss, 'Public and Private Self Consciousness: Assessment and Theory', *Journal of Consulting and Clinical Psychology*, 43, 4, 1975, p. 523.

[8] E. Klinger, S. G. Barta and M. E. Maxeiner, 'Motivational Correlates of Thought Content, Frequency and Commitment', *Journal of Personality and Social Psychology*, 39, 6, 1980, p. 1235.

Table A1: Significant loadings (greater than $+/-0.30$) in relation to the four factors extracted; factor pattern mix

Mode of reflexivity: question number	Factor 1 (Fractured)	Factor 2 (Meta-)	Factor 3 (Communicative)	Factor 4 (Autonomous)
Autonomous 2				0.665
Meta- 3		0.628		0.330
Fractured 4	0.452			
Autonomous 6	−0.434			
Meta- 7		0.742		
Fractured 8	0.645			
Communicative 9			0.668	
Autonomous 10	−0.540			
Communicative 11			0.665	
Fractured 12	0.762			
Communicative 13			0.519	
Meta- 15		0.604		
Fractured 16	0.845			

observation' (IAVAO).[9] Eight factors were extracted, but only the variance accounted for by the first factor, one 'substantially in line with all the items', was reported – at 28 per cent. This was followed by a table recording the loadings of the twenty-seven items on this principal factor. Finally, the currently popular 'Rumination–Reflection Questionnaire' (RRQ), devised by Trapnell and Campbell,[10] again gives no figure for the variance accounted for, but once more presents a table of factor loadings on items tapping into 'rumination' and 'reflection' respectively. In line with this practice amongst social psychologists, the parallel factor loadings of items on our four factors are presented in Table A1. These appear to meet the standards found acceptable for the use of research instruments in social psychology.

The selection of interviewees

The aim was to arrive at twelve interviewees for each of the communicative, autonomous, meta-reflexive and fractured categories, although the last sub-group will be reported upon in the following book. As will be

[9] A. Morin, J. Everett, I. Turcotte and G. Tardif, 'Le dialogue intérieur comme médiateur cognitif de la conscience de soi privée: une mesure de l'activité consistant à se parler à soi même à propos de soi et une étude corrélationnelle', *Revue Québécoise de Psychologie*, 14, 2, 1993, pp. 10, 12.

[10] P. D. Trapnell and J. D. Campbell, 'Private Self-Consciousness and the Five-Factor Model of Personality: Distinguishing Rumination from Reflection', *Journal of Personality and Social Psychology*, 76, 2, 1999, p. 293.

Table A2: Mode of reflexivity endorsed

Mode of reflexivity	Frequency	Percentage	Cumulative percentage
Communicative	27	21.1	21.1
Autonomous	35	27.3	48.4
Meta-	29	22.7	71.1
Fractured	28	21.9	93.0
Refuseniks*	3	2.3	95.3
Unclassified	6	4.7	100.0
Total	128	100.0	100.0

Note: * The term refers to subjects who scored less than 4 on C, A, M or F.

recalled, subjects were assigned to a dominant mode of reflexivity according to their highest score over 4.00 on the relevant sub-set of questions. Table A2 summarises the results for the 128 respondents.

For each mode, subjects were invited for interview by working downwards from the highest scorer(s) (at or closest to 7.0). In other words, 'extreme' practitioners were sought for each mode on the grounds that these subjects would supply the clearest exemplification of characteristics distinctive of that particular mode. Interviewees for every mode did not represent the highest scorers because some of those declined to be interviewed or appointments were not kept. Only ten interviews were completed for the 'communicatives' because two of those, who initially appeared genuinely willing, eventually asked to withdraw three months later because of marital breakdown and a difficult pregnancy, respectively. At that point, the next couple on the list had discontinued phone lines. The average scores of the sub-groups of interviewees were as follows:

Communicative reflexives   5.8
Autonomous reflexives   6.2
Meta-reflexives   6.4

The reason behind these differences in average scores is unclear and may reflect deficiencies in ICONI. Although that may still be the case, it was noticeable that no 'communicative' registered the maximum score of 7.0, whilst this was recorded in the other two groups. Thus, it could be that the 'autonomous' and 'meta-reflexives' were less hesitant – precisely because their modes of reflexivity did not involve receiving confirmation from others – in confidently expressing their personal views and thus using the strongest numerical indicator. Equally plausible, however, is the fact that as we move through the interviewees from the C to the A to the M sub-groups, the level of subjects' education also rises, on average. That, too, may be associated with greater confidence in the expression of opinion.

Selecting the 'highest scorers' could have upset the gender balance despite the fact that membership of these three sub-groups did not appear to be related to gender. It did not do so for the communicatives or meta-reflexives, where equal numbers of males and females were interviewed, but affected the autonomous category by producing only four women out of the twelve interviewees.

Subjects were offered the choice of venue for interviews, with the suggestion that this could be in their own homes, at a place of their choice in Coventry or at the Arts Centre on campus. The majority opted for me to visit their home addresses, with the Arts Centre being preferred by more of the younger subjects.

Index